The Great Father

When your GREAT FATHER and his chiefs see
those things, they will know that you have
opened your ears to your GREAT FATHER's voice,
and have come to hear his good Councils.

Lewis and Clark, in presenting American flags
and medals to Oto chiefs, 1804

They [the Indians] look to our government for
protection; rely upon its kindness and its power;
appeal to it for relief to their wants, and address
the president as their GREAT FATHER.

John Marshall in
Cherokee Nation v. *Georgia*, 1831

Nothing is more indispensable than the
protecting and guiding care of the Government
during the dangerous period of transition from
savage to civilized life. . . . [The Indian] is
overcome by a feeling of helplessness, and he
naturally looks to the "GREAT FATHER" to take
him by the hand and guide him on. That guiding
hand must necessarily be one of authority and
power to command confidence and respect. It can
be only that of the government which the Indian
is accustomed to regard as a sort of omnipotence
on earth. Everything depends upon the wisdom
and justice of that guidance.

Secretary of the Interior Carl Schurz in an
article in the *North American Review*, 1881

FRANCIS PAUL PRUCHA

The Great Father

The United States Government

and the American Indians

ABRIDGED EDITION

UNIVERSITY OF NEBRASKA PRESS

LINCOLN AND LONDON

Copyright 1984, 1986 by
the University of Nebraska Press
All rights reserved
Manufactured in the United States
of America
⊗
The paper in this book
meets the guidelines for permanence
and durability of the Committee
on Production Guidelines for Book
Longevity of the Council
on Library Resources.

Library of Congress
Cataloging in Publication Data

Prucha, Francis Paul.
The great father (abridged edition).

Bibliography: p.
Includes index.
1. Indians of North America –
Government relations.
I. Title
E93.P96542   1986
323.1′197′073   85-5875
ISBN 0-8032-3675-1 (alkaline paper)
ISBN 0-8032-8712-7 (pa.)

Contents

Maps and Tables

Preface to
the Abridged Edition

The present volume is an abridgment of the two-volume edition of *The Great Father*, published in October 1984. All the footnotes and illustrations and some of the maps and tables have been omitted and the remaining text cut by more than half, but the structure and sequence of the original are maintained. The only major modification is the moving of the discussion on government trading houses from a separate chapter to the section dealing with Indian trade. The shortening, however, has led to changes in chapter titles and subheadings and to some minor stylistic changes; the extensive bibliographical essay of the two-volume edition has been replaced by a shorter list of suggestions for further reading. Readers who are interested in a fuller treatment of topics than is presented here, in the exact source of a quotation, or in the documentation that lies behind my conclusions are referred to the two-volume edition, which is thoroughly annotated.

It is my hope that this version will serve students and general readers who desire a concise survey of the history of Indian-white relations in the two centuries of the nation's history.

Preface to
the Original Edition

The relations of the federal government of the United States with the American Indians through two centuries form a major component of American political history. From the beginnings of the nation, when some Indian tribes were political and military entities of power and independence with whom the young nation had to come to terms, to the present, when newly energized tribal organizations once again emphasize a government-to-government relation with the United States, Indians as tribes or as individuals have been persistently in the consciousness of officials of all three branches of the federal government.

I have long recognized the need for a comprehensive history of the relations between the United States government and the Indians. Excellent one-volume surveys of the subject exist, and there are now a great many scholarly studies of selected periods or particular aspects of American Indian policy. But what I have attempted here is a survey of the full scope of American Indian policy from the time of the Revolutionary War to 1980. I have sought to provide a reasonably complete discussion of the course of Indian policy development and implementation, with its many vicissitudes, and to indicate in the footnotes the essential documents and secondary works in which this history is set forth.

Because federal policies have rested on past experience, no full understanding of any part of the story is possible without seeing what went before or without examining the working out of the programs. I have learned from this comprehensive study that there was much more fundamental unity and continuity in the government's policy than I had previously thought from looking only at selected partial aspects or at limited chronological periods.

The officials of the federal government in the executive branch and in Congress faced a serious problem as greatly diverse cultures came into

contact and often conflict within the expanding terrritorial limits of the
United States. The Indian cultures were amazingly rich and diverse; but
the Indian groups quickly fell far behind the white society in numbers and
technical skills, and they were in general no match for the economically
and militarily powerful United States. When the Indian tribes, early in the
nineteenth century, lost their powerful European allies in the New World—
with whose assistance they might have hoped to hold off the onslaught of
white American advance—it was clear to both Indians and whites that the
United States dealt with the Indians from a position of dominance.

Cries for extermination of the Indians that were sounded by aggressive
frontiersmen and exasperated frontier commanders were rejected by United
States officials responsible for Indian affairs. These officials instead sought
to treat the Indians honorably, even though they acted within a set of circumstances that rested on the premise that white society would prevail.
The best term for this persistent attitude is *paternalism*, a determination
to do what was best for the Indians according to white norms, which translated into protection, subsistence of the destitute, punishment of the unruly, and eventually taking the Indians by the hand and leading them along
the path to white civilization and Christianity. The relationship was sometimes described, as it was by Chief Justice John Marshall in 1832, as resem-
bling that of a ward and its guardian. The modern emphasis on the trust
responsibility of the federal government toward the Indians has elements of
the same attitude.

In the nineteenth century, it was common for Indians to refer to the
president (head and symbol of the United States government) as the Great
Father, and the term was adopted by government officials as well. It was an
appropriate usage for the paternalistic attitude of the federal government
toward the Indians as dependent children. The Great Father rhetoric largely
disappeared after 1880, but paternalism continued and sometimes increased.
Federal concern for the education, health, and economic development of its
wards colored the history of Indian policy in the twentieth century. And
when, in the decades of the 1960s and 1970s, the renewal of Indian self-
determination came to the fore, it was protest against continuing governmental paternalism that gave form to the movement.

Paternalism was considered by its white practitioners as a humane,
Christian approach to the serious problems that faced the nation in its relations with the Indians, and it was accepted by many Indians as welcome
and necessary support. But paternalism also had its oppressive aspects, and
criticism of it has frequently arisen, sometimes in the form of a desire to
get the government out of the Indian business and let the Indians fend for
themselves within the larger white society and sometimes in the form of
criticism of the weakening of the Indians' ability to direct their own destiny. Throughout the two centuries covered by this study, however, the con-

trolling force in Indian-white relations has been the policy determined by the white government, not the wishes of the Indians.

This history is divided into two volumes at roughly 1880. The year is a neat chronological dividing point, for each volume thus covers a century, but it is more than that, too. Although nothing of startling historical importance happened in that precise year, the date can be used to note the end of an era marked by diplomatic dealings with the Indian tribes and marred by almost incessant military encounters with them in one region or another. The century after 1880, in contradistinction, was dominated by a new movement to destroy old tribal relations and traditional customs and to accomplish the ultimate acculturation and assimilation of individual Indians into white society.

As in my previous historical studies of Indian-white relations in the United States, large parts of which are incorporated in this book, I concentrate on the history of federal Indian policy and do not treat in detail the history of the Indian communities. I do this in part as a matter of expediency, because it is possible to survey the course of government policy in a single work, whereas it is not possible to treat the "Indian story" in such a unified way, given the great diversity of Indian groups and of individual responses within those groups. But my approach is justified also, I think, because the policies and programs of the United States have had a determining influence on the history of the Indian tribes. In the period of Indian-white contact that I cover, no history of a tribe can be understood without a detailed consideration of treaties, land cessions, the reservation system, and Indian educational programs, for example, which formed the substance of government policy and action.

I have boldly carried the story to 1980, for historical studies of Indian affairs have for too long emphasized events of the nineteenth century. Indian communities, like all human societies, have changed and developed through time, and their relations with the United States government have also changed. The policies and programs of the twentieth century are as important for understanding the status of Indians today in American society as are those of the nineteenth. There are difficulties, of course, in moving so close to the present in the writing of history, before the outcome of laws and decisions can be evaluated. Readers will appreciate that in the case of many recent events I have been unable to give the proportion of attention to them that later historians may find appropriate. But I have attempted to describe the multifarious developments that occurred and to indicate the arguments and purposes that lay behind them.

FRANCIS PAUL PRUCHA, S.J.
Marquette University

Acknowledgments

In a study of this scope, reliance on the work of other scholars and the assistance of archivists and librarians is manifest. I cannot begin to thank adequately the staffs of the National Archives, Library of Congress, Milwaukee Public Library, Harvard University Library, State Historical Society of Wisconsin, Newberry Library, Huntington Library, Department of the Interior Library, and Marquette University Library, as well as many others, who have helped in one way or another. Historians and other scholars who have contributed to my knowledge and understanding are altogether too many to name, for I have spoken or corresponded with a great many persons interested in Indian-white relations in the United States, and I have read their books and articles. I owe special mention, however, to Robert F. Berkhofer, Ray Allen Billington, William T. Hagan, Reginald Horsman, Robert M. Kvasnicka, Frederick Merk, Robert Pennington, Martin Ridge, Robert M. Utley, Herman J. Viola, Wilcomb E. Washburn, and Mary E. Young. To my students, too, I owe much gratitude.

My research in Indian affairs has been materially aided by grants and fellowships from the Social Science Research Council, National Endowment for the Humanities, John Simon Guggenheim Foundation, Charles Warren Center for the Study of American History, and Huntington Library. De Rance, Incorporated, generously provided research funds and added a sizable subvention for the publication of the original two-volume edition. Marquette University, the Marquette Jesuit Community, and the Wisconsin Province of the Society of Jesus have supported my studies in many ways. Much of the work on the abridgment was done while I enjoyed the facilities offered by the Thomas I. Gasson Professorship at Boston College.

In writing the two-volume edition, I drew on several of my own previously published studies. Some of that use is reflected also in this abridgment. I again thank the editors and publishers of those earlier studies for permission to copy sections verbatim from them.

The Colonial
Experience

The United States government in its relations with the American Indians built upon English colonial and imperial experience. The policy it developed was in many respects, of course, a response to specific conditions on the frontier, but little if anything was begun entirely de novo. Two centuries of English contact with the natives in the New World had provided a rich set of conceptions about the Indians and numerous examples of policies and programs concerning the interaction of the two cultures. There were colonial precedents for all the interfaces between white government and Indian groups—missionary contacts, military encounters, trade relations, and land transfers—upon which the new nation could draw. After individual colonies seemed unable to regulate the settlers and maintain honorable and tranquil relations with the Indians, imperial programs of control furnished models of centralized management of Indian affairs that were clear in the minds of the Founding Fathers.

IMAGES OF THE INDIANS

When Christopher Columbus struck the Western Hemisphere by chance in his attempt to sail west around the world to the riches of the Orient, he found not only land but peoples. Unable to comprehend that he was opening up a "new" world and confident that he had touched some outlying reaches of the Indies, he called the inhabitants Indians, a name that has lasted for five centuries despite its descriptive inaccuracy and the occasional attempts to substitute a more suitable name. These peoples were numerous and magnificently diverse, and it was immediately evident that they were different from the Europeans who came in contact with them. The Indians had to be accommodated into the intellectual patterns of the

Western European mind, and practical conventions for dealing with them had to be developed.

The Europeans dealt with the Indians as they perceived them, and this perception came ultimately from detailed observation. Explorers, churchmen, traders, governors, scientists, and casual travelers all were fascinated by the strange land and its inhabitants and produced a voluminous literature about the Indians. No aspect of Indian life and customs was unexamined or unreported. The early Spanish reports were eagerly devoured by curious Europeans, who translated them into their own languages. And as the Portuguese, French, English, and Dutch followed the Spanish to America, they created their own reservoir of facts, surmises, and fanciful tales about the Indians. The accumulated images of the Indians, however, were not free of preconceptions. The Europeans already had established patterns into which to cast the inhabitants of the New World, who, since they lived in or close to the state of nature, were commonly called "savages."

Two basic images developed, contradictory in content. The first was that of the "noble savage," natural man living without technology and elaborate societal structures. Naked without shame, unconcerned about private ownership and the accumulation of material wealth but sharing all things unselfishly, and free from the problems of government, the Indian represented an idyllic state from which the European had strayed or fallen. Dwelling in an earthly paradise, the Indians were a living example of a golden age, long past in European history but now suddenly thrust again upon the world's consciousness. This good Indian welcomed the European invaders and treated them courteously and generously. He was handsome in appearance, dignified in manner, and brave in combat, and in all he exhibited a primitivism that had great appeal to many Europeans.

The second pattern was that of the "ignoble savage," treacherous, cruel, perverse, and in many ways approaching the brute beasts with whom he shared the wilderness. In this view, incessant warfare and cruelty to captives marked the Indians. Ritual cannibalism and human sacrifice were the ultimate abominations; but countless descriptions of Indian life noted the squalor, the filth, the indolence, the lack of discipline, the thievery, and the hard lot accorded Indian women. Not a few Englishmen saw the Indians with their superstitions and inhuman practices as literally children of the Devil.

The threads of these two conceptions intertwined in strange ways, and one or the other was drawn upon as suited the occasion. What persisted, however, were the notions of otherness, dependency, and inferiority. "Savagism" (whether noble or ignoble) was contrasted with "civility"; natural life in the wilds was opposed to disciplined life in civil society. There was little doubt in the minds of the Europeans (pace those who used the noble savage concept to condemn evils in their own society) that savagism was an inferior mode of existence and must give way to civility (civilization). The Indians were "younger brethren," dependents whom persons in superior positions claimed the right and obligation to shape into a new and civilized mold, by persuasion if possible and ultimately by force.

The concept of savagism and inferiority did not imply racism, that is, a belief that the Indian was an inherently different kind of being incapable of rising out of an inferior condition. There was little question in the minds of Englishmen that the Indians were human beings like themselves, a belief firmly planted in the scriptural account of Adam as the single progenitor of all men. Nor was color an obstacle, for the brownness or tawny complexion of the Indians was considered to be the result of conditioning by the elements or by the use of cosmetics on persons born basically white. Not until the very end of the seventeenth century was there any reference to Indians as red, and then the term may have had symbolic meaning or arisen from the use of war paint.

As the English experience deepened, the theoretical concepts of noble and ignoble savagery (though long continued in imaginative literature) were replaced by more realistic and complex appraisals based on practical encounters. Remnants of Indian tribes remained in the developing colonies, often in a state of abject dependency, but the Indians who received the attention of the English colonial authorities in the century preceding the independence of the United States were separate groups existing outside the areas of concentrated English settlement. More or less independent "nations" (like the Cherokees and other southern Indians and the Six Nations of the Iroquois in the north) entered into the diplomatic relations of the age along with a multiplicity of other political entities—French and Spanish as well as English colonies. These Indian groups were recognized and dealt with as distinct political entities, and forms of political structure familiar to Europeans were frequently attributed to them whether or not they accurately reflected the actual political organization of the tribes. Yet the white goal continued to be the ultimate transformation of the Indians, a "civilizing" process that reached its apogee in the United States at the end of the nineteenth century.

CHRISTIANIZATION

The civility toward which the English hoped to bring the savages of the New World had as its companion Christianity. Although the two could be separated in theory, in practice they were nearly always combined. Despite fears and assertions that the Indians were the children of Satan, Europeans generally believed that conversion was possible and repeatedly asserted missionary motives for colonization. The first charter of the Virginia Company of 1606 included the declaration that propagation of the gospel was a principal purpose of the enterprise, and instructions to Governor Thomas Gates directed conversion of the natives "as the most pious and noble end of this plantation." The results, to be sure, were minimal, for the Indians remained attached to their old ways, and missionary enthusiasm waned in the face of so little success. Frontier settlers had little interest in converting the natives, and what initiative there was came from the coastal areas or England.

The Puritans of New England made conversion of the Indians a major justification of their undertaking, and the goal of conversion remained throughout the period of settlement. Impressive work was done by the missionary Thomas Mayhew on Martha's Vineyard, and John Eliot, the "apostle to the Indians," won fame for his missionary zeal and effectiveness among the Indians as he established "praying towns" of natives. Parliament promoted the good work by chartering in 1649 the Society for Propagation of the Gospell in New-England. Education was at the heart of the endeavor, and the establishment of an Indian college at Harvard was an indication of the Puritans' determination. But even with the zeal and notable success of a few missionaries, the total number of converted Indians remained small, in part, no doubt, because of the total transformation required by the Puritans of their converts.

Of particular note among Christians who preached to the Indians were the Quakers, members of the Society of Friends. They followed a policy of nonviolence toward the Indians and showed a willingness to accept Indian culture unknown among other groups of colonists; the common dichotomy between "savagery" and "civilization" had no place in their worldview. The Quaker colony established by William Penn had peaceful relations with the Indians, the result in part of Penn's insistence that lands be fairly purchased from the Indians; and the reputation of Penn and his followers for fair dealing was strong in the nineteenth century and has lasted to the present day.

The great missionary upsurge in the United States after 1800 had a long history of colonial efforts as precedent, but in the English colonies, as later, mundane affairs overshadowed missionary work and at times seemed to obliterate it altogether.

INVASION OF THE INDIAN LANDS

The great distinguishing feature of English relations with the Indian groups was replacement of the Indians on the land by white settlers, not the conversion and assimilation of the Indians into European colonial society. The

Spanish colonies to the south were marked by subjugation of a massive concentrated native population and its use as a primary labor force in exploiting the mineral and agricultural resources of the conquered lands. The Spaniards, in addition, carried on large-scale missionary efforts to Christianize the Indians, and the church was as significant as the state in the development of Spanish America. The preponderantly male Spanish colonists, moreover, took Indian women as wives and concubines, incorporating the Indians biologically as well as socially into Spanish society. None of these situations obtained in the English colonies to any large extent. The difference can be explained in part by the diverse attitudes toward other peoples of the southern and northern Europeans, but it was the fundamental nature and place of English colonization that determined the case. The Indians did not present the same usefulness to the English that they did to the Spanish. There were no heavy Indian populations to be turned into a labor force and at the beginning no real need, for the English came to settle and cultivate the land. Nor was intermarriage or other liaison between the whites and Indians called for on a large scale among the family-oriented English colonists.

An underlying condition of English settlement was the depopulation that had previously occurred among the Indian tribes with whom the first Englishmen had come in contact. European diseases, of which smallpox was only the most important among many, struck the Indians with devastating force, for the inhabitants of the New World had developed no immunity to Old World diseases. Large areas were stripped of once heavy populations, and the cleared fields of the former inhabitants were taken over by white settlers, who often saw the hand of Providence in their good fortune.

The replacement of the Indians on the land became the basis for enduring conflict with the Indians who remained, and Indian wars marked the English experience as they did that of the United States. In the very beginning, the natives received the English colonists hospitably, greeted them with signs of friendship, and supplied them with food. But the image of savagism in the minds of the Europeans included a strong element of treachery on the part of the savages, and English behavior toward the Indians soon brought real enmity to the surface.

It became evident to the Indians that the colonists were moving in to stay, and as the English expanded, encroaching upon Indian lands and in many cases treating the inhabitants despicably, the Indians resisted with force; sometimes young warriors acted without tribal approval, sometimes considered attacks were planned and executed by skilled tribal leaders. Indian rivalries, too, contributed to the conflicts, for by aiding one or another group that eagerly sought help against its enemies, the English became involved in intertribal wars. The Europeans for their part looked for Indian allies in their own conflicts. Sooner or later most tribes became attached in some fashion to French, Spanish, or British imperial systems. The pattern of hostility and open war thus began early and was a dominant part of Indian-white relations until almost the end of the nineteenth century.

The first case was the massacre of 1622 in Virginia, in which the Indians under Opechancanough rose up against the white settlers who had invaded their lands and quickly killed a quarter to one-third of the population. English reaction was immediate and vengeful; the massacre was used as an excuse for a massive retaliation against the Indians, for it was looked upon as proof that Indians could not be trusted, even when professing friendship. Soon after, in New England, the Pequot War of 1637 began formal conflicts between the Indians and the English. The Pequots, moving into the Connecticut River Valley, met Puritans migrating into the same region and posed a threat to the peaceful expansion of the Massachusetts Bay Colony. Pequot harassment of the settlements brought war as the English attacked the hostile Indians in order to protect the nascent colony in Connecticut.

Such conflicts set a pattern. A new surprise attack by Indians in Virginia in 1644, which killed five hundred whites, brought new reprisals, and Bacon's Rebellion of 1676 had strong anti-Indian origins. In 1675–1676 King Philip's War in New England furnished still another case of warfare instigated by the Indians in a desperate attempt to stop the advancing tide of English settlement.

There was much theoretical discussion about the rights of savage, non-Christian peoples to the land they occupied, about whether the Indians and similar people could claim lands against Christian nations; and the idea that the lands in the New World were a *vacuum domicilium*, a wasteland, open for the taking, had wide acceptance. The god-fearing Puritans of Massachusetts Bay Colony found religious justification for dispossessing the Indians, since the Indians did not seem to be cultivating the earth as God had commanded. The supremacy of the cultivator over the hunter was a classic weapon in the arsenal of the dispossessors.

Aside from conquest in a "just war" and the aggressive encroachment of individual settlers, however, the English colonies generally did not simply dispossess the Indians as though they had no rights of any kind to the land. The vast claims in the New World made by European monarchs on the slightest pretense of "discovery" were claims against other European monarchs, not against the aboriginal inhabitants of those lands, and the handsome grants made to trading companies or individual proprietors in the form of colonial charters (with their extravagant language of lands extending from sea to sea) were of the same nature. The English settlers took steps to "quiet the Indian title" to the land before they took possession—"extinguishing the Indian title" was the terminology commonly used in later times by the United States. But this did not solve all problems, for the Indian and white systems of land tenure were quite different. The Indians had a notion of communal ownership of land, the English one of individual ownership in fee simple; neither fully understood the concept of the other.

Many years of actual contact between the groups were necessary before settled relations were agreed upon. But as European exploration and colonization increased, a theory in regard to the territory in America gained general acceptance, a theory developed by the European nations without consultation with the natives but one that did not totally disregard the Indians' rights. According to this theory, the European discoverer acquired the right of preemption, the right to acquire title to the soil from the natives in the area—by purchase if the Indians were willing to sell or by conquest—and to succeed the natives in occupying the soil if they should voluntarily leave the country or become extinct. Discovery gave this right against later discoverers; it did not make claim against the original possessors of the soil, the native Indians. In practice, nevertheless, and eventually in theory, absolute dominion or sovereignty over the land rested in the European nations or their successors, leaving to the aborigines the possessory and usufructuary rights to the land they occupied and used.

Although there were many cases in which individual colonists acquired land directly from Indians by purchase or some other sort of deed, abuses arose in these private arrangements. Colonial laws struck at the difficulty by declaring null and void all bargains made with the Indians that did not have governmental approval. Not only did such laws seek to remove causes of resentment among the Indians by preventing unjust and fraudulent purchases, but they aimed as well at preserving the rights of the Crown or the proprietor to the land, which would be seriously impaired by extinguishment of Indian titles in favor of private persons.

A common vehicle for dealing with the Indians for land, as also for more generalized relations of trade and of peace and war, was the treaty negotiation. Formal and stately ceremonials marked the interchanges, in which the English colonists adapted their proceedings to the deliberate and highly metaphorical patterns of the Indians. The treaties in the eighteenth century with the Iroquois, for example, were dramatic documents indicating a shrewdness and eloquence on the part of the Indians that were often a match for the self-interest of the whites. It is in the treaties that one sees best the acceptance by Europeans of the nationhood of the Indian groups that became a fixed principle in the national policy of the United States.

The treaties did not solve the problem of the steady pressure of white settlers on the Indian hunting grounds, and it is difficult to explain the slowness with which the imperial government came to realize the danger of these white encroachments. Continuing to rely on presents in order to keep the Indians attached to the English cause, officials only gradually awakened to the realization that the way to keep the Indians happy would be to remove the causes of their resentment and discontent.

TRADE RELATIONS

Colonial bargaining with the Indians for land was but one aspect of the transactions between the two races. Trade was the great point of contact, and the exchange of goods became a complex mixture of economic, political, and military elements. Trade was of inestimable importance to the colonies economically, but political considerations came to overshadow all else. Peace and at times the very existence of the colonies depended on Indian attachment to the English. Presents to the Indians were long a favored method of ensuring the allegiance of the tribes, and constant efforts to prevent abuses in dealing with the Indians aimed to secure peace on the frontiers. But the fundamental policy in Indian affairs was to make the Indians dependent on the English in their trade. This was especially true in the case of the Iroquois, whom the English determined to attach to themselves at all costs in their conflict with the French.

Important as trade was to both the English and the Indians, it was also the source of almost endless trouble, and it became necessary for the colonial governments to protect the interests of the commonwealth against uncontrolled private gain. Fraud and illegal practices on the part of traders stirred up Indian indignation and anger and thus led to frequent retaliations against the white community. In an attempt to prevent abuses, multifarious legislation regulating the conditions of the trade was enacted. Different systems were tried, modified, abandoned, and tried again. Sometimes a strict public monopoly of the trade was set up; more often, the trade was in the hands of private traders, who were hedged about by detailed regulations.

The universal means of regulation was a licensing system. This was the only way to keep trade open to all qualified persons and at the same time provide protection against traders of bad character. Often bond was required of traders, and violators of the regulations were punished by revocation of license, forfeiture of bond and stores, or some specified fine. Frequently trade was restricted to designated localities, the better to enforce the licensing system. Commissioners and agents were appointed to manage trade, issue licenses, enforce laws, and adjudicate disputes arising from trade.

Regulation of trade was critical in the case of two items—firearms and liquor—because of their potential for creating trouble. Just as the colonists were forbidden to buy land from the Indians, so were they restricted in the sale of arms and rum. For obvious reasons it was necessary to prevent the supplying of hostile Indians with weapons, and laws were enacted for that purpose, especially in the early days of the colonies, when survival against the Indians was of primary concern. Of far greater moment, however, were the restrictions placed on the sale of liquor to the natives. The Indian propensity toward strong drink and the disastrous results that inevitably followed were universal phenomena.

In an attempt to meet the difficulty, the colonies enacted prohibitions against the sale of rum and other liquors to the Indians. Often the prohibition was absolute. Stiff fines were provided for violators, forfeiture of stores was common, and in some cases authorization was given to destroy the liquor. Such absolute prohibitions met with opposition even from respectable traders, who could not then compete with the irregular traders or the Dutch and the French. Prohibitions were often relaxed and sometimes removed altogether.

Despite all the concern, regulation of the Indian trade by the individual colonies was a failure. The frontiers were too extensive and the inhabitants too widely scattered to permit adequate control of intercourse with the Indians. The Indians could not be induced or forced to bring their furs to central markets where the trade could be supervised and regulations enforced, so trade was left practically free and unrestricted. Anyone could engage in it by obtaining a license. The fur trade was thus in the hands of a great number of individuals, many of them lawless, unprincipled, and vicious. Even if one leaves out of the picture the offensive traders and focuses on the respectable merchants and colonial officials, there is little to praise, for Indian regulations could become hopelessly entangled in factional politics. There was no uniformity among the colonies, no two sets of like regulations. Abuses prohibited by one colony were tolerated by the next, and the conditions could hardly be amended while each colony was left to govern its own trade and to be guided in part by rivalry with its neighbors. The failure was apparent to all. The corruption, fraud, and mischievous dealings of the traders continually aroused the resentment of the Indians.

BRITISH IMPERIAL POLICY

The only solution was imperial control, and in 1755 the first step was taken to remove Indian affairs from the incompetent hands of the colonists and center political control in the hands of the imperial government. On April 15 William Johnson, longtime friend of the Iroquois, was appointed superintendent of Indian affairs for the northern department. In the following year Edmond Atkin was named to a similar post in the south; he was replaced in 1762 by the more famous John Stuart. The superintendents had full charge of political relations between the British and the Indians. Their responsibilities were numerous: protecting the Indians as well as they could from traders and speculators, negotiating the boundary lines that were called for after 1763, distributing presents given to the Indians in the attempt to gain and maintain their goodwill, and enlisting Indians in wartime to fight on the British side. The superintendents, too, exercised what control they could over the fur trade, although management of the trade remained to a great extent in colonial hands.

The purchase of Indian lands also needed attention. Restrictions placed by individual colonies upon the purchase of Indian lands by private persons had not worked well, for single colonies could not grasp the overall pressure along the frontier, and the provincial governments themselves were causing alarm among the tribes by their own purchase of lands. Imperial control was imperative if peace and harmony with the Indians was to be maintained.

On December 2, 1761, a general order was issued to the governors in the royal colonies that forbade them to issue grants to any Indian lands. All requests to purchase land from the Indians would have to be forwarded to the Board of Trade and would depend upon directions received from the board. The governors, furthermore, were to order all persons who "either wilfully or inadvertently" had settled on Indian lands to leave at once and were to prosecute all persons who had secured titles to such lands by fraud. Little by little the idea grew of establishing an official and defined boundary line to separate Indian lands from lands of the whites.

Pontiac's Rebellion in 1763 hastened action. Something was needed at once to pacify the Indians. They must be convinced that the encroachment of the whites was at an end and that the British government meant to honor the commitments made to them in both the north and the south. A boundary line needed to be drawn quickly, and the ridge of the Appalachians was accepted as the dividing line. On October 7, George III incorporated it into his famous Proclamation of 1763. The document proclaimed three things: it established the boundaries and the government for the new colonies of Florida and Nova Scotia acquired by the Peace of Paris; it offered specific encouragement to settlement in the new areas to relieve pressures on the western frontiers; and it established the boundary line as a new policy in Indian affairs.

By this proclamation, the governors and commanders in chief of the new colonies were forbidden to issue any warrants for survey or patents for lands beyond the boundaries set for their colonies. The king's subjects were prohibited from making purchases or settlements in the restricted territory, and any person who had already moved into the Indian country was ordered to leave at once.

The Appalachian boundary line of 1763 was provisional. Almost immediately the laborious work began for a carefully drawn line, worked out by the agents with the Indians. In 1765 the line was marked out in South Carolina and continued into North Carolina in 1767. During 1768–1769 the line was drawn west of Virginia's settlements—with some reluctance on the part of Virginia, which did not want to appear to give up its claims to the western regions. In the north the responsibility lay with Sir William Johnson. At a conference with the Six Nations in the spring of 1765 he obtained the approval of the Indians, and in 1768, by the Treaty of Fort Stanwix, he settled the northern boundary line. The concept of such a line by then had become ineradicable; but the line itself moved constantly westward as new treaties and new purchases drove the Indians back before the advancing whites. The Proclamation of 1763 was not a carefully worked out plan for management of the West and regulation of affairs with the Indians. But a plan drawn up in 1764 for thoroughgoing imperial control of Indian trade was rejected because of its expense, and the regulation of the fur trade was returned to the colonies. It was a strange reversal. The Board of Trade was aware that the colonies had failed and that the misconduct of the ill-regulated traders had "contributed not a little to involve us in the enormous expences of an Indian war." Undaunted, with eyes consciously or unconsciously blinded to reality, the board trusted that the ill effects of past neglect and inattention would induce colonial officials in the future to more caution and better management.

The results were what might have been expected. The ministry perhaps thought the Indian boundary line alone would forever remove the causes of friction between the Indians and the English, but the American settlers could not be restrained. Control of the fur trade was no more exact. The failure of the colonies to enact the necessary legislation caused great restlessness among the Indians. Superintendent Stuart described the conditions in his department as chaotic, for the old lawless traders were still at work, and settlements were constantly appearing across the boundary line. The failure of the colonies to agree upon any sort of general regulations resulted in intolerable conditions in the West. Some interposition of Parliament for the regulation of the fur trade on an imperial basis was necessary, and one last attempt was made. By the Quebec Act of 1774 the western areas were placed under the Quebec government. It was a return to the former plan for imperializing the West, but it came too late. The Revolutionary War and the establishment of the independent United States threw these problems into the hands of the new nation.

CHAPTER I

The Revolutionary War and the Years Following

The colonies, engaged in a war with the mother country, were much concerned about the Indian nations at their back, and coordinated Indian policy began to take shape during the Revolutionary War, even before independence was declared. The individual colonies were well aware of Indian matters, and some of them sent commissioners to the tribes. But the Indian problem could not be handled adequately by disparate provincial practices.

THE POLICY OF THE CONTINENTAL CONGRESS

On July 12, 1775, less than three months after Lexington and Concord, the Continental Congress inaugurated a federal Indian policy with a report from a committee on Indian affairs. Declaring that "securing and preserving the friendship of the Indian Nations, appears to be a subject of the utmost moment to these colonies" and noting that there was reason to fear that the British would incite the Indians against the rebelling colonies, the committee recommended that steps be taken to maintain the friendship of the Indians. Congress thereupon established three departments: a northern department including the Six Nations and the Indians to the north of them; a southern department including the Cherokees and all others to the south of them; and a middle department containing the tribes living in between. It appointed commissioners for each department, who were to treat with the Indians "in the name, and on behalf of the united colonies"; they were to work to preserve peace and friendship with the Indians and, in the quaint understatement of the report, "to prevent their taking any part in the present commotions."

As with all the major questions involved in forming the new government, so with Indian policy the basic decision concerned the authority to be given to the federal government. The imperial experiment in unified management of the Indians had made its mark on the minds of the delegates to Congress, and a majority believed that Indian affairs belonged to the central government. Benjamin Franklin, the leading personality in the Congress, had offered a plan of union at Albany in 1754 that provided that the president-general, with the advice of the grand council, should control Indian affairs. Now he included the idea in a draft for a confederation that he proposed to Congress on July 21, 1775.

Congressional control of Indian affairs was not accepted by all, but in the end the need to control the Indians prevailed, for, as James Wilson pointed out, the Indians refused to recognize any superior authority, and only the United States in Congress assembled could have any hope of dealing with them successfully. Above all else, rivalries between colonies in treating with the Indians had to be avoided. In its final form, the Articles of Confederation declared: "The United States in Congress assembled shall also have the sole and exclusive right and power of . . . regulating the trade and managing all affairs with the Indians, not members of any of the States, provided that the legislative right of any State within its own limits be not infringed or violated."

Thus the management of Indian affairs and the regulation of Indian trade fell to the federal government. The principle was enunciated, but it was not crystal clear, for the proviso cast a heavy blur over the article and the power that it actually gave to Congress and prohibited to the states. James Madison in Number 42 of *The Federalist* poked fun at the article, ridiculing it as "obscure and contradictory," as "absolutely incomprehensible," and as inconsiderately endeavoring to accomplish impossibilities.

The debates over the Articles of Confederation and the subsequent practice under this frame of government, nevertheless, clarified one element of Indian relations: the concept of the Indian country was strengthened. Not only was the Indian country the territory lying beyond the boundary lines, forbidden to settlers and to unlicensed traders, but it was also the area over which federal authority extended. Federal laws governing the Indians and the Indian trade took effect in the Indian country only.

The Articles of Confederation were approved by Congress in 1777, but they did not take effect until 1781, for Maryland refused to ratify until the landed states had ceded their western claims to the United States. Meanwhile, the course of the war was in the hands of the Continental Congress and its committees.

The British had the more advantageous position in the war and in large measure retained the allegiance of the Indians. John Stuart and his deputies in the south and the successors of Sir William Johnson in the north made use of their authority and influence with the Indians to prevent them from following the colonists in opposition to the king. The British not only had better agents than the patriots could muster; they had powerful arguments, too, which they did not fail to exploit. It was plain that the causes of complaint among the Indians—the abuses of traders and the encroachment of white settlers—all came from the colonists. The British imperial officials, on the other hand, had a good record of trying to deal justly with the Indians, of protecting their rights to their lands and their peltries, and of furnishing the goods needed for trade. The British agents did not hesitate to call these facts to the attention of the Indians.

The ineffectiveness of the revolutionary government in supplying the Indians with essential trade goods was a serious disadvantage in seeking Indian support. It was all well and good to urge the Indians to desert the British by remaining neutral or by actively joining the colonial forces, but these positions (certainly the latter) meant loss of trade ties with the British, who alone could adequately supply the Indians' needs. The Americans could not honestly promise to replace the British as suppliers of goods, and this the Indians undoubtedly knew.

At first, the best the patriots could hope for was to keep the Indians neutral in the conflict, but that sentiment gradually changed, and the colonists, like the British, began to seek positive assistance from the Indians. In this they had little success. The only important groups to espouse the cause of the patriots were the Tuscaroras and Oneidas of the Six Nations, largely, it seems, because of the influence among them of the New England missionary Samuel Kirkland.

Although there was no consolidated uprising of Indians along the western frontier—which could have been a serious if not fatal blow to colonial aspirations—there were sporadic outbreaks, enough to keep settlers on edge and give consternation to the Congress that was directing the war. This phase of the Revolutionary War, perhaps, can best be considered a continuation of the tension between the two races that had already become a way of life in the West. But there is little doubt that the borderland warfare was aggravated by British encouragement of the Indians.

There were only a few instances of formal entry into the war by Indians. The Cherokees in 1776, against the advice of John Stuart, mounted an attack on the back country of the Carolinas. It was a disastrous venture. In an unusual show of intercolonial cooperation, militia from Virginia, North Carolina, and South Carolina united to crush the Indians. The Cherokees signed treaties in which they ceded large sections of land. This was the end of organized Indian harassment in the south.

In the north, the protagonists were members of the Iroquois confederacy who elected to side actively with the British. Ably directed by Guy Johnson, who had succeeded his uncle as superintendent in the north, and greatly influenced by the remarkable Mohawk chief Joseph Brant, the Mohawks and Senecas and their friends took an active part in the attempt in 1778 to cut off New England from the rest of the colonies. As General St. Leger drove east from Niagara along the Mohawk Valley to meet General Burgoyne coming from the north toward Albany, his army was heavily augmented by Indian allies. They played a significant role in the battle of Oriskany, as colonial troops sought to relieve the beleaguered garrison at Fort Stanwix.

Iroquois power was a distinct threat aimed at the heart of the colonies. It was to destroy this danger and show the Indians that the colonial government could and would strike strongly against the tribes who had decided to fight with the British that Washington sent a well-planned expedition into the Iroquois country in 1779 under General John Sullivan. Following a deliberate scorched-earth policy, Sullivan's army moved north into the heart of the Iroquois confederacy. Swinging wide through western New York, the troops destroyed villages and crops, without, however, managing to destroy the Indians, who faded away ahead of the approaching army. The policy of destruction left blackened ruins and a bitterness that was not easily erased.

The British from their post at Detroit instigated Indian war parties against the settlements south of the Ohio. To cut off this danger, George Rogers Clark, sent out by Virginia, attacked the Illinois towns and then recaptured Vincennes from the British commander Henry Hamilton, greatly bolstering the morale of western patriots. It was less than a total victory, for the Indians continued to be dependent on trade with the whites; and it was the British, not the Americans, who could provided the needed trading system. Moreover, Clark did not receive the reinforcements he required to proceed against Detroit, and for the last two years of the war he was on the defensive against continual Indian attacks.

Although the Indian campaigns in the war had little effect on the outcome, they did leave a lasting heritage. On the one side, Indian participation in the Revolutionary War had far-reaching effects upon the Indian communities themselves. The war, with the pull in opposite directions by the British and the colonists, fragmented the Iroquois confederacy and in general demoralized the eastern and southern tribes. Those who had agreed to aid Great Britain had succumbed to promises of support of land claims and generous provisions for trade. They discovered to their astonishment that at the end of the war these were disregarded, and they were left on their own to deal with the victorious colonists. Important, too, was the heritage of hostility between whites and Indians to which the war contributed so strongly. It is true that such fundamental causes of conflict as white desire for land existed independently of the war, but the atrocities on the frontiers, on the part of both Indians and whites, intensified antagonism and reinforced a pattern that might, in other circumstances, have been modified if not eliminated. It seemed only natural and proper to the founders of the nation that Indian affairs be placed under the War Department.

When the Revolutionary War ended, the Treaty of Paris signed with Great Britain in 1783 recognized the independence of the United States and designated the Mississippi River and the Great Lakes as the western and northern boundaries of the new nation. But because the treaty made no provision for the Indian tribes, they were considered technically still at war. It behooved the new nation to come to terms with the tribes at once, for the great desideratum was peace. Prolonged hostilities on the frontier could well have collapsed the young nation in the first precarious years of its existence.

Negotiations with the Indians came quickly. In the north and west were the treaties of Fort Stanwix on October 22, 1784, Fort McIntosh on January 21, 1785, and Fort Finney (at the mouth of the Great Miami) on January 31, 1786. The first, drawn up with the Six Nations, limited the Indians to an area in western New York and distributed goods to them pursuant to "the humane and liberal views of the United States." The second was a treaty with Delawares, Wyandots, Chippewas, and Ottawas by which these western Indians were allotted an area of land and by which they ceded to the United States other lands formerly claimed by them. The last was a similar agreement with the Shawnees. In these negotiations the idea of a boundary line was taken for granted; the basic problems were exact determination of the line, the conflict of state and federal authority in dealing with the tribes, and the grounds for demanding cessions from the Indians.

The United States in these first treaties after the Revolutionary War thought it was dealing with conquered tribes or nations. Although Congress spoke of liberality toward the vanquished and realized that some moderation of claims might be necessary to avoid a renewal of fighting, its commissioners dictated the boundary lines and offered no compensation for the ceded lands. To this highhanded arrangement the Indians, abetted by the British, continued to object. They had never asked for peace, they insisted, but thought that the Americans desired it, and they had no idea that they were to be treated as conquered peoples.

Furthermore, although the lands west of the boundary lines were guaranteed to the Indians and the United States promised to restrict the encroachment of whites, white aggressions continued. The government seemed powerless to hold back the onslaughts of the advancing whites, and by 1786 the northwest Indians, out of disgust with the whole policy of the United States, were ready to repudiate all the agreements made with them since the close of the war. In the south, the difficulties were, if anything, even greater because of the tenacity with which the Indians held to their lands, the mounting pressure of white settlers on the lands, the history of hostility of the tribes against the whites, and the serious interference by state officials in the federal government's handling of Indian affairs.

The new nation faced innumerable difficulties, and it was imperative that the Indians remain at peace. This happy end could be attained only by a policy of justice toward the Indians and protection of their rights and property against unscrupulous traders, avaricious settlers, and ubiquitous speculators. With this in mind, Congress on August 7, 1786, enacted an Ordinance for the Regulation of Indian Affairs. The ordinance established southern and northern Indian departments, divided by the Ohio River, and authorized a superintendent of Indian affairs for each. The superintendents and their deputies had power to grant trading licenses. They could not engage in the trade themselves, however, and had to take an oath to fulfill their obligations and to post a bond for the faithful discharge of their duties. All traders needed a license, good for one year at a fee of fifty dollars, and had to give bond of three thousand dollars for strict observance of the laws and regulations. Only citizens of the United States could reside among the Indians or trade with them.

Again, in the Northwest Ordinance of July 13, 1787, the federal government voiced its position: "The utmost good faith shall always be observed towards the Indians, their lands and property shall never be taken from them without their consent; and in their property, rights and liberty, they shall never be invaded or disturbed, unless in just and lawful wars authorised by Congress; but laws founded in justice and humanity shall from time to time be made, for preventing wrongs being done to them, and for preserving peace and friendship with them."

The continual reassertion by Congress of its ideas of justice toward the Indians began to have a hollow sound, for white encroachment on Indian lands continued. General Henry Knox, secretary of war under the Confederation, reported to Congress in July 1788 the unprovoked and direct outrages against Cherokee Indians by inhabitants on the frontier of North Carolina in open violation of the Treaty of Hopewell. The outrages were of such extent, Knox declared, "as to amount to an actual although informal war of the said white inhabitants against the said Cherokees." The action he blamed on the "avaricious desire of obtaining the fertile lands possessed by said Indians of which and particularly of their ancient town of Chota they are exceedingly tenacious," and he urged Congress to take action to uphold the treaty provisions and thus the reputation and dignity of the Union.

Knox came to realize that agreements with the Indians based on the right of conquest did not work and that adherence to such a policy would continually endanger the peace of the frontier. The British and colonial practice of purchasing the right of the soil from the Indians was the only method to which the Indians would peaceably agree, and Knox urged a return to that policy. He recommended, therefore, that the land ceded by the northwest Indians be compensated for and that future cessions be acquired by purchase. By the treaties signed at Fort Harmar on January 9, 1789, with the Six Nations and some of the northwest Indians, the lands granted to the United States at Fort Stanwix and Fort McIntosh were paid for. Small as the payments were, they marked the abandonment of the policy that the lands from the Indians had been acquired by conquest.

TREATY MAKING UNDER THE CONSTITUTION

After the concern of the Continental Congress with Indian affairs and the discussion aroused when the Articles of Confederation were drawn up, it is surprising to find so little about Indian matters in the Constitutional Convention of 1787. It was almost as if the presence of the Indians on the frontier had slipped the minds of the Founding Fathers and provisions were made for carrying on relations with them only as an afterthought. The lack of debate on the question indicated, perhaps, the universal agreement that Indian affairs should be left in the hands of the federal government.

James Madison proposed a broad grant of power "to regulate affairs with the Indians," but in the end the convention agreed to a simple phrase, "and with the Indian tribes," added to the commerce clause. These five words would seem to be scant foundation upon which to build the structure of federal legislation regulating trade and intercourse with the Indian tribes. Yet through them, plus treaty-making and other powers, Congress exercised what amounted to plenary power over the Indian tribes. John Marshall noted in *Worcester* v. *Georgia*: "[The Constitution] confers on Congress the powers of war and peace; of making treaties, and of regulating commerce with foreign nations, and among the several States, and with the Indian tribes. These powers comprehend all that is required for the regulation of our intercourse with the Indians. They are not limited by any restrictions on their free action. The shackles imposed on this power, in the confederation, are discarded."

The Constitution, with its division of powers among the three branches of government, necessitated a working out in practice of the grants of authority only briefly enumerated in the document itself. This was particularly true in regard to treaty making, which was stated in these terms: "[The President] shall have power, by and with the advice and consent of the Senate, to make treaties, provided two thirds of the senators present concur." Two questions arose: Were agreements with the Indian tribes to follow regular treaty procedures? How precisely did the Senate advise and consent in regard to treaties? Both questions were answered in 1789 and 1790 as President Washington dealt with the Senate concerning the treaties of Fort Harmar of January 1789 and the treaty with the Creeks at New York of August 1790.

The Fort Harmar treaties, although negotiated before the government under the Constitution was set up, were submitted to the Senate on May 25, 1789, by Henry Knox, who went to the Senate in person as a representative of the president to explain the circumstances under which the treaties had been concluded. When the Senate postponed action on the treaties, President Washington argued that it was the custom among nations to have the treaties negotiated by commissioners ratified by the government that had appointed them and that this practice should be followed also with the Indian tribes. The Senate, after some debate, accepted the president's view. Thus was the precedent established that Indian treaties—like those with foreign nations—be formally approved by the Senate before they took effect.

Washington and Knox went to confer in person with the Senate in regard to the treaty with the Creeks. The president outlined for the Senate his proposed solution to the complicated situation in the south, where Georgia was independently making treaties with the Indians and where the Creeks, under their astute leader Alexander McGillivray, were playing off the United States against the Spanish. The conferences between the president and the Senate were marked by constraint and tension, however, and the procedure proved unsatisfactory to both parties. The Senate wanted to examine the documents of the case at leisure, and Washington was irked by such delay. When he left the chamber, the president declared that "he would be damned if he ever went there again." And in fact he never did, although he continued to keep the Senate informed about the progress of negotiations with the Creeks.

The Creeks in the end signed a treaty with the United States at New York on August 7, 1790, in which they acknowledged themselves to be under the protection of the United States of America and agreed not to hold treaties with individual states or persons. For a small annuity, the Indians ceded lands actually occupied by Georgia settlers, but they refused to accede to the rest of Georgia's claims, and the United States solemnly guaranteed the Creek lands lying beyond the boundary line established by the Treaty of New York. It promised also to furnish "useful domestic animals and implements of husbandry," in order that the Creek nation might be led "to a greater degree of civilization and to become herdsmen and cultivators instead of remaining in a state of hunters." Secret articles to the treaty made McGillivray an agent of the United States in the Creek nation with the rank of brigadier general and an annuity of twelve hundred dollars and effectively guaranteed him control over Creek trade through American ports.

The United States government thus treated with Indian tribes with legal procedures similar to those used with foreign nations, a practice that acknowledged some kind of autonomous nationhood of the Indian tribes. As time passed, the practice became deeply ingrained. Many of the basic relations between the United States and the tribes were determined by treaties, and the obligations incurred endured after the treaty-making process itself ended.

Although Indian treaties and those with foreign nations had a legal similarity, it would be a mistake to push the sameness too far. In fact, the Indian groups were not foreign nations, and the negotiations with them often differed markedly from those with England or France. The Indian tribes, either willingly or because forced to do so, acknowledged in the very treaties themselves a degree of dependence upon the United States and a consequent diminution of sovereignty. In the treaties at Hopewell in 1785–1786, the Cherokees, Chickasaws, and Choctaws acknowledged themselves "to be under the protection of the United States of America, and of no other sovereign whosoever." Similar clauses appeared in the treaties of Fort McIntosh and Fort Harmar with the northwest Indians, in the Treaty of Fort Stanwix with the Six Nations, and in the Creek treaty at New York. And the Hopewell treaties proclaimed: "For the benefit and comfort of the Indians, and for the prevention of injuries or oppressions on the part of the citizens or Indians, the United States in Congress assembled shall have the sole and exclusive right of regulating the trade with the Indians, and managing all their affairs in such manner as they think proper." Other clauses specified provisions for trade and for the extradition of whites who committed crimes within the Indian nations.

Although the treaties did not touch the autonomy of the tribes in internal affairs, they made it clear that in relations with whites, the Indian nations accepted significant restrictions. The tribes were not free to deal directly with European nations, with individual states, or with private individuals.

One indication of the lack of full sovereignty among the Indian tribes was the insistence by the United States on the principle of preemption of Indian lands, inherited from the European nations who had developed it in the course of their New World settlement. Thomas Jefferson relied upon this accepted view when the British minister asked him in 1792 what he understood to be the American right in the Indian soil. The secretary of state replied: "1st. A right of pre-emption of their lands; that is to say, the sole and exclusive right of purchasing from them whenever they should be willing to sell. 2d. A right of regulating the commerce between them and the whites. . . . We consider it as established by the usage of different nations into a kind of *Jus gentium* for America, that a white nation settling down and declaring that such and such are their limits, makes an invasion of those limits by any other white nation an act of war, but gives no right of soil against the native possessors."

Henry Knox entertained the same views, although he based them less on theoretical reasoning about the law of nations than did Jefferson. "That the Indians possess the natural rights of man, and that they ought not wantonly to be divested thereof, cannot be well denied," Knox declared, and he recommended that these rights be ascertained and declared by law. "Were it enacted that the Indians possess the right to all their territory which they have not fairly conveyed," he wrote, "and that they should not be divested thereof, but in consequence of open treaties, made under the authority of the United States, the foundation of peace and justice would be laid."

Such views of Indian rights to the land were the basis of the dealings of the United States and the Indians. However great the pressures for dispossession of the Indians, the legal principles were clear. Judicial decisions regarding Indian rights to the land stressed either the possessory right of the Indians or the limitations of that right—the "sacred" right of occupancy or the "mere" right of occupancy—but all agreed that the aboriginal title involved an exclusive right of occupancy but not the ultimate ownership.

SUBJUGATING THE INDIANS

The goal of Washington and Knox was peace, to be obtained and preserved by just and humane treatment of the Indians. Yet there was undeclared war on the frontiers between frontiersmen and Indians in raids and counterraids. The federal government soon came to realize that military might was an indispensable ingredient of the policy it pursued. When treaties, laws, proclamations, and trade provisions by themselves failed to ensure tranquility on the frontier, military force was needed to enforce the stipulations of the treaties and the legislation and to back up the decisions of the agents and the War Department. Moreover, from time to time it was employed to crush resisting hostile tribes and force them to submit to land cessions and other demands of white society.

A crisis came first in the Old Northwest as waves of white settlers appeared along the Ohio, floating down the river by the thousands in flatboats and barges. The Indians refused to accept the invasion. The Americans were intent on settling north of the Ohio, and the Indians were equally resolved that the Ohio was to be a permanent and irrevocable boundary between the white settlers and themselves.

Although the War Department was not to be pushed precipitously into military action, pressure for war became too strong for Knox to resist as reports of Indian incursions and atrocities poured in from the frontier, and military engagements with the northwest tribes began. General Josiah Harmar on September 20, 1790, launched a punitive attack against the Miami towns. His expedition, formed mostly of militia from Kentucky and Pennsylvania, was routed by the Indians. The next to try to chastise the Indians was Governor Arthur St. Clair, who was given command with a commission as major general. His chances of success in an expedition against the Indians were greater than those of the hapless Harmar, but delays in getting supplies and in establishing a chain of posts north of Fort Washington led to a late fall campaign, and the troops, still largely militia, fared no better than Harmar's. An attack by the Indians on November 4, 1791, destroyed St. Clair's army.

St. Clair's defeat was a national disaster, and it proved that a makeshift force was not enough to face the competent chiefs and warriors of the Indians. Knox called for an adequate military force of disciplined troops, and Congress in March 1792 authorized more regular infantry and militia cavalry. President Washington appointed another Revolutionary War general, Anthony Wayne, to lead a new campaign against the Indians. After organizing and disciplining his troops, Wayne moved north from Fort Washington and spent the winter building a post he called Fort Greenville. From there in the spring and summer of 1794 he prepared his advance against the tribes, and on August 20 at the Battle of Fallen Timbers the Indians fled headlong in defeat. The British at nearby Fort Miami, not willing to risk open conflict with United States troops, closed their gates in the face of the retreating Indians and with this action ended the Indians' hope of succor from those who had encouraged their defiance of the Americans.

Wayne at once consolidated his victory. He built Fort Wayne at the headwaters of the Wabash and by November was back at his headquarters at Greenville. He negotiated with the Indians, who were stunned by their defeat and the failure of the British to support them. Their hope of maintaining the Ohio boundary was now gone, and on August 3, 1795, at the Treaty of Greenville, they agreed to Wayne's terms, giving up once and for all two-thirds of Ohio and a sliver of Indiana.

Peace with the Indians in the northwest was supported by diplomatic negotiations with the British, whose occupation of military posts on American soil after the Revolutionary War had encouraged the Indians and exasperated the United States. Jay's Treaty, signed in 1794, although highly unpopular among some segments of the population because it failed to settle maritime grievances against Great Britain, promoted peace in the West, for the British agreed to evacuate the troublesome posts and turn them over to the United States on June 1, 1796. The provision in the treaty that permitted Indian traders from Canada to operate unrestricted within American territory was a continuing threat to American sovereignty because of the inimical influence of the traders upon the Indians, yet the transfer of Fort Mackinac, Detroit, and the other posts was a significant recognition of American authority that was not lost upon the Indians.

In the region south of the Ohio River, American sovereignty was maintained as precariously as in the Old Northwest, for much of the present state of Tennessee, most of Alabama and Mississippi, and large parts of Georgia were held by the Cherokees, Creeks, Chickasaws, and Choctaws. Spain possessed the Floridas and Louisiana and claimed jurisdiction as far north as the Tennessee River; it sought to control the trade of the southern tribes and, by entering into alliances with them, to use the Indians as a barrier against the advancing American settlers. Yet despite serious provocation and the clamor for military support from whites in the region, the federal government refused to fight in the south. It had committed its meager regular army to resolving the question of effective American sovereignty in the Northwest Territory, and had no resources to commit in another direction. Nor could the United States afford to antagonize or irritate Spain while delicate negotiations were under way over the southern boundary of the United States and navigation of the Mississippi. The Indian problem was merged with the boundary dispute, and one could not be negotiated or solved without the other.

In the Treaty of San Lorenzo (Pinckney Treaty), signed with Spain on October 27, 1795, the United States won recognition of the thirty-first parallel as its southern boundary and navigation rights on the Mississippi. Then the Louisiana Purchase in 1803 changed the whole complexion of Mississippi Valley defense and Indian relations, for the withdrawal of the Spanish from New Orleans and the acquisition of the right bank of the Mississippi from its source to its mouth removed the obstacles to western commerce that had long irritated frontiersmen. Spain, however, was still present in the Floridas, and the southern Indians maintained their hold on vast stretches of territory. The Creeks, supported by British traders and the Spanish, remained a special problem, but there was relative quiet until the approach of the War of 1812.

PROBING THE NEW WEST

The Louisiana Purchase had nearly doubled the territorial size of the United States and provided a new empire of unmeasured extent and unknown character. Occupying and establishing American sovereignty over the land and its people brought new problems and new opportunities in government relations with the Indians.

In the southern part of the Louisiana Purchase, with its concentrations of white population in New Orleans and outlying regions, the United States moved quickly to replace the Spanish and French and to institute civil government of its own. There were few Indians in the area. But north of the thirty-third parallel, a region organized as the Territory of Louisiana, the land was largely wilderness and, aside from St. Louis and a few other small settlements along the Mississippi and its tributaries, the Indians were the lords of the land.

To serve as first governor of the new territory, President Jefferson appointed General James Wilkinson, who combined in his one person both civil and military authority over the region. Although Wilkinson's fame has been tarnished by his association with Aaron Burr and his machinations with Spanish officials in the western regions, he had a fundamental grasp of the problems facing the United States with its new empire, problems that came from British and Spanish influence upon the Indians. His experience in campaigns in the Old Northwest had given his mind a distinctly anti-British set, and what he learned at his post in St. Louis did little to change it. Of immediate concern was the danger from British traders. Wilkinson knew that he could not suddenly cut off the British merchandise that furnished the regular supplies of the Indians, but he urged the secretary of state and the secretary of war to warn the British that the trade would be stopped and to make the warning public.

Meanwhile, President Jefferson, fired by a dream of empire of his own, set about to gain accurate information about the land and its inhabitants. The most daring and dramatic of the expeditions was that of Meriwether Lewis and William Clark and their corps of discovery to the Pacific and back in 1804–1806. Along with the gathering of scientific data, trade with the Indians and peaceful relations with them were uppermost in Jefferson's mind as he sent the explorers out. When they ascended the Missouri, Lewis and Clark carefully informed the Indians that the French and Spanish had withdrawn from the waters of the Missouri and the Mississippi and that the "great Chief of the Seventeen great nations of America" was now the one to whom they must turn. The chiefs were told to turn in their French, Spanish, and British flags and medals, for it was no longer proper for them to keep these emblems of attachment to any great father except the American one.

While Lewis and Clark were still working their way across the Great Divide, General Wilkinson himself sent out two exploratory expeditions with similar goals. On July 30, 1805, he sent Zebulon Montgomery Pike up the Mississippi River to seek its source. Pike was told to gather geographical and scientific knowledge, to locate proper points for military posts, and "to spare no pains to conciliate the Indians and to attach them to the United States." Pike got as far as Leech Lake (somewhat short of the source of the Mississippi), where he found a British trader operating on American soil. He asserted American rights in no uncertain terms in a letter to the trader, and in council with the Chippewas he directed them to turn in their British medals and flags.

In 1806 Pike made a second trip, this time to probe the activities of the Spanish and their influence over the Indians in the southwest. He was instructed to make contact with the Comanches, to make peace between them and other tribes, and to induce some of their chiefs to visit Washington, where their friendship could be cultivated and they could be impressed with the power and authority of the United States. Pike found clear evidence of Spanish influence over the Indians; and when he ventured too far west, he was arrested by Spanish troops, taken into Mexico, and not released for several weeks.

As the century advanced, there were new signs of Indian unrest on the frontiers, and the fragile peace achieved by a combination of negotiation and military force began to crumble. William Clark, who on his return from the expedition of discovery began a long career as Indian agent and superintendent at St. Louis, noted in late 1807 that the Indians on the upper Missouri "Shew Some hostile Simtoms," which he attributed to British action, and he feared that British traders had already made inroads on the upper Missouri.

Soon the celebrated Shawnee chief Tecumseh and his brother, the Prophet, appeared on the scene. The Prophet preached resistance to the whites and a return to primitive ways, and Tecumseh became a political leader, determined to stop the westward advance of the whites. Arguing that no sale of Indian land could be valid unless approved by all the tribes, he set about to form a confederacy that would unite the Indians in blocking white aggrandizement. For aid in this great project Tecumseh depended upon the British and from them drew arms and ammunition.

Tecumseh and his brother won support among the northwest Indians, and in 1808 the Prophet and his followers moved to the upper Wabash River at the mouth of Tippecanoe Creek. This concentration of warriors on the Wabash alarmed William Henry Harrison, governor of Indiana Territory, who was convinced that serious trouble was brewing. Then, in the face of growing Indian intransigence, Harrison concluded a treaty at Fort Wayne on September 30, 1809, with the Miamis, Weas, and Delawares by which he purchased a large tract of land in Indiana. The treaty greatly agitated Tecumseh even though no Shawnee lands were involved, and in 1810 he visited Harrison at Vincennes, where he threatened the governor with hostile gestures and announced that he would never submit to the Fort Wayne treaty. The following summer Tecumseh appeared again with a large retinue. He told Harrison he was on his way south to bring the southern nations into his confederacy.

Harrison made use of the opportune absence of the Shawnee leader to advance against the Prophet's town. With regular troops, militia, and volunteers, he moved north from Vincennes in September 1811. On November 7 the Indians attacked Harrison's army and were repulsed only after severe fighting in which Harrison's losses were heavy. This Battle of Tippecanoe was described by Harrison as "a complete and decisive victory," but in the end it settled nothing. The Prophet's town was burned and his followers were scattered, but enmity against the whites only increased. Another step had been taken toward all-out war to see who would control the Old Northwest.

THE WAR OF 1812 AND AMERICAN DOMINION IN THE WEST

When the War of 1812 broke out, the British and their Indian allies immediately reasserted control in the territory stretching west of Lake Michigan. Fort Mackinac fell on July 17, 1812, and Fort Dearborn (established in 1802 on the site of future Chicago) was evacuated on August 15 and most of its inhabitants massacred by the Indians as they marched out. More important was the disastrous surrender of Detroit on August 16 by General William Hull, who feared the massacre of the women and children by the Indian allies of the British if the city were taken by force.

The surrender of Hull's army left consternation and confusion on the frontier, and the Indians were emboldened by the American disaster. In Ohio, where settlement was heavy and concentrated, little was to be feared, but in thinly settled Indiana and Illinois fears of Indian raids were well-founded. Clearly a new northwestern army would have to be organized to repair the damage done by Hull's defeat. The work fell to William Henry Harrison, who moved successfully against the British in upper Canada as soon as Admiral Oliver H. Perry had won control of the supply lines in the Great Lakes. At the Battle of the Thames on October 5, 1813, Harrison defeated Colonel Henry Proctor and his Indian allies. The Indians, ably led by Tecumseh, offered stiff resistance, but Tecumseh was soon killed and the Indians followed the British in flight.

Meanwhile a parallel story unfolded in the south, where the Creeks developed a hostile faction that posed a serious threat. Certain of the young Creeks were influenced by Tecumseh, who visited the nation in 1811 and again in 1812 to solicit southern Indian support. Although older chiefs warned against Tecumseh, the great Shawnee came with a bagful of magic tricks and on his second visit brought encouraging news of American defeats. With promises that Spanish and British aid would support the Indians, he won over the young warriors, or Red Sticks. When a part of Red Sticks returning from a trip to Pensacola (where the Spanish governor had supplied them with ammunition) were attacked by white frontiersmen, the Indians retaliated by massacring the men, women, and children at Fort Mims, a stockade forty miles north of Mobile. The United States was electrified, and campaigns to crush the hostile Red Sticks were immediately mounted.

The most important of these was led by Andrew Jackson, commander of the Tennessee militia. He quickly assembled volunteers, augmented them with regular infantry, and prepared to strike the Creeks in their stronghold in eastern Alabama. On March 27, 1814, aided by a contingent of Cherokees, Jackson crushed the hostile Creeks at Horseshoe Bend, a fortified position on the Tallapoosa River in the heart of the Creek country. Then on August 9 he forced the Creeks to sign a treaty at Fort Jackson, in which the Indians ceded large sections of land west of the Coosa River and along the Florida border, to serve as buffers against the Chickasaws and Choctaws on the west and the Spanish on the south.

The treaty of peace signed at Ghent on December 27, 1814, provided for a return to the status quo before the war and left unmentioned the basic maritime problems that had done so much to bring on the conflict, and it is easy to assert that the war accomplished nothing. This was certainly not the case on the frontier in the northwest and the southwest. The defeat of the Indians at the Thames and at Horseshoe Bend and the failure of the British (or the Spanish) to substantiate Indian claims against the Americans put a new complexion on the Indian problems in the West.

The Indians, against whom so much of the American force in the War of 1812 had pressed, were not a party to the Treaty of Ghent. The treaty, however, provided that the United States would undertake to put an end to all hostilities with Indian tribes with whom it might still be at war at the time of ratification of the treaty and to restore to those tribes "all the possessions, rights, and privileges" that they had enjoyed previous to the war. Accordingly, the United States signed peace treaties with western tribes in 1815 at Portage des Sioux, a convenient spot on the west bank of the Mississippi above St. Louis. Meanwhile, other negotiations were carried on with the Indians of Ohio, Indiana, and Michigan, and a treaty was signed with them at Spring Wells near Detroit, in which peace was reaffirmed and the Indians who had continued hostilities after 1811 were pardoned.

These treaties of friendship would be no more than paper documents unless the United States carried out its resolve to establish military posts on the Great Lakes and in the upper Mississippi Valley. Such action was imperative if the United States did not want to forfeit for a second time its control over the Indian tribes of the northwest. Americans in the West pleaded for military establishments that would check the Indians, weaken or destroy their adherence to the British, and protect and extend the American fur trade in the region.

The War Department quickly moved to establish new military posts and reestablish old ones at strategic spots. In 1816 the post at Chicago (Fort Dearborn) was reoccupied and Fort Howard at Green Bay was constructed. At the same time troops pushed up the Mississippi to build Fort Crawford at the mouth of the Wisconsin River. Indian agencies were established in the shadows of these posts. A further extension of the military frontier occurred when Secretary of War John C. Calhoun directed the building of posts on the upper Missouri and the upper Mississippi. The establishment of Fort Atkinson above Omaha and Fort Snelling at the confluence of the Mississippi and Minnesota rivers in 1818–1819 to a considerable extent answered Calhoun's purpose of overawing the Indians, cutting off their intercourse with British traders, and throwing "the most valuable fur trade in the world" into American hands.

In the south, the federal government presumed that all Indian difficulties had ended with the Treaty of Fort Jackson with the Creeks. Besides the huge land cession, the Indians had promised to abandon all communication or intercourse with any British or Spanish posts and to permit the establishment of American forts and roads in the territory they still retained. It was a harsh peace, imposed, as the preamble to the treaty stated, because of the "unprovoked, inhuman, and sanguinary war" waged by the Creeks against the United States. But many Indians, unwilling to accept defeat, joined the Seminoles in Florida, where they continued to be a lively threat to white settlers moving onto the vacated lands. Here they were encouraged by British adventurers in their erroneous belief that the lands taken away from them at Fort Jackson would be returned now that the War of 1812 had ended.

To maintain peace on this perilous frontier was the task of General Edmund P. Gaines, who attempted to overawe the warlike Indians with a show of force. He built Fort Scott at the confluence of the Flint and Chattahoochee rivers, almost on the Florida border, and from there and from Fort Montgomery in Alabama Gaines carried on a running war with recalcitrant Indians along the border. He was soon joined by General Andrew Jackson, who, convinced that the Spanish were encouraging the Indians, boldly invaded Florida. There he seized two British traders, tried them by court-martial, and summarily executed them.

Unmindful of the storm of controversy that would soon arise because of his execution of the two British subjects on Spanish soil, Jackson moved next against Pensacola. On May 25 he invested the Spanish post and three days later accepted its surrender. His justification was explicit: "The Seminole Indians inhabiting the territories of Spain have for more than two years past, visited our Frontier settlements with all the horrors of savage massacre—helpless women have been butchered and the cradle stained with the blood of innocence. . . . The immutable laws of self defense, therefore compelled the American Government to take possession of such parts of the Floridas in which the Spanish authority could not be maintained."

Jackson returned to Nashville in triumph, leaving the diplomats to pick up the pieces. The Spanish minister, Don Luis de Onís, demanded the prompt restitution of St. Marks, Pensacola, and all other places wrested from Spain by Jackson's forces, as well as an indemnity for all losses and the punishment of the general. The posts were returned, but Jackson was not punished, and resolutions in Congress condemning his action were voted down. General Gaines meanwhile kept watch on the southern frontier, where the problems were not solved as completely as Jackson had asserted. The Indians had not been decisively beaten in combat, and until Florida finally passed into American possession in 1821, there was a continual threat of Spanish intrigue with the Indians.

CHAPTER 2

Regulating Trade and Intercourse

Military action against the Indians to push them back before the advancing whites was not a suitable basis for governing the relations between the United States and the Indians. Washington and Knox, both men of high integrity and experienced in Indian affairs, rejected an all-out war of subjugation against the tribes. The alternative was conciliation of the Indians by negotiation, a show of liberality, express guarantees of protection from encroachment beyond certain set boundaries, and a fostered and developed trade. But it was not enough to deal only with the Indians, for white settlers and speculators ignored the treaties and guarantees. Plainly, something more was needed than the treaties, which had been so largely disregarded.

TRADE AND INTERCOURSE LAWS

In response to the insistent pleas of the executive, Congress supplied a series of laws for regulating trade and intercourse with the Indians. These laws, originally designed to implement the treaties and enforce them against obstreperous whites, gradually came to embody the basic features of federal Indian policy. The first law was approved on July 22, 1790. Continuing the pattern set in the Ordinance of 1786 and earlier colonial legislation, it first of all provided for the licensing of traders and established penalties for trading without a license. Then it struck directly at the current frontier difficulties. To prevent the steady eating away of the Indian country by individuals who privately acquired lands from the Indians, it declared such purchases invalid unless made by a public treaty with the United States. To put a stop to the outrages committed against Indians by whites who invaded the Indian country, the act provided punishment for murder and other crimes committed by whites against the Indians in the Indian country.

Despite the legislation, frontier disturbances continued in both north and south, and military force had to be used to restrain the Indians and defend the whites. Washington hoped that legislation could be provided that would eliminate the causes of the conflict, and in his annual message of 1790 he again urged the matter upon Congress. It was necessary first of all, he told the lawmakers, to enforce the laws on the frontier and to check the outrages committed by the whites, which led to reprisals on the part of the Indians. The government should employ qualified agents, promote civilization among the friendly tribes, and develop some plan for carrying on trade with them "upon a scale equal to their wants."

A new law, approved March 1, 1793, was a considerably stronger and more inclusive piece of legislation than its predecessor. New sections authorized the president to give goods and money to the tribes "to promote civilization . . . and to secure the continuance of their friendship," and a long section was aimed at horse stealing, but the bulk of the new material was intended to stop criminal attacks of whites against the Indians and the irregular acquisition of their lands.

The trade and intercourse laws were necessary to provide a framework for the trade and to establish a licensing system that would permit some control and regulation, but this was merely a restatement of old procedures. The vital sections of the laws were in answer to the crisis of the day on the frontier, and the provisions pertained to the tribes of Indians with whom the nation dealt as independent bodies. Neither President Washington nor the Congress was concerned with the remnants of tribes that had been absorbed by the states and had come under their direction and control. The laws sought to provide an answer to the charge that the treaties made with the tribes on the frontiers, which guaranteed their rights to the territory behind the boundary lines, were not respected by the United States. The laws were not primarily "Indian" laws, for they touched the Indians only indirectly. The legislation, rather, was directed against lawless whites and sought to restrain them from violating the sacred treaties. Even when severe crises were resolved by force, the restrictive elements of the intercourse laws were maintained, augmented, refined, and applied to later frontiers.

By the end of 1795 the hostile Indians north of the Ohio had been defeated by General Wayne, but the largely unrestrained invasion of the lands of the Creeks and Cherokees in Tennessee and Georgia caused a constant disruption of the peace, and Washington again asked Congress to act. He repeated his plea for measures to protect the Indians from injuries inflicted by whites and to supply the necessities of the Indians on reasonable terms. In response Congress passed the intercourse law of May 19, 1796. The new law specified in detail the boundary line between the whites and the Indians, the first designation of the Indian country in a statute law. The delineation was meant to indicate once again the government's intention to uphold the treaties, and though the line met with opposition in the House, efforts to remove it from the bill failed. Violent debate erupted over sections in the law aimed specifically at intruders on Cherokee lands, but again the supporters of the bill were able to maintain their ground. As the bill finally emerged, unscathed by the attacks upon it, it was almost double the length of the law it replaced.

When Thomas Jefferson sent his first annual message to Congress in December 1801, he could remark that "a spirit of peace and friendship generally prevails" among the Indian tribes. The new president saw no need to depart from the Indian policies of his predecessors, and when temporary laws expired, he asked Congress to renew them. The only modification he suggested was some restriction on the liquor traffic among the Indians, which he said the Indians themselves wanted. Accordingly, on March 30, 1802, a new trade and intercourse law was passed; it was to remain in force, with occasional additions, as the basic law governing Indian relations until it was replaced by a new codification of Indian policy in 1834.

For the trade regulations in the trade and intercourse laws, Congress simply adopted the principles of the licensing system used for decades past, although it softened somewhat the requirements set forth in the Ordinance of 1786. The new laws required licenses of all traders, bonds for the faithful observance of regulations governing the trade, and forfeiture of goods taken illegally into the Indian country. From time to time the legislation was strengthened by additional restrictions or increased fines, and the law of 1796 and subsequent laws authorized the use of military force to apprehend offenders. These laws supplemented and strengthened the treaties signed with the tribes, which often dealt with trade and the federal government's right to regulate it.

The provisions of both the laws and the treaties seem unexceptionable. The licensing system was meant to furnish a check on the traders and make them abide by the rules of the trade. The bonds were high enough to eliminate the unstable, and the threat of confiscation of goods—with one-half to the informer—should have dampened any hopes for profitable trading outside the law. The facts, however, belied the surface impression. Year after year reports poured in about illegal trading and the inability of anyone to prevent it. Both north and south of the Ohio the territorial governors, serving ex officio as superintendents of Indian affairs, found it impossible to cope with the illicit trade. With the addition of the Louisiana Purchase, the problems of regulating the trade spread over a vaster area and one where the legal lines were even less clearly drawn.

It seemed well-nigh impossible to stop the illegal trading by judicial process. The intercourse laws provided machinery, designating the action to be taken and the courts to be used, but the machinery was shaky and not very effective. Distances were too great, the time lag too long, and the difficulties of arranging for witnesses too serious for the laws to provide an effective deterrent or remedy for the illicit traffic. If some diligent and conscientious officer or agent did make the effort to bring a violator to trial, chances were that the judges would dismiss the case on a technicality or the jury side with the defendant. Too often the only reward for an officer who attempted to enforce the law was to be called into court himself to answer to charges of illegal trespass or arrest.

A further problem came from British traders who had deeply infiltrated the northwest area after the French were driven out in 1763. Operating under the direction of powerful companies, they exerted great influence over the Indians, who accepted their presents and depended upon them for goods. These traders were unmolested after the Revolutionary War, chiefly because the Americans were not prepared to replace them, and Jay's Treaty of 1794 specifically guaranteed their right to be there. Their posts of Michilimackinac and Prairie du Chien were important gathering points for Indians, and in the War of 1812 American eyes were opened to the danger, for it was through the influence of traders that the Indians fought with the British against the United States in the war.

It is understandable that agitation should have arisen to eliminate the British traders altogether. By a law of April 29, 1816, licenses to trade with the Indians within the territorial limits of the United States were refused to noncitizens, although the president could permit such licenses if he thought the public interest demanded it. All goods taken into the Indian country by foreigners were subject to seizure and forfeiture if not yet traded to the Indians, and all peltries purchased from the Indians by foreigners were liable to seizure while still in the Indian country. The president was authorized to use military force to seize the goods or furs and to arrest violators of the act. Even foreigners who wished merely to pass through the Indian lands were required first to obtain a passport. The discretionary power of the president permitted some foreigners to continue in the trade, and boatmen and interpreters were allowed. Yet, by the effects of the restrictive legislation and the steady growth of the power and influence of the American Fur Company, the British were generally forced out of the trade within the territory of the United States.

In 1822 an amendment to the intercourse law of 1802 tightened the restrictions on all traders, and two years later Congress directed that all trading be done at designated sites, thus permitting a more efficient enforcement of the laws. But an attempt to give the agents discretionary authority in issuing licenses, which would have enabled them to turn back unsavory characters, was successfully blocked by the trading interests.

THE FACTORY SYSTEM

Running parallel to restrictions on the trade and regulation of private traders was another attempt to remove abuses in the trade and thus maintain the friendship of the Indians. It was a system of government-run trading houses (factories), a pet scheme of Washington, who wrote, "I think, if the Indian Trade was carried on, on Government Acct., and with no greater advance than what would be necessary to defray the expence and risk, and bring in a small profit, that it would supply the Indians upon much better terms than they usually are; engross their Trade, and fix them strongly in our Interest." Washington insisted that the trade must be free of fraud and extortion, supply goods plentifully and without delay, and provide a market for Indian commodities at a stated and fair price. Private traders were motivated by hope of profit and took advantage of the Indians to gain their end, he argued; therefore the government, which was interested only in reimbursement of costs, should undertake the trade itself.

The factory system that Washington envisaged was soon begun. Congress was cautious, but it was willing to let the president try the matter as an experiment. It appropriated $50,000 to purchase goods for the Indians in 1795 and directed that the goods be sold under the direction of the president.

With such small funds, only a small and experimental beginning could be made. Passing over the Six Nations, which were closely surrounded by white settlements, and the tribes north of the Ohio River, still negotiating for peace after Wayne's victory, the War Department decided to apply the money among the southern Indians only. For the Creeks a factory was set up at Colerain, on the St. Marys River in Georgia, a point of easy access for goods. To supply the Cherokees, and to a lesser extent the Chickasaws, another trading house was begun at Tellico Blockhouse in eastern Tennessee, where there was already a military post to which the Indians were accustomed to resort.

The success of this initial outlay prompted Congress in the next session to formalize the program, and in a law of April 18, 1796, it authorized the president to establish such trading houses on the southern and western frontiers or in the Indian country as he judged best for carrying on a "liberal trade" with the Indians. Money was provided for agents and clerks, who were prohibited from engaging in any trade on their own account. To the fund of the previous year Congress now added $150,000, and the law directed that prices were to be set at such a level that this capital stock not be diminished. Lest the trade in any way hinder the ultimate goal of civilizing the Indians in the white man's pattern, the law forbade agents to accept in trade guns, clothing, cooking utensils, or "any instrument of husbandry" obtained by the Indians in their intercourse with whites. The act was to run for two years.

President John Adams did not push the system aggressively, but Thomas Jefferson, who had a deep and abiding interest in Indian affairs, established new trading houses in both the south and the west. He pointed out to Congress that the system was succeeding with its liberal trade policies. Private traders, both foreign and domestic, were undersold and driven from the field, and the nation was ridding itself of a class of men who constantly endeavored to excite the Indian mind with suspicions, fears, and irritations toward the Americans.

Congress kept the system afloat by periodically renewing the authorization, and in 1805 it appropriated $100,000 for additional trading houses. A new factory appeared in 1805 at Chicago, and three more were built west of the Mississippi. With such far-flung and increasing activity, it was necessary to do more than revive from time to time the original law of 1796, and in 1806 Congress supplied more comprehensive legislation for the system. In addition to repeating the main provisions of the earlier legislation, it authorized a superintendent of Indian trade to take charge of the whole business under the direction of the president.

The creation of the Office of Indian Trade was a milestone in developing the federal machinery for dealing with Indian problems. Before 1806 there had been no official in the government whose full duties concerned the Indians; the secretary of war, under the president, looked after what business there was. The goods for the factories were purchased by a succession of purchasing agents operating in Philadelphia. Now, with the superintendent of Indian trade, there was someone who could attend to the important trading functions and who gradually became the focus for nonmilitary Indian matters.

The factories enjoyed an active and thriving business, and Congress continued the system in 1811 with a new basic law. Repeating most of the 1806 act and its supplements, the new law specifically provided for the factors and in a very general way described their duties. Capital stock of $300,000 was furnished, and the president was authorized to open additional houses. An indication of the growing responsibility of the superintendent of Indian trade was the directive that in future he was to purchase and distribute, in addition to the goods for the trading houses, all the goods needed for annuities and presents to the Indians and for treaty purposes.

The factory system was very closely associated with the frontier military posts. The success of the government trading operations was due in part to the protection and assistance given to the factories by the regular army garrisons. All but four of the twenty-eight trading houses were in the shadow of an existing military post or were themselves the occasion for the building of a fort. The forts protected the factories, the presence of the soldiers enhanced the factors' prestige in the eyes of the Indians, and the

MAP 1: United States Factory System, 1795–1822

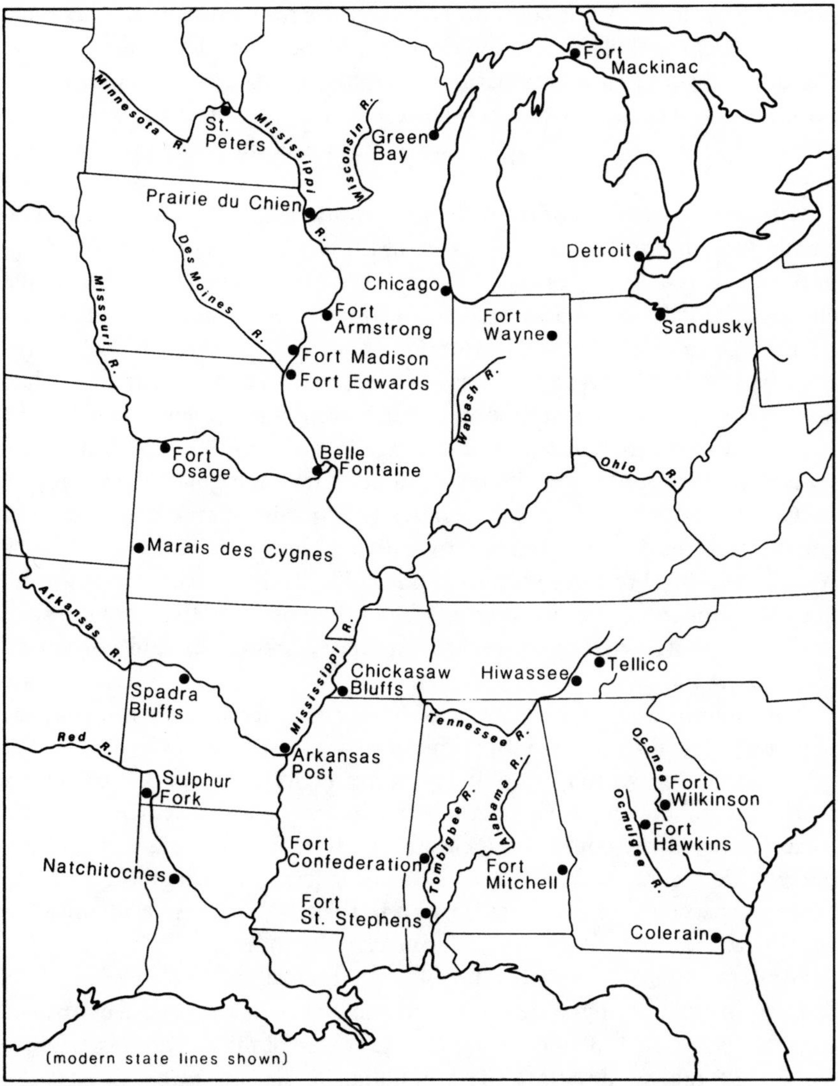

Fort Mackinac
Minnesota R.
St. Peters
Mississippi R.
Wisconsin R.
Green Bay
Prairie du Chien
Des Moines R.
Detroit
Chicago
Missouri R.
Fort Armstrong
Fort Wayne
Sandusky
Fort Madison
Fort Edwards
Wabash R.
Fort Osage
Belle Fontaine
Ohio R.
Marais des Cygnes
Arkansas R.
Mississippi R.
Chickasaw Bluffs
Hiwassee
Tellico
Spadra Bluffs
Tennessee R.
Oconee R.
Red R.
Arkansas Post
Fort Wilkinson
Ocmulgee R.
Sulphur Fork
Tombigbee R.
Alabama R.
Fort Hawkins
Natchitoches
Fort Confederation
Fort Mitchell
Fort St. Stephens
Colerain

(modern state lines shown)

troops were sometimes the only labor force on hand to build the factories, transport their goods, and aid in the beating and packing of furs.

The War of 1812 interrupted the work of the factories, but the economic loss caused by the British seizure of some of the western trading houses was quickly overcome after the war. More dangerous to the future of the system were the changed conditions of the American fur trade after the Treaty of Ghent. The spirit of enterprise blossomed forth with the rise of American nationalism that came at the end of the war. When foreign traders were prohibited from the fur trade in 1816, the American Fur Company of John Jacob Astor began to push steadily for control of the fur trade in the area of the Great Lakes and the upper Mississippi. The years after the War of 1812 were years of dramatic conflict between the increasingly powerful private fur trading interests—powerful both economically and politically—and the embattled but defiant supporters of the government trading houses.

Criticism of the factories came also from western officials. One such person was Ninian Edwards, governor of Illinois Territory since 1809, who flatly told the secretary of war: "For my part, I have never been able to discover, and I defy any man to specify, a solitary public advantage that has resulted from it [the factory system] in this country." Another critic was the governor of Michigan Territory, Lewis Cass. As early as 1814 Cass had noted that the trading factories and "our economy in presents" had led the Indians to scorn the United States. "The Government," he told the secretary of war, "should never Come in contact with them, but in cases where its Dignity, its strength or its liberality will inspire them with respect or fear." After the War of 1812 he argued that there was sufficient private American capital to carry on the fur trade effectively and that there was no need then for the government to engage in the business; that, in fact, such mercantile enterprise made the government "obnoxious and contemptible" to the Indians.

The government officials responsible for the program were not so ready to give up. The most important of the advocates was Thomas L. McKenney, who became superintendent of Indian trade in 1816. He was one of the key figures in the development of American Indian policy, a sentimental and romantic man who could not always keep his accounts straight, who lived beyond his means, and who was continually trying to advance his importance in the political circles of the day, but withal a sincere humanitarian committed to the welfare and betterment of the Indians.

McKenney used his office to further two intense and abiding views. One was an abhorrence of private traders, whom he saw as the source of immeasurable evil in the Indian country. "In the course of my Superintendence of the trade established with the several Indian Tribes," he wrote in 1818, "it has become part of my duty to take cognizance of such checks as are known to operate against it. Among these, and foremost in this train, is the conduct of the private traders, than which it is impossible to conceive of any thing more obnoxious, if viewed in relation to the morals of the Indians; or more destructive of that pacific result which the U.S. factories are or may be calculated to produce." The second was the use of the factories as positive agencies for promoting the education and civilization of the Indians. He expected the factors to be more than tradesmen; they were to be key men in spreading the gospel of agriculture and domestic arts, to supply necessary tools and information, and to be models of what could be done in taming the wilderness. But in addition to his instructions to the men at the trading houses, McKenney hoped to inaugurate a federal policy of education and civilization, and in this he broadly expanded his position as superintendent of Indian trade.

McKenney continued to insist on an expanded factory system and to emphasize the humanitarian effects of the government program, which were simply impossible under private traders motivated only by gain. He declared in 1818 that an end to the government factory system would cause the whole system of Indian reform to "tumble into ruins, and blast, at once, the happiness of thousands of Indians who now enjoy its benefits." He concluded, "The existing Government system has its foundation in *benevolence,* and *reform.* Those are the two pillars, on which it rests."

In the long run, McKenney's vision of benevolence and reform was overcome by John Jacob Astor and his political friends, who were alarmed by McKenney's efforts to maintain and expand the government system at the expense of private traders. The opponents of the factories were aided greatly by the strong support of Senator Thomas Hart Benton, who railed against the government trading houses in 1822. He asserted that great abuses had been committed in the purchase of goods by the superintendent, who had bought some goods ill suited to the Indian trade and others of bad quality and had purchased goods at high prices in eastern markets when they would have cost less in western ones. He accused the superintendent of mismanagement in the disposition of goods to the Indians and in the sale of the furs and peltries taken in trade.

Congress heeded the arguments and by an act of May 6, 1822, abolished the factory system. The American Fur Company congratulated Senator Benton on the victory: "The result is the best possible proof of the value to the country of talents, intelligence, & perseverance; and you deserve the unqualified thanks of the community for destroying the pious monster, since to your unwearied exertions, and sound practical knowledge of the whole subject, the country is indebted for its deliverance from so gross and [un]holy an imposition." The trade now became the unimpeded domain of the private traders and the powerful fur company.

It cannot be said that the conduct of the Indian trade by the federal government was a failure, for the system was never really given a full chance. Unable to concede that circumstances might demand a government monopoly of the trade in order to end abuses and to supply the Indians fairly with the goods they needed, the government admitted a dual system, allowing private traders to engage in the trade (under a licensing system) while at the same time engaging in the trade itself on a nonprofit basis.

Once the private traders came into their own after the War of 1812, they squeezed out the factory system, which had never had more than half-hearted support from Congress, despite the strong rational arguments made in its behalf by McKenney and other ardent supporters. The ineffectiveness of the factories, which their critics charged, was belied by the opposition itself, for the violence of the attacks is indication enough that the factories were offering serious competition. It may be that the proponents put too much burden on the system. Instead of working to correct recognized economic weaknesses, they intended to use the trading houses as a measure for benevolence and reform, humanitarian notions that could not stand up against the hardheaded, if not ruthless, economic policies of John Jacob Astor.

THE CRUSADE AGAINST ARDENT SPIRITS

One of the great sources of difficulty in the Indian trade was whiskey. The "ardent spirits" smuggled into the Indian country made madmen of the Indians, yet the flow could not easily be stanched. It was an elemental problem, rooted in strong human drives—the Indians' fondness for drink and the heartless avarice of the whites. To protect the Indian from his own weakness the government needed to clamp down on the whiskey dealer.

The problem of the liquor traffic was as old as white settlement in America. Yet the first federal laws governing intercourse with the Indians made no mention of intoxicating liquors, just as there had been no discussion of the matter in the Continental Congress and no specific enactments in regard to it. This may seem like a strange omission in view of the past troubles that had grown out of laxness in the matter, but it is likely that the legislators hoped that the licensing provisions of the laws would supply the necessary restraints. They looked to the superintendents of Indian affairs and to the Indian agents to place the necessary brake upon the liquor trade. Nor was it clear at first that state or territorial ordinances could not take care of the problem. Officials on the frontier were in fact well aware of the whiskey menace, even though territorial governors and legislators took little action. That their steps were halting was due more to the dim twilight of authority between federal and local governments and to hesitation to act against the economic interests of the infant communities than to any malice toward the Indians or indifference to their plight.

The inability or unwillingness of the territorial governments to cope with the whiskey problem brought numerous complaints to the federal officials as the nefarious traffic flourished. Even the Indians themselves, becoming aware of the evil effects of the liquor on their morals, health, and very existence, pleaded with President Jefferson for protection. When Jefferson in turn recommended to Congress that it restrict the trade, Congress inserted a special provision in the intercourse law of 1802 that authorized the president "to prevent or restrain the vending or distributing of spirituous liquors among all or any of the said Indian tribes."

This law was followed by a succession of ever stronger measures aimed at controlling or eliminating the liquor menace. The 1822 amendment to the intercourse act of 1802, for example, authorized the president to direct Indian agents, superintendents of Indian affairs, and military officers to search the goods of all traders in case of suspicion or information that ardent spirits were being carried into Indian lands. If liquor was found, all the goods were to be forfeited, the trader's license was to be canceled, and his bond put in suit. But the amendment availed little. There were still ambiguities and loopholes in the law, and the American Fur Company was able to overreach the government agents and army officers in executing it when they received permission from Governor Cass to import liquor in order to compete with British traders along the northern border.

There were other ways to take liquor into the Indian country under the protection of authority. Permission was granted to carry in whiskey for use of the boatmen employed in trading, as the prohibition under the laws of 1802 and 1822 was only against introducing the article for use in trade with the Indians. This was a loophole through which large amounts of liquor poured into the Indian country, and any ruse to get by inspecting officers seemed to succeed. A second method was to demand liquor for the white settlements, such as Green Bay or Prairie du Chien, which were not, strictly speaking, Indian country.

However diligent the agents and army officers were, the whiskey merchants were always one step ahead. The licensed traders used whatever schemes they could concoct to gain permission to take in liquor, and they slipped easily into illegal practices. The unlicensed traders operated altogether beyond the law. No section of the frontier was free of disturbance. From Florida, Alabama, Mississippi, Michigan, Arkansas, and Missouri reports flowed into the War Department from officers and agents lamenting the state of affairs, which all the current laws were quite inadequate to remedy. The legislation to date had concentrated on regulating the trade; because such measures were ineffective, the next step would be absolute prohibition of spirituous liquor in the Indian country.

This step was taken in 1832, when Congress bluntly declared: "No ardent spirits shall be hereafter introduced, under any pretence, into the Indian country." It was an all-inclusive prohibition that allowed for no exceptions and that applied to traders and nontraders alike.

CRIMES IN THE INDIAN COUNTRY

Another essential part of the Indian trade and intercourse laws concerned criminal court procedures. When the white and red races met on the American frontier, there occurred innumerable violations of the personal and property rights of one group by members of the other. Murders and robberies were all too frequent between peoples who were nominally at peace, and some provision had to be made to preserve law and order or constant warfare would result. If private retaliation was not to be the rule, then crimes had to be defined and legal machinery established to mete out justice.

The earlier laws, in an attempt to guarantee respect for the treaties on the part of whites, were concerned particularly with whites who committed crimes against Indians in the Indian country. The act of 1790 equated a crime against an Indian with the same deed committed against an inhabitant of one of the states or territories. The white offender was to be subject to the same punishment and the same procedure was to be followed as though the offense had been committed outside the Indian country against a white. Procedures for apprehending, imprisoning, and bailing in such crimes were to follow the Judiciary Act of 1789.

These basic provisions of 1790 were expanded in succeeding acts. In the intercourse law of 1793, "murder, robbery, larceny, trespass or other crimes" were named, and a new section specified the proper courts to be used. Yet this was not strong enough. Washington bluntly told Congress in December 1795: "The provisions heretofore made with a view to the protection of the Indians from the violences of the lawless part of our frontier inhabitants, are insufficient. It is demonstrated that these violences can now be perpetrated with impunity, and it can need no argument to prove that unless the murdering of Indians can be restrained by bringing the murderers to condign punishment, all the exertions of the Government to prevent destructive retaliations by the Indians will prove fruitless and all our present agreeable prospects illusory."

Acting on Washington's recommendation, Congress wrote into the intercourse law of 1796 detailed provisions for restraining outrages on both sides, including the death penalty for anyone convicted of going into Indian country and there murdering an Indian. Property taken or destroyed was to be paid for by the culprit or by the United States Treasury, and if Indians crossed over the line into white lands and committed crimes, satisfaction was to be demanded from the tribe. All of this was predicated on the condition that no private satisfaction be exacted. The provisions of the 1796 law were reenacted with little change in the permanent law of 1802. But it was not until 1817 that Congress ordained punishment for Indians who committed crimes against whites within the Indian country.

The United States government was determined to provide an adequate judicial system for the Indian country and intended that Indians and whites be treated with equal justice. In practice, however, there were serious discrepancies, for the universal resort to legal procedures to gain satisfaction and justice envisaged by the laws simply did not obtain. The laws, however, were by no means completely ineffective. Against Indian criminals they were invoked again and again. If an Indian committed a crime against a white—and murder was the offense foremost in mind—the criminal was demanded from the tribe for punishment by the United States. If the accused Indian was not delivered up, a military expedition was sent to apprehend him or hostages were seized and held until the criminal appeared. The culprit was guarded by the federal troops and turned over by them to a civil court in a nearby territory or state for trial.

For crimes committed by whites against Indians the laws made specific provisions, which gradually became more explicit. If the offenses were committed within a territory or a state, the criminal code of that civil jurisdiction sufficed. Within the Indian country, offenses of whites against Indians were punishable in federal courts when the offenses were specified in federal statutes, and the intercourse laws declared that crimes in any of the states or territories against a white citizen should also be considered crimes if committed in the Indian country against an Indian. But the crimes were so numerous and widespread that their control by judicial means proved impossible. The frequency of offenses committed against Indians by frontier whites, among which outright murder was commonplace, was shocking.

One measure taken to appease the Indians was to issue a proclamation in the name of the president, offering a handsome reward for the apprehension of the criminal. The ineffectiveness of such proclamations in actually bringing the criminals to justice in the frontier communities can be presumed, and the government more frequently resorted to compensating the families of murdered Indians by payment of a fixed sum of money or goods. The War Department directed the Indian agents to offer such pecuniary satisfaction in cases where the murderers could not be apprehended, in order to satisfy the families and show the willingness of the government to do justice. A sum of one to two hundred dollars for each Indian murdered by whites was suggested by the secretary of war in 1803, and this amount was regularly given.

Theft was another cause of conflict, and the chief concern was horses. Aside from outright murders and massacres by the Indians, nothing was so likely to embroil the two races on the frontier as horse stealing, for horses were of elemental necessity for the frontiersman. The white's need and the Indian's cupidity and stealth made for an explosive combination that threatened to blow up one frontier after another. The petitions that reached the War Department regularly coupled horse stealing with murder as the scourge of living near the Indians. The intercourse laws attempted to meet the problem by requiring a license to purchase horses from Indians or whites within the Indian country and then by providing compensation for the owners of stolen stock.

Because it was generally admitted that offenses among Indians within the tribe or nation were tribal matters that were to be handled by the tribe and were of no concern to the United States government, crimes committed by Indians against other Indians did not fall within the scope of the intercourse laws. The sovereignty of an Indian tribe, no matter how it might be circumscribed in other respects, was certainly considered to extend to the punishment of its own members. Up to the mid-nineteenth century, indeed, there were no laws or treaty provisions that limited the powers of self-government of the tribes with respect to internal affairs. Intertribal wars, however, were of a continuing interest to the United States, for they could endanger the lives and property of white citizens on the frontier. Indian agents were directed to use whatever advice, persuasion, or presents might be needed to prevent hostilities between tribes, but they were not to involve the United States on either side.

REMOVAL OF INTRUDERS

The conflict between the whites and Indians that marked American Indian relations was basically a conflict over land. Although the American government recognized Indian rights to the land and attempted by law, treaty, and special proclamation to ensure justice to the aborigines, the views of the frontiersmen were of a different nature altogether. Theorizing about rights of preemption played little part in the thinking of the settler or of the eastern speculator in western lands; they saw the rich lands of the Indians and they wanted them.

In the conflict with the frontiersmen, the government did not back down in its principles, and it tightened its restrictions and strengthened the machinery of enforcement. But as the spearhead of settlement fluctuated back and forth across the West, driving ever deeper into territories once solely Indian, the pious principles of the legislators ran into the unprincipled practices of the settlers. The men actually on the land generally had the better of it, for they again and again deflected the enforcing arm of government and in the end forced the Indians off the land. The Indians, however, were not completely deserted. Explicit treaties were made guaranteeing their rights, and stringent laws were enacted to ensure respect for the treaties. Various measures were undertaken to enforce the laws, and what order and peace there was on the frontier came in large part from the enforcement of the intercourse laws against unlawful encroachment on Indian lands.

The prohibition of private purchase of lands from the Indians, which had been part of the colonial and imperial policy, continued as a fixed policy of the United States. The First Congress incorporated this principle into the intercourse law of 1790: "no sale of lands made by any Indians, or any nation or tribe of Indians within the United States, shall be valid to any person or persons, or to any state, whether having the right of preemption to such lands or not, unless the same shall be made and duly executed at some public treaty, held under the authority of the United States." The principle was clearly stated, and the practice had been uniform for decades. Federal commissioners were appointed to treat with the Indians for their lands, and Congress appropriated funds for compensating the Indians.

Treaties entered into with the Indians for cessions of land had the universal corollary that the unceded lands would be guaranteed against invasion by whites. Thus all the treaties entered into by the Continental Congress guaranteed the remaining lands of the Indians, and the later ones expressly forbade whites to settle on Indian land under sanction of forfeiting the protection of the United States and becoming subject to punishment by the Indians. The same provisions were written into the first treaties made under the Constitution. Congress, therefore, in drawing up the intercourse law of 1790, considered it unnecessary to make specific prohibition of encroachment on the Indian country.

The open violations of the treaties, however, necessitated additional legislative measures against the illegal settlers, and the intercourse law of 1793 provided a maximum fine of one thousand dollars and imprisonment for twelve months for anyone who settled on Indian lands or surveyed or marked boundaries on such lands with a view to settlement. The president, furthermore, was authorized to remove all unlawful settlers by such measures as he might judge necessary. From that time on, the successive laws included sections aimed specifically at the aggressive frontiersmen.

The federal government was determined to defend the integrity of the Indian country, but the United States itself was sometimes forced to seek concessions from the Indians. This occurred particularly in two cases: the acquisition of land within the Indian country for military posts, agencies, and trading houses, and acquisition for roads connecting important settlements or major segments of American territory. Getting land for the military posts and other government establishments caused little trouble because the troops of the United States were generally looked upon with respect by the Indians. Military forces within the Indian lands were more a protection than a threat and did not form a wedge for whites to intrude into the forbidden lands. The agencies and factories also worked for the benefit of the Indians.

The running of roads through the Indian country was a more controversial question, for the Indians frequently objected to such invasion of their lands. The War Department instructed its agents to proceed with great caution in persuading the Indians to grant permission for the roads and to offer suitable inducements and compensation. With requests for the roads also went requests for sites of land on which "houses of entertainment" might be set up for the refreshment of travelers, and one inducement used to win the agreement of the Indians was that the Indians themselves might profit from running such establishments. Although permission was sometimes delayed, the United States generally won its point, and treaties with the Indians contained specific articles authorizing the roads.

Such small and authorized encroachments on Indian lands were insignificant in comparison with the illegal onrush of settlers, whose pressure was usually so great that the United States could not enforce the intercourse laws with any complete success. The laws of Congress, the proclamations of the president, and the orders issued by the War Department did provide a brake on the westward-rolling juggernaut. But in the end, the force of the intruders was too great to be held back. Temporarily it could be halted, but the intruders were a mobile lot. They had moved in easily the first time, and if they were removed by military force, they could just as easily return. The more frequently the government acquiesced in the illegal settlements, the more difficult it became to take effective action. The settlers had little fear that civil action would succeed against them, and there was an increasing number of examples of government action to cover such settlements through formal treaties that extinguished the Indian title.

The history of intrusions on Indian lands, of course, raises the difficult question of the sincerity of the government in its policy of protecting Indian rights to the land. Certainly the legal basis was firm enough, and the doctrines of preemption and of Indian sovereignty were endorsed by the Supreme Court in a series of famous decisions. In *Fletcher* v. *Peck*, in 1810, the court asserted that the "nature of the Indian title, which is certainly to be respected by all courts, until it be legitimately extinguished, is not such as to be absolutely repugnant to seizin in fee on the part of the State." In 1823, in *Johnson and Graham's Lessee* v. *McIntosh*, the court expanded this doctrine when it considered the case of two claimants to the same piece of land, one of whom had received title directly from the Indians, the other by a patent from the government. Chief Justice Marshall, in giving the decision of the court, furnished a long disquisition about the nature of the Indian title to land and expatiated on the traditional doctrine of preemption. "It has never been contended that the Indian title amounted to nothing," he said. "Their right of possession has never been questioned."

Yet in the long run, the settlers nearly always won out. Why did the government not take more effective measures to prevent encroachment? The answer lies partly in the insufficiency of the forces available to carry out the legislative measures and executive decisions. Indian agents simply lacked the necessary means. The civil authorities could not be relied upon to prosecute or convict violators; and the army on the frontier was too small to police the whole area successfully.

But behind these failures was a larger issue. The federal government was sincerely interested in preventing settlement on Indian lands only up to a point, and it readily acquiesced in illegal settlement that had gone so far as to be irremediable. The policy of the United States was based on an assumption that white settlement should advance and the Indians withdraw. The federal government was interested primarily in seeing that this process was as free of disorder and injustice as possible. It meant to restrain and govern the advance of the whites, not to prevent it forever. It supported Indian claims as far as it could out of justice and humanity to the Indians and above all as far as it was necessary to keep a semblance of peace and to maintain Indian goodwill so that land would continue to be ceded by the tribes. In the early decades of the nineteenth century the federal government was convinced that once the Indians had been permanently settled on lands west of the Mississippi, the problems of encroachment and of removing intruders would be unhappy memories of the past. And in the end it looked for the civilization of the Indians and their assimilation into white society.

The energy of the government in removing intruders was, in fact, proportionate, either directly or inversely, to a number of other circumstances: to the length of time during which the Indian claims were expected to be maintained; to the seriousness of Indian objections to the intruders, as removal was often the only way to prevent an Indian war; to the necessity of convincing the Indians of the government's good faith in order to keep them in a proper frame of mind for some impending treaty at which more concessions of land were to be sought; to the pressures of white settlement, for full-scale drives into an area usually led to new treaties of cession rather than to removal of the whites; to the boldness and aggressiveness of the agents and military commanders in enforcing the laws; to the military forces available in the area where encroachment was threatened; to the strength of frontier opposition to military action against the intruders; and to the color of title that the settlers on Indian lands could display, as well as the character of the settlers themselves.

CHAPTER 3

Civilization and
Education

Much of the legislative program that established Indian policy aimed to avoid conflicts between white citizens and the Indians. It was thus largely negative and restrictive, in an attempt to regulate trade and intercourse between the two races. Even the government trading houses, although they contained positive features in supplying the Indians with useful goods at fair prices and with good example, had as their primary objective the elimination of abuses in the fur trade.

Parallel to these restraining activities was a positive constructive attempt to change the Indians and their cultural patterns. Operating under the principles of the Enlightenment and of Christian philanthropy, government officials proposed to bring civilization to the Indians. It is here that the benevolent and paternalistic aspects of Indian policy appear most clearly. Although the first attempts were feeble and sporadic, they foreshadowed increasingly powerful efforts through the nineteenth century to Americanize the Indians.

CIVILIZATION AND CHRISTIANIZATION

The proposals made to better the condition of the Indians all gave evidence of a deepseated and common conviction of what *civilization* meant, even though most of the officials concerned never bothered to think philosophically about the concept. They relied on the accepted wisdom of the day, which reflected ideas that were part of their Western European heritage. *To civilize* meant to bring to a state of civility out of a state of rudeness and barbarism, to enlighten and refine. It meant as a minimum to lead persons who lived a natural life in the wilderness, relying upon hunting and gathering, to a state of society dependent upon agriculture and domestic arts (spinning and weaving); to this was added instruction in reading, writing, arithmetic, and the truths of the Christian religion.

The place of American Indians in the scheme of civilization depended on the way Americans viewed the Indians. Opinions varied from the extreme disdain of the aggressive frontiersman, who equated the Indians with wild beasts of the forest fit to be hunted down at will, to the romantic ideas of novelists like James Fenimore Cooper and poets like Henry Wadsworth Longfellow, who exalted the qualities of the "noble savage." But in between, among the responsible and respected public figures in the first decades of United States development, there was a reasonable consensus that was the underpinning of official policy toward the Indians.

Among the first generation of American statesmen, Thomas Jefferson was surely the most important theorizer about the aborigines. He was a man of tremendous speculative interests, a scientist (according to the definition of his age) as well as a political philosopher, and one who so influenced his generation that we correctly speak of his age in American history as "Jeffersonian." Jefferson, setting a pattern that was not to be successfully challenged, wrote unequivocally in 1785: "I believe the Indian then to be in body and mind equal to the whiteman."

His arguments rested on two principles. In the first place, he believed in an essential, fixed human nature, unchangeable by time or place, and he applied his principle of unity of mankind to the Indians. In the second place, as an ardent American, Jefferson could not accept a position that would have made the American natives a basically ignoble breed. In fact, his most detailed and most eloquent defense of the qualities of the Indians came in his *Notes on the State of Virginia*, in which he refuted the criticism of things American that appeared in the celebrated work of the French naturalist Georges Louis Leclerc de Buffon, who described the Indian as deficient in stature, strength, energy, mental ability, and family attachments. These aspersions Jefferson answered fully, and he entered a point-by-point refutation of the slanders. He insisted that the Indian's "vivacity and activity" of mind was equal to that of the white in similar situations. He quoted from the famous speech of Chief Logan and declared that the orations of Demosthenes and Cicero could not produce a single passage superior to the chief's oratory. Physically, too, the Indians were a match for the whites. They were brave, active, and affectionate.

Unable to ignore weaknesses in Indian life and customs as they existed before his eyes, Jefferson (like most of his contemporaries) explained the difference by environment. If the circumstances of their lives were appropriately changed, the Indians would be transformed. So convinced was he of the racial equality or uniformity that he urged physical as well as cultural amalgamation of the Indians with the whites. "In truth," he wrote to the Indian agent Benjamin Hawkins, "the ultimate point of rest & happiness for them is to let our settlements and theirs meet and blend together, to intermix, and become one people."

Since the Indian by nature possessed the capacity for civilization, Jefferson admitted the responsibility of the whites to aid the natives in attaining that great goal. He knew, of course, that the Indians could not be transformed at a single stroke; but the movement toward civilization he held to be inexorable, and unless the Indians moved with the tide, they would surely be destroyed. That they would indeed move and eagerly accept white aid was judged to be a corollary of their rational nature. If there was a sense of urgency in Jefferson's hope for Indian melioration, it came from his conviction that haste was necessary because of the extraordinary pressures of white civilization.

Jefferson had a linear view of civilization; he saw an inevitable movement from the savagery of the Indians toward the European culture of his own coastal region. Jefferson accepted the "stages of society" theory that dominated the minds of the nineteenth century, the idea that the set stages of savagery, barbarism, and civilization followed one another inevitably, as the history of all human societies had shown. If the whites had gone through the process over the centuries, there was no reason to doubt that the Indians would follow the same route.

Jefferson and his contemporaries did not think that the Indians would take as long to reach civilization as had their own European ancestors. The process could be speeded up by radical changes in the conditions of Indian society, and the Jeffersonians and their heirs set about to make those changes. Jefferson strongly urged the Indians to accept the white man's ways. And for this he had a single formula. The hunter state must be exchanged for an agricultural state; the haphazard life dependent upon the chase must give way to a secure and comfortable existence marked by industry and thrift; private property must replace communal ownership. By example and by education these changes could be wrought. The central point was conversion to farming, which was proper enough in light of Jefferson's agrarian propensities.

In Jefferson's mind there was no contradiction or equivocation in working for the Indians' advancement and at the same time gradually reducing the land they held. It was not an opposition of policies, one working for the education and civilization of the Indians, the other seeking to relieve them of their land for the benefit of the whites. These were two sides of the one coin. At the same time that the whites called for more land, the Indians, by conversion to an agricultural existence, would need less land, and they would exchange their excess land for the trade goods produced by the whites. Nor was Jefferson unmindful of benevolence toward the Indians. "In leading them thus to agriculture, to manufactures, and civilization," he told Congress on January 18, 1803; "in bringing together their and our sentiments, and preparing them ultimately to participate in the benefits of our Government, I trust and believe we are acting for their greatest good."

Although Jefferson was the chief theorist, his view was common. Thus President Washington had asked Congress in 1791 to undertake experiments for bringing civilization to the Indians and in the following year repeated his plea. Thereupon Congress in the intercourse law of 1793 provided that "in order to promote civilization among the friendly Indian tribes, and to secure the continuance of their friendship," the president might furnish them with domestic animals and the tools of husbandry, as well as other goods and money. Washington noted with pleasure that the results of the law seemed promising, and the laws of 1796, 1799, and 1802 retained the civilization provision.

Emphasis on the Enlightenment thought of the Jeffersonians in the formation of American policy, however, overlooks an even more important and enduring influence: the dominance of evangelical (that is, biblical) Christianity in American society. The views about the nature of the Indians and the possibility of their transformation held by the rationalists and the churchmen were much the same if not identical. But the basis was different. One built on the philosophy of the Enlightenment, on the laws of nature discovered in God's creation by rational man. The other was a product of a surge of evangelical religion that came with the Second Great Awakening at the turn of the century, a new missionary spirit, a revivalism that was to be a mark of Protestant Christian America for a full century and more. The unity of mankind, firmly anchored in the story of man's creation in Genesis, became and remained a fundamental tenet in the nation's Indian policy.

The civilization of the Indians by instructing them in agricultural and household arts, of course, received vigorous support from Thomas Jefferson. In his first annual message to Congress, he enthusiastically reported success in the program under the intercourse laws. He noted that the Indians had already come to realize the superiority of these means of obtaining clothing and subsistence over the precarious resources of hunting and fishing, and that instead of decreasing in numbers they were beginning to show an increase. The president expressed his views freely in his talks to the Indians. He told the Miamis, Potawatomis, and Weas, for example, on January 7, 1802: "We shall with great pleasure see your people become disposed to cultivate the earth, to raise herds of useful animals and to spin and weave, for their food and clothing. These resources are certain, they will never disappoint you, while those of hunting may fail, and expose your

women and children to the miseries of hunger and cold. We will with pleasure furnish you with implements for the most necessary arts, and with
persons who may instruct how to make and use them."

Jefferson, as he neared the end of his administration, saw in the state of
Indian affairs a vindication of the policy of civilization. Those tribes who
were "most advanced in the pursuits of industry" were the ones who were
most friendly to the United States. The southern tribes, especially, were far
ahead of the others in agriculture and the household arts and in proportion
to this advancement identified their views with those of the United States.

The annual fund provided by the intercourse laws for promotion of civilization among the Indians was not the only source from which the government could draw in providing plows and looms, blacksmiths and carpen-
ters; many of the treaties signed with the tribes also provided for such aid.
The Treaty of New York with the Creeks and the Treaty of Holston with
the Cherokees were early examples. The Delawares in 1804 were promised
a yearly sum "to be exclusively appropriated to the purpose of ameliorating
their condition and promoting their civilization," plus the employment of
a person to teach them how to build fences, cultivate the earth, and practice the domestic arts. In addition, the United States agreed to deliver draft
horses, cattle, hogs, and agricultural implements. Similar arrangements
were made with other tribes, and sometimes the tribes were allowed to
choose between annuities in the form of goods or money and special aids
for developing agriculture. Furthermore, treaties often stipulated blacksmiths or other artificers and teachers in agricultural or domestic skills.

The United States government accepted as allies in its work of civilization the Christian churches of the land, whose missionary energies were
directed in part toward the Indians. These were in the main Protestant
efforts; the early Catholic missionary work within the boundaries of the
United States was sparse, and not until the end of the nineteenth century
did Catholic missionaries come into prominence. Even Protestant missionaries at the beginning of the new nation were not much in evidence;
only a dozen missionaries survived at the end of the Revolutionary War to
Christianize the Indians. But the Second Great Awakening stimulated new
endeavors, and soon there was a group of eager missionary societies whose
purpose it was to evangelize the heathen, including the Indians in their
own nation. The most important of these groups was the American Board
of Commissioners for Foreign Missions, founded in Boston in 1810 by Pres-
byterians and Congregationalists. Their goal was to bring the gospel to the
unenlightened.

The churches engaged in a long and inconclusive debate over the prece-
dence to be given to civilizing and to Christianizing. Did an Indian need to
be civilized first, so that Christianity could "take"? "The Gospel, plain and

simple as it is, and fitted by its nature for what it was designed to effect," one missionary wrote, "requires an intellect above that of a savage to comprehend. Nor is it at all to the dishonor of our holy faith that such men must be taught a previous lesson, and first of all be instructed in the emollient arts of life." Others held as firmly that the gospel itself was the greatest civilizing power. "Instead of waiting till Civilization fit our Indian neighbors for the gospel," one advocate said, "let us try whether the gospel will not be the most successful means of civilizing them." But it was largely a theoretical squabble, for the two processes, civilizing and Christianizing, were inextricably mixed. When missionaries went among the Indians, they went to educate and to convert, and it would be difficult to tell where one activity ended and the other began. Nor did it matter to the government, which came to depend upon the church societies for civilizing work among the Indians without intending to promote any particular religion.

The mission stations among the Indians were primarily educational institutions, instructing the Indian children not only in piety, but in traditional learning and in industrious work habits. As such, they were actively encouraged and supported by the United States government. Thus when the Presbyterian missionary Gideon Blackburn approached Jefferson and Secretary of War Henry Dearborn in 1803 about aid for a school among the Cherokees, he was warmly received and permitted to open his school. Although he was told that he could expect no compensation from the government for his services, the secretary of war nevertheless instructed the Cherokee agent to erect a schoolhouse and to give necessary aid to start the project.

The first mission of the American Board of Commissioners for Foreign Missions was founded at Brainerd, Tennessee, in 1816 and received similar assistance from the government. Cyrus Kingsbury, founder of the school, applied to the War Department for support on the grounds that extending to the Indians the blessings that whites enjoyed was "not only a dictate of humanity, and a duty enjoined by the Gospel, but an act of justice." Kingsbury had explicit goals, which could easily be seconded by the War Department and the Indian agents. "I considered it to be the grand object of the present undertaking," he wrote to the American Board on November 26, 1816, "to impart to them that knowledge which is calculated to make them useful citizens, and pious Christians. In order to do this, it appeared necessary to instruct them in the various branches of common English education, to form them to habits of industry, and to give them competent knowledge of the economy of civilized life."

THOMAS L. MCKENNEY AND INDIAN EDUCATION

The close union of minds between government and the churches was exhibited in the attempt to make the factory system into a primary civilizing
agency. Such was the dream, if not the obsession, of Thomas L. McKenney
while he was superintendent of Indian trade from 1816 to 1822. McKenney
used his office to further his paramount interest, the civilization and Christianization of the Indians, and he sounded at times more like a missionary
than a public official. "It is enough to know that Indians are Men," he
wrote to a missionary of the American Board early in his tenure, "that like
ourselves they are susceptible of pleasure, and of pain—that they have
souls, the term of whose duration is co-extensive with our own—that like
us they must live forever; and that we have the power not only to enhance
their happiness in this world, but in the next also; and by our councils, and
guidance, save souls that otherwise must perish!" He declared that the government was founded on pillars of mercy, that it was run by men who
"would joyfully administer to them [the Indians] the cup of consolation,
nor withhold it because of the color which an Indian Sun has burned upon
their brothers." As superintendent of Indian trade McKenney worked in
close concert with missionaries to the Indians, prodding, encouraging, and
supporting their efforts and interceding for them with the secretary of war.

McKenney's first goal was to turn the Indians toward agriculture, which
would promote an interest in private property, stimulate hard work, and
provide the stability and settled existence that the missionaries needed to
build Christian communities. Despite a considerable lack of enthusiasm
on the part of the Indians, he sent agricultural equipment and seeds to the
factories and wanted the factors to encourage the Indians to trade for such
goods by setting up model gardens and farms. "This is the way you will
most effectually promote the *great object of the Govt.* towards these unenlightened people," he wrote. "Invite their attention to agriculture and
the arts, and help them, for they are helpless. Our object is not to keep
these Indians hunters eternally. We want to make citizens out of them, and
they must be first anchored to the soil, else they will be flaying about
whilst there is any room for them in the wilderness or an animal to be
trapped."

Working with Henry Southard, chairman of the House Committee on
Indian Affairs, and other sympathetic congressmen, McKenney fought hard
for a national school system for the Indians, to be supported by profits from
an expanded factory system. "I certainly think," he told Southard, "Congress has it completely in its power to erect out of the materials of Indian
reform a monument more durable and towering than those of ordinary dimensions, a monument as indestructible as justice, interesting as human-

ity—and lasting in time." He and his missionary friends lobbied earnestly for the measure, and the House committee reported a bill to extend the factory system with the addition of eight new factories and to provide schools for the Indians.

Congress refused to turn the factory system into an educational enterprise, but this was only a temporary delay, for McKenney did not waver in his resolve, and he stimulated a flood of petitions to Congress from religious groups in behalf of a measure (now left unspecified) for "the *security, preservation,* and *improvement* of the Indians." President Monroe asserted the need to civilize the Indians, and the House committee reporting on the president's message in January 1819 praised the successful work being done by missionary societies among the Indians, asserting that "a more energetic and extensive system is necessary, to improve the various Indian tribes, in agriculture, education, and civilization."

The result was not an elaborate school system tied to the factories, but an annual appropriation for a civilization fund independent of the factories, which continued after the factories themselves were destroyed. An "act making provision for the civilization of the Indian tribes adjoining the frontier settlements" became law on March 3, 1819. It appropriated ten thousand dollars annually for use at the president's discretion to further the civilization of the tribes wherever practicable by employing "capable persons of good moral character, to instruct them in the mode of agriculture suited to their situation; and for teaching their children in reading, writing, and arithmetic." The president and the secretary of war decided not to use the fund directly, but rather to spend it through the "benevolent societies" that had already established schools for the education of Indian children or would do so in future (under the encouragement of the fund). Secretary of War Calhoun issued a special circular that invited interested individuals or groups to apply for a share of the fund and called for information about their resources, the kind of education they proposed to impart, and the number of students to be instructed.

When McKenney was appointed to head the Office of Indian Affairs in 1824, he continued to fight aggressively for the program. One of his early acts was to send a blistering circular to the Indian superintendents and agents reminding them of the solicitude of the government for the improvement of the Indians by means of the school system and the ten thousand dollars annually appropriated for its support. It was the duty of the superintendents, McKenney declared, to "*sanction,* and *second,* this plan of renovating the morals and enlightening and improving these unfortunate people." Those who opposed the plan were opposing the government itself, paralyzing its program, and bringing the program into contempt in the eyes of the Indians, whom it was designed to benefit.

McKenney continued to be enthusiastic about the program and its salutary effects, and his annual reports showed a steady increase in the number of schools, the enrollment of Indian pupils, and the religious groups taking part. These groups, encouraged by the government aid, devoted more and more from their private funds to the enterprise.

Indian schools were materially aided also by special treaty provisions. Treaties with the Chippewas and Potawatomis in 1826, for example, authorized an annual grant for schools, to be continued as long as Congress thought proper. Similarly, treaties with Winnebagos, Menominees, Kickapoos, Creeks, Cherokees, and others stipulated money for education. As the policy continued, sizable funds were provided. In the year 1834, thirty-five thousand dollars was due for schools under treaties.

Of special note among the attempts to provide white education for Indian youths was the Choctaw Academy, established in 1825 under the sponsorship of Richard M. Johnson, representative and senator from Kentucky and later vice president of the United States. Under the Choctaw Treaty of Doak's Stand in 1820, funds for education were provided from the sale of ceded lands, and in 1825 a new treaty added a six-thousand-dollar annuity for twenty years to support Choctaw schools. The chiefs desired to use part of the funds for a school outside the Choctaw nation, where the influence of white civilization would be stronger. When the federal government approved the request, Johnson quickly seized upon the occasion to have the school established on his property near Great Crossings, in Scott County, Kentucky. The Baptist General Convention undertook the venture, and the Reverend Thomas Henderson was engaged to superintend the school. What developed was a boarding school for Indian boys that taught the standard elements of an English education and supplied training in mechanic arts. The students were primarily Choctaws, sent from the Indian Territory, but the school was open to other Indians and to local white boys as well. Johnson was a good promoter, no doubt in part because he profited from the venture, and Henderson an able director, and the school flourished for fifteen years. It reached its top enrollment of 188 in 1835.

The Indian schools were a mere beginning. In the formative years the system was inadequate, and even enthusiastic promoters like Thomas McKenney came to realize that. Because of the small number of schools provided, only a few children in each tribe could be educated, and they were not enough to influence the character of the whole tribe. Even those who enrolled in school often did not profit because at the completion of their studies they had no means and little incentive to pursue a new life. So the student's only alternative was, as McKenney noted, "to turn Indian again, and too often by his improved intelligence he becomes the oppressor of his less cultivated brothers." McKenney wanted to furnish the educated Indians with land, a house, and agricultural implements, but no funds for the purpose were available.

As the 1820s advanced, the initial expansion of Indian education occasioned by the civilization fund began to slacken. By 1830, there were fifty-two schools with 1,512 students, but that was not a large proportion of the total number of Indian children, even of the tribes where schools had been established. It had been McKenney's hope that once the system had proved itself, Congress would increase the annual fund, but Congress refused to do so. When he left office in 1830, McKenney saw how far short of his optimistic goals the reality was, but the goal of civilizing and Christianizing the Indians remained an important element in government policy well into the twentieth century and helped to give that policy its strongly paternalistic bent.

THE INDIAN DEPARTMENT

The education and civilization of the Indians, as well as other aspects of United States Indian policy, depended upon the special personnel within the War Department appointed to deal with the Indians. The aggregate of these persons was given the general designation "Indian department," a term covering the officials and clerks in the office of the secretary of war who were assigned to Indian matters and the superintendents, agents, sub-agents, interpreters, clerks, and mechanics who carried on the work in the field. The term at first did not necessarily indicate a fixed organization, but as the laws governing intercourse with the Indians expanded in scope and were expressed with greater precision, so the official standing and duties of the men in the Indian department also became more clearly defined, until in 1834 a definitive organization was established by law.

Antecedents of the Indian department are found in the colonial agents sent among the Indians, the British superintendents, the special commissioners sent out by the Continental Congress, and the Indian superintendents authorized by the Ordinance of 1786. Most directly concerned were the superintendents, for their office was quietly carried over when the Constitution replaced the Articles of Confederation. On September 11, 1789, Congress provided two thousand dollars for the governor of the Northwest Territory, both as his annual salary and "for discharging the duties of superintendent of Indian affairs in the northern department," thus beginning the practice of making territorial governors ex officio superintendents of Indian affairs. In 1790 the law establishing the Territory South of the River Ohio declared that "the powers, duties and emoluments of a superintendent of Indian affairs for the southern department, shall be united with

those of the governor." Subsequent laws setting up new territories included similar clauses.

The first trade and intercourse law (1790) authorized the superintendents to issue licenses for trade and to enforce the licensing provisions, and
it referred to "such other persons as the President of the United States shall
appoint" to issue and recall licenses. But no specific provision was made
for appointing agents or establishing agencies. To care for particular Indian
problems, however, special agents were appointed in 1792. These men—
three sent to the southern Indians and one to the Six Nations—had no connection with the intercourse law but were charged instead with special
diplomatic missions.

A new turn in the development of Indian agencies came with the second
intercourse law (1793). A section dealing with measures to civilize the Indians authorized the president "to appoint such persons, from time to
time, as temporary agents, to reside among the Indians, as he shall think
proper." The commissions and instructions sent to these agents emphasized their responsibility to civilize the Indians by means of agriculture
and domestic arts and referred to them officially as "temporary agents."
The duties assigned them ran the wide range of Indian relations set forth in
the intercourse laws, and eventually the word *temporary* was dropped from
their title. Under this authorization appeared the permanent Indian agents,
assigned to particular tribes or areas, who became indispensable in the
management of Indian affairs.

An agent's duties were in large part reportorial. He was to keep an eye
out for violations of the intercourse laws and to report them to the superintendents, to the military commanders of the frontier posts, or to the War
Department. Action and further directions to the agent in most cases came
from his superior officers. But the critical work of dealing with the Indians
and the frontier whites devolved upon the agent, and the success of the
work depended upon the character of the man, the respect he won from the
tribes among whom he lived, and the authority of his position in the eyes
of the whites. Fortunately the United States had a number of capable and
distinguished men of a character and integrity that gave stature to the
office of Indian agent and that enabled the agents by their personal influence alone to ease the conflicts between whites and Indians without reliance on either civil court procedures or military force.

The work of directing the superintendents and agents rested upon the
secretary of war and the clerks of the War Department whom he chose to
assign to the task, for in the first decades of the new nation there was no
formally established office charged specifically with Indian affairs. Dealings with the Indians were considered a special category of the War Department's activities, however, and separate letterbooks were maintained for
correspondence concerned with Indian matters.

When the office of superintendent of Indian trade was established in 1806, it became an unofficial focus for Indian affairs, supplying information and advice to the secretary of war and corresponding with citizens who were interested in the Indians. But the abolition of the factories in 1822 removed even this semblance of an Indian center in the War Department.

Then on March 11, 1824, Secretary of War Calhoun, by his own order and without special authorization from Congress, created in the War Department what he called the Bureau of Indian Affairs (but designated usually the Office of Indian Affairs). Calhoun appointed Thomas L. McKenney to head the office and assigned him two clerks as assistants. The duties of the new position were set forth in the letter of appointment: to take charge of the appropriations for annuities and current expenses, to examine and approve all vouchers for expenditures, to administer the fund for the civilization of the Indians, to decide on claims arising between Indians and whites under the intercourse laws, and to handle the ordinary Indian correspondence of the War Department. This set-up was formalized by Congress in 1832 when it authorized the president to appoint a commissioner of Indian affairs, under the secretary of war, who was to have "the direction and management of all Indian affairs, and of all matters arising out of Indian relations."

The superintendents and agents were assisted by the military officers and men on the frontier. The army had an important role as the power behind the decisions and policies of the Indian agents and as the last resort of the territorial governors in dealing with hostile Indians or recalcitrant whites. It was no accident that Indian agencies and government trading houses were usually in the shadow of a military post.

Close cooperation was required of the agents and the military commanders, not only by the intercourse laws, but also by the repeated directives coming from the secretary of war, the general in chief, and the head of the Office of Indian Affairs. Unfortunately, the official directives could not smooth out all the rough edges in human relations between the army officers and the civilian Indian agents. Both groups were under the direction and surveillance of the secretary of war, but frequent conflicts of authority arose, to the detriment of efficient enforcement of the intercourse laws. Many army officers were unwilling to take orders directly from civilian officers of the government, and specific directives coming explicitly from the secretary of war or down through the chain of command to the post commandant were considered necessary before military officers would heed the request of agents for help. Difficulties sometimes arose, too, because of interference in Indian affairs on the part of army officers, who did not always wait to get a cue from the agents and whose garrisons were at times a point of infection in the Indian country, to which the Indians flocked for free food and even liquor.

Yet the disputes and controversies between agents and officers were more than balanced by the energy and zeal with which most of the frontier commanders undertook to carry out the federal government's Indian policy. In removing intruders, confiscating liquor, restraining Indian hostilities, and conducting treaties and conferences, the army officers were able and devoted supporters of the government and of the intercourse laws.

PRESENTS AND ANNUITIES

Whatever the legal formality of treaties between sovereign nations, the relations between the United States government and the Indian tribes called forth procedures and practices that indicated special relationships which hardly existed even analogously between the United States and the nations of Europe. One was the widespread use of presents to Indian leaders. It had been European practice during the colonial era and continued to be British practice among the Indians in Canada and along the border to provide gifts to Indian tribes and their chiefs. As the Indians came to depend more and more upon European goods, such gifts formed an indispensable diplomatic tool in gaining the goodwill and allegiance of Indian tribes. Great amounts of money were expended to "brighten the chain of friendship," and as the outlay of free goods continued, many Indians became almost completely dependent upon them.

The young United States could not eliminate the practice, and President Washington was alert to the need for presents. In the six-point program for advancing the happiness of the Indians and attaching them to the United States proposed in 1791, he asked that the president "be enabled to employ the means to which the Indians have been long accustomed for uniting their immediate interests with the preservation of peace." The presents were to be employed also as a means of bringing the Indians around to the civilization of the whites. Secretary of War Henry Knox, in his first long report on Indian affairs, recommended gifts of sheep and other domestic animals for chiefs and their wives in an attempt to instill in the Indians a "love for exclusive property." And the intercourse laws provided that "in order to promote civilization among the friendly Indian tribes, and to secure the continuance of their friendship," the president could furnish them with domestic animals and the implements of husbandry.

Competition with the British offered a strong incentive for distributing presents to Indians. Lewis Cass, as governor of Michigan Territory, gave the matter great emphasis, for he saw a moral obligation to provide for the Indians who had given up "the fairest portion of their Country" to the whites and who now found it difficult to subsist by means of hunting. Without the "annual gratuities" they had come to expect from the government, he found it "difficult to conceive how they could support and clothe themselves." Cass looked upon the distribution of presents as essential for peace on the frontier. "Whatever has a tendency to conciliate the minds of the Indians and to render less unpleasant those obnoxious circumstances in our intercourse with them, which cannot be removed," he wrote, "will have a powerful effect in continuing our existing relations with them. The importance of presents in this point of view is too striking to require any particular illustration." This was especially true in competition with the British, and Cass pointed to the experience of the War of 1812, in which the British had used presents to great advantage.

When annuities under treaties and trade goods from the factory system provided alternatives, the use of presents as a wholesale means of supplying the needs of the Indians declined. The annuities, in fact, together with rations and other gratuities that continued through the decades, became an essential means of support for many tribes. The distribution of the annuities—either in cash or in goods—became one of the primary activities of the Indian department and one of its biggest headaches.

To procure the goods needed for annuity payments and to account for goods and money distributed were major tasks. When the annuities and presents were added to funds appropriated for the salaries of agents and their supporting personnel, for transportation, for buildings, and for contingent expenses, the sums involved were large, and it seemed impossible (granted the problems of communication and the incompetence of some of the men who handled accounts) to keep the records straight. Accounting procedures seemed to give officials in the Indian department more trouble than did the actual dealings with the Indians. Henry R. Schoolcraft, the longtime Indian agent at Sault Ste. Marie, expressed a general view when he wrote graphically in 1828, "The derangements in the fiscal affair of the Indian department are in the extreme. One would think that appropriations had been handled with a pitchfork. . . . And these derangements are only with regard to the north. How the south and west stand, it is impossible to say. But there is a screw loose in the public machinery somewhere."

The distribution of annuities usually took place at the Indian agencies, to which the Indians were summoned for the occasion. There the agent, with the support of the military post commander, gave the money or goods to the chiefs, who in turn distributed them to the Indians. In some cases the annuities went directly to individuals, but in 1834 Congress stipulated that annuities were to be paid to the chiefs or to such other persons as the tribe designated. Cash annuities, although easier to provide than goods, came under frequent attack, for the money quickly passed from the Indians' hands into the pockets of traders. McKenney called the payment of money a "radical defect." It was a practice, he said, that "furnished a lure to the avaricious—and gives the means of indulgence to these untutored people, in all their propensities to drunkenness & idleness; & is known, to have produced from the beginning, *no other fruits."* Annuities continued to be of great concern to the government officials responsible for Indian affairs.

Besides presents and annuities, the United States (following the practice of Great Britain and other European nations) gave silver medals to chiefs and warriors as tokens of friendship and as signs of allegiance and loyalty on the part of those who accepted them. These so-called Indian peace medals came to play a prominent part in American Indian policy. Medals were given to Indian chiefs on such important occasions as the signing of a treaty, a visit of Indians to the national capital, or a tour of Indian country by some federal official. They were distributed, too, by Indian agents on the frontier at their own discretion but according to established norms.

The practice became so firmly established that it was impossible to conduct satisfactory relations with the Indians without medals. McKenney made this clear to the secretary of war at the end of 1829. "So important is its continuance esteemed to be," he wrote, "that without medals, any plan of operations among the Indians, be it what it may, is essentially enfeebled. This comes of the high value which the Indians set upon these tokens of Friendship. They are, besides this indication of the Government Friendship, badges of power to them, and trophies of renown. They will not consent to part from this ancient *right*, as they esteem it; and according to the value they set upon medals is the importance to the Government in having them to bestow."

When the United States was in competition with the British for the friendship of the tribes, the medals were of special importance, for the chiefs signified their switch from adherence to the British to loyalty to the United States by formally turning in their British medals and accepting in their place those bearing the likeness of the American president. Within the tribes, too, possession of a medal gave rank and distinction; and despite protestations of government officials to the contrary, by awarding medals the United States commissioners sometimes designated or "made" the chiefs with whom they dealt.

President Washington presented large oval silver medals to Alexander McGillivray and his Creek associates by the secret clauses of the Treaty of New York in 1790 and sent similar medals to the Cherokees, Choctaws, and Chickasaws in subsequent years and to the Seneca chief Red Jacket in 1792. General Wayne distributed Washington medals at Greenville. When Lewis and Clark ascended the Missouri in 1804, they took along a large supply of medals, mostly Jefferson medals (in three sizes) with the bust of the president on the obverse and clasped hands with the words PEACE AND FRIENDSHIP on the reverse. As the years passed, medals flooded the frontier, especially after the War of 1812, when they played a significant part in the campaign to gain the loyalty of the Indians of the Great Lakes region and on the upper Mississippi and Missouri.

Another device for attaching Indians to the United States government was to invite delegations of important tribal leaders to the seat of government to confer with the president, the secretary of war, and the commissioner of Indian affairs. These Indian delegates sometimes came to negotiate treaties and sometimes to present grievances, but the occasions were used also to impress them with the size and power of the United States and its people. The Indians visited the sights of the capital, met dignitaries at the White House, inspected navy yards and fortifications, and often stopped to see Philadelphia and New York before they returned home. The trials of entertaining the Indians in Washington were many, but the practice continued—often at the insistence of the Indians.

The Indian Office, which entertained the delegations and performed the steadily increasing duties that federal relations with the Indian entailed, was a modest bureau in the early years of the nineteenth century. Its organization and much of its work began informally, but as the years passed its role became ever more critical, and like other bureaucracies it grew and grew. The Indian Office assumed the paternalistic mantle that theoretically belonged to the Great Father, the president.

CHAPTER 4

The Policy of Indian Removal

American Indian policy is sometimes thought of as a movement between two extremes. On one hand was the idea of assimilating the Indians into white American society through the acculturative processes of private property, an agricultural (as opposed to a hunter) economy, formal education in English letters, and Christianization. On the other was the idea of segregation or separateness; the Indians could maintain their limited political autonomy, their special languages, and their customs and religions but only outside the limits of white society, either in protected enclaves or, preferably, beyond the western frontier of white settlement. In the nineteenth century, at least, there was no concept of a truly pluralistic society.

FORMULATION OF THE POLICY

The removal of the eastern Indians that dominated the second quarter of the century falls on the side of separateness. It was an admission that the speedy acculturation and absorption of the Indians into white society (and even the biological intermingling of the races) that was the goal of the Jeffersonians had not been attained and was perhaps unattainable. Yet this was not a simple matter of either assimilation or segregation. Removal was the policy adopted to solve the problem of alien groups claiming independence within established states and territories of the United States, the problem of groups of human beings with communal cultures still only partially dependent upon agriculture owning large areas of land that were coveted by the dynamic white agricultural systems of both the north and the south, and the problem of friction that occurred along the lines of contact between the two societies and the deleterious effect that contact almost universally had upon Indian individuals and Indian society.

These problems were real problems both for the United States government and for the Indian tribes. They could not be easily waved aside simply by appeals to public morality and justice. They resulted in a great complexity of practical situations that confounded sincere Christian statesmen as well as zealous missionaries and for which even aggressive and ruthless white expansionists found no easy answers. Indian leaders, too, saw the complexity, and they arrived at a variety of adaptive responses as they sought to maintain some degree of self-determination in the face of the obvious power and advantages of the United States. Nor was removal complete segregation, a cutting off of the Indian groups from white contact and connections by banishment beyond the Mississippi. In some respects the policy and the process brought increased rather than lessened interference in domestic Indian affairs on the part of the Great Father. And when the emigrant Indians were settled in their western homes, the drive for educating, civilizing, and Christianizing them took on new vigor. Acculturation and to a large extent assimilation were still the ultimate goals.

Although it has been common to ascribe the removal of the Indians in the 1830s to Andrew Jackson, his aggressive removal policy was in fact the culmination of a movement that had been gradually gaining momentum in government circles for nearly three decades. Whites had steadily encroached upon Indian lands, and new treaties of cession had been negotiated from time to time to validate the incursions. But this was a piecemeal process, and there were dreams that the problems could be eliminated once and for all by inducing the eastern Indians to exchange their lands for territory west of the Mississippi, leaving the area between the Appalachians and the Father of Waters free for white exploitation.

The idea of exchange of lands originated with Thomas Jefferson in 1803, when the addition of the vast Louisiana Purchase created conditions that would make removal feasible. Before the end of Jefferson's administration gentle pressure was being placed on the Cherokees to introduce to them the notion of exchanging their present country for lands in the West. Some Cherokees did go west, at first to hunt and then to settle, but the War of 1812 crowded out any serious thought of orderly emigration of the tribes. Not until President Monroe's administration was the proposal discussed again in earnest.

Monroe and Secretary of War John C. Calhoun worked sincerely for a change in the enduring situation of the Indians. The anomaly of large groups of savage or semicivilized tribes surrounded by civilized whites struck them with special force. The solution was either removal to the open western regions or a change from the hunter state. In a letter to Andrew Jackson in October 1817, Monroe asserted that "the hunter or savage state requires a greater extent of territory to sustain it, than is compatible with the progress and just claims of civilized life, and must yield to it."

The prickly question of land tenure would disappear if only the Indians could be removed beyond the Mississippi, and the War Department authorized its commissioners to make liberal offers to the eastern tribes in an attempt to induce them to accept willingly an exchange of lands.

The removal question was given a new and dangerous twist by special circumstances surrounding the Cherokees in Georgia (and to a lesser extent the Creeks, Chickasaws, and Choctaws in Alabama and Mississippi). The Cherokees were settled within the boundaries of Georgia on lands that they had always held. These Indians were not nomads; they had an abiding attachment to their lands and were determined to hold them at all costs, no matter what the United States might offer them as an inducement to move. The United States, through government officials directly and through the encouragement given to missionary societies, had urged the Indians to adopt white ways by tilling the soil and developing the domestic arts of spinning and weaving. Formal education in English-language schools, also, had led to a cadre of leaders—mostly mixed-bloods—who could deal effectively with white society. The remarkable invention of a Cherokee syllabary by Sequoyah made it possible for great numbers of Cherokees to learn to read in their native tongue. Assisted by missionaries of the American Board of Commissioners for Foreign Missions, the Cherokees at the end of the decade of the 1820s began to publish their own newspaper, the *Cherokee Phoenix*, which printed material in English and in the Cherokee language and which became an important vehicle for disseminating views of the Cherokees, both within their own nation and to the white world. Some of the Indian leaders, too, had adopted the whites' system of black slavery and had established extensive plantations rivaling their white counterparts'.

Georgia and the United States had signed a compact on April 24, 1802, by which Georgia ceded to the United States its western land claims. In return, the United States agreed to extinguish the Indian title to lands within the state and turn them over to Georgia as soon as this could be done peaceably and on reasonable terms. As the land greed of the Georgians increased through the years, the federal government was accused of failing in its part of the bargain, for the government had not extinguished the Indian title to Georgia lands. To these criticisms President Monroe replied in a special message to Congress on March 30, 1824, defending the course of the government, asserting that the Indian title was in no way affected by the compact of 1802, and denying any obligation on the part of the federal government to force the Indians to move against their will. He reiterated his strong opinion that removal would be in the best interests of the Indians, but he refused to be pushed by Georgia beyond the strict import of the compact.

As Monroe neared the end of his term, he increased his insistence that steps be taken to preserve the rapidly degenerating tribes, now increasingly threatened by Georgia and other southern states. He told Congress on December 7, 1824, of the Indians' deplorable conditions and the danger of their extinction. To civilize them was essential to their survival, but this was a slow process and could not be fully attained in the territory where the Indians then resided. Monroe had no thought of forceful ejection; even if it aimed at the security and happiness of the Indians, he said, it would be "revolting to humanity, and utterly unjustifiable." There was only one solution: the Indians must be invited and induced to take up their home in the West.

In a special message on removal, January 27, 1825, the president urged a liberal policy that would satisfy both the Cherokees and the Georgians. He asked for "a well-digested plan" for governing and civilizing the Indians, which would not only "shield them from impending ruin, but promote their welfare and happiness." He was convinced that such a plan was practicable and that it could be made so attractive to the Indians that all, even those most opposed to emigration, would accede to it in the near future. The essence of his proposal was the institution of a government for the Indians in the West, one that would preserve order, prevent the intrusion of the whites, and stimulate civilization. "It is not doubted," Monroe told Congress, "that this arrangement will present considerations of sufficient force to surmount all their prejudices in favor of the soil of their nativity, however strong they may be."

Because Congress failed to act on Monroe's proposal, President John Quincy Adams faced the continuing Indian problem. His secretary of war, James Barbour, submitted a new removal plan, which was read and discussed in a cabinet meeting. Although Adams noted that Barbour's paper was "full of benevolence and humanity," he wrote: "I fear there is no practicable plan by which they can be organized into one civilized, or half-civilized, Government. Mr. Rush, Mr. Southard, and Mr. Wirt all expressed their doubts of the practicability of Governor Barbour's plan; but they had nothing more effective to propose, and I approved it from the same motive." But again Congress took no action.

On July 26, 1827, the Cherokee Nation adopted a written constitution patterned after that of the United States, in which the Indians asserted that they were one of the sovereign and independent nations of the earth with complete jurisdiction over their own territory. This move on their part caused great alarm. The secretary of war wrote to the Cherokee agent, warning that the constitution could not be understood as changing the relations that then existed between the Indians and the government of the United States. Georgia, of course, was indignant and angered by the "presumptuous document," and the state finally began to move against the

Cherokees, contending that it could not abide an *imperium in imperio* within its boundaries. Georgia's line of action was to extend the authority of the state and its laws over the Cherokee lands. This would in effect withdraw the Cherokee territory from the status of Indian country, bring control of the lands into Georgia's hands, and by overt as well as subtle pressure force the Indians out.

ANDREW JACKSON AND REMOVAL

Then Andrew Jackson became president of the United States. He was a man of forthright views who did not hesitate to speak his mind and a man who had ample Indian experience to give weight to his utterances. He had early decided that it was farcical to treat with the Indian tribes as though they were sovereign and independent nations, and he could point to considerable evidence to show that treaties had never been a success. Jackson brought these views with him when he entered the White House. He was convinced that the Indians could no longer exist as independent enclaves within the states. They must either move west or become subject to the state laws.

Assured of presidential sympathy, Georgia took new action against the Cherokees. At the end of 1828 the Georgia legislature added Cherokee lands to certain northwestern counties of the state. A year later it extended its laws over these lands, effective June 1, 1830. Thereafter the Cherokee laws and customs were to be null and void. The Cherokees immediately protested and made representations to the president and to Congress.

Through the instrumentality of Secretary of War John H. Eaton, Jackson answered the Cherokees. Bluntly he told them that they had no hope of succor from the federal government. A letter of Eaton to the delegation of the Cherokees on April 18, 1829, was an unequivocal statement of the Jackson policy. Eaton informed the Indians that by the Declaration of Independence and the treaty of 1783 all the sovereignty which pertained to Great Britain had been conferred upon the states of the Union. "If, as is the case," he told the Indians, "you have been permitted to abide on your lands from that period to the present, enjoying the right of the soil, and privilege to hunt, it is not thence to be inferred, that this was any thing more than a permission, growing out of compacts with your nation; nor is it a circumstance whence, now to deny to those states, the exercise of their original sovereignty." The treaties with the Indians, which for the supporters of Indian rights were a great arsenal of arguments, were turned to his own uses by the secretary of war. The "emphatic language" of the Treaty of Hopewell, he told the Cherokees, could not be mistaken. The United States *gave peace* to the Indians and took them again into favor and under its protection. The treaty *allotted* and *defined* the hunting grounds. It secured to the Indians the privilege of pursuing game and protection from encroachment. "No right, however, save a mere possessory one, is by the provisions of the treaty of Hopewell conceded to your nation. The soil, and the use of it, were suffered to remain with you, while the Sovereignty abided precisely where it did before, in those states within whose limits you were situated." The compact of 1802, Eaton added, had nothing to say about sovereignty. Both parties to the compact knew well where it lay: with the state. There was nothing to be offered to the Cherokees but the urgent recommendation that they move west of the Mississippi.

Jackson moved ahead boldly. In his first message to Congress, on December 8, 1829, he addressed himself to the problems of the "condition and ulterior destiny of the Indian tribes within the limits of some of our States." He called attention to the fact that some of the southern Indians had "lately attempted to erect an independent government within the limits of Georgia and Alabama," that the states had countered this infringement on their sovereignty by extending their laws over the Indians, and that the Indians in turn had appealed to the federal government. Did the federal government have a right to sustain the Indian pretensions? he asked. His answer was forthright. The Constitution forbade the erection of a new state within the territory of an existing state without that state's permission. Still less, then, could it allow a "foreign and independent government" to establish itself there. On these grounds, he told Congress, he had informed the Indians that their attempt to establish an independent government would not be countenanced by the executive of the United States, and he had advised them either to emigrate beyond the Mississippi or to submit to the laws of the states.

Jackson denied any intention to use force and declared, "This emigration should be voluntary, for it would be as cruel as unjust to compel the aborigines to abandon the graves of their fathers and seek a home in a distant land." The protestation had a hollow ring, for the Indians were to be informed that if they remained they would be subject to the state laws and would lose much of their beloved land. With a touch of sarcasm, the president pronounced it visionary for the Indians to hope to retain hunting lands on which they had neither dwelt nor made improvements "merely because they had seen them from the mountain or passed them in the chase."

In line with the president's recommendation, an Indian removal bill was introduced in Congress. The measure, like the president's message, made no mention of coercion to remove the Indians, and on the surface it seemed harmless and humane enough, with its provisions for a permanent guarantee of possession of the new lands, compensation for the improvements left behind, and aid and assistance to the emigrants. But those who knew the policy and practice of Jackson and the Georgians and the adamant stand of the Indians against removal understood that force would be inevitable.

MOTIVATION FOR REMOVAL

The proponents of removal of the Indians from Georgia and the other southeastern states had diverse motivations. The strongest pressure came from the land hunger of the whites. When the cotton plantation system began its dynamic drive west across the gulf plains after the War of 1812, a movement stimulated by the invention of the cotton gin and the seemingly endless demand for cotton to feed the new mills in England and the Northeast, the land held by the Indians seemed an enormous obstacle. All of the Five Civilized Tribes—Cherokee, Creek, Choctaw, Chickasaw, and Seminole—had sloughed off rims of territory by treaties of cession in the period 1815–1830, a paring down that opened much good land to white exploitation. But the tribes insisted on retaining their heartlands, sizable blocks of territory that seemed to Georgia and the new states of Mississippi and Alabama (admitted to the Union in 1817 and 1819, respectively) to be alien enclaves in their midst.

It was possible for some years to postpone the conflict, as free land was taken up and as Georgia continued to expect action from the federal government in regard to Cherokee lands under the compact of 1802. But in the 1820s the push for new lands intensified, and the vehemence of the demands of the southern states increased. An added element was the discovery of gold within the Cherokee Nation in 1829. As would be the case with strikes in the Far West later in the century, the word of gold fired the Georgians with new enthusiasm for Cherokee lands, and many rushed into the region in violation of the Indians' territorial rights.

There was no effective check upon the covetousness for land. Land was the most important commodity in early-nineteenth-century America, and the sale of the public domain was a major source of funding for the national government before the Civil War. White society, both northern and southern, had a fundamental belief that the land was there to be exploited and that the Indians were not making full use of its possibilities. Governor George C. Gilmer of Georgia declared in 1830 that "treaties were expedients by which ignorant, intractable, and savage people were induced without bloodshed to yield up what civilized peoples had a right to possess by virtue of that command of the Creator delivered to man upon his formation—be fruitful, multiply, and replenish the earth and subdue it."

Strong arguments were made for the rights of the Indians to their lands, but they ultimately foundered on the deepseated conviction that the white man had a superior right to the land. The Jacksonian and Georgian contention that the Indians had only a possessory right to the soil—a "mere right of occupancy"—was not a spur-of-the-moment argument to cover white cupidity for Indian lands. There had long been an overriding reluctance to admit any title in fee for Indians. Despite the Jeffersonian principle that the salvation of the Indians lay in private ownership of land, treaties negotiated with them generally had fallen short of providing fee simple ownership either to individual Indians or to tribes.

By liberal terms and inducements, the promoters of removal hoped to persuade the Indian tribes that it would be to their benefit to move away from the stresses and pressures that came from existence within the state and that the advantages would overcome the attachment to their ancestral lands. Such a voluntary move was made by considerable numbers of Indians, but the great majority preferred to stay where they were, and they insisted on their right to do so.

A second motivation for removal was concern about states' rights and the fear of a bitter federal-state jurisdictional contest that might even lead to military conflict. The demands made for federal protection of the Indians in their own culture on their ancestral lands within the states in the East ran up against the hard fact that the United States government could not risk an all-out confrontation with Georgia. The jurisdictional dispute cannot be simply dismissed. Were the tribes independent nations? The question received its legal answer from the Supreme Court when John Marshall defined the Indian tribes as "domestic dependent nations." But aside from the judicial decision, were the Indians, in fact, independent, and could they have maintained their independence without the support—political and military—of the federal government? The answer, clearly, was no, as writers at the time pointed out. The federal government could have stood firm in defense of the Indian nation against Georgia, but this would have brought it into head-on collision with a state that insisted its sovereignty was being impinged upon by the Cherokees.

There was also, it must be admitted, genuine humanitarian concern for the Indians, in which their voluntary removal out of contact with whites appeared to be a viable, indeed perhaps the only, answer. Despite the optimism of supporters of the programs for civilizing the Indians, an uncomfortable conclusion had become increasingly clear: the contact of Indians with white civilization had deleterious effects upon the Indians. The efforts at improvement were vitiated or overbalanced by the steady pressure of white vices, to which the Indians succumbed. Instead of prospering under white tutelage, Indians in many areas were degenerating and disappearing. The promoters of the program argued that only if the Indians were removed beyond contact with whites could the slow process of education, civilization, and Christianization take place. Insofar as removal was necessary to safeguard the Indian, to that extent the intercourse laws had failed.

A shift of attitude can be seen in Thomas L. McKenney. His enthusiastic reports on the progress of the Indian schools and Indian civilization in general were replaced by more dismal reporting. Although he had for some time been favorable to the voluntary removal of groups of Indians, he asserted that his tour through the Indian country in 1827 had opened his eyes to the degradation of the eastern tribes. When asked to report in 1830 on the previous eight years of the program for civilizing the Indians, he no longer considered salvation possible in the present location of the tribes. The condition of the Florida Indians he described as "in all respects truly deplorable. It is not known that they have advanced a single step in any sort of improvement; and as to the means of education, when offered to them, they were refused." The Indians in the Northwest, he reported, "pretend to nothing more than to maintain all the characteristic traits of their race. They catch fish, and plant patches of corn; dance, paint, hunt, get drunk, when they can get liquor, fight, and often starve." Their condition, however, was far better than that of the Creeks and better than that of most of the Choctaws.

In a typically paternalistic frame of mind McKenney wrote in 1829: "Seeing as I do the condition of these people, and that they are bordering on destruction, I would, were I empowered, take them *firmly* but *kindly* by the hand, and tell them they must go; and I would do this, on the same principle that I would take my own children by the hand, firmly, but kindly and lead them from a district of Country in which the plague was raging." President Jackson expressed a similar view in private correspondence in 1829. He said: "You may rest assured that I shall adhere to the just and humane policy towards the Indians which I have commenced. In this spirit I have recommended them to quit their possessions on this side of the Mississippi, and go to a country to the west where there is every probability that they will always be free from the mercenary influence of White men, and undisturbed by the local authority of the states: Under such circumstances the General Government can exercise a parental control over their interests and possibly perpetuate their race."

CONTROVERSY AND DEBATE

The Cherokees and their white advocates strenuously opposed removal. The Indians protested Georgia's action and carried their arguments to the federal government. Politically astute leaders, generally mixed-bloods who were wise in the ways of whites, kept delegations in Washington to watch developments and to present the Cherokee position to federal officials.

They pointed to the tribe's national and territorial rights and to Georgia's violations of these rights in extending jurisdiction over the Indian lands, and they asked the federal government to protect them in their legal rights and to uphold the treaty obligations that the United States had entered into with the tribe. The Indian action, however, was ineffective in reversing the position of the Jackson administration. The removal bill introduced in February 1830 was reported favorably by the Committee of Indian Affairs in both the House and the Senate.

Even before the congressional committees had made their formal reports, a campaign to support the Cherokees' rights got under way in the North. It sought to arouse the public conscience against the removal scheme and to persuade Congress to support the Indian nations against Georgia and the other states. The campaign, although on the surface a great outpouring of Christian sentiment and a spontaneous upsurge of public opinion, was in fact largely the inspiration and the work of one man, the secretary of the American Board of Commissioners for Foreign Missions, Jeremiah Evarts.

Evarts, born in Vermont in 1781 and a graduate of Yale University, was a lawyer, but he devoted most of his short life to the cause of religion and especially Christian missions. He became associated with the American Board shortly after its founding in 1810 and in 1821 became its secretary. Evarts had close acquaintance with the Cherokees and other southern tribes because of the American Board's missions among them. He had traveled through the Indian country, counted numerous Indian leaders among his personal friends, and had studied their history and legal claims. But he was also a man with a vision of a world fully evangelized, of universal conversion to Christ, and he saw the new American nation as the vehicle of this great work. The movement of Christian benevolence, reaching its height as the Indian question came to the fore, became for Protestant Americans of Evarts's persuasion a great national mission. Evarts insisted upon Christian influence on civil society and upon the obligation of committed Christians to call to task civil rulers if they departed from the path of justice and morality. It was a profound patriotic view that God had called this nation to a special mission—to be a special beacon of goodness in a corrupt world—and that God in his vengeance would rain disaster and destruction on America if it, as a nation, sinned against that covenant.

Evarts was convinced that the federal government's refusal to protect the Cherokees against the clamors of Georgia would be a moral wrong, a sin of great magnitude. The only way to prevent it would be through an outcry by the Christians of the nation, protesting against the threatened action with such a loud and persistent voice that the nation's leaders would turn aside from their sinful plans. Evarts set about to stir up the conscience of the nation and to direct its indignation and sense of outrage into effective channels in the national councils.

His most important work in support of the Cherokees was a series of twenty-four articles that appeared in the *National Intelligencer* between August 5 and December 19, 1829, under the pseudonym William Penn. The articles began with a statement of the moral crisis facing the nation in the removal question, the national sin that would bring God's sure punishment if the obligations to the Indians were cast aside, and then moved to a detailed analysis of the Cherokee treaties and their recognition of the Cherokees as a nation. The Penn essays were the fullest and best statement of the Cherokee case and the obligations of the United States to support it. They were reprinted in numerous newspapers and periodicals and widely circulated in pamphlet form. Churchmen and congressmen alike drew their arguments from Evarts's writing, and they looked to him to instruct them as they moved against the Jackson policy and Georgia's actions.

Evarts also initiated a widespread campaign of submitting memorials to Congress in favor of the Cherokees and against the removal bill. His strategy was to enlist individuals or groups to organize in major cities public meetings that would endorse a memorial written by Evarts. The first such memorial came from New York City at the end of December 1829. It presented information on the rights of the Indians and their treaties, drawn largely from the Penn essays, and ended with an earnest plea that Congress intervene on the behalf of the Indians in order to "save the nation, by prompt and decisive measures, from the calamity that hangs over it." Another long memorial, prepared in Boston, was submitted on February 8, 1830; then short petitions in the same vein were distributed to friends around the country, to be signed by concerned Christians and forwarded to Congress.

The final argument of Evarts and other opponents of Indian removal shifted away from the question of legal rights to the inexpediency of emigration. While the supporters of the policy spoke of exchanging eastern lands for lands of equal or better quality in the West, the critics described in the most dismal terms those districts set aside to receive the emigrants. Thus Evarts in the final number of the Penn essays spoke of the misery that removal would bring to thousands of innocent persons, and a memorial he prepared in early 1831 described how the despondent Indians would sink into anarchy and how the temptations of the open land to the west would counteract the forces that had led them to adopt agriculture in the East. Vagrant white men and savage Indians would press upon them, and the very nature of the land assigned them was unknown. That little was in fact known about the lands in the West did not stop fanciful descriptions to suit the purpose of Jackson's opponents.

Jeremiah Evarts and his friends tried to make the removal question simply a moral issue. Would the United States government honor its treaty obligations to the Cherokees, recognize their nationhood, and protect them against the illegal pretensions of Georgia? Or would Jackson and the Georgians drive ahead in their evil ways and make the nation liable to God's punishment? Yet beneath the surface was a strong party feeling; each side accused the other of operating not on moral principles but on political ones. Evarts was particularly pointed in charging the supporters of removal with acting in "the spirit of party." It is clear, nevertheless, that Evarts got all his support from Whigs and other anti-Jackson men and that the fight against removal was used as one means to embarrass the Jackson administration.

The opposition was in vain; the Senate passed the removal bill 28 to 19 on April 24 and the House by the narrower margin of 102 to 97 on May 26, and Jackson signed it on May 28, 1830. On its face it was a "liberal" measure, which Jackson hoped would win over the Indians. It authorized the president to mark off lands west of the Mississippi "not included in any state or organized territory, and to which the Indian title has been extinguished" and to exchange such districts for lands held by the eastern Indians. The president was "solemnly to assure the tribe or nation with which the exchange is made, that the United States will forever secure and guaranty to them, and their heirs or successors, the country so exchanged with them." The act provided payment for improvements made on present lands, for aid and assistance in emigrating and for the first year after removal, and for protection of the Indians in their new home and the "same superintendence and care" over the tribes that was authorized in their present places of residence. The act specifically noted that it did not authorize or direct the violation of any existing treaties. For carrying out these provisions, Congress appropriated five hundred thousand dollars.

The symbol that the act had become was perhaps more important than its specific provisions. Its passage meant congressional authorization of the removal policy that Jackson's administration had announced, and steps were quickly taken to begin treaty negotiations for removal.

Having failed in their appeals to the president and to Congress, the Cherokees took their case to the Supreme Court, with former attorney general William Wirt as their legal adviser. The Cherokee Nation filed suit in the Supreme Court against the state of Georgia; it sought an injunction against Georgia's encroachment on the Indian territory in violation of the tribe's treaty rights. Wirt contended that the Cherokees were a sovereign nation, not subject to Georgia's territorial jurisdiction, and that the laws of Georgia were null and void because they were repugnant to treaties between the United States and the Cherokees, to the intercourse law of 1802, and to the Constitution by impairing contracts arising from the treaties and by assuming powers in Indian affairs that belonged exclusively to the federal government.

Chief Justice John Marshall's decision in *Cherokee Nation* v. *Georgia*,

March 18, 1831, began with a statement of concern for the Cherokees. "If
Courts were permitted to indulge their sympathies," he said, "a case better
calculated to excite them can scarcely be imagined." But rather than look
at the merits of the case, he moved instead to "a preliminary inquiry." Did
the Supreme Court have jurisdiction? Was the Cherokee Nation a foreign
state and thus, under the Constitution, able to sue as a plaintiff in the Supreme Court? Marshall admitted that the Cherokees formed "a distinct political society, separated from others, capable of managing its own affairs
and governing itself." He noted the treaties by which the United States recognized the tribes as capable of maintaining the relations of peace and war
and of being responsible for violations of their political engagements. But
were the Indians, in fact, a *foreign* state? Marshall's answer was no, that the
relation of the Cherokees and the United States was something different,
"perhaps unlike that of any other two people in existence." He declared
that the Indians were "domestic dependent nations" and noted that they
occupied territory to which the United States asserted a title independent
of the Indians' will, which would take effect when the Indians gave up possession. "Meanwhile," he said, "they are in a state of pupilage. Their relation to the United States resembles that of a ward to his guardian."

Thus the court for the present sidestepped a critical confrontation with
Jackson and Georgia, and the Jacksonites looked upon the decision as a vindication of their position. But anti-Jackson agitation took on new life, and
Jackson was painted as a "nullifier" who refused to enforce the intercourse
law. At the meeting of the National Republicans in Baltimore in December
1831, called in order to name candidates for the 1832 election, much was
made of Jackson's villainy regarding the Cherokee issue.

The legal cause of the Indians, meanwhile, entered a new stage. Georgia
under a law that took effect on March 1, 1831, forbade whites to reside in
the Cherokee country without a license, for the state hoped to remove the
missionaries who encouraged and advised the Indians in their adamant
stand against removal. When the missionaries did not leave, they were
arrested and imprisoned. Two of them, Samuel A. Worcester and Elizur
Butler, refused to accept pardons or licenses. The American Board of Commissioners for Foreign Missions, with which these men were affiliated,
hired William Wirt and John Sergeant to bring the Cherokee cause against
Georgia to the Supreme Court. Here was a case to test the Georgia-Chero-
kee controversy that was clearly within the jurisdiction of the court.

Marshall's decision in the case of *Worcester* v. *Georgia*, delivered on
March 3, 1832, was a forthright vindication of the Cherokee position, for
he declared unconstitutional the extension of state law over Cherokee
lands. In his long opinion, the chief justice again examined the status of
the Indian tribes and now came to a conclusion that emphasized the political independence of the Cherokees considerably more than had his deci-

sion of the previous year. Marshall argued that the nationhood of the Indians was not destroyed by treaties acknowledging the protection of the United States, for "the settled doctrine of the law of nations is, that a weaker power does not surrender its independence—its right to self-government, by associating with a stronger, and taking its protection." The Cherokee Nation, therefore, was "a distinct community, occupying its own territory, with boundaries accurately described, in which the laws of Georgia can have no force, and which the citizens of Georgia have no right to enter, but with the assent of the Cherokees themselves, or in conformity with treaties, and with the acts of Congress." All intercourse with the Indian nations was vested, not in the state, but in the federal government.

The Supreme Court issued a special mandate ordering the Georgia court to reverse its conviction of Worcester and release him, but there were loopholes in federal laws that made the court's action ineffective. United States marshals could not be sent to free the prisoners until the state judge had refused formally to comply with the order. But Georgia completely ignored the court's proceedings, and no written refusal was forthcoming. Anyway, the Supreme Court adjourned before it could report Georgia's failure to conform. Nor was there any other procedure that Jackson could adopt, even if he had wanted to. He himself declared that "the decision of the supreme court has fell still born, and they find that they cannot coerce Georgia to yield to its mandate."

Jackson hoped that the impossibility of enforcing the Supreme Court's decision might help to convince the Indians that voluntary removal would be the only practicable solution. He urged Governor Wilson Lumpkin of Georgia not to act in any way what would exacerbate the conflict, and Lumpkin agreed to act in concert with the federal government. The president asked Georgia to pardon the missionaries, and the American Board persuaded them to accept the release.

The rapprochement was due in large part to the nullification threat from Georgia's neighboring state South Carolina, which came in the critical months after *Worcester* v. *Georgia*. Jackson moved cautiously lest he drive Georgia into the nullification camp; but more important, Jackson's opponents saw the danger to the Union that arose from South Carolina's action, and they tempered their criticism of Jackson as he stood firm against nullification. In the end, unionist sentiment proved greater than sympathies for the Cherokees, and the Indians' devoted friends on the American Board urged them to sign a removal treaty.

Undoubtedly the Cherokee controversy lost votes for the Democratic Party in the election of 1832, but it was not an issue of sufficient weight to defeat the popular president. When Jackson was handily reelected in November 1832, hope for preserving the Cherokees in their old homes practically vanished.

CHAPTER 5

Emigration of
the Tribes

The test of the removal policy was not the passage of the Removal Act or the legal decisions in the Cherokee cases of the Supreme Court. It came in the implementation of the policy during the administrations of Jackson and Martin Van Buren. The decade of the 1830s was matched by no other in American history as a dramatic period in relations between the United States government and the Indians. Removal treaties with the Five Civilized Tribes were negotiated—under various levels of duress—between 1830 and 1835, and by 1840 the bulk of the southeastern Indians, some sixty thousand tribesmen, were settled in the Indian Territory, now the state of Oklahoma, to continue their national existence.

CHOCTAWS, CREEKS, CHICKASAWS

The first of the southern Indians to emigrate were the Choctaws, who moved from their homes in Mississippi to the region assigned them in what is now southeastern Oklahoma. Their removal was a sort of test case that exhibited the governmental pressures, tribal factionalism, hardship on the march, and troubles in establishing the nation in the West that marked the whole removal process.

The Choctaws had long experienced white pressures upon their nation. In 1801, 1803, 1805, and 1816 they had reluctantly signed treaties of cession with the United States by which large areas passed into the hands of the whites. The Indians had retained most of central Mississippi, but the creation of the state in 1817 brought increased demands for the Indian lands, and by the Treaty of Doak's Stand, October 18, 1820, the Choctaws, in exchange for five million acres in west central Mississippi, received some thirteen million acres between the Arkansas and Canadian rivers and the Red River, partly in Arkansas Territory and partly to the west. The residents of Arkansas were hostile to the treaty, which would bring more Indians into the territory, and the Choctaws for their part were reluctant to leave Mississippi. In 1825, by a treaty signed in Washington, a new boundary line was drawn along the western border of Arkansas and additional annuities were provided for the Choctaws.

Under the Removal Act of 1830, Jackson sought to eliminate the remaining Choctaws from Mississippi by the cession of all the lands they still owned in the state. By providing generous land allotments and other benefits to tribal leaders, United States commissioners were able to sign a treaty with the Choctaws on September 27, 1830. The Indians agreed to relinquish all their lands east of the Mississippi and in return received "in fee simple to them and their descendants, to inure to them while they shall exist as a nation and live on it" the territory that had already been marked out in the treaty of 1825.

The national existence of the Indians was strongly guaranteed, and the United States agreed to protect the Choctaws from domestic strife and from foreign enemies "on the same principle that the citizens of the United States are protected." Annuities from older treaties would continue, and the treaty authorized an additional twenty thousand dollars for twenty years. In addition, the United States was to provide houses for chiefs, schools, mechanics, and miscellaneous goods, and to educate forty Choctaw youth for a period of twenty years. But the treaty showed the ambivalence of the removal policy: whereas it made every effort to clear Mississippi of tribal Indians and included all sorts of inducements to encourage emigration, it at the same time allotted lands to Indians within the ceded territory east of the Mississippi. The disposition of these lands and the settlement of claims arising from their sale led to nearly interminable conflicts between the Indians, bona fide settlers, and land speculators that delayed removal and unsettled land titles for years following the treaty.

The treaty specified emigration in three groups, the first in the fall of 1831 and the others in 1832 and 1833. The operation, directed by the army's commissary general of subsistence, George Gibson, was carefully planned, with supplies accumulated along the route of travel and civilian agents and army officers appointed to oversee the actual movement. But confusion soon appeared, as the agents and army officers bickered among themselves and as maldistribution of rations caused delays. Late departures exposed the emigrants to unusually severe winter storms, and the Indians experienced great misery en route, even though the army officers who met them in the West exerted extraordinary efforts to meet the needs of the desperate travelers.

In an attempt to better organize the removal process, Secretary of War Cass in April 1832 relieved all civilian agents and put the entire removal operation in military hands under General Gibson. The removals of 1832 and 1833 went more smoothly, but jurisdictional disputes disrupted the emigration, and in 1832 the appearance of cholera in the Mississippi Valley caused still further alarm and hardship. Altogether about 12,500 Choctaws settled in the Indian Territory; some 600 more remained in Mississippi on allotments provided by the treaty or simply as vagrants.

The situation of the Creeks in Alabama and Georgia was much like that of the Choctaws. The massive cession of territory by the Treaty of Fort Jackson in 1814 was followed in 1818 and 1821 by the cession of other parcels of land. Then in 1825 a new cession was made at the Treaty of Indian Springs, which included a provision for a grant of land in the Indian Territory in exchange for the ceded lands. This treaty had been negotiated by a small pro-removal faction led by William McIntosh against the clear stipulation of Creek law providing for the execution of any chief who subscribed to an unauthorized land cession, and McIntosh and some of his associates were killed by order of the Creek council. When President John Quincy Adams learned of the fraudulent nature of the treaty, he determined to make a new treaty, which he did in Washington in 1826. This treaty validated the cession of land in Georgia, sought to adjust amicably the dissension between the Creek factions, and provided for removal to lands to be selected in the West. Prosperous mixed-blood members of the McIntosh faction migrated to the Indian Territory and laid out plantations in the Arkansas and Verdigris valleys.

The Creeks who remained in Alabama were soon subjected to pressures from the state and from white intruders on their lands. Federal officials used such actions to support their arguments that the only salvation for the Creeks lay in removal from the state. Finally, on March 24, 1832, Chief Opotheyahola and other Creek leaders signed a treaty in Washington with Lewis Cass. The treaty was not specifically a removal treaty. Although the Creeks ceded to the United States all their lands east of the Mississippi, they were to receive allotments within the cession. They were authorized to sell these allotments or to remain on the lands themselves and after five years receive a fee simple title. The Creek territory west of the Mississippi was solemnly guaranteed to the Indians, and their right to govern themselves free from interference by any state or territory was recognized "so far as may be compatible with the general jurisdiction which Congress may think proper to exercise over them."

In Alabama whites defrauded and intimidated the Indians, who looked in vain for protection from the United States. The whole Creek Nation was in a state of turmoil and bitterness resulting from the premature and illegal

MAP 2: Land Cessions of the Five Civilized Tribes

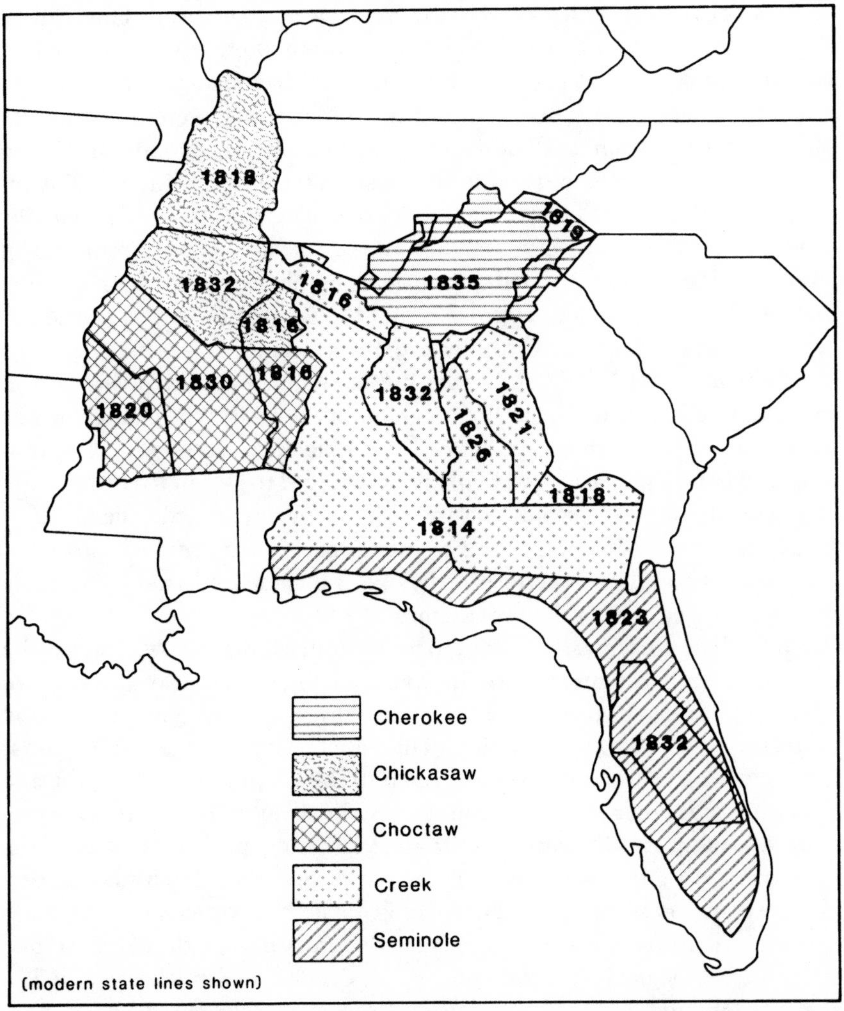

action of the whites, and a government attempt to get the Creeks to sign a new treaty that would provide for immediate removal came to nothing. The tension on both sides mounted, and destitute Indians sought refuge wherever they could find it, some moving into Cherokee country in Alabama and Georgia. The smoldering situation broke into open fire in the spring of 1836. Georgia militia attacked Creeks who had encamped on Georgia soil, and roving bands of Creeks began to attack and kill whites and destroy their property.

As the alarming reports reached Washington, Secretary of War Cass issued orders to remove the Creeks as a military measure. General Thomas S.

Jesup inaugurated a military operation against the Indians, and the Creeks, quickly subdued, were removed to the West. Dejected warriors, handcuffed, chained, and guarded by soldiers, left Fort Mitchell on July 2, followed by wagons and ponies carrying the children and old women and the sick. On July 14 almost 2,500 Indians, including 800 warriors, were embarked at Montgomery and conveyed down the Alabama River to Mobile, thence to New Orleans and up the rivers to the western lands of the Creeks. The remainder of the hostiles left Montgomery on August 2. The friendly Creeks soon followed their brothers west. In all, 14,608 Creeks were removed in 1836, including 2,495 enrolled as hostile. A number of Creek warriors who had enlisted for service in Florida against the Seminoles were released too late to emigrate in 1836 and followed the next year.

The Chickasaw Nation in northern Mississippi and northwestern Alabama suffered the same disabilities in relations with its white neighbors as did the other southern tribes. Because they blocked white expansion into rich lands, the Chickasaws were ultimately forced to give in to the pressure put upon them by the states and the federal government to cede all their lands east of the Mississippi and to move west. Their removal, however, was more tranquil and the return they got for their lands more equitable than was the case with the other tribes.

The will of the Chickasaws not to move from Mississippi was broken by encroachments of whites on their lands and by the action of the state in extending jurisdiction over the nation, erasing the tribal government and destroying the power of the chiefs. The Indians' appeal to Jackson against these evils met the same response given to the Cherokees, Choctaws, and Creeks: "To these laws, where you are, you must submit;—there is no preventive—no other alternative. Your great father cannot, nor can congress, prevent it. . . . [Your great father's] earnest desire is, that you may be perpetuated and preserved as a nation; and this he believes can only be done and secured in your consent to remove to a country beyond the Mississippi."

By a treaty signed on October 20, 1832, Chickasaw lands were ceded to the government; they were to be surveyed immediately and placed on sale, to be sold for what the market would bring. Meanwhile, each adult Indian received a temporary homestead (ranging from one section to four sections depending on the size of the family). The money from the sale of these temporary reservations and of the surplus lands would be placed in a general fund of the Chickasaw Nation, and from it would come the costs of survey and of removal.

As the survey and sale of the lands in Mississippi proceeded, Chickasaw commissioners sought a satisfactory territory in the West. It was the intention of the United States that the Chickasaws share the western land assigned to the Choctaws, but the two tribes had trouble reaching an agreement. Finally, on January 17, 1837, a treaty signed at Doaksville in the Choctaw Nation provided for the purchase by the Chickasaws of the central and western sections of the Choctaw lands for $530,000, and it granted the Chickasaws certain privileges within the Choctaw Nation. The Chickasaws then began their emigration; a roll of the tribe prepared for the removal showed 4,914 Chickasaws and 1,156 slaves.

As the removal process moved into full gear with the treaties made with the Choctaws, Creeks, and Chickasaws, the United States government took steps to ease the process by turning its attention to the lands to which the emigrating Indians were directed. In order to make sure that the Indians located on suitable lands and that no conflicts arose among the different tribes, Congress in July 1832 authorized the appointment of three commissioners to investigate the western lands, to select tracts for the incoming Indians, and to adjudicate conflicting claims. The commission, headed by Montfort Stokes, former governor of North Carolina, received from Secretary of War Cass a detailed set of instructions, in which Cass urged them to satisfy the Indians and thus preserve peace in the area. He told them particularly to welcome the Indian delegations sent to look at the land and to see that they were pleased.

The commission, in its report of 1834, judged the land favorably and declared: "There is a sufficiency of good first rate soil, now belonging to those tribes who already have lands assigned to them, and in sufficient quantity still undisposed of, to assign to such tribes as may hereafter choose to remove there, to support them, if they will settle down like our white citizens and become agriculturists." This appraisal agreed substantially with earlier reports on the quality of the country in the West to which the Indians were removed. The negative reports brought back by some Indian groups who went west to look at the lands are understandable, however, for the Indians found undeveloped wilderness in contrast with the improved lands in their old homes. The Indians after relocation found the agricultural potential of the region sufficient for their economic well-being and development. The injustice came, not from having to settle on poor lands, but from the ultimate lack of secure and permanent enjoyment of the lands they did receive.

SEMINOLES AND THE FLORIDA WAR

The Seminoles, an amalgam of Creeks who had gradually drifted into Florida and native tribes there with whom they mixed, numbered no more than five thousand, but they showed a resistance to removal that kept the United States army occupied for seven years and that was never completely overcome. The United States government had made a decision that the Seminoles were to be removed; then it tried with main force to carry out the decision, even though it soon became apparent that the land thus to be freed of the Indians was not of significant value to the whites and that if the Seminoles had been left alone the expense and grief of the conflict might have been avoided.

The removal of the Seminoles was complicated by the problem of black slaves. For many years slaves from the southern states had fled as fugitives to the Indian settlements in Florida, where they often became slaves of the Seminoles, and they enjoyed a less restrictive existence there than with white masters in Georgia or Alabama. They lived in a kind of semi-bondage, more like allies than slaves of the Indians. Many lived in their own villages as vassals of the chief whose protection they enjoyed, contributing shares of the produce from their own fields rather than labor on the lands of the owner.

The demands of the white masters of the fugitives became increasingly insistent. Claims were presented that the Seminoles, who kept no legal records of their slaves, could not easily refute in court. More and more frequently raiding parties from the north invaded the Seminole lands and attempted to carry off by force the blacks who were claimed as slaves. The Seminole War was perhaps as much a movement on the part of the slave-owners to recover the property they claimed as it was a war to acquire Indian land for white use. And the blacks clearly sensed that fact. Although about a tenth of the Seminoles sided with the United States in the conflict over removal, the blacks all fought bitterly against the whites until assurance was given that enrollment for removal to the West did not mean placing oneself within the clutches of some white slaveowner who stood by waiting to enforce his claims.

A removal treaty was signed with the Seminoles on May 9, 1832, at Payne's Landing. The Indians were near destitution, and the promise of food and clothing in the treaty eased the negotiations. But the Seminoles would not agree to removal until they had had an opportunity to inspect the land and determine its suitability. A Seminole delegation sent to the West was persuaded to sign an agreement stating that they approved the land. This Treaty of Fort Gibson, March 28, 1833, although it was not accepted by the nation as a whole, was considered by the United States as fulfilling the provisions of the Payne's Landing treaty, and the government demanded that the Indians carry out the treaty and move out of Florida. The usual impasse had arrived. The government pointed to the treaty and insisted that it be fulfilled. The Indians denied that they had made the agreements specified and refused to move. As the tension increased, the stage was set for war.

The war, known as the Second Seminole War to distinguish it from Andrew Jackson's foray into Florida in 1818, began on December 28, 1835, when the Indians murdered Indian Agent Wiley Thompson outside Fort King and ambushed and destroyed a company of troops under Major Francis L. Dade. The uprising electrified the Florida frontier, and the War Department hastened to act, but the Indians could not easily be routed from their fastnesses in the Everglades. One commander after another tried his best to bring the embarrassing affair to a successful conclusion, yet the war dragged on and on, despite optimistic announcements from the commanding generals and the War Department that the war had finally been brought to an end. It was a sad and distressing affair, and it included episodes—such as the capture and imprisonment of the Seminole leader Osceola when he came in to parley under a white flag and the hiring of bloodhounds from Cuba to track down the elusive Indians—that roused strong public criticism of the war.

Little by little, however, some bands of Indians gave up and were moved from Florida, and by the end of the war in August 1842, an estimated 2,833 Seminole Indians had been located in new lands in the Indian Territory, leaving an irremovable remnant in Florida.

CHEROKEES AND THE TRAIL OF TEARS

Just as the Cherokee Nation was the chief focus of the controversy over the removal policy, so it furnished the most controversial episode in the actual emigration to the West. The agitation of the 1830s, however, obscures the fact that many Cherokees had already emigrated and established themselves in the Indian Territory. Some had migrated west with the permission of the government during the administrations of Jefferson and Madison, and by 1816 the agent estimated that at least two thousand Cherokees were in Arkansas. Their status there was precarious, for they were challenged by Osage Indians in the region and by incoming white settlers as well. To regulate the situation the Cherokees, by treaties in 1817 and 1819, ceded large sections of their holdings in the East in return for a guaranteed tract in Arkansas. The treaties provided that all white citizens were to be removed from the western districts, but there were the usual difficulties as the whites looked with covetous eyes upon the rich Indian lands. Then in 1828 the western Cherokees exchanged their lands in what is now Arkansas for seven million acres in the northeastern corner of the present state of Oklahoma, and they were granted as well the so-called Cherokee Outlet, extending west to the limits of United States jurisdiction at the hundredth meridian.

The Indians west of Arkansas were known as the Old Settlers or Cherokees West, and they developed their own government and a prosperous agricultural economy along the rivers of the area. Here they were joined from
time to time by small parties of eastern Cherokees who enrolled for emigration before a total removal treaty had been negotiated. By 1836 more
than six thousand Cherokees had moved west.

Despite the success of these Cherokees, the great bulk of the nation adamantly refused to consider removal. Encouraged by the favorable decision
of the Worcester case and influenced by political leaders who controlled
the national councils, they repeatedly importuned the federal government—
both the executive and Congress—to protect them where they were.

Jackson's administration was embarrassed by the Cherokees' failure to
accept the inducements to emigrate. Secretary of War Cass met again and
again with the Cherokee delegations and explained the president's desire to
aid them, but he insisted that if they chose to remain in the East, they
must accept both the privileges and disabilities of other citizens. Jackson
himself in March 1835 spoke firmly to the Cherokees:

> I have no motive, my friends, to deceive you. I am sincerely desirous
> to promote your welfare. Listen to me therefore while I tell you that
> you cannot remain where you now are. Circumstances that cannot be
> controlled and which are beyond the reach of human laws render it
> impossible that you can flourish in the midst of a civilized commu-
> nity. You have but one remedy within your reach. And that is to re-
> move to the west and join your countrymen who are already estab-
> lished there. And the sooner you do this the sooner will commence
> your career of improvement and prosperity.

The condition of the Cherokees in the East steadily worsened, as white
encroachments continued to destroy their property and threaten their lives,
and the federal government showed no signs of weakening its stand. A part
of the Cherokees, thereupon, decided to face the inevitable and prepared to
negotiate for removal. This group, known as the "treaty party," was led by
Major Ridge, who had fought with Andrew Jackson against the Creeks at
Horseshoe Bend, his educated and politically active son John Ridge, and his
two nephews, the brothers Elias Boudinot and Stand Watie. Its appearance,
beginning in 1832–1833, split the Cherokee Nation into factions of bitter
opposition that persisted for decades. The "anti-treaty party," representing
the bulk of the nation, was led by the elected principal chief John Ross, a
mixed-blood who was one-eighth Cherokee.

The factionalism was used by the federal government to promote its designs, and a removal treaty was signed with the Ridge party at New Echota
on December 29, 1835. By the treaty, the Cherokees ceded all their lands

east of the Mississippi and for five million dollars released their claims upon the United States. The seven million acres of land granted the Cherokees in the treaty of 1828 plus the outlet to the west were confirmed, and additional lands were granted. Other articles excluded the western lands from state or territorial jurisdiction and granted protection against unauthorized intruders and against domestic and foreign enemies. Provision was made also for the emigration, for one year's subsistence, and for allotments for Indians who desired to stay in the East. The treaty specified that the removal was to be accomplished within two years after ratification.

The treaty party emigrated with little trouble; the state officials treated them considerately, and they were, in general, economically well-off. They established their farms and plantations among the western Cherokees. The remainder, having rejected the treaty as a valid instrument, refused to move, and Ross used every opportunity in his attempts to reverse the treaty's provisions. He encouraged his followers to stand firm, and few enrolled for emigration. Numerous petitions poured into Congress from religious and philanthropic supporters of the Cherokees, protesting the execution of the 1835 treaty.

The appeals had no effect. When the deadline for removal, May 23, 1838, approached and the Indians were still on their old lands, the government ordered General Winfield Scott to the Cherokee country "with a view to the fulfillment of the treaty." The emigrating Indians were organized into detachments, but only about three hundred had departed when Scott called a halt to the exodus for the rest of the hot summer season. The Cherokee leaders then made an agreement with Scott whereby they themselves would take charge of the emigration when it began again in the fall, and the operation became a project of the Rosses. Officers were appointed by the Cherokee council, and a quasi-military order was maintained on the march. When the drought that had further delayed the departure was broken in October, the caravans began their march overland through Nashville and Memphis. The emigrants numbered about thirteen thousand, including black slaves; they carried along whatever of their belongings they had managed to save. The Indian leaders themselves were responsible for the good behavior of the nation, and no military escort was deemed necessary. Because the journey, with its late start, occurred during the hardest months of the year, this Trail of Tears reaped a heavy harvest of misery and death.

CLEARING THE OLD NORTHWEST

Public attention focused on the removal of the Five Civilized Tribes from the southeastern states. It was the Cherokees' conflict with Georgia that held the attention of the federal government and of the public in the development of the removal policy and in the Removal Act of 1830. But this removal policy was also intended to apply to the Indians north of the Ohio River, who remained on lands sought by the expanding agricultural society of the North. They, like their southern brothers, with the notable exceptions of groups that migrated to Canada and others that remained on reservations within their old territories, were removed to the Indian country west of the Mississippi River.

Whereas the southern Indians were organized into five sizable Indian nations, with relatively well defined land holdings that stretched back to time immemorial, the northern tribes were numerous, sometimes fractionalized into scattered bands, and often with land claims overlapping or ill-defined as the result of frequent migrations. In the removal period a great variety of Indian communities in the Old Northwest (Kaskaskias, Peorias, Shawnees, Ottawas, Wyandots, Miamis, Potawatomis, Menominees, Delawares, Sacs and Foxes, Piankashaws, Weas, Kickapoos, Chippewas, Sioux, and New York Indians) negotiated treaties with the United States, and in the same period treaties were signed with Indians holding lands in Iowa, Missouri, and Minnesota in order to clear those regions, or parts of them, of Indian inhabitants. It was a continuous and complicated process.

Most of the Indians involved had a long history of shifting locales. The Delaware Indians, for example, at the beginning of the historic period were located in what is now New Jersey and Delaware, but at the end of three centuries of movement Delawares were found in Oklahoma, Kansas, Wisconsin, and Ontario. The Shawnees had a similar history, perhaps even more diverse. None of the Indians north of the Ohio occupied precisely the same lands in 1830 that their ancestors had held when French traders first came in contact with them in the seventeenth century. The emigration of these tribes in the Jacksonian era was part of their migration history, which continued even after their first settlement west of the Mississippi.

Nor was the relation of the United States government with these groups in the 1830s, after the passage of the Removal Act, a new departure. Rather, it was a continuation of policies and actions that had been going on for more than three decades (although without doubt new impetus was given by the 1830 legislation). Removal, in the sense of an exchange of lands within the states and territories east of the Mississippi for lands in the West, was only one part of the story. Many of the treaties provided for cession of Indian lands to the United States and the concentration of the displaced Indians on remaining lands, with the privilege of hunting on the ceded lands until they were surveyed and sold—a process that had been taking place for many years. Indeed, by 1830 most of Ohio, Indiana, and

Illinois had already been freed of Indian title in a succession of treaties between Indian groups and the United States government. What remained in these states were enclaves of natives, subsisting on agriculture and government annuities, surrounded by whites. Pressures for the release of these final Indian holdings became irresistible. In the northern territories, Michigan and Wisconsin, on the other hand, white settlement, even after the opening of the Erie Canal in 1825, was confined to the southern and central tiers of counties. The rest of the region retained much of its Indian population and in addition became a refuge for Indians displaced from other areas.

The situation in the Old Northwest also differed from that in the South because of the proximity of Canada. Many of the tribes in the region had had close economic and political ties with the British. They had sided with the British in the War of 1812 and after the war continued to frequent the British posts (notably at Malden across from Detroit). For many Indians in the United States Canada offered an open haven. Thus it would be wrong to think of removal from the Old Northwest only as a migration to the future states of Iowa, Kansas, or Oklahoma, for large numbers of Potawatomis, Ottawas, and Chippewas, as well as smaller numbers of other tribes, moved into Canada.

In treaties with the Indians of the Old Northwest, provision was frequently made for reserves of land within the cession for individuals or small bands. The practice began with the treaties of 1817 and continued thereafter, but the guaranteed reserves were an awkward intrusion into the removal policy. At first they were patented in fee to the individuals; then the Senate, in ratifying treaties, came to look askance at this procedure, and later treaties specified either that these lands were to be held "in the same manner as Indian reservations had been heretofore held," with pre-emption rights in the United States government, or that individual grants could not be disposed of without the approval of the president.

Once the practice of setting up reserves had been established, it was almost impossible to obtain a treaty of cession from the northwest Indians without them. The reserves were not only a hedge against removal; they were also a means to individual profit, for the Indians could dispose of them for a reasonable price and sometimes more. Traders and other land speculators hoped to get the lands from the Indians by sale or in payment of debts. To the federal government, desirous of clearing the states of Indians altogether, the reservations became an irritant and an obstacle, yet so insistent were the Indians that there was great temptation to allow the individual grants in order to obtain new cessions.

The passage of the Removal Act stimulated increased action in regard to the northern tribes, and little by little the tribes succumbed. In a series of treaties the Potawatomis gave up their lands in Michigan, Indiana, Wiscon-

sin, and Illinois in exchange for reservations in the West, at first in Iowa and
then in Kansas, while many migrated to Canada. The Miamis and Winnebagos, too, were eliminated from lands desired by whites in Indiana and
Wisconsin. The Sioux ceded their lands east of the Mississippi; the Chippewas sold large areas, although they retained reservations in Michigan
and Wisconsin; and the Menominees, after threats of removal to Minnesota, settled for a restricted reservation in north central Wisconsin.

At the very time the United States government was trying to extinguish
the titles of the resident tribes, however, Indians from New York State were
moving to the Old Northwest. Secretary of War John C. Calhoun had spoken
of the region west of Lake Michigan as a refuge for Indians from the East,
and pressure on their lands in New York motivated some groups to move.
Under the active leadership of a mixed-blood named Eleazar Williams, a
group of Oneida Indians migrated to Wisconsin in the early 1820s. There
they were joined by a number of Stockbridge Indians (who had a small
admixture of Munsees) and some Brotherton Indians. These tribes received land from the Menominees and remained in Wisconsin on reduced
reservations.

THE BLACK HAWK WAR

The movements of the Indians were accomplished by and large without a
need for military force. The notable exception was the Black Hawk War of
1832, a military conflict that in its small way was as embarrassing to the
Jackson administration as the Seminole War. Black Hawk, the chief pro-
tagonist, was a Sac warrior with a long history of anti-American views and
actions. In the War of 1812 he had joined with the British, and after the war
he made regular trips to the British at Malden, which reinforced the hostility toward the Americans of his followers, who became known as the
British band. Black Hawk rejected the treaty made by William Henry Harrison with Sacs and Foxes at St. Louis in 1804 by which the chiefs on hand
ceded their extensive holdings in western Illinois and southwestern Wisconsin. Although later treaties confirmed the cession and Black Hawk
himself signed at least one of them, he refused to depart from his village of
Saukenuk and the lands in Illinois near the mouth of the Rock River.

After agreeing temporarily to move west of the Mississippi with other
bands of Sacs and Foxes, Black Hawk and his band on April 6, 1832, recrossed
the Mississippi into Illinois. There were about five hundred mounted warriors, together with the old men and the women and children of his band,
who swelled the total number to an estimated two thousand. These Indians
were pursued up the Rock River by General Henry Atkinson with a small
regular force, augmented by mounted Illinois militia. The undisciplined

MAP 3: Indian Land Cessions in the North

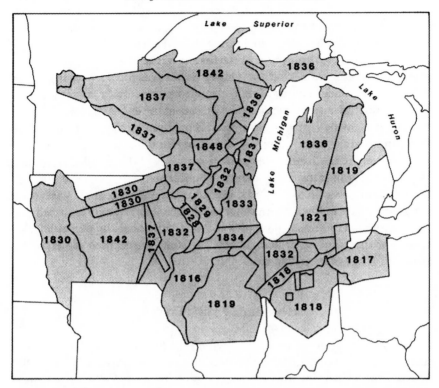

horsemen moved faster than Atkinson's foot soldiers and overtook the Indians near the Wisconsin border. Here Black Hawk sought to surrender, but the party he sent under a white flag was set upon by the excited volunteers. Believing that his peace overtures had been rejected, Black Hawk attacked and routed the militia camp. The war had now become a bloody affair, and there was no drawing back on either side.

Atkinson began a slow pursuit of the Indians into Wisconsin. Suffering desperately from want, the Indians were finally overtaken just as they reached the Mississippi and were cut down at the mouth of the Bad Axe River. Black Hawk, who had escaped the final carnage, was captured by a party of Winnebagos and turned in to the Indian agent at Prairie du Chien. He and his sons and two associates were sent in irons to Jefferson Barracks.

The Black Hawk War need never have occurred, had there been honorable dealings with the Indians and a firm policy toward both the Indians and the whites. Squatters had been allowed to violate treaty obligations by invading the Sacs' ancient lands before the area had been sold by the government. An earlier concentration of regular troops on the upper Mississippi might have kept the Indians better in check, and a less cautious com-

mander than Atkinson might have successfully stopped the movement of
Black Hawk's band up the Rock River before hostile acts occurred. The
shameful violation of the flag of truce by the volunteers precipitated open
warfare just as Black Hawk had decided to surrender.

The war was a turning point in the history of the Sacs and Foxes. Once a
powerful confederation that the United States was forced to respect, the
Indians now succumbed to liquor, declined precipitously in population,
and were rent by internal factions. By a treaty at the end of the war the tribe
surrendered a wide strip along the Mississippi running almost the length of
the future state of Iowa, "partly as indemnity for the expense incurred, and
partly to secure the future safety and tranquillity of the invaded frontier."
This was the beginning of the complete liquidation of the estate of the Sacs
and Foxes in Iowa. In 1836, 1837, and 1842 the Indians parted with their
remaining lands in Iowa in return for assignment of a "tract of land suitable
and convenient for Indians purposes . . . for a permanent and perpetual residence for them and their descendants" at some unspecified place on the
Missouri River or its tributaries.

THE ROLE OF THE TRADERS

It is easy to think of the treaties by which the Indian title to land was extinguished as compacts between two parties, the Indian tribe and the
United States government—and such, legally, they were. But in fact there
was sometimes an influential and occasionally dominating third party:
white traders. When the fur trade flourished, traders supplied the Indians
with goods in return for furs, but as the hunting lands were circumscribed
and the fur-bearing animals disappeared, the Indians paid the traders from
their annuities, or the government bought large quantities of goods for the
Indians directly from the traders. As cessions multiplied and annuities and
other payments grew, the traders became more and more involved in the
treaty process. Indians were indebted to the traders for goods received on
credit; the debts could be recovered only by provisions in the treaties for
cash annuities, by which the Indians could pay the debts, or by direct allotment of funds in the treaties to cover specified debts.

The allowance of traders' claims in the treaties began with the Osage
treaty of 1825, in which the Indians, as a mark of friendship toward favorite
traders, agreed to payment of certain debts by the United States. The practice became almost universal in the treaties signed in subsequent years
with the Indians in the Old Northwest. And as the pressures for removal
increased and removal treaties seemed necessary at any price, the rewards
for the Indians and for the traders were considerable.

In addition, because the treaty negotiations were usually eased by generous handouts to the attending Indians and because the treaties often specified large payments in goods as well as in cash, the traders profited by furnishing these supplies, often at inflated prices. The traders, moreover, had a deep interest in the lands allotted individual Indians in the treaties, for such lands often quickly fell into their hands. So much influence did traders have over the Indians that in many cases the government would have been unable to procure the treaties of cession it wanted without providing adequately for the traders' interests.

The attitude of the traders toward removal was often ambivalent. These men shared the sentiments of other white settlers that the Indians should be moved to the west to clear the land for white exploitation, and often they had a direct interest in the ceded lands. Yet it was not easy to part with the large profits they made in supplying the Indians where they were. Even though most traders realized that removal was inevitable, they worked to delay the emigration as long as possible. Each new treaty could be another bonanza. In 1838 the commissioner of Indian affairs asserted that disturbances arising in the removal of the Indians were caused "by the large indebtedness of the Indians to their traders, and [by] the undue influence of the latter over them."

It was the government's unwavering objective to rid the East of Indians, and since it was necessary to get the traders' acquiescence if not active support, measures were taken to circumvent any obstructionism. Thus in the Potawatomi removal the government threatened to pay no more claims until the Indians had emigrated. Then on March 3, 1843, the Senate resolved that in future negotiations of treaties with the Indians "no reservations of land should be made in favor of any person, nor the payment of any debt provided for." But many old debts were still outstanding, and claims dragged on and on, much to the irritation of the overburdened Indian Office. In later treaties the claims of the traders against the Indian had to be recognized if the desired cessions were to be obtained. Even though the government did not pay the traders directly, large sums were provided to enable the Indians "to settle their affairs and comply with their present just engagements."

CHAPTER 6

The Aftermath of Removal

Advocates of removal justified the policy on the grounds that emigration to the West would benefit the Indians. Out of the reach of established states and territories, the Indian tribes could continue their national existence unmolested by encroaching whites and jurisdictional controversies. West of the Mississippi the federal government could provide for the protection and improvement of the Indians.

Because of the dramatic nature of the removal, especially of the southern tribes, it is easy to ignore the sequel of the removal itself and to assume that once the Indians had been shipped out of the way of the whites, the government breathed a sigh of relief and washed its hands of the whole affair. That was far from the case, for in the decade following removal the United States diligently—although not always effectively—worked to fulfill the vision Jackson had enunciated in his first annual message to Congress: "There [in the West] they may be secured in the enjoyment of governments of their own choice, subject to no other control from the United States than such as may be necessary to preserve peace on the frontier and between the several tribes. There the benevolent may endeavor to teach them, to raise up an interesting commonwealth, destined to perpetuate the race and to attest the humanity and justice of this Government."

TRANSPLANTED INDIAN NATIONS

The Indian nations were not destroyed by removal, for the utter degradation and collapse predicted by the opponents of Jackson's removal program did not occur. Although most of the northern tribes that emigrated to the West were small in population and economically and politically weak, the Indian nations from the southeast moved to the Indian Territory in strength and with treaty guarantees that protected their land holdings and their political autonomy. The turmoil of removal brought great hardships to those who were forced to depart their traditional homes against their will, and tribal divisions occasioned or aggravated by removal disrupted the tranquility of the communities. Yet the southern nations showed tremendous resilience in reestablishing an orderly and productive existence beyond the Mississippi. Organized governments continued, agricultural development quickened, school systems were established, and missionary endeavors were renewed and encouraged.

The Cherokees were the most important of the Indian nations in the West, and they best exemplified the rapid establishment of a viable society in the new lands. Yet they were sharply divided politically. The Old Settlers, Cherokees who had voluntarily emigrated to Arkansas and then into the Indian Territory before the agitation for removal in the 1830s, were economically well established in their western homes and had a loosely organized but effective government that dealt with the federal government as a distinct entity. In 1834 they numbered fifty-eight hundred. A second division was the treaty party of the Ridges, Elias Boudinot, and Stand Watie. Having promoted the Treaty of New Echota in 1835, they emigrated peacefully under its provisions and settled in the West with the Old Settlers. Because they had cooperated with the removal policy, they were generally favored by United States officials who became entangled in Cherokee intratribal conflicts. Finally, there was the Ross party, the group that had opposed removal and emigrated only when forced to do so in 1838. This was the most populous faction, with perhaps fourteen thousand adherents. John Ross considered himself the principal chief of *all* the Cherokees, thus irritating the treaty party and the Old Settlers, who feared his domination. The arrival of this anti-treaty group in the West brought dissension and conflict.

The conflict was severely exacerbated by the vengeance taken by the Ross party against treaty party leaders for having ceded the eastern lands. On June 22, 1839, Major Ridge, John Ridge, and Elias Boudinot were brutally murdered; Stand Watie, also marked for death, escaped. Although it was clear that this was a planned political assassination, John Ross denied any complicity or approval of the deed, but he could not completely shake the accusations made against his party. The federal government remained critical of him and continually called for punishment of the murderers. Under the rubric of maintaining domestic peace within the Cherokee Nation, Matthew Arbuckle, commander at Fort Gibson in the Cherokee country, took an active part in Cherokee political affairs and openly represented the interests of the Old Settlers.

Although members of the Cherokee factions agreed to an Act of Union in 1839 and 1840, the groups were still at odds among themselves and with United States military commanders, and the following years were filled

Map 4: Location of Indians in the Indian Territory after Removal

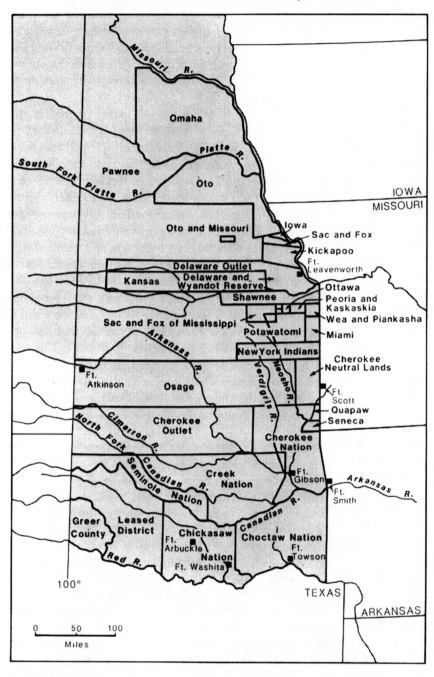

with turmoil at times approaching civil war. All three parties sent delegations to Washington to plead their causes and to seek a settlement by the
federal government. President James K. Polk, convinced that there was no
possibility that the conflicting groups could live together in peace and harmony, advocated separate governments for them as distinct tribes. But such
a solution led John Ross, who above all wanted a unified nation, to persuade Polk to approve a treaty that would keep the Cherokees intact. With
able advisers and a firm intent to settle past differences, the three factions
worked out an agreement in 1846.

This treaty provided for a unified Cherokee Nation and that "the lands
now occupied by the Cherokee Nation shall be secured to the whole Cherokee people for their common use and benefit." A general amnesty and an
end to party distinctions was proclaimed, and the treaty declared that "all
difficulties and differences heretofore existing between the several parties
of the Cherokee Nation are hereby settled and adjusted, and shall, as far as
possible, be forgotten and forever buried in oblivion." The United States
government agreed to adjust claims and pay indemnities to the treaty party.
The treaty was a compromise measure, for Ross now agreed to the legitimacy of the 1835 treaty, and the Old Settlers admitted that the Ross party
had rights to the lands in the West. Quiet then returned to the Cherokee
Nation, and a decade and more of prosperity and development ensued.

The Choctaws, the first to sign a removal treaty, reestablished themselves in the southeastern section of the Indian Territory, west of Arkansas
and along the Red River. This land had been assigned to them in 1820, and
an agency had been established for the western Choctaws, but not until the
Treaty of Dancing Rabbit Creek in 1830 did the Choctaws move en masse
to the West. A government based on the three districts of the Choctaw Nation was then set up, and agricultural development was promoted. Using
funds specified in their treaties, the Choctaws built anew a flourishing
school system, and Protestant missionaries zealously provided schools and
churches.

The Choctaws were joined by the Chickasaws, who settled on the western section of the Choctaw lands, with certain privileges in the Choctaw
Nation. This condition dissatisfied the Chickasaws, for they wished to live
under a strictly independent government, and in 1848 they adopted a formal constitution, in part as a means to prevent the diversion of their large
tribal funds to the Choctaws. By 1854 contention between the two tribes
had reached such a point that commissioners were appointed to seek agreement on separate jurisdictions and a set boundary line. A treaty signed that
year defined the boundary; in 1855 a new treaty more carefully established
relations between the two tribes.

Chickasaw development in the West proceeded slowly, for with the death of Levi Colbert in 1834 there was no effective unified leadership, and the scattering of the settlements further fragmented the tribe. More serious was the general debilitation brought on, ironically, by the good terms received by the Chickasaws in their removal treaty. The Indians seemed to lapse into a kind of apathy, depending on treaty annuities for their subsistence, but by the mid-1850s the tribe appeared regenerated, with new leadership and social and economic development.

The Creek Indians moved to lands in the Indian Territory between the Cherokees and the Choctaws, although at first they clustered near Fort Gibson because they feared the wild tribes of the prairies. Like other tribes, they were divided, the Lower Creeks settling along the Arkansas River and the Upper Creeks along the Canadian. In 1840 the two groups united in a general council, but only later were the animosities between them quieted. Their factionalism, together with heavy population losses occasioned by the removal, delayed Creek development in the West.

A further complication was the emigration of the Seminoles who had been forced out of Florida by the Seminole War. They were assigned a district within the Creek lands, between the Canadian River and its North Fork. But they objected to a union with the Creeks, and many stayed encamped near Fort Gibson. A principal bone of contention was the status of black slaves among the Seminoles, for these slaves enjoyed a good deal more freedom than the slaves of the Creeks, and they seemed to the Creeks to pose a threat to their own slave society. In a treaty signed on January 4, 1845, the difficulties were at least partially resolved, although the slavery problem continued and the Seminoles were irked by their incomplete independence. Finally, in 1856, following the pattern of separating the Choctaws and Chickasaws, a treaty was concluded in Washington by which the Seminoles received a new tract of land west of the Creek settlements. Once they had moved to these lands there were no longer subject to Creek laws.

In spite of internal dissension, the growth of these nations in the Indian Territory presaged an era of peace and prosperity that was taken as a sign of the wisdom of removal and the potentialities of the Indians to adapt to white ways.

Development of the Indian communities in the West depended upon a peaceful existence, free of attacks by outside enemies whether white or Indian. Critics of the removal policy had voiced a fear that the emigrant Indians would be insecure in their new homes, facing wild Indians of the plains who would resist the intrusion of tens of thousands of eastern Indians, most of them unprepared to fend off attacks. The emigrant Indians, moreover, would need protection against the encroachments of whites, protection that the Jackson administration had asserted was impossible in the East because of state jurisdictional problems but which the federal government could and would provide beyond the Mississippi, where its authority was unchallenged. The federal government was mindful, also, of white citizens on the western frontier, who, rightly or wrongly, feared the new heavy concentration of Indians on their borders. As removal proceeded, therefore, the United States developed elaborate plans for western defense to meet these needs.

All the plans provided for a military cordon in the West. In 1844 Fort Wilkins was established on Keweenaw Peninsula in Lake Superior to meet defense needs arising from the influx of miners into that copper region. With Fort Wilkins the top link in the chain, the exterior line of posts in that year comprised Fort Snelling, Fort Leavenworth, Fort Scott, Fort Gibson, Fort Towson, and Fort Washita. The interior posts were Fort Mackinac and Fort Brady on the Great Lakes, Fort Winnebago at the portage between the Fox and Wisconsin rivers, Fort Crawford at Prairie du Chien, Forts Atkinson and Des Moines in Iowa, and Jefferson Barracks. In the south Fort Smith and Fort Jesup also served the Indian frontier.

The officers and men of these posts gave a sense of security to the whites in the West, and they furnished an available military force that was called upon to restrict white encroachments on Indian lands and lessen (although they could not control) the machinations of whiskey venders. In this they carried out the stipulations of Indian treaties and fulfilled many promises made by the United States to the tribes. Although there were clashes between the plains Indians and the emigrants, there were no serious intertribal wars, and the line of forts restrained white advance.

Army commanders on the frontier played a significant role in the management of Indian affairs, both between the Indians and the federal government and within the tribes themselves. Imbued with the same paternalistic spirit that marked the civilian officials of the government, the army officers felt called upon to impress and control Indians as they would unruly children. But they were also a buffer between the frequently helpless Indians and unscrupulous frontier whites or warlike Indians to the west, and they could be a source of support and influence that was cultivated by tribal factions for their own purposes.

BENEVOLENCE AND REFORM

When Indian removal was over—or nearly so—the federal government returned to a concentrated effort at civilization and Christianization. By 1840 the bulk of the eastern Indians had emigrated, and as they settled into their new lives, new humanitarian efforts were made to move them rapidly into the white man's ways. With relative tranquillity on the frontier and the trauma of the removal process over, the wounds began to heal as the tribes adjusted to their new conditions. Under such circumstances, it is understandable that concerns for Indian advancement should have assumed something of their old prominence.

The 1840s were a decade of intense reforming spirit in America, a high point in reform movements that began about 1815 and continued to the Civil War. Betterment for all mankind seemed within easy reach, and concern for society's unfortunates (the delinquent, the insane, the indigent poor, the deaf, and the blind) appeared everywhere. Crusades for peace, women's rights, temperance, education, and the abolition of slavery marched with reforming zeal and a strange naiveté through the land. Words like *benevolence, philanthropy,* and *perfectibility* slipped easily from men's tongues. The plans for civilizing and Christianizing those Indians who had been moved from the main arena of American life partook of this evangelizing spirit.

Indian welfare in the 1840s was not the object of a formal "reform movement," with voluntary organizations and national attention—as were temperance, women's rights, or abolition, and as Indian reform became in the last decades of the century. But the men who directed Indian affairs reflected their times. They spoke the same evangelical Protestant perfectionist rhetoric that distinguished the other reformers. They shared in the vital optimism of the age and hoped for no less for the Indians than the professional reformers did for other unfortunate groups within the nation.

The great means to bring about the transformation in the Indians that the reformers wanted—as it had been since early in the century—was education. There continued to be no doubt in the minds of responsible officials of the federal government that the Indians were ultimately educable. These men admitted that the present state of many of the Indians was one of semi-barbarism, but they did not believe in a racial inferiority that was not amenable to betterment. "It is proved, I think, conclusively," Commissioner of Indian Affairs T. Hartley Crawford remarked of the Indian race, "that it is in no respect inferior to our own race, except in being less fortunately circumstanced. As great an aptitude for learning the letters, the pursuits, and arts of civilized life, is evident; if their progress is slow, so has it been with us and with masses of men in all nations and ages." Circumstances and education alone made the difference between them and the whites; and Indian agents, missionaries, and traders contributed evidence that the Indians were susceptible of improvement. There would be no racial obstacle to their eventual assimilation into the political life of the nation.

The promotion of schools took on new exuberance when the Indians were safely ensconced in the West, where the "experiment" could be carried out unhindered. Education, Commissioner Crawford asserted in 1839, formed "one of the most important objects, if it be not the greatest, connected with our Indian relations. Upon it depends more or less even partial success in all endeavors to make the Indian better than he is."

The initial problem was how to intrigue the Indians, both the youths to be educated and their parents, into accepting the schooling. It was all too evident that simply duplicating white schools in the Indian country or sending Indians to the East for formal education was not the answer. Learning in letters alone was not appreciated by the Indians and did not give any practical advancement to young Indians, who became misfits within their own communities. The answer, rather, lay in manual labor schools, and the practical model for the Indian Office was the manual labor school established at the Methodist Shawnee mission in eastern Kansas in 1839, which seemed to embody all the characteristics needed to reach the goal.

The school, built with church funds aided by substantial grants from the Indian civilization fund of the government, drew students from several tribes—Shawnee, Delaware, Kansas, Peoria, Potawatomi, Wyandot, Ottawa, and a scattering of others—and provided training for both boys and girls in useful agricultural and domestic skills, as well as in the English language. Crawford considered the school "the strongest evidence I have yet seen of the probability of success, after all our failures, in the efforts made by benevolent and religious societies, and by the Government, to work a change in Indian habits and modes of life; while it is conclusive proof that these sons of the forest are our equals in capacity." For its good work, and even more as a harbinger of greater things to come within the Indian country, the school won praise from the highest sources. Manual labor schools for the Indians became the goal of the War Department and the Indian Office.

Two other principles in connection with manual labor education were adopted by the Indian Office. One was that Indian schools should teach girls as well as boys, if civilization were to be forwarded. The other, gradually developed during the decade, was that Indian youths should be taught in the Indian country where they lived and not sent off to eastern schools. This reversed the tradition of sending selected Indian boys to schools in the East, where it was supposed that they could more quickly absorb the white man's civilization and take it back to their tribes.

Although the number of students in the Indian schools was small, the optimism of the Indian Office and the missionaries was not without foundation. The Choctaws, who were more interested in education than many of the tribes, offered an example of what was possible. They began to build schools as soon as they arrived in the West. The missionaries of the American Board reported eleven schools with 228 Choctaw students in 1836, in addition to which there were five schools supported by the Choctaw Nation and the three district schools provided by the 1830 treaty. In 1842 a comprehensive system of schools was begun. Spencer Academy and Fort

Coffee Academy were opened in 1844, Armstrong and New Hope academies two years later. The national council also supported four schools established earlier by the American Board. By 1848 the Choctaws had nine boarding schools supported by tribal funds, and neighborhood schools had been opened in many communities. The commissioner of Indian affairs reported progress as well among the other tribes. The Cherokees especially made remarkable advances and had a better common school system than that of either Arkansas or Missouri.

These schools could not have existed without the devoted work of Christian missionaries, and Indian education was a beneficiary of the missionary impulse of the Protestant churches that was an important element in the reform ferment of the age. The Indian Office felt this influence strongly, for its goals and those of the missionary societies were identical: practical, moral, and religious education of the Indians that would bring both Christianity and civilization to the aborigines. Reliance on the missionaries, indeed, was an important part of federal policy.

The general reports of Indian progress were highly optimistic. Government officials held firm to views of Indian perfectibility, of the ability of the tribesmen to attain the civilization of the whites. They eagerly seized upon whatever evidence pointed in that direction, convinced as they were that the advances in education among some of the tribes proved conclusively that all Indians were amenable to such attainments, immediately or in the near future.

By the end of the decade success seemed assured. Commissioner Orlando Brown reported in 1849: "The dark clouds of ignorance and superstition in which these people have so long been enveloped seem at length in the case of many of them to be breaking away, and the light of Christianity and general knowledge to be dawning upon their moral and intellectual darkness." Brown gave credit for the change to the government's policy of moving the Indians toward an agricultural existence, to the introduction of the manual labor schools, and to instruction by the missionaries in "the best of all knowledge, religious truth—their duty towards God and their fellow beings." The result was "a great moral and social revolution" among some of the tribes, which he predicted would be spread to others by adoption of the same measures.

Brown's optimism was extreme, for the Indians did not reach utopia. But it was quite in tune with the age, when zealous reformers saw no limit to the possibilities for ameliorating and perfecting the human condition, when the insane were to be cured, the slaves freed, the prisons cleansed, and women's rights recognized, and when Sunday schools would flourish. Government officials and their missionary allies hoped for no less for the American Indians.

DEVELOPMENT OF THE INDIAN DEPARTMENT

The removal of the eastern Indians not only meant the relocation of tens of thousands of Indians in the trans-Mississippi West, radically changing the distribution of the tribes with whom the United States government dealt, but it also necessitated a modification and codification of the laws and regulations governing Indian relations. The Indian bureaucracy (which had grown piecemeal during the previous decades) was regularized, an up-to-date trade and intercourse law was enacted, and plans were proposed for Indian government in the West.

The first step was congressional authorization in 1832 of a commissioner of Indian affairs to replace the head of the Indian Office appointed by the secretary of war on his own authority. Congress specified that the new official, under the direction of the secretary of war, would manage all Indian affairs.

In 1834 Congress went far beyond the establishment of the commissionership by undertaking a wholesale revamping of the Indian department and its activities. Here it was helped by a detailed report prepared for the secretary of war in 1829 by Lewis Cass, governor of Michigan Territory, and William Clark, superintendent of Indian affairs at St. Louis. They submitted the draft of a bill incorporating essential provisions from previous laws but embodying also their own views for ameliorating the existing state of affairs. The proposed bill was accompanied by a set of "Regulations for the Government of the Indian Department," which added details of procedure for carrying the law into effect. A third item was a bill to consolidate into one statute all the provisions for payment of annuities due from the United States to the Indians. This was a sensible proposal, intended to eliminate the unnecessary complications of accounting for funds under diverse headings. The work of Cass and Clark bore witness to their competence in Indian affairs, and much of their report was incorporated into the bills that became law in 1834.

The first law put a firm legislative foundation under the Indian service, made explicit provisions for Indian agents (whose status had been somewhat irregular), and established systematic accounting procedures in order to eliminate the confusion and embarrassment that had frequently arisen in financial matters.

The second measure, the trade and intercourse law of 1834, was a good example of continuity in American Indian policy. It offered no sharp break with the past but embodied, occasionally in modified form, the principles that had developed through the previous decades. The act began with a definition of the Indian country. The principles of the earlier intercourse laws, in which "the boundary of the Indian country was a line of metes and bounds, variable from time to time by treaties," was rejected because the multiplication of treaties made it difficult to ascertain just what was the Indian country at any given moment. Instead, the new law declared: "All that part of the United States west of the Mississippi, and not within the states of Missouri and Louisiana, or the Territory of Arkansas, and also, that part of the United States east of the Mississippi river, and not within a state[,] to which the Indian title has not been extinguished, for the purposes of this act, be taken and deemed to be the Indian country." The law accepted the removal of the Indians as an accomplished fact. The Indians in the southern states were no longer considered to be in Indian country, and in territories east of the Mississippi, as Indian titles were extinguished, the lands would cease automatically to be Indian country.

The licensing system for trading with the Indians was continued, but it was strengthened by the grant of discretionary authority to the agents in issuing licenses and by the requirement that all trading be done at designated sites. The use of presidential authority to withhold goods from certain tribes and to revoke licenses to trade with them, which Cass and Clark had proposed as a means of bringing pressure to bear on the Indians when the public interest demanded it, became part of the new law. To protect the integrity of the Indian country, restrictions were made more explicit and fines were often increased.

In one respect the 1834 law marked a new direction in the relations of the United States and the tribes. The War Department in the past had been careful not to interfere in purely Indian squabbles. Although it deprecated the hostilities that frequently broke out between tribes, it had adopted a hands-off policy. Now, as hostilities increased because of the emigration of eastern Indians to the West, the government took a direct interest in suppressing such wars, both to protect American citizens who fell in the way of war parties and to preserve the Indians themselves. The law of 1834 gave the War Department authority, under the direction of the president, to use military force to end or prevent Indian wars.

The House Committee on Indian Affairs in 1834 submitted a third bill, one for organizing a western territory to provide a political system for the emigrant Indians. The committee intended this bill to meet "the obligations of the United States to the emigrant tribes"; it was "to provide for the establishment of the Western Territory and for the security and protection of the emigrant and other Indian tribes therein." The three bills were considered "parts of a system," and the committee urged that they all be passed together.

The third bill established boundaries for an Indian territory west of Arkansas and Missouri that would be reserved forever for the Indian tribes. It pledged the faith of the United States to guarantee the land to the Indians and their descendants. Each of the tribes was to organize a government for its own internal affairs, and a general council would be established as a governing body for the voluntary confederation of the tribes envisaged by the bill. A governor, appointed by the president, would have a veto over acts of the council, power to reprieve offenders sentenced to capital punishment, and considerable authority in settling difficulties between tribes, executing the laws, and employing the military forces of the United States. The confederation would send a delegate to Congress, and the committee expressed a hope of eventual admission of the territory as a state into the Union.

The three bills of the committee, although introduced in the House on May 20, 1834, were not debated until June 24, close to the adjournment of Congress on June 30. The lateness of the session may well have enabled the first two bills to be pushed through without much change, but strong opposition arose to the bill on the western territory, which had no real precedents. After considerable and violent debate, it foundered in the House and was postponed to the next session and to ultimate failure.

There were repeated attempts to resurrect the idea of a western Indian state. President Jackson himself thought in terms of a confederacy of the southern Indians in the West, developing their own territorial government, which should be on a par with the territories of the whites and eventually take its place in the Union. He backed the suggestions of the commissioner of Indian affairs and the secretary of war for developing a confederated Indian government. But in the end all the suggestions and recommendations came to nothing.

Even if the paternal plans for a regulated confederated government in the western territory had passed congressional barriers, it is not likely that such an organization could have been set up effectively, for strong Indian groups were also vehemently opposed. If to many whites a unified Indian state seemed wise and feasible, to the Indians it violated tribal nationalism. The Five Civilized Tribes, the most politically sophisticated of the emigrated Indians, upon whom any successful confederated government would have had to depend, refused to consider such a move. Though they met in occasional intertribal councils, they held fast to their own tribal identities and independent governments, and their removal treaties gave a legal foundation to their position.

ANNUITIES AND LIQUOR REGULATION

The settlement of the Indians in the Indian country west of the Mississippi and the new legislation organizing the Indian department did not eliminate all problems in Indian-white relations. The Indians, unfortunately, were not sequestered from contact with evil men. Traders under license were permitted in the Indian country, and they came to the emigrant Indians principally to provide goods in return for annuity money. Concern for the Indians in the 1840s included a critical attack upon the exiting system of annuity payments and strenuous efforts to change the system.

Commissioner Crawford complained in 1841: "The recipients of money are rarely more than conduit pipes to convey it into the pockets of their traders." The annuities aggravated the very conditions that the Indian Office was trying to correct. So long as the Indians were assured of receiving their annual stipend, they did not exert themselves to earn a living, thus defeating the efforts of reformers to turn them into hardworking farmers. Much of the annuity money was spent for worthless goods or trivial objects, so that the bounty of the government was misappropriated. The annuity problem, furthermore, was closely tied to the problem of intemperance among the Indians, for the money was easily drained off into the pockets of whiskey venders.

The attack on the problem was made on several fronts, all aimed at directing the annuities toward the benefit of the Indians. A change was demanded, first, in the method of payment. The act of 1834 that reorganized the Indian department provided for payment to the chiefs, but the funds often were siphoned off by the chiefs and their friends for purposes that did not necessarily benefit the tribe as a whole. To correct this deficiency, Congress on March 3, 1847, granted discretion to the president or the secretary of war to direct that the annuities, instead of being paid to the chiefs, be divided and paid to the heads of families and other individuals entitled to participate, or, with the consent of the tribe, that they be applied to other means of promoting the happiness and prosperity of the Indians.

The new law, in addition, struck boldly at the liquor problem. No annuities could be paid to Indians while they were under the influence of intoxicating liquor or while there was reason for the paying officers to believe that liquor was within convenient reach. The chiefs, too, were to pledge themselves to use all their influence to prevent the introduction and sale of liquor in their country. Finally, to protect the Indians from signing away their annuities ahead of time, the law provided that contracts made by Indians for the payment of money or goods would be null and void.

All problems or obstacles in improving the Indians' condition seemed to stem from or to be aggravated by intemperance. The cupidity of white men, who were eager to sell vile concoctions to Indians at exorbitant prices, could not be struck at directly, and restrictions on the sale of liquor to Indians were impossible to enforce. A primary justification for removing the Indians to the West had been to place them in a home free from temptations. In an age of reform, when many considered excessive drinking an important factor in the problems of delinquency and dependency among the general public, temperance was to be one of the means that would open up "the fountains of hope" for Indians in the new lands.

But removal alone did not prevent intemperance among the Indians. The whiskey venders were if anything more virulent on the western frontier than in the settled regions in the East, and the means of stopping their nefarious commerce were less effective. Temperance societies were organized in several of the tribes, and some tribes passed laws of their own to put down the sale and use of whiskey, but more federal legislation seemed imperative.

In 1847 a new law provided up to two years' imprisonment for anyone who sold or disposed of liquor to an Indian in the Indian country, and up to one year's imprisonment for anyone who introduced liquor, excepting such supplies as might be required for the officers and troops of the army. In all cases arising under the law, Indians were to be competent witnesses. The commissioner of Indian affairs and the secretary of war were not satisfied to let the law serve by itself, however. New regulations were promulgated by the War Department, which spelled out in detail the duties of the military officers and the Indian agents—who were enjoined to be vigilant in executing their duties and were threatened with removal from office if they did not succeed.

The efforts to prevent whiskey from reaching the Indians met with some success. But all the laws of Congress and the strenuous efforts of the Indian agents and military officers on the frontier to enforce them did not end drunkenness. The frontier was too extensive and the profits to whiskey dealers too large to make complete prohibition possible. Abuse of liquor remained an abiding plague in Indian affairs.

CHAPTER 7

American Expansion and Indian Affairs

The removal of the Indians from east of the Mississippi and their settlement beyond Arkansas and Missouri was accomplished by mid-century. The Five Civilized Tribes maintained their national identity in the Indian Territory, and the smaller tribes along the Missouri border were encouraged by government officials and Christian missionaries to strive for the good life, cultivating farms, learning mechanical arts, and educating their children in white schools. The Indians and the whites were generally at peace.

Just when the education and civilization of the border tribes seemed to be bearing such good fruit, however, dramatic events in the 1840s overturned the premises upon which American Indian policy had been based. The formal removal program had followed the earlier policy, more or less unplanned, of simply moving the Indians west out of the way of advancing white settlement. The line separating the Indian country from white lands, which had been defined in the intercourse law of 1796, had been gradually pushed westward, as the Indian tribes ceded land in exchange for annuities and for newly designated and newly guaranteed lands to the west. Some thought that the removals of the 1830s had culminated this process, and that the removed Indians were finally secure behind a permanent line running from the Red River north and northeast to Lake Superior.

Then, suddenly, before the end of the 1840s the concept of such a line was shattered, and it was not long before the barrier itself was physically destroyed. The expansion of the United States that in three short years added Texas (1845), the Oregon country (1846), and California and the rest of the Mexican Cession (1848) radically changed the relationship between the United States and the Indians.

The government now came face to face with new groups of Indians. There were the nomadic buffalo Indians of the northern and southern plains—Sioux, Cheyennes, Arapahos, Crows, Kiowas, Comanches, and Pawnees—warlike and untamed and uninterested in transforming themselves into English-speaking farmers. There were Indians like the Utes, Shoshones, and Paiutes, subsisting at minimal levels in the mountains and in the wastelands of the Great Basin. There were the oasis Indians of the Southwest with their age-old patterns of life in the pueblos, warlike Apaches and Navajos raiding their peaceful Indian neighbors and the Mexican settlements, and numerous bands of California Indians, some affected by the Spanish mission experience but others living still undisturbed in the mountains. To the north were the Indians of the Pacific Northwest, fishing along the coast and hunting in the intermountain basins. These tribes were not totally unknown, of course, for early explorers had encountered and observed them; traders had met them on the Pacific coast, in the Rocky Mountains, and along the Santa Fe Trail; and some military reconnaissance expeditions had come upon Indian warriors.

In Texas the white population that had created the Republic of Texas in 1836 had already challenged Indian occupation of the region. With the acquisition of the Oregon country and the Mexican Cession, American population in those areas swelled greatly, and the aboriginal inhabitants were increasingly pressed upon by aggressive pioneers who had scant concern for Indian rights of person or property. And to get to the riches of the Pacific coastal regions, emigrants cut across the hunting grounds of the plains Indians. The Indian country was invaded, crossed and crisscrossed, and it was no longer possible to solve the question of the Indians' destiny by the convenient scheme of repeated removal.

A RESERVATION SYSTEM

The commissioner of Indian affairs in 1856 looked into the future with considerable perception. He saw railroads moving into the Great Plains as far as good lands extended and at the same time other railroads moving east from the Pacific coast settlements, followed in both cases by an active white population that would open farms and build cities.

> When that time arrives, and it is at our very doors, ten years, if our country is favored with peace and prosperity, will witness the most of it; where will be the habitation and what the condition of the rapidly wasting Indian tribes of the plains, the prairies, and of our new States and Territories?
>
> As sure as these great physical changes are impending, so sure will these poor denizens of the forest be blotted out of existence, and their

dust be trampled under the foot of rapidly advancing civilization, unless our great nation shall generously determine that the necessary provision shall at once be made, and appropriate steps be taken to designate suitable tracts or reservations of land, in proper localities, for permanent homes for, and provide the means to colonize, them thereon.

So reservations—in most cases small parcels of land "reserved" out of the original holdings of the tribes or bands—developed as an alternative to the extinction of the Indians. The reservations, however, were thought of as a temporary expedient, for whites dealing officially with the Indians in the 1850s all accepted the idea that the nation within its new continental limits would become the abode of enterprising and prosperous American citizens. They had no notion of a pluralistic society or a divided land occupied in part by European immigrants and their descendants and in part by American Indians adhering to their own customs. The goal was to ease the immediate conflicts between the two cultures and to prevent, as far as it was in their power to do so, the utter destruction of the weaker party.

It was for this end that segregation on reservations and application of the intercourse laws were considered so essential for Texas, Utah, New Mexico, California, and the Pacific Northwest and that revision of the intercourse laws was incessantly called for to make them more applicable to the new conditions. But beyond protection and preservation there was the ultimate goal of transformation: to induce the Indians all to become cultivators of the soil, to adopt the white man's language, customs, and religion, and finally to be self-supporting citizens of the commonwealth, a goal that all but a few believed was entirely practicable if only the proper means were applied. Agriculture, domestic and mechanical arts, English education, Christianity, and individual property (land allotted in severalty) were the elements of the civilization program that was to be the future of the Indians.

The policy makers were firm in their views of what constituted humanitarian concern and benevolence for their Indian charges. Having judged the civilization programs among the Five Civilized Tribes and the border Indians as marked with signs of ultimate success, they saw no reason why the same causes would not produce the same effects among the new tribes that had fallen under United States jurisdiction.

The United States government had only one pattern for dealing with the Indians. It held that Indians retained title to the lands they occupied (although there was considerable question whether this principle applied to the Indians and land that came to the United States from Mexico) and that these titles could be extinguished only by treaties, which would specify the lands ceded and the payment to be made for them. Yet the treaties with most of the tribes with whom the government now came into contact, following the precedent already well established in the East, were not the result of negotiations between two sovereign and independent powers. They were instead a convenient and accepted vehicle for accomplishing what United States officials wanted to do under circumstances that were frequently difficult.

By treaty the government could provide Indian segregation on small reservations, throwing open the rest of the territory to white settlement and exploitation. On the reservations the restrictions and protection of the intercourse laws could be applied to restrain if not prevent deleterious contacts between the two races and to protect the remaining rights of the Indians. By treaty, too, the United States sought to provide the means for transforming the life of the Indians, for the negotiations were used to gain the acquiescence, at least nominal, of the Indians to an agricultural existence and "moral improvement and education."

The system was applied with indifferent success. In many cases the treaty procedure came too late, after the destruction of the Indians was already far advanced, and the federal government was inexcusably slow in looking after Indian affairs in the remote regions of the Far West. The single pattern was applied with little appreciation of the varying Indian cultures it was supposed to replace, and on occasion the treaties signed in the field were not ratified by the Senate, leaving the status of the Indians and their lands in a sort of limbo. Often, application of the treaty provisions was possible only after resisting Indians had been overwhelmed and crushed by military force.

The men in the Indian service whose lot it was to seek solutions for the new Indian problems facing the nation after the territorial acquisitions of the 1840s took faltering steps, and Congress was no more sure-footed. But out of it all developed a reservation system that became a staple of United States Indian policy for the future.

ADMINISTRATIVE CHANGES

The changed relations with the Indians that came with American expansion to the Pacific were accompanied by changes in the administration of Indian policy. One of these was the transfer of Indian affairs in 1849 from the War Department, which had been responsible for them since the beginning of the nation, to a newly created executive department called the Department of the Interior. Congress, in organizing the government after the Constitution had been adopted, had put Indian relations into the hands of the War Department with hardly a second thought, for the Revolutionary War had placed the Indians for the most part on the side of the British, and contact with them had been as adversaries.

As circumstances changed and the Indians were no longer looked upon primarily as military foes, the logical reasons for having the secretary of war direct Indian affairs disappeared. What held the management of the Indians within the War Department was bureaucratic inertia and strong congressional disinclination to increase the size of the executive branch of the government by creating a new department and a new cabinet officer.

The eventual success in gaining a new department came largely as a result of America's expansion in the 1840s, which so greatly increased the "interior" concerns of the United States. On March 3, 1849, President Polk signed the bill creating a new department to assume responsibility for the Office of Indian Affairs and for the General Land Office, the Patent Office, and the Pension Office.

There was no objection from the War Department about giving up its control of Indian affairs; no doubt the secretary was happy to be rid of the onerous duty. For the Indian Office, the new law of itself did not create any great problems. The work had been a civilian operation reporting to the secretary of war; the office continued as it was, but it reported now to the secretary of the interior. The end of the 1840s was one of those times of rare tranquillity on the frontier, when it was easy to believe that Indian wars were a thing of the past and that Indians were no longer a military matter.

The commissioners of Indian affairs under the new Interior Department developed a strong and consistent reservation policy. Luke Lea, appointed by President Zachary Taylor in 1850, adopted the unequivocal stand that the civilization of the Indians was a necessary and practicable goal of the federal government. Although he admitted the difficulties of the task and his own insufficiency in carrying it out, he declared that civilizing the Indians was "a cherished object of the government" and that any plan would have to provide for the Indians' "ultimate incorporation into the great body of our citizen population."

The immediate means to Lea's humanitarian end would be a national system of reservations, and he worked out a clear statement of that policy in regard to "our wilder tribes."

It is indispensably necessary that they be placed in positions where they can be controlled and finally compelled by sheer necessity to resort to agricultural labor or starve. Considering, as the untutored Indian does, that labor is a degradation, and that there is nothing worthy of his ambitions but prowess in war, success in the chase, and eloquence in council, it is only under such circumstances that his haughty pride can be subdued, and his wild energies trained to the more ennobling pursuits of civilized life. There should be assigned to each tribe, for a permanent home, a country adapted to agriculture, of limited extent and well-defined boundaries; within which all, with occasional exception, should be compelled constantly to remain until such time as their general improvement and good conduct may supersede the necessity of such restrictions. In the mean time, the government should cause them to be supplied with stock, agricultural implements, and useful materials for clothing; encourage and assist them in the erection of comfortable dwellings, and secure to them the means and facilities of education, intellectual, moral, and religious.

George W. Manypenny, who replaced Lea in March 1853, was strongly committed to a reservation system as a means of promoting the civilization of the Indians in the Far West. Of the Indians in New Mexico and Utah, he wrote at the end of 1854: "Conventional arrangements are necessary . . . for the purpose of fixing them in proper locations, and giving to the department such influence and control over them as will enable it, as far as possible, to confine them thereon, and to induce them to resort to agriculture and kindred pursuits, instead of relying, as they now do, for support upon the uncertain and precarious supplies of the chase; and when that fails, upon the more hazardous and injurious practice of theft and plunder."

It was clear to Manypenny that it was no longer possible to solve the question of the Indians' destiny by the convenient expedient of repeated removal. He hoped at first in dealing with the emigrated tribes along the border in Kansas and Nebraska to move them into the "colonies" established north and south, but he noted the Indians' resistance and ultimately promoted instead the assignment of permanent reservations, reduced in size to be sure, where the Indians already were. The reservation policy that was developing in the 1850s, therefore, included as an essential component the establishment of fixed and permanent homes for the Indians.

The allotment of land in severalty was a necessary corollary of the reduced permanent reservations, and it was recommended strongly by Manypenny and his successors. The doctrine of private property was, of course, an essential part of the American way that the Indian had long been expected to accept. But it took on a special urgency as the reservation system got under way, for it lay "at the very foundation of all civilization."

While the commissioners were developing and promoting a reservation policy for the Indians in the West, they were also concerned about the insufficiency of the administrative machinery they had to work with. One serious defect was the lack of a sufficient number of superintendents to handle Indian affairs in regions remote from the seat of government, regions where discretionary authority frequently needed to be exercised and where superintendents could give "immediate and rigid supervision" to agents and subagents. A remedy came in a law of February 27, 1851, that repealed all previous authorization for Indian superintendents east of the Rockies and north of Texas and New Mexico and provided instead three superintendents for the Indians in those areas. A new assignment of agents was made, and the intercourse laws were extended over the tribes in New Mexico and Utah territories.

The separation of the territorial governors from ex officio duty as Indian superintendents, another reform proposed, came slowly, as Congress acted piece by piece. In 1850 a separate superintendency for Oregon was created. In 1856 the Minnesota Superintendency, in which the governor served as superintendent, was discontinued and its agencies added to the Northern Superintendency. And in 1857 the two offices were separated in the territories of Utah and New Mexico.

What bothered the commissioners of Indian affairs was the general inapplicability of old laws to new circumstances and especially the inadequacy of the trade and intercourse law of 1834 to protect the persons and property of the Indians. Manypenny saw what was happening to the Indians as they succumbed to the pressures of the invading whites, and he remarked, "The rage for speculation and the wonderful desire to obtain choice lands, which seems to possess so many of those who go into our new territories, causes them to lose sight of and entirely overlook the rights of the aboriginal inhabitants." He concluded: "Humanity, Christianity, national honor, unite in demanding the enactment of such laws as will not only protect the Indians, but as shall effectually put it out of the power of any public officer to allow these poor creatures to be despoiled of their lands and annuities by a swarm of hungry and audacious speculators, attorneys, and others, their instruments and coadjutors." The same plea was made by Manypenny's successors, but nothing came of it.

There was a perennial problem with annuities, especially if they were paid in money. Commissioner Manypenny declared that the money-annuity system had done "as much, if not more, to cripple and thwart the efforts of the government to domesticate and civilize our Indian tribes, than any other of the many serious obstacles with which we have had to contend." He wanted payments to the Indians to be in the form of goods, agricultural implements, and stock animals or in the form of "means of mental, moral, and industrial education and training." As he set about to negotiate treaties with the Indians, he saw to it that payments were not permanent, but that they would gradually be reduced over a set period of years. A provision was inserted in most of the treaties in this or similar form:

All which several sums of money shall be paid to the said . . . tribes, or expended for their use and benefit under the direction of the President of the United States, who may, from time to time, determine, at his discretion, what proportion of the annual payments, in this article provided for, if any, shall be applied to and expended, for their moral improvement and education; for such beneficial objects as in his judgment will be calculated to advance them in civilization; for buildings, opening farms, fencing, breaking land, providing stock, agricultural implements, seeds, &c., for clothing, provisions, and merchandise; for iron, steel, arms and ammunition; for mechanics, and tools; and for medical purposes.

Because Manypenny negotiated a large number of treaties, his policy had significant effect. Moreover, the policy inaugurated in the previous decade of paying annuities semi-annually was revived. It appeared to have a good effect in countering the tendency of many Indians to spend their funds wastefully and then sink back into a long period of misery until the next annual payment arrived.

The old problem of the liquor traffic continued, for even the new and tighter strictures of the law of 1847 were not enough. "The appetite of the Indian for the use of ardent spirits," Manypenny lamented in 1855, "seems to be entirely uncontrollable, and at all periods of our intercourse with him the evil effects and injurious consequences arising from the indulgence of the habit are unmistakably seen. It has been the greatest barrier to his improvement in the past, and will continue to be in the future, if some means cannot be adopted to inhibit its use." The federal system was in large part to blame, for the federal government had done almost all it could to end the sale or use of liquor in the Indian country, but it could not make laws for the states and territories that were adjacent to or surrounded the tribal lands. All it could do was to urge proper legislation, but nothing truly effective was provided.

A PATHWAY TO THE PACIFIC

The territorial acquisitions of the 1840s were both the result of and a stimulus to population movements to the Pacific slope. Although large numbers moved by sail around Cape Horn and others risked the shorter distance through the Isthmus of Panama, great hordes of emigrants chose the course across the continent. In 1843 the first mass movement to Oregon took place, jumping off from Independence, Missouri, and moving along the overland route to the Willamette Valley in Oregon. The spectacle was repeated in 1844 and 1845, and by 1848 more than fourteen thousand emigrants had impressed the Oregon Trail indelibly on the landscape and on the American consciousness. Some turned south from Fort Hall and sought California instead of Oregon; the trickle became a torrent when news of the discovery of gold in California in 1848 reached the East. Meanwhile, there was heavy traffic as well on the Santa Fe Trail, which had been laid out in 1822 and which became a major passageway to the Southwest and California.

These great movements of population had two effects on Indian affairs. In the first place, they cut directly through the lands of the Indians, making a wide swath that upset the ecological patterns by destroying large numbers of game (chiefly buffalo) and forcing the Indians to seek new hunting grounds; this in turn led to increased intertribal irritations. Although direct conflicts between the Indians and the Oregon and California emigrants were few, and in many cases the Indians offered vital assistance to the intruders, the ultimate results shook apart the existing economic and political structures on the plains into an irreparable shambles—with which the federal government had to deal. In the second place, the increasing population of the West (the population of California in the census of 1850 was ninety-three thousand, that of Oregon Territory thirteen thousand, and that of Utah Territory eleven thousand) meant that the Indians were surrounded. No longer was it possible to keep moving the tribesmen vaguely "to the west." Whites and their lines of communication moved upon the Indians with seemingly inexorable force from both east and west, and the process speeded up still more after the Civil War.

To meet the crisis, the officials of the federal government intended to free the great middle section of the plains of its Indian inhabitants by moving them to two great "colonies," one already well established in the south as the Indian Territory and a comparable one to be laid out north of the lines of travel. The idea had been slowly developing. Commissioner of Indian Affairs T. Hartley Crawford in 1841 spoke of "an Indian territory in the northern part of Iowa" as a "counterpoise to the southwestern Indian territory," with a "dense white population . . . interposed between the two settlements." And his successor, William Medill, in 1848 noted that the government had "commenced the establishment of two colonies for the Indian tribes that we have been compelled to remove; one north, on the head waters of the Mississippi, and the other south, on the western borders of Missouri and Arkansas." These officials were thinking primarily of locations for the Indians transferred from east of the Mississippi, but no great mental gymnastics were required to expand the notion to the tribes of the plains.

All the proposals for colonization had a second component or argument, for humanitarian concerns of the previous decade were not suddenly dropped in the face of the new circumstances. Consolidating the Indians was necessary in order to preserve them and to civilize them. The interest in settling the Indians in conditions where they could be "improved" by education and manual labor, which had been an essential part of the civilization plans from the beginning of the century, continued to be viewed as a kind of panacea for the Indian problem.

The federal government took steps to carry out its designs—to open up the passage to the Far West and to promote the civilization of the Indians— by a series of Indian treaties in the early 1850s. The first of these was the Treaty of Fort Laramie, signed September 17, 1851, with the Sioux, Cheyennes, Arapahos, Crows, Assiniboins, Gros Ventres, Mandans, and Arikaras. The treaty was negotiated by David D. Mitchell, a onetime fur trader who was superintendent of Indian affairs at St. Louis and an active advocate of clearing a central passageway to the Pacific. He was aided by Thomas Fitzpatrick, Indian agent for the Upper Platte Agency. The Indians agreed to cease hostilities among themselves and "to make an effective and lasting peace." They recognized the right of the United States to establish roads and military posts in their territory, and they agreed to make restitution for wrongs committed on whites lawfully passing through their lands. The treaty spelled out in detail the boundaries for each of the tribes in an attempt, generally unsuccessful, to keep them apart. In return the United States promised to protect the Indians from white depredations and to pay annuities of fifty thousand dollars a year for fifty years (reduced to ten years, with a possible five-year extension, by an amendment proposed by the Senate and later ratified by the tribes). The annuities were to be paid in "provisions, merchandize, domestic animals, and agricultural implements, in such proportions as may be deemed best adapted to their condition by the President of the United States."

In 1853 Thomas Fitzpatrick by himself negotiated a treaty with the southern plains tribes—Comanches, Kiowas, and Apaches—at Fort Atkinson on the Santa Fe Trail in southwestern Kansas. The provisions were similar to those of Fort Laramie: agreements of peace among the Indians and with the whites, right of passage through the territories for the whites, and permission for military and other posts on Indian lands. The annuities were set at eighteen thousand dollars a year for ten years, with a possible five-year extension; a special article provided that if the United States decided it would be wise to establish farms among the Indians for their benefit, the annuities could be changed into a fund for that purpose.

Agitation for a railroad to the Pacific was an important force in clearing the central region of its Indian inhabitants. Some sort of transcontinental road linking the Mississippi Valley with the Pacific, and thus with the riches of the Orient, had been urged by Asa Whitney in the mid-1840s; by 1853 the need was so universally agreed upon that Congress authorized surveys to determine the most appropriate route. The search for a railroad route had deep political implications, for each section had strong advocates of a railroad. A southern route would pass through politically organized areas that would offer protection and encouragement to settlement along the road. It was therefore incumbent upon the proponents of a central route to see that the lands through which it would pass were also organized.

In addition to the need for a railroad, there was continued pressure for settlement of the lands west of the Indian frontier line from restless farmers who felt unjustly obstructed from the "normal" development of the West by the Indian barrier.

In response to the pressures for territorial organization, Congress passed the Kansas-Nebraska Act in May 1854. The law, while repealing the Missouri Compromise prohibition on slavery, provided for two territories whose inhabitants themselves under "popular sovereignty" would decide for or against slavery. Whatever the ultimate motivations of the men who voted for the bill, the long agitation for territorial organization that culminated in the act provided a tremendous impetus to the new direction in Indian policy. While the territorial debate engaged Congress in 1853–1854, in fact, the Indian Office was taking steps to free the region of Indian title and thus open it for settlement.

That difficult task was the responsibility largely of Commissioner Manypenny, who believed that for the Indians' sake the western territories should be organized and that the Indians should be placed as much as possible out of the paths of emigrants to the Pacific. "Objections have been urged to the organization of a civil government in the Indian country," he wrote in 1853; "but those that cannot be overcome are not to be compared to the advantages which will flow to the Indians from such a measure, with treaties to conform to the new order of things, and suitable laws for their protection."

Manypenny energetically moved ahead to fit the Indians into "the new order of things." He visited most of the border tribes, held councils with them, and did his best to get agreement from them for the cession of their lands. The Indians were ill-disposed to such a measure, having been excited and irritated by exploring parties of whites already invading their territory. At first they were opposed to any sale at all, but eventually they agreed on condition that they could keep small reserves in the areas where they were then situated. In Washington between March 15 and June 5, 1854, the commissioner negotiated nine treaties with the Indians who lived along the eastern border of the new territories: Otos and Missouris, Omahas, Delawares, Shawnees, Iowas, Sacs and Foxes of the Missouri, Kickapoos, Kaskaskias, Peorias, Piankashaws, Weas, and Miamis.

The treaties were pretty much of a piece; the Oto and Missouri treaty of

March 5 can be taken as an example. It provided for the cession of the tribes' holdings west of the Missouri River and designated a reduced area within the old reservation to which the Indians agreed to remove within a year. A significant characteristic of this treaty, as of all these treaties, was the provision for allotting lands in the newly designated reserve in farm-sized plots to individual Indians. The president was given the discretionary authority to survey the land, set it off in lots, and assign the lots in specified amounts (a quarter section to a family, eighty acres to single adults, and so on) to all Indians who were "willing to avail of the privilege" and would make permanent homes on the lots. Any residue of land after all the Indians had received an allotment was to be sold for the benefit of the Indians.

In return, the United States agreed to pay the Otos and Missouris annuities on a sliding scale from twenty thousand to five thousand dollars over the next thirty-eight years. The president would decide what proportion, if any, was to be paid in money and what proportion expended for education and other means to civilization. Another twenty thousand dollars was granted to help the Indians to move, subsist for a year, and establish themselves on their farms. Moreover, the government would build a grist and saw mill and a blacksmith shop and for ten years would employ a miller, a blacksmith, and a farmer. Thus were these Indians, who had been subjected to the civilizing policies of the government for a number of decades, to be finally incorporated into white society.

The continued Indian residence in Kansas and Nebraska was not intended to impede the westward movement of the whites, for the Indians agreed in the treaties to allow "all the necessary roads and highways, and railroads, which may be constructed as the country improves" to run through their lands, with just compensation to be paid in money.

Good as the intentions of the federal officials were in attempting to provide permanent homes for the Indians in eastern Kansas and Nebraska (as much as possible on individual homesteads), they did not reckon fully with the special problems facing Kansas in the mid-1850s and with what Manypenny called "the wonderful desire to obtain choice lands" on the part of individuals, land companies, and railroads that "causes them to lose sight of and entirely overlook the rights of the aboriginal inhabitants." The conflict between the pro-slavery and anti-slavery forces that turned the southern territory into Bleeding Kansas caught the hapless Indians in a devastating situation.

Manypenny hoped that with the return of peace and order to the territory the good citizens would hasten to repair the wrong and injury done to the Indians by lawless men. But he was much too sanguine in his expectations. The Indian reserves were extraordinarily attractive to designing speculators; leaders of Indian factions made use of the uncertain times for their own benefit; and the federal government was powerless—or lacked the will to exert power—to fulfill its promises to protect the Indians.

The plans of federal officials for opening a wide passageway west through the plains were interrupted by Indian hostility, brought on by the inexorable pressure of white population sometimes compounded by the imprudent and foolish actions of a few men. Indian resistance became so general by the end of the 1850s that one could speak of a plains Indian barrier of Sioux, Cheyennes, Arapahos, Kiowas, and Comanches extending from the Canadian to the Mexican border, a barrier that did not crumble until a decade or more after the Civil War. The United States army, maintaining small forts along the trails and in trouble spots in the West, at first followed a defensive strategy, acting the role of policeman. Then, as Indian raids multiplied, it modified its policy to consider the whole tribe or band responsible for the raids of its members, and it mounted offensive campaigns against them.

The first encounter arose out of the chance Indian killing of a cow belonging to an emigrant Mormon on the trail near Fort Laramie. A rash young lieutenant, John L. Grattan, marched out of the fort on August 19, 1854, to arrest the Indian accused of the cow's death. When the Brule chief Conquering Bear, at whose camp the culprit was sought, failed to deliver him, Grattan opened fire, killing the chief. The Sioux fought back and quickly destroyed Grattan and his whole detachment. Emboldened, other Indians attacked the trail along the Platte. The Indian Office criticized the army's action, for under the intercourse law there should have been recourse to the Indian agent for compensation for the butchered animal. But the army decided to teach the Sioux a lesson.

Secretary of War Jefferson Davis placed Colonel William S. Harney in command, and in the summer of 1855 Harney moved against the Brules. Early in September he destroyed the Indians' village near Ash Hollow on the North Platte in western Nebraska. Then the troops marched through the heart of the Sioux lands from Fort Laramie to Fort Pierre on the Missouri. At Fort Pierre in March 1856 Harney held a council with the Sioux chiefs and cowed them into agreeing to refrain from hostilities. But the harsh action did little to encourage genuinely peaceful sentiments among the Indians. Harney's expedition was simply the first major challenge to the powerful Sioux advance on the northern plains, a movement that paralleled the advance of white Americans into the same region.

Cheyenne Indians, continuing their raids on the Pawnees despite the Treaty of Fort Laramie in 1851, disturbed the central plains, and they soon became the target of army action. The Cheyennes struck at emigrants on the trail along the Platte, and the army chastized them in a spring offensive in 1857. Their defeat kept the Cheyennes quiet even during the Pike's Peak gold rush of 1858–1859, when hordes of gold seekers cut across the central plains from the Missouri to the Rockies. But the increased emigration and its effect upon the Indians gave the Indian Office one more argument for its reservation policy.

While a precarious peace settled on the northern plains, the Kiowas and Comanches continued their raids on the Texas frontier. Although they suffered numerous casualties inflicted by United States cavalry and the Texas Rangers, the Indians kept up their hostility throughout the decade. Even an extensive summer campaign of regular troops in 1860 through southern Kansas and western Indian Territory failed to quench the fires.

Thus in the antebellum years neither the army with its offensive operations on the plains and its network of military posts nor the Indian Office with its treaties of peace and civilization and its commitment to a reservation system had completely opened the way for unharassed travel or settlement on the Great Plains.

CHAPTER 8

Developments in
the West

The developing reservation policy of the United States met severe challenges in the West. There was no lack of resolve on the part of federal officials in Washington or the superintendents and agents they sent into the field. These men held fast to the notion that the Indians must be forced to end their nomadic habits and their raids against the settlements and accept a new existence by living within specified boundaries and depending for subsistence on cultivation of the soil and stock raising. Only thus would there be order in the land and the Indians be protected against extermination. But wherever the federal government turned there were special problems that came close to shattering the humanitarian dreams of the policy makers.

THE INDIAN SITUATION IN TEXAS

The government's reservation policy in Texas failed utterly, for it could not be built securely on the foundation inherited from the Republic of Texas. After Texas gained its independence from Mexico in 1836, its Indian policy vacillated between two extremes. President Sam Houston (1836–1838 and 1841–1844) and the last president of the Republic, Anson Jones (1844–1845), followed a policy of friendship and conciliation, even in the face of continuing Indian raids upon the settlements. President Mirabeau Bounaparte Lamar, who served between Houston's two terms, on the other hand, was determined to remove or exterminate the Indians, and he organized volunteer troops and rangers to subjugate the hostile tribes. Although agents and commissioners were appointed from time to time to deal with the Indians, the Republic of Texas acknowledged no Indian rights to the land. The Indians roamed over the central and western regions of Texas, following their nomadic hunting life, and passed freely between Texas and the lands still under Mexican jurisdiction, complicating the relations of Texas with Mexico. When Texas was annexed in 1845, the United States inherited an unsolved Indian problem of serious dimensions.

The federal government worked under special handicaps. In the first place, the annexation provisions left control of the public lands in Texas in the hands of the state, not the federal government, and the United States assumed responsibility for Indian affairs in the new state without ownership and jurisdiction over lands that could be granted and guaranteed to the Indian tribes as reservations. It was unable, without the consent of Texas, to extend the federal trade and intercourse laws (which applied to federally controlled Indian country) for the protection of the Texas Indians from white crimes, encroachment, and trade abuses.

Second, by the Treaty of Guadalupe Hidalgo in 1848 the United States agreed to restrain the Indians from incursions into Mexico and to exact satisfaction for incursions that could not be prevented. The treaty made it unlawful for the inhabitants of the United States to purchase captives or property seized by the Indians in Mexico, and the United States government agreed to rescue Mexican captives brought into the country and return them to Mexico. Given the lack of federal control over the affairs of Texas and New Mexico, these stipulations were never effectively carried out, and the United States, with a sigh of relief, extricated itself from the responsibilities in the Gadsden Treaty of 1853. A large part of the payment under that treaty was considered an indemnity for Indian incursions.

Finally, the military forces available to the federal government, by which it might have enforced by military might what persuasion and diplomacy failed to accomplish, were never numerous enough to patrol the long frontier lines and the even longer international boundary with anything more than minimal effect. A string of posts along the Mexican boundary and cordons of forts along the lines of white settlement were unable to restrain the Indians, nor were they effective in holding back the tide of white settlers.

Despite the peculiarities of the situation, the federal government proceeded according to the main outlines of its developing policy for dealing with the new Indians it encountered as the result of western territorial acquisitions. A peace commission dispatched to conciliate the Indians signed a treaty with them in May 1846, by which the Indians acknowledged themselves to be under the exclusive protection of the United States and agreed to keep peace with the Americans and with other Indians. And on March 3, 1847, Congress authorized a special Indian agent for Texas.

The agent appointed, Robert S. Neighbors, was an especially happy choice. He had moved to Texas in 1836 when he was twenty and had served with distinction in the Texas Revolution and under the Republic of Texas (as army officer and Indian agent). He understood the Indians' situation, was sympathetic to their plight, and stood irrevocably committed to protecting their interests; he acted as an effective and persuasive diplomat under conditions that gave him little to work with.

There seemed to be only one practicable solution for the Indian problems in Texas. The state must grant lands for reservations on which the Indians could be settled and turned into farmers and where the federal government could protect them from lawless whites. But not until February 6, 1854, did the Texas legislature offer such reservations for the Indians. In the summer of that year two reserves were established, one at the main fork of the Brazos River about ten miles south of Fort Belknap, another on the Clear Fork of the Brazos at Camp Cooper.

It took some time to gather the Indians, but in March 1855 the semi-agricultural tribes—Caddos, Wacos, Tawakonis, Anadarkos, Tonkawas, Keechies, and a few Delawares—began to colonize the Brazos reserve. In September Neighbors counted 794 Indians located there, and he spoke enthusiastically of their agricultural progress. This reservation appeared to fulfill all the agent's hopes, as year by year he reported more Indians settled, more fields under cultivation, and more crops harvested. The Comanche reserve, with Indians less ready to settle down, made much less progress, both in numbers and in agricultural production.

The location of hundreds of Indians on the two reserves did not solve the Indian problem in Texas. Nonreservation Indians, many if not most of whom came into the state from Mexico, New Mexico, or the Indian Territory, continued their depredations. In the minds of the enraged Texans it was difficult to draw a sharp distinction between those Indians and the Indians on the reservations. Indeed, many Texans believed that reservation Comanches were guilty of raids and other outrages. Tension increased as the border warfare heightened, for neither state nor federal officials were able to end the attacks. The futility of the government's reservation policy was thus apparent, and in February 1859 Neighbors urged the immediate removal of the reservation Indians outside the borders of Texas to land recently obtained from the Choctaws and Chickasaws. Even if the United States poured in military forces to protect the reserves, the Indians under the circumstances could hardly progress in the arts of civilization. In August, protected by United States cavalry on the march, 1,050 Indians from the Brazos reserve and 380 Comanches migrated to the Indian Territory—out of the "heathen land of Texas," "out of the land of the Philistines," as Neighbors described it to his wife.

INDIAN AFFAIRS IN NEW MEXICO

The United States began its formal relations with the Indians of New Mexico during the Mexican War, and its relations in the first instance were primarily military. The advance of General Stephen Watts Kearny into the region in 1846 as part of the American strategy in the Mexican War set the pattern for government action. Kearny's column came as a conquering army, promising to bring peace and order to a land torn by depredations and fear. The Pueblo Indians in their settled towns along the Rio Grande were beset by their hostile Navajo neighbors and threatened periodically by the warlike Apaches and Comanches raiding from the southern plains, and they hastened to greet the American soldiers with gestures of friendship. The Americans looked upon the Pueblos, who had been considered citizens by the Mexican government, as "civilized Indians," living in organized communities and dependent upon agriculture for subsistence.

Quite different were the "wild" Apaches and Navajos, tending their sheep and horses but living in large part by raids on the Mexicans. It was these Indians who created such an uproar in the region and who were the basic problem for the United States government. Kearny came with a strong feeling of American superiority, which he expected the Indians to recognize, and he hoped to gain support for his occupation from the Mexicans by his offers of protection against the hostile Indians.

Peace seemed to be at hand as Kearny proceeded on to California, leaving Charles Bent on the spot in charge of a provisional territorial government. But it did not take long for Indian unrest to reappear. Mexicans, unhappy with the American occupation, plotted to overthrow the government and enlisted Pueblo support. An uprising at Taos on January 19, 1847, killed Governor Bent and other officials and ended the idea of peaceful occupation, although the revolt was quickly put down by military force. Soon the wild Indians renewed their depredations, and Indian affairs in New Mexico deteriorated, as the success of Navajo and Apache raids emboldened other tribes to attack the Americans, especially along the Santa Fe Trail. American military force in New Mexico was not enough to guarantee the peace that Kearny had so sanguinely promised.

When President Zachary Taylor entered office in 1849, the United States provided for civilian administration of Indian affairs in New Mexico by appointing a South Carolina politician, James S. Calhoun, to be Indian agent. Calhoun proved to be a man of marked ability who exhibited deep concern for the Indians and intelligently promoted an Indian policy that would end the troubles in the Southwest. His proposal for adjusting Indian affairs in New Mexico was a display of military force that would end Indian depredations, then settlement of the Indians on reservations modeled after the

Pueblo towns. When Congress established the Territory of New Mexico as part of the Compromise of 1850, Calhoun became the first territorial governor and ex officio superintendent of Indian affairs. At the end of February 1851 Congress authorized four Indian agents for New Mexico and extended the trade and intercourse laws over the territory.

The military component of Indian affairs, nevertheless, continued to be of great moment. In 1851 the army established Fort Union east of Santa Fe, as a depot for supplies coming into the territory and as a base for troops sent out to protect the Santa Fe Trail, and Fort Defiance in the Navajo country. New posts near El Paso (Fort Fillmore) and at Valverde south of Albuquerque (Fort Conrad) placed more troops among the Indians.

While the military policy was being implemented, Calhoun began assigning his agents. Early in 1852 a Navajo agency was established at Fort Defiance and one was opened near Ojo Caliente for the southern Apaches. Here the agents began to distribute the seeds and farming implements that were to start the Indians on the way to becoming farmers. At the time of Calhoun's death in June 1852, the application of the new policy in New Mexico was well begun. There were sporadic wars, however, and new military posts had to be built along the Rio Grande and in other trouble spots.

In 1855 treaties were negotiated with the New Mexico Indians that embodied Commissioner Manypenny's principles. The treaty with the Capote Utes on August 8 can be taken as an example. In it the Utes agreed to peaceful relations, a cession of all their land claims, and the acceptance of a specified reserve of about two thousand square miles at the headwaters of the San Juan River; but the more crucial articles imposed a regimen of civilization upon the Indians, who agreed to settle on the reservation within a year after ratification of the treaty and to "cultivate the soil, and raise flocks and herds for a subsistence." Furthermore, the president of the United States, at his discretion, could survey the reservation and allot parcels of land to individual Indian families. In return for the cession and the promises of the Indians, the United States would pay annuities: $5,000 annually for the first three years, $3,000 for the next three, and $2,000 for the following twenty years. The payments were to be made at the direction of the president, who could determine what proportion, if any, would be paid in money and what proportion might be expended for moral improvement and civilization.

Here was a clear indication of the theoretical policy of the government to turn the Indians of the newly acquired territories into settled agriculturalists, no matter what the Indians' traditions and inclinations might be or what the capabilities of the land for farming. The governor reported the Utes "very reluctantly consented to commence the cultivation of the soil for a subsistence"; but he had strong hopes that success with this relatively amicable band would have "a powerful effect upon all the other bands of this savage tribe." The Senate failed to approve the treaties, yet the negotiations appear to have had some effect, for Manypenny reported at the end of 1856 that depredations in New Mexico had been less serious than in any of the previous years.

While plans for peaceful settlement of the Utes and Apaches proceeded, the Navajos were engaged in war—predatory raids by the Indians and retaliation by federal troops. Only after a vigorous campaign in the winter of 1860–1861 were the Indians subdued and a peace negotiated. By then the Civil War had brought new circumstances, as both the military and civilian officials were forced to neglect Indian affairs for more pressing concerns.

INDIANS AND MORMONS IN UTAH

In Utah Territory, stretching from the Rocky Mountains to the Sierra Nevada north of the thirty-seventh parallel, Indian affairs were complicated by relations between the Mormons and the federal government. The Mormons were deeply interested in the Indians from a theological standpoint, for the Book of Mormon described them as Lamanites, descendants of Israelites who had migrated to the New World and who had fallen from grace. They were to be redeemed in the new age, and the Mormons actively sought Indian children for upbringing in their own families as a means of conversion. The Mormons, moreover, had practical interests in Indian relations in the Great Basin, where the Utes, Shoshones, and Paiutes occupied the lands into which Mormon immigrants poured in the 1840s and 1850s. The security and well-being of the settlements depended upon peaceful accommodation with the Indians, and Brigham Young repeatedly directed his followers to treat the Indians well. There was genuine concern for the civilization of the Indians that differed little from that exhibited by Christian humanitarians in the East, and Young appreciated the futility of war with the natives. The peaceful policy, of course, did not always work, and Mormon frontiersmen experienced Indian wars and depredations as they encroached seriously upon the Indians.

Added to the problems of Indian-white relations common to all American frontiers was the question of Mormon domination of life in Utah, a serious irritant to the agents of the federal government who were responsible for Indian affairs there. The United States, as the decades of the 1850s advanced, became greatly concerned that its authority in the territory was not respected by Brigham Young and the Mormons. Under these unfavorable circumstances, the United States attempted to provide an Indian policy for Utah.

Some stability came with the establishment of the Territory of Utah in September 1850 and the appointment of Brigham Young as territorial governor and ex officio superintendent of Indian affairs. In February 1851 Congress extended the intercourse laws over Utah and provided an agent for the Utah Superintendency, who with two subagents reached Salt Lake City in the summer. But these men almost at once became embroiled in the controversies between the Mormons and non-Mormons.

A great problem in Utah was the lack of any treaty with the Indians by which some recognition of their lands and other rights against the whites might have been officially established. Negotiation of a treaty was repeatedly urged by the agents and by Brigham Young, too, but the whole movement was abortive. Not until 1863 were treaties signed with Indians in Utah Territory, and not until 1865 was a treaty negotiated (but never ratified) with the Utes. In the meantime, the agent moved ahead with an alternative to formal reservations by establishing a farming system for the Indians' benefit. Building on some early moves by Brigham Young to provide farmers to instruct the Indians, he undertook to teach them to farm in order to ease their destitution, an action cautiously approved by Commissioner Manypenny.

In 1857 relations between the United States and the Mormons in Utah approached a breaking point. Brigham Young's plan for a Mormon-dominated state, with economic and political as well as religious control, was in many ways a fact. Non-Mormons in Utah were antagonized, and their hostility spread across the nation. The announcement in 1852 that polygamy was a basic doctrine and practice of the Mormon church added an emotional fervor to the cries of lawlessness and rebellion against the Mormons. President James Buchanan, over-hastily heeding complaints from a few federal officials in Utah and the public outcry, replaced Young as governor of Utah Territory with Alfred Cumming and sent a military expedition west to put down the alleged rebellion and to make sure that the new governor was accepted and respected. Congress on March 3, 1857, had already provided for independent superintendents of Indian affairs in the western territories, and Jacob Forney was appointed to the new office for Utah Territory.

As the Utah Expedition moved toward Utah, the Mormons geared for war. Buchanan had neglected to inform Young of his replacement and of the military expedition, and the Mormon governor and his followers, when they received news of the advance of the troops, believed that the army was coming to destroy them. They prudently sought to engage the Indians on their side against the federal troops and the non-Mormon oppressors. Thus Young instructed one of the Mormon missionaries to the Indians in August 1857: "Continue the conciliatory policy towards the Indians, which I have ever recommended, and seek by works of righteousness to obtain their love and confidence, for they must learn that they have either to help us, or the United States will kill us both."

The "Mormon War" in the end was bloodless. The troops, arriving in the West too late in the year to move directly into Utah, wintered near Fort Bridger with some discomfort, for the Mormons had applied a scorched-earth policy to the vicinity. Conciliatory measures were begun, and Brigham Young, who had ordered the evacuation of Salt Lake City with directions to burn the city if the hostile troops moved in, agreed to accept peace. In the spring the troops passed peacefully through the nearly deserted city and established a military post forty miles to the west, where they stayed until called back by the Civil War. Governor Cumming was amicably accepted by the Mormons, and Forney took over the duties of Indian superintendent.

Brigham Young continued to use his considerable influence with the Indians to further peaceful relations with them and to work for their civilization. When treaty negotiations with the Utes were undertaken in 1865, the agent did not hesitate to call upon Young for support. Yet peaceful relations were not enough, for the white encroachment on Indian lands came faster than the government's plans for civilization and self-support could be carried out, and at the end of the decade many of the Indians were hungry, naked, and in desperate straits.

A RESERVATION POLICY FOR CALIFORNIA

The movement of American citizens to the Pacific coast and the incorporation of California and the Pacific Northwest into the American nation illustrate the deleterious effect upon the Indians of a policy applied from a great distance without a sound appreciation of local conditions and without adequate concern to protect Indian rights against the onslaught of American invaders. The relations of the United States with the Indians of California, particularly, were disastrous for the Indians, for the attempt of the federal government to protect them through treaty machinery was abortive, and the Indians were no match for the aggressive and often lawless gold seekers who flooded the region in 1849 and after.

The United States, to begin with, was almost entirely ignorant of the Indians in the new acquisition. It knew neither the population, the number and organization of the bands and tribes, nor the status of the Indians under Mexico—a status that presumably was to be continued under the provisions of the Treaty of Guadalupe Hidalgo. The Americans, logically enough, grouped the Indians roughly into two categories. One comprised the mission Indians, who had come under the influence of the Franciscan friars in the mission establishments that dotted the coast from San Diego to San Francisco Bay. These Indians had been drawn to live at the missions in order to be trained in agriculture, stock raising, and simple crafts, as well as to be instructed in Christianity. But by the time the Americans arrived the missions had been secularized by the Mexican government and the Indians dispersed. The rest of the native inhabitants were "wild Indians," who had little or no contact with whites and who subsisted by hunting, fishing, and gathering acorns.

After California was seized by United States troops under Stephen Watts Kearny in 1847, it was the military who first sought to establish some sort of official relations with the Indians and to prevent as much as possible the raids and counterraids between Indians and whites that threatened the peace of the country. The federal government only slowly proceeded to provide a civil arrangement for the Indians, based on its reservation policy. Three commissioners were appointed to negotiate treaties with the Indian groups, and between March 1851 and January 1852 eighteen treaties were drawn up and signed.

The treaties were much alike. The Indians recognized the United States as sole sovereign over the land ceded by Mexico in 1848, and they placed themselves under the protection of the United States and agreed to keep the peace. By each treaty a definite reservation was set aside for the tribes, and subsistence in the form of beef cattle was provided for them while they were moving and settling on the reservations. Annuities in the form of clothing, agricultural implements, and livestock were authorized, and farmers, blacksmiths, and schoolteachers were provided for a period of years. The eighteen treaties set aside 11,700 square miles (7,488,000 acres) of land, about 7.5 percent of the state.

The three commissioners did their work rapidly. Indeed, haste was necessary if conflicts between the onrushing whites and the Indians were to be prevented and the Indians protected in their rights. But they acted without the detailed knowledge of the Indians that modern anthropologists can provide. Although 139 tribes or bands were represented in the eighteen treaties, an enumeration in 1926 indicated that more than 175 tribes were not included in the treaties. Thirty years later, a study conducted under Indian Claims Commission litigation reported that of the 139 signatory groups, 67 were identifiable as tribelets, 45 were merely village names, 14 were duplicates spelled differently without the commissioners having been aware of the fact, and 13 were either personal names or unidentifiable.

The irregularities, although indicative of the lack of precise information with which the whole process was carried out, in the end did not matter, for the Senate refused to ratify the treaties. There is some question whether, even at the beginning, a majority of the Senate intended to authorize treaties of cession rather than mere treaties of peace and friendship, for there was considerable feeling in Congress that the California Indians had no land titles and therefore that no treaties were needed to extinguish them. But whatever the status of Indian titles, other aspects of the treaties drawn up by the three commissioners militated against their ratification. There was strong opposition from Californians, who saw large regions to be snatched from their grasp and reserved for the Indians, whom they despised. Furthermore, the costs of the treaties had grown to nearly a million dollars, far beyond the total of $50,000 that had been appropriated.

The rejection of the treaties left Indian affairs in California in an uncertain state. For one thing, many of the claims made under the contracts let by the treaty commissioners were later declared fraudulent and never paid. More serious was the worsening condition of relations between the Indians and the miners and other settlers. This became the responsibility of Edward F. Beale, a highly competent and benevolent man with navy and army experience who was appointed the first Indian superintendent in California under congressional authorization of March 3, 1852. Beale wanted to reestablish the mission system on a secular basis, for he thought the missions had been an ideal means for channeling Indian labor into useful projects, and he began to implement his plan on a piece of land on the San Joaquin River, land passed over by the settlers as unworthy of their labor. He wanted no treaties and insisted that the land should be a government reservation to which the Indians would have no title and from which they could be moved as occasion demanded.

Congress authorized military reservations for the Indians, and Beale and his successor reported some success, but then doubts arose about the success of the California experiment. In 1858 a special agent, dispatched to visit the reservations, concluded that Beale's plan of collecting the Indians on the reserves where they would be supported by their own labor was "a lamentable failure." And the Indian Office agreed that too much money had been expended and too much done for the Indians, with negligible results.

On June 19, 1860, Congress authorized the secretary of the interior to divide California into northern and southern districts. Two superintending agents were provided, and Indians were to be placed on small reservations, to which they would move by simple agreements, not by formal treaties. The new arrangement seemed little better than the old. None of the reserves in the southern district were free of white claims and none were adequate in extent to serve the Indians' needs, and in the northern district conditions were just as bad. The result was utter defeat of the purposes for which the reservations had been set up.

Many of the California Indians, nevertheless, settled on the reservations and developed a rancheria existence—little spots of poor land within the rich state to which they had no clear title and on which they were under constant threat of encroachment from white Americans. These so-called mission Indians and their rights became a special subject of attention of the post–Civil War humanitarian Indian reformers.

INDIAN AFFAIRS IN OREGON AND WASHINGTON

In the Oregon Country, the vast area lying north of California and west of the Rocky Mountains, the United States was slow to vindicate its claims and thus to assume responsibility for Indian relations. Not until 1846, after the large immigration of Americans into Oregon had persuaded the British to give up their claims, did the United States gain undisputed dominion over the region between California and the forty-ninth parallel.

The United States, however, made no immediate move to establish a territorial government or any administrative machinery to attend to Indian affairs. Only after the Cayuse Indians murdered the missionary Marcus Whitman did Congress act, and in August 1848 President Polk signed a bill that created the Territory of Oregon. The law specifically protected the rights of the Indians in the new territory "so long as such rights shall remain unextinguished by treaty between the United States and such Indians," and it asserted the right of the United States to make laws and regulations regarding the Indians. As a stopgap measure, it provided funds for such presents to the Indians as might be required for the "peace and quietude of the country."

Anson Dart of Wisconsin was appointed Indian superintendent in 1850, and Commissioner Luke Lea instructed him to urge the Indians to live in peace and harmony among themselves, to induce them to engage in agricultural pursuits (encouraging them by prizes offered for the best crops), and to cooperate with the Christian missionaries working among the Indians without getting involved in sectarian disputes. The Indian, Lea said, has "but one alternative—early civilization or gradual extinction. The efforts of the government will be earnestly directed to his civilization and preservation, and we confidently rely upon their Christian teachers, that, in connection with their spiritual mission, they will aid in carrying out this policy." He declared that if the Indians could be "taught to subsist, not by the chase merely, a resource which must soon be exhausted, but by the rearing of flocks and herds, and by field cultivation, we may hope that the little remnant of this ill-fated race will not utterly perish from the earth, but have a permanent resting-place and home on some part of our broad domain, once the land of their fathers." Lea seemed to have no awareness that the Indians with whom Dart had to deal subsisted largely by fishing and that a change to an agricultural existence was neither wise nor easily accomplished.

When the commissioners opened negotiations with the Oregon Indians, they found them adamant in their refusal to move to the region east of the mountains, and the six treaties signed in April and May 1851 allowed the Indians to keep small reservations and a portion of their fishing grounds where they were. None of the treaties, however, were ever ratified. The failure to eliminate the Indians completely from west of the Cascades was an important reason. Some of the treaties, too, were negotiated with mere remnants of once more populous tribes. The Wheelappa band of Chinooks, with whom Dart signed a treaty on August 9, 1851, for example, had only two male survivors and a few women and children. The cost of the annuities may have been another point of objection.

The first round of treaties, then, did not bring a firm settlement of Indian problems facing the federal government in Oregon, and critical conditions remained. Whites moved into the territory in ever-increasing numbers, eager to lay hands on the rich lands. Congress on September 27, 1850, by the so-called Donation Land Law, without concern for Indian titles, had provided grants of 320 acres to American citizens or prospective citizens who had resided in Oregon and cultivated the land for four years, and settlers felt entitled to take land wherever they chose.

A new round of treaties followed, negotiated by Dart's successor, Joel Palmer. These treaties, which were ultimately ratified, were much alike and fitted well into the pattern established throughout the West in the 1850s. There was little indication in them that two sovereign equals were negotiating. For lack of other acceptable and established procedures, the treaties were the vehicle chosen to accomplish what the United States government wanted as it reacted to cries from western settlers and to the philosophical principles dominant in government circles. The Indians were to be moved out of the way of the whites—not, as in the case of the removal of the eastern tribes, to open spaces in the West, but to limited reserves within their old, more extensive territorial claims or to other specified locations within the territory. Most of the treaties were made with "confederated tribes and bands," an often more or less arbitrary grouping for convenience. In all of them the chiefs and headmen of these bands acknowledged "their dependence on the Government of the United States" and promised to stay on friendly terms with the citizens, sometimes consenting "to submit to, and observe all laws, rules, and regulations which may be prescribed by the United States for the government of said Indians."

All the treaties spoke specifically of "civilization." Annuity payments for ceded lands, set for a limited term of years, were not to be in money, but in goods conducive to the agricultural development of the Indians and for their moral improvement and education. The United States, moreover, agreed to erect blacksmith shops, hospitals, and schoolhouses and to furnish for a period of years the necessary mechanics, physicians, and teachers. The treaties authorized the president to survey the reservations and assign lots in severalty to Indians "willing to avail themselves of the privilege, and who will locate thereon as a permanent home."

In 1853 Washington Territory was broken off from Oregon Territory, and Isaac Ingalls Stevens was appointed territorial governor and ex officio superintendent of Indian affairs. Stevens, from Massachusetts, was a West Point graduate with service in the Mexican War, who resigned his commission in March 1853 to accept the new position in the West; he was thirty-five years old. At his request the War Department placed him in charge of the party surveying the northern route for a Pacific railroad, and he met with Indian groups as he moved west from St. Paul to Olympia, the territorial capital.

Governor Stevens was an energetic and highly organized man, and his career as superintendent of Indian affairs was marked by a series of dramatic councils with the Indians at which treaties of peace, cession, and civilization were signed. Armed with a treaty already prepared, the governor and his commissioners met first on Christmas Day 1854 with a number of tribes at Medicine Creek at the mouth of the Nisqually River. This was not to be a negotiation between two political powers, of course, but an imposition upon the Indians of the treaty provisions Stevens brought with him, for he held a highly paternalistic view of his relations with the tribes. The prepared treaty was explained point by point to the Indians, who signed it on December 26 without objection. The terms were very similar to those in the treaties signed by Joel Palmer and the Oregon Indians, but in addition specific provision was made to protect the fishing rights of the Indians.

In quick succession, Stevens and his assistants signed similar treaties with other groups of coastal Indians at Point Elliott (January 22, 1855), Point No Point (January 26), and Neah Bay (January 31). With that of Medicine Creek, these treaties cleared a wide area of land around Puget Sound.

The summer and fall of 1855 were taken up by three great councils with the Indians of the interior in which Stevens, with his usual drive and energy, expected to impose on them his vision of their future. The first, the Walla Walla Council held in late May and early June, was made up of delegations of Walla Walla, Cayuse, Umatilla, Yakima, and Nez Perce Indians. The Indians, aside from the generally friendly Nez Perces, were hostile, and concessions (including special cash annuities for the chiefs) had to be made to get signatures on the treaties.

In mid-July Stevens moved on to Hell Gate on the Clark Fork near the northern end of the Bitterroot Valley for a council with Flathead, Kutenai, and Pend d'Oreille Indians. The treaty, similar to those at Walla Walla, was signed on July 16, 1855. At Hell Gate, too, there was much agitation among the Indians as they argued about a proper location for the reduced reservation they were expected to accept. The deep Indian attachment for traditional homelands was not sufficiently appreciated by the whites, who looked chiefly at the economic potentialities of a reservation for sustaining the Indians in a peaceful agricultural existence, and the treaty was signed by the Indians with the understanding that the president would survey the region and designate an acceptable spot.

The final grand council was held in October with Blackfeet, Flatheads, and Nez Perces at the mouth of the Judith River in present-day Montana. The treaty began with formal statements of perpetual peace between the United States and the Indians and between the signatory tribes themselves and with other tribes. Boundaries were specified for common hunting grounds for the Indians for a period of ninety-nine years, and the lands belonging exclusively to the Blackfeet were described. The United States agreed to provide the Blackfeet with certain annuities and to instruct them in agricultural and mechanical pursuits, to educate their children, and in other ways to promote their "civilization and Christianization."

There was delay in the ratification of some of the treaties made in Oregon and Washington because of war that broke out in 1855. Increasing penetration of their country by whites stirred up both the Rogue River Indians in Oregon and the Yakimas and their allies in central Washington, and fighting continued for several years. Quarrels between Stevens and the military commander John Wool and recriminations over action of the volunteers did little to bring the war to a close, and the first military encounters brought only temporary pacification of the hostile Indians. Not until 1858, when defeat of a column under Lieutenant Colonel Edward J. Steptoe called forth strong punitive action by troops under Colonel George Wright, did peace return to the Northwest. Wright traversed the Indian country, executing culprits accused of inciting attacks and gaining the submission of the defeated chiefs.

The military action was decisive in Oregon and Washington. The Indians, unlike those in many parts of the nation, had moved beyond guerrilla warfare and, with well-defined war aims, met their enemy in open battlefield encounters, in which they were soundly defeated. The ending of the war opened the way for ratification of the treaties by the Senate in March 1859. The movement to the reservations and the advance toward the white man's way of life that those treaties specified became the lot of the Indians in the Pacific Northwest.

CHAPTER 9

The Civil War Years

Indian affairs during the years of the Civil War were marked by two distinct situations. In the first place, the Civil War had a direct bearing on Indian relations in the Indian Territory and the neighboring state of Kansas. The defection of the slave-holding Indian nations from their treaty obligations to the Union and their signing of treaties of allegiance and alliance with the Confederate States of America brought them into the Civil War as formal participants, while loyal factions that fled to Kansas created additional problems for the federal government.

In the second place, this period in the West was one of continuing development and settlement, with throngs of whites moving into new areas in search of precious metals or agricultural riches. It was almost as though westerners were unaware of the great battle raging between the North and the South. The Pike's Peak gold rush of 1859 and the concurrent discoveries in Nevada were soon followed by the establishment of Colorado and Nevada territories in 1861; and Nevada achieved statehood in 1864. Then the mining frontier moved rapidly both north and south, with political organization of new territories coming quickly in the wake of the first major strikes. Arizona Territory was created in 1863, and in the same year Idaho Territory was set up to satisfy the whites who had rushed into the Snake River region. New discoveries of precious metals in what is now western Montana led to thriving centers of population at Virginia City and Helena. In May 1864 Congress created Montana Territory. These advances cut deep into Indian lands, and the increased traffic they occasioned between the mining settlements and the more established sections of the country further exasperated the Indians. Meanwhile, growing white population on the central plains brought new pressure upon the Indian tribes there. Kansas grew in population from 107,206 in 1860 to 364,399 in 1870 and Nebraska (which became a state in 1867) from 28,841 to 122,993.

The Civil War years were filled with Indian-white conflicts growing out of white invasion of Indian lands. These serious encounters were aggravated by the weakening of federal authority in the West as regular troops were withdrawn and replaced by volunteers, who were often few in number, inexperienced in Indian control, and too frequently imbued with frontier hostility toward Indians. Yet the federal government, despite the fact that its energies were fully engaged in the great sectional struggle, could not totally ignore the Indians, and both the Indian service (working under the weight of a patronage system that placed political appointees in sensitive positions) and the army had to worry about the "second front."

THE SOUTHERN INDIANS AND THE CONFEDERACY

The Indian country in the West was of strategic importance in the Civil War. Of vital concern to both the North and the South was the attitude of the southern Indians—especially the Cherokees, Creeks, Choctaws, Chickasaws, and Seminoles—now living in the area to which they had been removed, north of Texas and west of Arkansas. The Five Civilized Tribes, or at least significant portions of them, were southern in sympathy as well as location. They were dominated by mixed-bloods, many of whom were slave-owners, and cultural affinity to the southern states as well as practical political interests tilted them toward the seceding states. Even so, it is difficult to understand how Indian groups so recently uprooted from their traditional lands by Georgia, Alabama, Mississippi, and Tennessee— action vigorously opposed and condemned by northern states—could now forswear their allegiance and treaty obligations to the Union and ally themselves with the South. Despite large Unionist factions, especially among the Creeks and the Cherokees, all of the Five Civilized Tribes signed formal treaties with the Confederate States of America, and some of the smaller Indian groups in the Indian Territory joined them in this switch of loyalty.

Geographical location had a significant influence. The Choctaws and Chickasaws were located along the Red River adjacent to Texas, and the Choctaws were bordered on the east by Arkansas. Thus caught in a vise between two ardent members of the Confederacy, there was little likelihood that they could maintain a neutral or Unionist position even if they had been inclined to do so. The Creeks and Seminoles and even more the Cherokees, located farther north, could for a while think of neutrality and at least hope for effective support and succor from the North. The Cherokees held out the longest, and only under extreme pressure did the Union faction, led by John Ross, succumb.

The Indian department officials in the Indian Territory at the outbreak of the Civil War were largely southern sympathizers, for the federal patronage system had long emphasized local men. The agents, the agency employees, and the traders were southerners, in many cases from Arkansas and Texas. There were, moreover, financial considerations. The trust funds of the Indians, invested by the federal government for the benefit of the tribes, were almost entirely in southern stocks and bonds. There was a fear, played upon heavily by the secessionists, that these funds would be forfeited if the tribes maintained their attachment to the North.

The southern Indians questioned the genuineness of the support of their interests by Lincoln's Republican administration. They were aware, too, of the defenseless nature of their situation as far as northern military support was concerned. In the late 1850s the War Department, despite vigorous protests by the secretary of the interior, had persisted in a general withdrawal of troops from the Indian Territory. When the war broke out, the remaining Union forces were withdrawn, and the military posts were occupied by Confederate forces. The Indians were left at the mercy of the Confederacy, and southern officials were quick to capitalize on all the points in their favor.

The Confederacy was energetic in its concern for Indian affairs. It saw at once the strategic necessity of drawing the Indian Territory into its camp and the need to act expeditiously before the withdrawn federal troops could be replaced by volunteers, who might shore up any sagging Union sentiment among the Indians. In May the provisional Congress passed an act for the protection of the Indian tribes, under which Albert Pike was appointed special agent for negotiating treaties with the Indians. A native of New England, Pike had become a prominent lawyer in Arkansas; he had also gained military experience in the Mexican War, and he was even a poet of some renown. He was an excellent choice for dealing with the Indians, for he respected their rights and was generous in the guarantees he wrote into the treaties he signed with them.

Pike failed in his first attempt to persuade John Ross to align the Cherokee Nation with the Confederacy, but he passed on to quick success with the other tribes. The Creeks signed a treaty on July 10, 1861, the Choctaws on July 12, and the Seminoles on August 1. All these treaties transferred allegiance and loyalty from the Union to the Confederacy, and the tribes agreed to offensive and defensive alliances with the South. The treaties recognized the existing territorial limits of the tribes, and they guaranteed fee simple ownership of the lands within the boundaries. The lands were never to be included in any state or territory, nor would a tribe, without its consent, be organized as a territory or state. In many respects the treaties were the same as the earlier treaties with the United States, but the new treaties were more generous to the tribes, and the tone was one of conciliation rather than dictation, for Pike promised the Indians many things that they had been contending for with the United States. The Indians were allowed more control of their trade, property rights in slaves were guaranteed, and financial benefits were promised.

Pike moved on from his success with these major tribes, which he treated with great solicitude, to negotiate with the lesser tribes in the Indian Territory, which received few concessions. Two treaties, signed on August 12 with the Wichita and Comanches tribes, were primarily treaties of peace and of promoting civilization, in large part to satisfy the citizens of Texas, who were ravaged by Indian raids. They contained little if anything to distinguish them from treaties made by the United States with the western tribes except, of course, that the Indians placed themselves "under the laws and protection of the Confederate States of America."

The Cherokees were still outside the southern fold, but as Pike was negotiating in the west, John Ross threw in his lot with the Confederacy. This was a surprising move, for Ross had formally declared his neutrality and his intention of holding firm to his treaty relationship with the United States. But there were strong forces undermining Ross's position of neutrality. The factionalism of the Cherokees was revived. The old treaty party, now led by Stand Watie and his nephew Elias C. Boudinot and supported by many half-bloods, among whom most of the slave-owners were found, were sympathetic to the southern cause. Ross's great dream of unity in the Cherokee Nation might be shattered if a North-South split grew, and he could lose his position of leadership if the Confederacy chose to deal with Watie, as indeed Pike hinted in June that it might do. Unionist Indian agents and northern missionaries had departed, and the treaties Pike had made with the other tribes still further undercut Ross. The attractive offers made by Pike no doubt also played a part, for the Confederate agent was promising things that Ross had sought for years to obtain from the federal government without success.

The treaty with the Cherokees was signed on October 7. It was similar to those with the other Five Civilized Tribes and included the promises made by Pike: Cherokee Nation control over its lands, the right to incorporate other tribes into the nation, rights of self-government, control over the appointment of agents, a Cherokee court, a delegate in the House of Representatives, and provision for sale of the Neutral Lands, which the Cherokees owned in Kansas. As a kind of anticlimax, the Cherokee Council on October 31 adopted a declaration of independence, written by Pike, that stated the reasons for joining the Confederacy and declared the Cherokees a "free people, independent of the Northern States of America and at war with them by their own act."

The Confederacy successfully recruited and organized military units among the Indians, but this could not hide the division within some of the tribes between northern and southern factions. The Choctaws and Chickasaws were strong supporters of the South, but the Cherokees and the Creeks were seriously rent by the tenacity of Union factions. The full-blood Cherokees of the Ross party had joined the South without enthusiasm under the press of circumstances, and latent Union sentiment came to the surface whenever conditions seemed promising. Among the Creeks large numbers led by Opothleyohola resisted attempts to force them into the southern camp and fled as refugees into Kansas, where similar discontented refugees from other tribes joined them. These Indians crowded across the border in a state of destitution, for which there seemed to be no remedy.

At length the Indian Office moved to provide aid. Commissioner of Indian Affairs William P. Dole went to Kansas in late January 1862 and purchased supplies on credit for the Indians. Congress sustained that action and on July 5 provided that the annuities of the hostile Indians in the Indian Territory should be applied for the relief of the refugees. The solution of the refugee problem, however, was not relief, but return of the Indians to their homes in the Indian Territory and protection of them there.

When at length a Union expedition moved south from Kansas in June, the Confederate Indian forces were in sad disarray. The advancing army moved easily into Tahlequah, the Cherokee capital. John Ross, arrested by the army, went north to Kansas with his family and other Cherokee refugees and then on to Washington and Philadelphia, where he waited out the war. During the late summer and fall the Union forces generally routed the Confederates they met, and large numbers of Indians deserted to the Union side. Only Stand Watie's soldiers seemed to hold together.

The last years of the war were disastrous for the Indian Territory. Guerrilla warfare caused widespread destruction, and political disorganization resulted in corruption and exploitation. The ground gained by the Five Civilized Tribes, as they had developed economically and socially in the Indian country between removal and the Civil War, was lost. The physical destruction was enormous, and the factionalism and political upheaval were equally demoralizing. The Indians were considered by many northerners to have lost all rights by their adherence to the Confederacy. But the Confederacy, which had made such grand promises of protection and financial benefits, had been unable to live up to those promises. When the war ended, mammoth problems of reconstruction faced the Indian Territory.

RECONSTRUCTION TREATIES

The United States government intended to deal strongly with the tribes that had joined the Confederacy. The Indians had thrown over their treaty obligations and concluded formal alliances with the South, and many of them had fought tenaciously for the Confederate cause. Stand Watie was the last Confederate general to surrender.

In September 1865 the United States called the tribal leaders to a conference at Fort Smith, Arkansas. There the Indians met with a special commission headed by Dennis N. Cooley, whom Andrew Johnson had appointed commissioner of Indian affairs in July. The goal of the commission was well summarized in a telegraph from Secretary of the Interior James Harlan to Cooley en route to Fort Smith: "The President is willing to grant them peace; but wants land for other Indians, and a civil government for the whole Territory." At the conference Cooley outlined for the Indians in seven points the stipulations that were to be included in the treaties.

1. Each tribe must enter into a treaty for the permanent peace and amity with themselves, each nation and tribe, and with the United States.

2. Those settled in the Indian territory must bind themselves, when called upon by the government, to aid in compelling the Indians of the plains to maintain peaceful relations with each other, with the Indians in the territory, and with the United States.

3. The institution of slavery, which has existed among several of the tribes, must be forthwith abolished, and measures taken for the unconditional emancipation of all persons held in bondage, and for their incorporation into the tribes on an equal footing with the original members, or suitably provided for.

4. A stipulation in the treaties that slavery, or involuntary servitude, shall never exist in the tribe or nation, except in punishment of crime.

5. A portion of the lands hitherto owned and occupied by you must be set apart for the friendly tribes in Kansas and elsewhere, on such terms as may be agreed upon by the parties and approved by government, or such as may be fixed by the government.

6. It is the policy of the government, unless other arrangement be made, that all the nations and tribes in the Indian territory be formed into one consolidated government after the plan proposed by the Senate of the United States, in a bill for organizing the Indian territory.

7. No white person, except officers, agents, and employees of the government, or of any internal improvement authorized by the government, will be permitted to reside in the territory, unless formally incorporated with some tribe, according to the usages of the band.

The Indian delegates were strongly opposed to some of the points Cooley proposed. They were hesitant about incorporating the blacks into their nations, and they were especially hostile to the scheme of a territorial govern-

MAP 5: The Indian Territory, 1866–1888

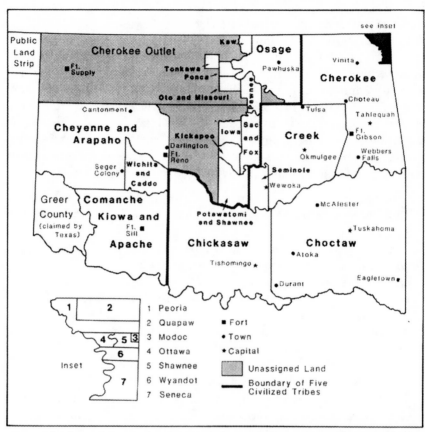

ment. The best that Cooley's commission could accomplish at Fort Smith was an agreement of amity between the tribes and the United States. In it the Indians acknowledged once more that they were under the exclusive jurisdiction of the United States, and they canceled and repudiated the treaties they had made with the Confederacy. In its turn the United States promised peace and friendship and renewed protection of the tribes.

The Fort Smith council adjourned on September 21, to meet again at the call of the secretary of the interior. In Washington in the spring and early summer of 1866 the representatives of the Five Civilized Tribes met to sign new treaties with the United States. The treaties had common provisions and built upon the points laid out by Cooley at Fort Smith, but considerable modifications were made to meet the protestations of the Indians. The tribes gave up sections of their land to make homes for Indians to be removed from Kansas and elsewhere; slaves were emancipated and slavery forever prohibited, and provisions were made for the freedmen; stipulations were included for a general council of all the tribes in the Indian Territory (looking toward territorial government, but for the present stopping short of it); and rights of way for railroads were provided for. The Seminoles gave up their entire territory and accepted a new region to the east. The Choctaws and Chickasaws sold their interests in the Leased District to the United States, and the Creek land was cut in two. But the Cherokees, although they sold the Neutral Lands and the Cherokee Strip and gave the United States an option on the Cherokee Outlet, lost none of their lands; they agreed, however, to admit other Indians to their territories west of the ninety-eighth meridian.

The Civil War was a crucial experience in the history of the southern Indians. Even though they could argue that their attachment to the Confederacy was the result of abandonment by the Union and duress from the Confederate government, it placed them in the position of conquered foes at the end of the war. Northern sentiment in the post–Civil War years, even among notable friends of the Indians, never quite shook off the conviction that the treaty rights of the Indians had been destroyed by the tribes' defection.

A SERIES OF OTHER WARS

The Civil War was accompanied by military engagements that the United States government was forced to fight concurrently—wars with the Sioux in Minnesota and Dakota, with the Apaches and Navajos in Arizona and New Mexico, and with the Cheyennes, Arapahos, Kiowas, and Comanches in Kansas and eastern Colorado. Unlike the action of the southern tribes in the Indian Territory, which was an inextricable part of the Civil War, the Indian wars in the north and west were only indirectly related to the main event. They nevertheless put an additional strain on the resources of the Lincoln administration and were significant events in the history of the government's relations with the Indian tribes.

On August 18, 1862, without warning, the Sioux Indians of Minnesota rose up in fury against the white settlers. This was an outbreak of peculiar violence, and it tested severely the Indian policy of the federal government.

Minnesota was the homeland of important Indians: in the north bands of Chippewas (Ojibwas) and in the south the Santee Sioux (Mdewakanton, Sisseton, Wahpeton, and Wahpekute bands). In 1851 the United States had made treaties with the Sioux, by which the bands gave up most of their land in Minnesota in return for small reservations along the Minnesota River and annuities in cash and goods. The treaties were "civilizing" treaties, for the reservations were intended to be the site of increased agricultural development for the Indians.

As the Indians moved to the reservations in 1853 and 1854, agency buildings were erected at both the Upper Sioux Agency and the Lower

Sioux Agency, and the agent divided his time between them. Here the successive agents, aided by Christian missionaries, worked to change the Indians into white farmers. Then in 1858 new treaties further restricted the reservations, as the lands lying north of the Minnesota River were ceded to the United States. These treaties provided for the allotment of eighty acres to heads of families and to single individuals over twenty-one. The secretary of the interior, moreover, was given discretionary power over expenditure of the annuities, to use them in a way "best calculated to promote their interests, welfare, and advance in civilization."

Although there were encouraging reports of success in the civilization program, there was in fact a deep division among the Sioux and growing hostility between the "farmer" Indians and the "blanket" Indians, who intended to keep their old ways. Persecution of the agriculturalists by the traditional party made it difficult for the former to adhere to the programs of the agents and the missionaries. Conditions were becoming ripe for an explosion.

The Indians had specific grievances. The Great Father's promises in the treaty negotiations had never fully materialized, for the sums listed were drained away to pay traders' debts, and the Indians were further irritated by the attempts to substitute goods for money payments. The Civil War, too, had a decided effect. Withdrawal of regular troops was not unnoticed by the Indians. Although the men were replaced in part by Minnesota volunteers, the number of companies was cut in half and the new soldiers were inexperienced. The Sioux were restless, and there were rumors that the war would put an end altogether to the money coming from the federal government. Many men at the time also suspected machinations of Confederate agents among the Indians.

In 1862 there was unreasonable delay in the annuity payments. This would have remained only an irritation, no doubt, had not the Indians come to depend so heavily on the annuities. Because of bad crops they were in a state of near starvation. The agent and the missionaries made some moves to provide subsistence for the tribes, but at the time of the uprising many of the Indians were desperate.

The outbreak began with a simple enough event. On August 17, for inconsequential reasons and without premeditation, four Indians killed five whites settlers in Acton Township. The Indians knew that the rash action would bring retaliation by the whites, and the chiefs debated about what course to pursue. In the end they decided for war. Led by Little Crow, the Indians stormed the Lower Agency in a surprise attack. The outbreak spread rapidly, as the Indians decimated the outlying settlements and attacked Fort Ridgely and the town of New Ulm.

The state of Minnesota and the United States reacted quickly to the outbreak. On August 19 Governor Alexander Ramsey placed Henry Hastings

Sibley in command of a relief expedition; Sibley, with hastily gathered militia and volunteers, moved against the Indians. Lincoln created a Department of the Northwest and sent General John Pope to command it. The general arrived in St. Paul on September 16 and immediately took a hard line toward the Indians. "It is my purpose utterly to exterminate the Sioux if I have the power to do so," he wrote to Sibley, "and even if it requires a campaign lasting the whole of next year. Destroy everything belonging to them and force them out to the plains, unless, as I suggest, you can capture them. They are to be treated as maniacs or wild beasts, and by no means as people with whom treaties or compromises can be made."

The Indians, although they had the initial advantage of surprise, were in the end no match for the forces of Sibley and Pope. A decisive victory by Sibley at Wood Lake on September 23 was the end of organized fighting by the Sioux in Minnesota. Indians who remained hostile fled west, and friendly chiefs arranged for the release of white captives. Large numbers of Sioux were captured or surrendered, and day by day more Indians, many of them on the point of starvation, gave themselves up.

Cries of vengeance filled the air, and a five-man military commission was quickly appointed to try the captive Indians. The commission worked with great haste; in ten days it tried 392 prisoners, condemning 303 to death. Pope and Sibley wanted the condemned men executed at once, and they telegraphed the names to Lincoln for confirmation of the sentences. Lincoln would not move so precipitously and directed that the full records of the trials be sent to him for review. It was not an easy question for Lincoln. He decided finally to uphold the sentence of death for only thirty-nine of the convicted men, and on December 6 he sent Sibley their names. One of the thirty-nine men was reprieved at the last minute; the thirty-eight were hanged at Mankato, Minnesota, in a spectacle attended by a large crowd on December 26, 1862.

Mass execution was not the only thing Minnesotans wanted. They demanded the total removal of the Sioux from the state, and the Lincoln administration acquiesced. On March 3, 1863, Congress authorized the removal of the Sioux from Minnesota, requiring that they be located outside the limits of any existing state. In May and June 1863 the Sioux who had been encamped at Fort Snelling in the wake of the uprising were loaded on steamboats for the long journey down the Mississippi and up the Missouri to their new reservation at Crow Creek in Dakota Territory. It was a miserable, barren spot, and after three years the Sioux were moved to a new and better reservation at the mouth of the Niobrara River in Nebraska.

The Sioux who fled Minnesota in 1862 were not quickly pacified. They roamed the Dakota prairies and found some support among the Yankton and Yanktonai Indians. General Pope feared a new attack by these Indians on the Minnesota frontier, and he mounted a punitive expedition into Dakota Territory against them. In 1863 General Sibley moved west from Minnesota, while General Alfred Sully proceeded up the Missouri. They scattered the Indians they met, but the expeditions settled nothing. In 1864 Sully led another expedition into Dakota, where he was joined by Minnesota forces. In the Battle of Killdeer Mountain on July 28, 1864, the Sioux were defeated. Military posts were established along the Missouri, and the Indian raids gradually ceased.

In the Southwest, a Confederate invasion of the Rio Grande Valley was driven back by Colorado volunteers under Major John M. Chivington at Glorieta Pass on March 28, 1862. The Civil War years in Arizona and New Mexico were then filled with military action of Union forces against hostile Indians. The key figure was Brigadier General James H. Carleton, who arrived on the Rio Grande in August 1862 with a column of California volunteers. A man of ability and zeal, he was also arrogant and arbitrary, and he stubbornly pushed for the fulfillment of his vision of what New Mexico needed.

With the Confederate threat removed, Carleton turned his attention to subduing the Indians. Joining with an old associate, Colonel Christopher (Kit) Carson of the New Mexico cavalry, he set out to accomplish his objective: to end once and for all the depredations of the Apaches and the Navajos. To do this Carleton intended to adopt the guerrilla tactics of the Indians themselves. He intended to make no treaties short of total surrender and when subjugation was achieved to move the Indians to an isolated reservation away from all contact with the white inhabitants of the territory, where they could be supported by the government until they could be transformed into agriculturalists and enlightened by teachers and Christian missionaries.

Carleton turned first to the Mescalero Apaches in south central New Mexico. These Indians had been subdued in the mid-1850s, and Fort Stanton had been erected on the Rio Bonito in May 1855. But when the post was abandoned in the face of Confederate attack in 1861, the Apaches began to prey upon the white settlers. The general moved vigorously. He ordered Carson to reactivate Fort Stanton and directed the officers to kill the Indian men and capture the women and children and to hold no council of peace with them. The troops kept up incessant pressure on the Apaches, and in November the chiefs appeared with the agent at Santa Fe to make peace.

BOSQUE REDONDO

At Santa Fe Carleton revealed to the Indians what he had in store for them. He had established a new military post (Fort Sumner) on the Pecos River in eastern New Mexico at a spot called Bosque Redondo, after the round grove of cottonwoods there. The Indians who wanted peace were to move to the Bosque Redondo and take up a life of agriculture; the government would provide their subsistence and protect them until they could raise crops for themselves. By the end of March 1863 more than four hundred Apaches— the great bulk of the tribe—were at Fort Sumner.

Carleton next gave his attention to the Navajos, a far more numerous tribe with an estimated ten thousand people. His plan for them, however, was the same as for the Apaches: to subdue the hostile elements of the tribe and move all to some distant reservation. Carleton soon decided that the Navajos as well as the Apaches were to settle at the Bosque Redondo. On June 15, 1863, he ordered Kit Carson to move into the Navajo country and "to prosecute a vigorous war upon the men of this tribe until it is considered at these Head Quarters that they have been effectually punished for their long continued atrocities." The army was to have only one message for the Indians: "Go to Bosque Redondo, or we will pursue and destroy you. We will not make peace with you on any other terms."

As winter set in, Carleton planned an attack into the Canyon de Chelly, the final citadel of the Navajos. The Indians could not withstand the insistent attacks and the destruction of their crops, orchards, and livestock. After the invasion, they surrendered in large numbers, for they faced starvation and had lost all hope of turning back the determined white soldiers. By mid-March six thousand had come in. They were transported across New Mexico to the reservation on the Pecos in a Long Walk that recalled the Cherokees' Trail of Tears more than a quarter-century before. By the end of 1864, three-fourths of the total tribe—some eight thousand people— were at the Bosque Redondo. The remainder, refusing to surrender, fled westward to the deserts, out of contact with the settlements.

Carleton was now ready to begin the massive experiment in Indian transformation that he had planned for the Bosque Redondo. There was much in favor of his dream of building a model reservation there. The site was distant enough from the concentrations of white settlement to prevent contact between the two races, and the open plains in which it was located made it difficult for Indians to flee unnoticed. The land along the Pecos was suitable for irrigated farming, and Carleton estimated that enough food could be grown to feed the large number of Indians. He was sanguine about the possibilities, and he looked ahead ten years to see the Navajos as the "happiest and most delightfully located pueblo of Indians in New Mexico—perhaps in the United States."

Carleton had a number of strong supporters, but from the start weaknesses in the scheme began to appear, and outspoken critics condemned the operation. There were, in fact, serious problems on the reservation.

The Navajos, used to a largely pastoral existence, objected to being cooped up on farms, with no provisions for extensive flocks and herds. They objected to Carleton's plans to have them live in concentrated villages, when they were used to smaller and more mobile units of habitation. But it was the forces of a harsh nature that ultimately destroyed the Bosque Redondo experiment, for year after year the crops failed, destroyed by insects or drought. Goods supplied by the government were never adequate, and reduced rations were frequently the lot of the Indians. The Navajos were destitute, demoralized, and weakened by disease—far from the happy farmers that Carleton had predicted. Nor was the general able to develop his plans for education. The reservation life, moreover, did not bring an end to Indian raiding in New Mexico, for dissident Apaches and Navajos still struck the settlements, and as conditions worsened at the Bosque Redondo, members of both tribes slipped away to join in the depredations.

So the great experiment failed. New crop disasters precluded cutting the tremendous costs of maintaining the reservation Indians, and the dissatisfaction of the Navajos increased. In December 1866 General Ulysses S. Grant instructed the commander of the Department of the Missouri to turn over the Navajos, "now held as prisoners" at the Bosque Redondo, to the Indian Office, but it was ten months before the actual transfer was accomplished. The Indian Office, unfortunately, was even less prepared financially than the War Department to continue the operation, and it announced at the end of 1867 that it was prepared to take care of the Indians at the Bosque Redondo for only three months and then additional appropriations would be necessary.

Congress authorized a Peace Commission in 1867, which, although mainly concerned with the hostile tribes on the southern and northern plains, also turned its attention to the Navajos. General William T. Sherman and Samuel Tappan, members of the commission who were sent to the Bosque Redondo, met with the Indians in late May 1868 and heard from them about the terrible conditions on the reservation and their earnest desire to return home. They could see for themselves the tragedy of the enforced stay at Fort Sumner, and on June 1 they signed a treaty with the Navajo chiefs providing for the Indians' return west. Boundaries were set for a reservation there; $150,000 was provided for removal and for the purchase of livestock; and all the customary stipulations for advancing the Indians in civilization were included.

There was little problem in the return trip of the Navajos to their old lands, for they were eager to go, and they rejoiced as they saw the familiar landmarks. But it was not a simple return to the past, for the years at the Bosque Redondo left an indelible mark on the tribe. The Indians' clothing and housing had been influenced by the close contact with whites on the reservation, and a new sense of tribal unity had been fostered. More fundamentally, the Navajos put behind them their longtime raiding and depredations and settled on the reservation to work out their future. There was never again a Navajo war.

SAND CREEK

When the Indians in Minnesota rose up against the white settlers in 1862, there was great consternation, for whites feared a widespread conspiracy among the Indians to attack all along the frontier while the nation was engaged in the great struggle of the Civil War. There were, in fact, scattered raids along the emigrant and mail routes crossing the plains, and the general restlessness among the Sioux, Cheyennes, and Arapahos worried the Indian Office and the War Department and unnerved the territorial officials in the West, even though there was no general uprising.

In 1861, at Fort Wise on the upper Arkansas, peaceful chiefs, including Black Kettle and White Antelope of the Cheyennes and Little Raven of the Arapahos, had agreed to give up the lands assigned them in the Treaty of Fort Laramie of 1851 and accept a reservation along the Arkansas. But most of the Indians continued to rely on hunting the buffalo that still roamed between the Platte and the Arkansas. Governor John Evans of Colorado Territory expected and planned for war. In his aggressive policy he was eagerly joined by the military commander of the District of Colorado, Colonel John M. Chivington, the hero of Glorieta Pass. Chivington, a Methodist minister turned soldier and politician, enjoyed unusual autonomy while his superiors were occupied with the Civil War.

The Civil War did not seriously interrupt the great migration of people to the West. The explosion of the mining frontier that followed the strikes in Colorado in 1858 continued unabated and largely unconcerned with the dramatic events taking place in the East. Stage and freight lines moved west across Kansas, and the burgeoning traffic of men and materials continued to cut sharply into the hunting grounds of the Indians, who reacted with sporadic raids on stations and settlements. Although the raids were often isolated and of limited destruction, the depredations over a wide area made it difficult to separate hostile Indians from peaceful ones. It was enough to alarm the Colorado settlements to the point of panic, and Evans and Chivington urged military action to crush the offending Indians and restore security to the territory.

One group of Cheyennes under Black Kettle and White Antelope, joined by a small number of Arapahos, wanted peace with the whites. They turned in their arms at Fort Lyon (the former Fort Wise) and moved north to a camp along Sand Creek. There on the morning of November 28, 1864, they were attacked without warning by Colonel Chivington with troops of the First Colorado Cavalry and one-hundred-day enlistees of the Third Colorado Cavalry. Black Kettle raised an American flag and a white flag before his tent to indicate the peaceful nature of the camp, and White Antelope stood with his arms folded in a peaceful gesture as the whites advanced, but to no avail. The soldiers slaughtered the defenseless Indians in a most brutal manner, killing men, women, and children indiscriminately and mutilating in revolting fashion the bodies of those who fell. Black Kettle and others escaped, but about one hundred and fifty Indians, including White Antelope, were killed in this Sand Creek Massacre.

The atrocities at Sand Creek were celebrated with jubilation in Denver, where the returning volunteers were cheered in the streets and in the theaters as they displayed the grisly trophies of the campaign. But the savage treatment of the peaceful Indians brought nothing but revulsion and outcry in the East. There was no dearth of information, for three formal investigations of the event collected extensive testimony and spread it before the public in official reports. Here was a barbaric affair that sickened those who had hoped for Christian treatment of the Indians.

The voluminous hearings furnished tremendous ammunition for those who were aghast at the government's handling of Indian affairs and wanted immediate reform. No matter that the testimony on Sand Creek was often contradictory, that evidence was admitted without any critical norms, and that the investigators made no claim to objectivity. No matter that the attack was undertaken by local troops and was not the result of official United States policy or plans. The Sand Creek Massacre became a never-to-be-forgotten symbol of what was wrong with United States treatment of the Indians, which reformers would never let fade away and which critics today still hold up to view. Sand Creek intensified Indian hostilities on the plains if it did not, indeed, set off new Indian warfare. Black Kettle and others who escaped were aided by the Northern Cheyennes and Arapahos and by the Comanches and Kiowas, and the Indians fought off the troops sent out to quiet them. The army planned an extensive campaign, but humanitarian outcries over Sand Creek and the desire of the Indians themselves for peace led to negotiations. A United States commission met with chiefs of the Cheyennes and Arapahos, Comanches, Kiowas, and Kiowa-Apaches on the Little Arkansas River. On October 14, 1865, the Cheyennes and Arapahos present signed a treaty in which they agreed to give up their lands in Colorado and accept a reservation that lay partly in Kansas and partly in the Indian Territory. Although they were permitted to range over their old lands, they agreed not to disturb the roads, military posts, and towns of the whites. The government agreed to pay annuities for forty years. Three days later a similar agreement was concluded with the Kiowa-Apaches, and on the following day one with the Comanches and Kiowas, who were to get a reservation in the Indian Territory and in the panhandle of Texas. The treaties, although they brought a temporary peace, did not solve the problem because the reservations to be established never materialized. The control of Texas over its lands nullified the agreement with the Comanches and Kiowas, and Kansas refused to allow a reservation within its boundaries.

At the end of the Civil War, when full attention could once more be directed to Indians problems, the nation was ready for a major overhaul of Indian policy.

CHAPTER 10

The Peace Policy

The Civil War was an economic conflict between competing agrarian and industrial societies and a great nationalistic drive on the part of the North to crush rising southern nationalism and thus preserve the Union. But it was also a great Christian crusade, a moral mandate fulfilled, a wiping away of the hideous blot of sinful slavery from the conscience of the nation. The war, despite the carnage and destruction, was, in the minds of many, America's finest hour. It reinforced the evangelical aspirations and sentiments of the nation, touching many with a new revivalist ardor that could not be suddenly cooled by Appomattox.

The end of the Civil War freed new energies, and America embarked upon expansion and development of a scope that few in antebellum days would have thought possible. Northern industry, stimulated by the war and encouraged by sympathetic and benevolent legislators, absorbed the energies and talents of many men, and the exuberance that came when the crushing burden of war was removed covered over the traumas of that past event. Exploitation of land and mineral resources moved at new speeds, and transcontinental railroads, rapidly becoming a reality, tied the nation together in new unity.

Evangelical reformism thrived in this new and ebullient atmosphere, for evils still abounded that reforming spirits could not ignore. One of the most obvious and pressing at war's end was the condition of the Indians, now made manifest as never before. Even before the war had run its course, the trail of post–Civil War Indian reform had begun, for the massacre at Sand Creek in November 1864 became a popular symbol of what was wrong in the Indian service, and a great humanitarian outcry was the result.

The formal answer to the demands for reform came in the administration of Ulysses S. Grant. It has been called "Grant's peace policy," but the principles it embodied antedated 1869 and continued to the end of the century and beyond. The peace policy was almost as many-faceted as the Indian problem it hoped to solve. Basically it was a state of mind, a determination that since the old ways of dealing with the Indians had not succeeded, a new emphasis on kindness and justice was in order.

An official description of the policy in its early days appeared in a statement in 1873 by Grant's secretary of the interior, Columbus Delano, that listed the aims and purposes of the administration's policy. In the first place, Delano noted, the policy aimed to place the Indians on reservations. There they could be kept from contact with frontier settlements and could be taught the arts of agriculture and other pursuits of civilization through the aid of Christian organizations cooperating with the federal government, and there "humanity and kindness may take the place of barbarity and cruelty." Second, the policy sought to combine with such humane treatment of the Indians "all needed severity, to punish them for their outrages according to their merits, thereby teaching them that it is better to follow the advice of the Government, live upon reservations and become civilized, than to continue their native habits and practices." Third, it meant a determination to see that the supplies furnished to the Indians were of high quality and reasonably priced so that funds appropriated for the Indians would not be squandered. Fourth, through the aid of religious organizations, it aimed to procure "competent, upright, faithful, moral, and religious" agents to distribute the goods and to aid in uplifting the Indians' culture. Finally, "through the instrumentality of the Christian organizations, acting in harmony with the Government," it intended to provide churches and schools that would lead the Indians to understand and appreciate "the comforts and benefits of a Christian civilization and thus be prepared ultimately to assume the duties and privileges of citizenship."

Underlying this new departure in Indian policy was the conscious intent of the government to turn to religious groups and religion-minded men for the formulation and administration of Indian policy. The peace policy might just as properly have been labeled the religious policy. Building on the long history of close relations between the federal government and missionary groups in Indian matters, the nation now went far beyond simple cooperation of church and state in educational and religious activities. It welcomed official church societies and church-related individuals into fuller partnership; and to a large extent these groups came to dominate official government policy and administration of Indian affairs, at first by direct participation, then by stirring up and channeling public opinion. In turning to religious organizations, the federal government abdicated much of its responsibility. Specific governmental functions were handed over to the churches, a development that indicated not only the failure of the governmental processes in regard to the "Indian question" but also the pervasive moral and religious influences on the national outlook.

The soil for the seeds of reform was prepared by formal investigations of evil conditions in the West. The first of these was made by the Joint Special Committee created by Congress on March 3, 1865, "to inquire into the present condition of the Indian tribes, and especially into the manner in which they are treated by the civil and military authorities of the United States." The committee, composed of three senators and four represen-tatives, was chaired by Senator James R. Doolittle and is commonly called the Doolittle Committee. The committee toured the West to investigate conditions among the Indians and sent a detailed questionnaire to military commanders, Indian agents, and others acquainted with the West asking about causes of the deterioration of the Indians, the best forms of land ten-ure, the effects of schools and missions, the use of annuities, and whether the Indian Office should be transferred to the War Department. The volu-minous answers were attached to the committee's report, which, after long delay, was submitted on January 26, 1867. The committee noted that, ex-cept for the tribes in the Indian Territory, the Indian population was rapidly declining as the result of disease, intemperance, war, and the pressure of white settlement. The wars, it asserted, came in large part because of "the aggression of lawless whites." Viewing the loss of Indian hunting grounds as an important cause of decay, it spoke of the powerful effect of the rail-roads on the destruction of the buffalo.

The importance of the Doolittle Committee lay, not in immediate legis-lation, but in the effect its report had upon the Christian conscience of re-form-minded humanitarians in the East. Its bulky appendix was full of charges of fraud and corruption indicating the need for a new policy. The statements were inconsistent, the charges often unsubstantiated, and the facts many times in error. The large volume hardly presented an accurate picture of the "condition of the Indian tribes," but no matter, for it fur-nished ammunition for those seeking a change.

Even while the Doolittle Committee was formulating its report, re-newed warfare in the West drove home the need for some better Indian pol-icy. War broke out along the Bozeman Trail, which had been built through the Powder River hunting grounds of the Sioux to link the new mining re-gions of Montana with the Oregon Trail near Fort Laramie. The state of siege in which the Indians held the military posts established in 1865 and 1866 to protect the miners' wagon trains caused apprehension, but few saw it as a prelude to white defeat. Then on December 21, 1866, a rash lieuten-ant, William Fetterman, ignoring the admonitions of his superiors not to go beyond the protective range of Fort Phil Kearny, was ambushed by the Indians. He and his command of eighty men were wiped out, and the Fetterman Massacre made clear in the East the seriousness of the Indian situation in the West. A special committee appointed to investigate the disaster reinforced the conclusions of the Doolittle Committee.

The central plains, too, were on fire, and the news of the Fetterman ambush and of parties raiding into Texas brought near panic. To prevent what he believed would be a major outbreak in the spring of 1867, General Winfield Scott Hancock moved to overawe the Indians by striking at a Cheyenne village. The action only stirred up the Indians more, and the peace of the spring turned into war as the hostile Indians terrorized the regions on both sides of the Platte.

To meet the crisis, Congress created the United States Indian Peace Commission. The purpose was to take the business of negotiating with the Indians out of the hands of the executive and give it instead to a special group of civilian and military leaders with interest and competence in Indian affairs. The act of June 20, 1867, set the commission's tasks in unmistakable language. The body had authority to call together the chiefs of the warring tribes, find the causes of hostility, and negotiate treaties that would "remove all just causes of complaint on their part, and at the same time establish security for person and property along the lines of the railroad now being constructed to the Pacific and other thoroughfares of travel to the western Territories, and such as will most likely insure civilization for the Indians and peace and safety for the whites." For Indians who did not then occupy reservations under treaty agreements, the commissioners were to select reservations that would become their permanent homes. But there was an iron hand in this velvet glove: if the commissioners failed to get the Indians to settle on reservations and thus secure peace, the secretary of war was authorized to call for volunteers for "the suppression of Indian hostilities."

The chairman of the commission was Nathaniel G. Taylor, who had been appointed commissioner of Indian affairs by President Johnson on March 26, 1867. Taylor was a man of deep religious sentiment who served for a time as a Methodist minister. He had strong views about Indian policy, which dominated his annual reports and the initial report of the Peace Commission; there was not the slightest doubt in his mind about either the obligation or the possibility of civilizing the Indians in a Christian pattern. The most important army officer on the commission was General William T. Sherman, commander of the Division of the Missouri, who had overall responsibility for peace on the frontier. A reasonable mixture of military firmness and humanitarian leniency, the commission boded well for a successful move toward peace.

The Peace Commission went right to work. At Medicine Lodge Creek in southern Kansas in October 1867 it signed treaties with the Cheyennes,

Arapahos, Kiowas, Comanches, and Kiowa-Apaches that assigned the Indians to two reservations in the western part of the Indian Territory, where the United States would furnish rations and other goods needed to turn them into happy farmers. There was less success in the north, for Red Cloud refused to come in to Fort Laramie, declaring that he would not consider peace until the military forts along the Bozeman Trail were removed. The commission decided on a new council in the spring and adjourned.

On January 7, 1868, the commission submitted its first report, which was clearly from Taylor's hand although it was signed by all the members. The report was a jeremiad, a denunciatory tirade against the evils in the Indian system. It found that an Indian sought to gain all his ends by war, the only means he knew. "If he fails to see the olive-branch or flag of truce in the hands of the peace commissioner and in savage ferocity adds one more to his victims, we should remember that for two and a half centuries he has been driven back from civilization, where his passions might have been subjected to the influence of education and softened by the lessons of Christian charity." In councils with the Indians the commission inaugurated "the hitherto untried policy in connection with Indians, of endeavoring to conquer by kindness."

The evangelical sentiment that suffused the report is seen best in the goal for the Indians that it proposed. The Indians must accept the civilization of the whites. To transform the Indians, to break down the antipathy of race, the commission set forth its recommendations: districts in the West set aside for the Indians, organized as territories, where agriculture and domestic manufactures should be introduced as rapidly as possible; schools to teach the children English; courts and other institutions of government; farmers and mechanics sent to instruct the Indians; and missionary and benevolent societies invited to "this field of philanthropy nearer home."

Settlement with the northern tribes came at Fort Laramie in 1868. The way had been prepared by the government's willingness to withdraw its posts from the Powder River country, for as the Union Pacific moved westward, it would soon be possible to supply a new route to Montana west of the Big Horn Mountains. Little by little the tribes came in. A treaty was signed with the Brule Sioux on April 29, with the Crows on May 7, and with the Northern Cheyennes and Northern Arapahos on May 10. But the other bands of Sioux appeared only slowly to affix their signatures to the treaty. The offending forts were dismantled and burned during the summer, and Red Cloud finally signed the treaty in November. The treaty set aside the Great Sioux Reserve west of the Missouri River in Dakota, and the chiefs agreed to settle at the agencies and accept reservation life.

The treaties were political documents of significance, for they declared that war between the tribes and the United States would "forever cease" and that peace between the parties would "forever continue," made arrangements for the punishment of wrongdoers, and established reservations with well-defined boundaries on which the Indians agreed to reside. But they were also reformist documents aimed at attaining the humanitarian civilizing goals of the Peace Commission. They were intended to turn the nomadic warriors into peaceful farmers, and to educate their children in English schools, as the provisions for encouraging farming and for the building of schools clearly indicate.

The peace party could at first claim success, and for a time there were no serious disturbances. Then in August 1868 a group of Cheyennes with a few Arapahos and Sioux shattered the agreements made at Medicine Lodge Creek by an outbreak on the Saline and Solomon rivers in Kansas. Roving war parties killed and burned and raped on the frontiers of Kansas and Colorado. General Sherman and General Philip Sheridan decided on a winter campaign to drive the tribes to their reservations, and they determined to harry and kill those who refused to settle down, with none too great care in separating those who were actually hostile from those who hoped to remain at peace. Hostile Indians were pursued until most of them were defeated and returned to the reservations. But the reservations for many of the southern plains Indians were merely places to recoup their strength between raids.

The initial report of the Peace Commission and the continuing warfare on the plains both gave new impetus to reformers interested in the Indians—the report because it gave hope that the government would listen to men and women who promoted peace and justice, the warfare because it reemphasized the urgency to do something radical to end conditions that caused war.

Many persons of humanitarian and philanthropic bent turned to Indian reform once they had been awakened to the needs. One such response was the formation in 1868 of the United States Indian Commission in New York City under the instigation of Peter Cooper. The purpose of this collection of Protestant ministers and other benevolent gentlemen was "to array on the side of justice and humanity the influence and support of an enlightened public opinion, in order to secure for the Indians that treatment which, in their position, we should demand for ourselves." These men condemned the failure of the government to fulfill its treaty obligations, the outrages upon Indians by white citizens and soldiers (especially Sand Creek), the degradation and deterioration of the Indians by venereal disease brought in with military troops in Indian country, and the lack of honest and faithful Indian agents. Once the nation was informed about Indian wrongs, they thought, "their united voice will demand that the honor and the interests of the nation shall no longer be sacrificed to the insatiable lust and avarice of unscrupulous men."

Of all the groups concerned about a Christian approach to Indian policy, none was more symbolic (if not actually influential) than the Society of Friends, who from colonial days on showed an interest in just and humane treatment of the Indians. When disturbances on the frontier in the late 1860s attracted the attention of the nation, the Quakers did not fail to react. The conference of the Yearly Meetings of the Liberal Quakers (Hicksite) at Baltimore in 1868 sent a memorial to Congress praying "that the effusion of blood may cease, and that such just and humane measures may be pursued as will secure a lasting peace, and tend to the preservation and enlightenment of those afflicted people, whom we regard as the wards of the nation." The assembly urged "benevolent efforts to improve and enlighten the Indians" and that only persons "of high character and strict morality" be sent among them as agents. The next year, shortly after the release of the Peace Commission's report, these Quakers renewed their appeal to Congress for the Indians.

THE BOARD OF INDIAN COMMISSIONERS

By 1869 the Indians were in the forefront of reformers' minds. The drive to protect them from avarice and corruption and to draw them ultimately into the Christian civilization of the humanitarians gathered momentum as one group after another turned with new interest toward them. The first sign of a change came from President Grant himself, who in his inaugural address on March 4, 1869, declared: "The proper treatment of the original occupants of this land—the Indians—is one deserving of careful study. I will favor any course toward them which tends to their civilization and ultimate citizenship."

Encouraged by this clear sign of Grant's willingness to listen to Christian advocates, a group of Philadelphia philanthropists led by William Welsh determined to press for an independent commission to watch over Indian affairs, an idea that had frequently been recommended as a means of rectifying the corruption and attendant evils in the Indian service. Stimulated by Welsh's continuing efforts, Congress on April 10, 1869, authorized the president to "organize a board of Commissioners, to consist of not more than ten persons, to be selected by him from men eminent for their intelligence and philanthropy, to serve without pecuniary compensation," who under the president's direction should "exercise joint control with the Secretary of the Interior" over the disbursement of Indian appropriations.

The establishment of this Board of Indian Commissioners set post–Civil War Indian policy ever more firmly in the pattern of American evangelical revivalism, for the men appointed to the board were Christian gentlemen who had been caught up in the awakening represented best by the Young Men's Christian Association. The YMCA, first organized in the United States in 1851, was a laymen's group of interdenominational scope with a concern for pragmatic ethical action. During the Civil War its great work had been the United States Christian Commission, which was devoted to care for the religious needs of the Union troops. The Christian Commission was a voluntary, benevolent organization that worked closely with the government, and the idea of the Christian Commission and its work was much in the air when the Board of Indian Commissioners was conceived and set up. It was no coincidence that nearly all the board's first members had been important officials of the Christian Commission.

The relation of the board to the churches was not defined in the law, but it was obviously very close. Although the original members were not official representatives of their particular denominations, they all reflected the dominant Protestant character of American Christianity. And when new members were appointed after 1875, they asserted that they had been nominated by and therefore represented their particular churches. There were no Roman Catholics on the board, even though Catholics were heavily involved in Indian missionary work, and it seems reasonable to suppose that none would have been welcome.

The Board of Indian Commissioners entered upon its duties with energy and goodwill. It appointed a purchasing committee to cooperate with the government in purchasing supplies for the Indian department, and three of the members made an extensive trip to the Indian country during the summer. At the end of the year, the board submitted a long and outspoken report. The report was a powerful denunciation of past Indian relations and, although it admitted that recommendations should not be the "result of theorizing," a remarkably complete prospectus of policies and programs to come.

The righteous indignation of these Christian philanthropists pervaded the report. "Paradoxical as it may seem," they said, "the white man has been the chief obstacle in the way of Indian civilization. The benevolent measures attempted by the government for their advancement have been almost uniformly thwarted by the agencies employed to carry them out." The board members saw no inherent problem in the Indians themselves, who had been made suspicious, revengeful, and cruel by the treatment they had received from the whites. They denied that the Indians would not work and pointed to the example of the Five Civilized Tribes and the Yankton Sioux.

For men with little experience in Indian affairs, the members of the board confidently set forth preliminary recommendations for future dealings with the tribesmen. They urged that Indians be collected on small contiguous reservations making up a large unit that would eventually become a state of the Union. On the reservations the Indians should be given land in severalty, and tribal relations should be discouraged. They recommended the abandonment of the treaty system and the abrogation of existing treaties "as soon as any just method can be devised to accomplish it." Money annuities should cease, for they promoted idleness and vice. The board urged the establishment of schools to teach the children English and wanted teachers nominated by religious bodies. Christian missions should be encouraged and their schools fostered. "The religion of our blessed Saviour," they said, "is believed to be the most effective agent for the civilization of any people." They insisted upon an honest observation of treaty obligations, appointment of agents "with a view to their moral as well as business qualifications, and aside from any political consideration," and fair judicial proceedings for Indian criminals. "The legal status of the uncivilized Indians," they decided, "should be that of wards of the government; the duty of the latter being to protect them, to educate them in industry, the arts of civilization, and the principles of Christianity; elevate them to the rights of citizenship, and to sustain and clothe them until they can support themselves."

It was just the sort of platform one would expect from the Christian merchant princes who made up the Board of Indian Commissioners. Whether they were conscious of it or not, they intended to apply to the "uncivilized" Indians of the plains and mountains the same prescriptions made for more eastern Indians in antebellum days.

THE CHURCHES AND THE AGENCIES

The second component of Grant's peace policy was the apportionment of the Indian agencies among church groups, with the understanding that the missionary boards would nominate the agents and other employees at the agencies. By such an arrangement, it was hoped, the evils resulting from dishonest and incompetent agents would be obviated. This extreme measure, an admission by the government that it was unable to carry out its obligations by ordinary procedures, was a striking example of the conviction in public as well as private circles that only by emphasis on moral and religious means would the Indians be led along the path to civilization.

The postwar allotment of agencies to religious bodies began with the Quakers. On February 15, 1869, Ely S. Parker, then Grant's aide-de-camp, wrote to the secretary of the Quaker conference, asking for a list of Quakers whom the Society of Friends would endorse as suitable persons to be Indian agents. The Quakers, after some hesitation about accepting posts on the distant and exposed frontier, responded favorably, and by mid-June both the Orthodox and Hicksite Friends had appointed superintendents and agents and organized special committees to deal with Indian matters. The

Hicksite Friends were given the Northern Superintendency, comprising six agencies in Nebraska; the Orthodox Friends received the Central Superintendency, comprising the Indians in Kansas and the Kiowas, Comanches, and a number of other tribes in the Indian Territory.

For the other agencies Grant appointed army officers, a move that was not surprising in the light of the reduction of the army that had come in 1868. He did this for reasons of economy, since the officers otherwise would be on pay but not on duty; and they were thought to be a "corps of public servants whose integrity and faithfulness could be relied upon, and in whom the public were prepared to have confidence." But this solution to the problems of political patronage was soon upset, for Congress on July 15, 1870, forbade army officers to accept civil appointments. When the army agents were removed, it was a logical step to expand the Quaker system, to offer the agencies to other religious groups, who could be expected "to Christianize and civilize the Indian, and to train him in the arts of peace."

The difficult task of allotting the agencies to the various church denominations fell to Vincent Colyer, secretary of the Board of Indian Commissioners. The only enunciated principle for Colyer to follow appeared at the end of 1870 in Grant's annual message to Congress, in which he declared his determination "to give all the agencies to such religious denominations as had heretofore established missionaries among the Indians, and perhaps to some other denominations who would undertake the work on the same terms, i.e., as a missionary work." But this was much too vague to be satisfactory, and Colyer was forced to make an initial division on the basis of his own scanty information about the agencies and the missionary work being performed at them. In 1872, when the system was fully established, the following division existed.

Denomination	Number of agencies	Number of Indians
Methodist	14	54,473
Orthodox Friends	10	17,724
Presbyterian	9	38,069
Episcopalian	8	26,929
Catholic	7	17,856
Hicksite Friends	6	6,598
Baptist	5	40,800
Reformed Dutch	5	8,118
Congregationalist	3	14,476
Christian	2	8,287
Unitarian	2	3,800
American Board	1	1,496
Lutheran	1	273

What the government wanted from the churches was a total transformation of the agencies from political sinecures to missionary outposts. The
religious societies were expected not only to nominate strong men as
agents but to supply to a large extent the subordinate agency personnel.
Teachers especially were desired, men and women with a religious dedica-
tion to the work that would make up for the low pay and often frightening
conditions. The churches, too, it was assumed, would pursue more energetically and more effectively the strictly missionary activities already begun now that conflicts between government agents and missionaries would
no longer be an obstacle. Agency physicians, interpreters, and mechanics,
if they were of solid moral worth, could all contribute to the goal of civilizing and Christianizing the Indians. Utopia seemed to be within grasp. The
reports of the secretaries of the interior, the commissioners of Indian affairs, the Board of Indian Commissioners, and Grant himself rang loud
with praise for the new policy.

Yet, despite the early praise, both the Board of Indian Commissioners
and the church-run agencies were soon in trouble. The romantic ideal of
depoliticizing the Indian Office and the administration of the agencies by
the appointment of high-minded, religiously motivated individuals ran up
against the hard rock of practical operations within an old political system.

The Board of Indian Commissioners felt the pressures first, for its attempts to do good were blocked by powerful forces and its advice and recommendations ignored or contradicted. Goodwill and integrity on the part
of the board's members met greed in the "Indian ring" and corruption
among public officials. By 1874 matters had come to an impasse, and all
the original members of the Board of Indian Commissioner resigned. New
members were appointed who were less inclined to set themselves up in
opposition to the official government departments.

The assignment of agencies to churches that had looked so promising in
principle did not work well in practice. Fundamentally, the missionary
societies were not prepared to handle the tremendous responsibility suddenly cast upon them. It was not as simple as many sanguine persons had
thought to supply competent Christian men to run the agencies. Such men
were not available in large numbers, and the missionary boards were none
too astute in selecting agents. Of the eight hundred agency employees
under control of the churches, many did not display Christian character,
and some of them were from the worst social classes in the country. Until
such difficulties were overcome, the work of Christianization would yield
little fruit.

Nor were the auxiliary services of education and missionary work effectively pursued, for most of the missionary boards found that providing for
the Indian service was a distasteful responsibility. Among many of the
churches, the Indians had to compete with foreign infidels, who captured

the imagination of the communicants and most of the missionary funds. In truth, the internal effectiveness of the whole policy was open to serious doubt. Equally as serious as the lack of sustained interest on the part of the churches was interdenominational rivalry. Maintaining a position against a conflicting group was, unfortunately, often a more powerful motivation than concern for the welfare of the Indians. Examples of these fights abounded; they were all disedifying if not scandalous. If many could be explained by pettiness and denominational bias, the conflict between the Protestant mission groups and the Roman Catholics was nothing less than flagrant bigotry.

It quickly became clear that the assignment of agencies to the churches did not solve the "Indian problem." Good intentions of Christian men were not enough to correct evils of a complex nature or overcome a long history of mismanagement. Failure to study or appreciate the Indian side of the question, to adopt or build upon the societal forms that persisted in the Indian communities, weakened all the missionary efforts. Although most of the church groups professed a sincere regard for the well-being and advancement of the Indians, all this was thought of completely in terms of transforming them into acceptable Christian citizens.

External forces, too, were at work. The policy of church agencies would have brought difficulties in times of the highest moral rectitude in government circles; in fact, it was attempted in a decade noted in American history as a low point in public morals. "Grantism" became a term for fraud and corruption in high federal office, and the Indian service was one of the more lucrative areas in which politicians and spoilsmen could grow rich. It is understandable that rapacious individuals would not stand idly by when the source of rich spoils was cut off by the missionary policy. Almost from the very start of the program, pressures of political patronage were at work, undermining the system.

When Rutherford B. Hayes succeeded Grant in 1877, the policy of church-appointed agents was clearly on a downhill course. Carl Schurz, the reform-minded Liberal Republican whom Hayes appointed secretary of the interior, developed quite a different tone from that of the previous administration, and the religious character of the men in office did not seem any longer to be of prime importance. The board of inquiry that Schurz appointed soon after taking office to investigate irregularities in the Indian service criticized the appointment of agents "because of a sentiment" rather than on the basis of business qualifications, and it said that to entrust the church-appointed agents with such great power and responsibility was to "undertake through pigmies the solution of a problem that has engaged the best efforts of statesmen and philanthropists ever since the days of the republic."

The churches became less and less involved in appointing the agents, and the denominations that had been in the forefront in instigating the policy became disillusioned. By 1882 all the churches had withdrawn.

A concomitant movement for fundamental change in American Indian policy that culminated early in Grant's administration was an attack on the treaty system. From President Grant down, reformers called for abandonment of the system that had been an essential element in the relations between the United States government and the Indian tribes from the inception of the nation.

Those who had some historical sense realized that the treaties at first had been a good deal more than "a mere form to amuse and quiet savages, a half-compassionate, half-contemptuous humoring of unruly children," as Commissioner Francis A. Walker observed in 1873. The Indians at one time had had enough power to make a favorable cession of lands a diplomatic triumph for the United States. But from the early nineteenth century on, perceptive men had seen the incongruity of treating the Indian tribes as equals, and as demands for reform in Indian affairs grew during and immediately after the Civil War, the treaty system came under increasing scrutiny. The attack was part of the movement to end Indian tribal organization and make Indians wards of the government and then ultimately individualized citizens.

The Board of Indian Commissioners in its first report recommended unequivocally: "The treaty system should be abolished." The highest government officials agreed with the reformers. Commissioner of Indian Affairs Ely S. Parker, who had a long career of upholding the rights of the Seneca tribe, to which he belonged, declared flatly in 1869 that the treaty system should no longer be continued. He considered the Indians to be wards of the government, whose title to the land was a "mere possessory one," and he condemned the treaty procedures for falsely impressing upon the tribes a notion of national independence. "It is time," he said, "that this idea should be dispelled, and the government cease the cruel farce of thus dealing with its helpless and ignorant wards." President Grant believed that the treaty system had been a mistake and ought to be abandoned.

Before the reformers could organize effectively enough to bring an end to treaty making, however, the system was destroyed by Congress for reasons that had little to do with humanitarian reform. The end came as the result of a conflict of authority between the House of Representatives and the Senate. The fundamental problem was that making treaties was a function of the president and the Senate, and if dealings with the Indians were con-

fined to treaties, the House of Representatives was left out completely except to appropriate funds for arrangements it had no hand in making.

One crucial point at issue was the disposition of Indian lands. The Indian Office, by negotiating treaties with the Indians, could manipulate Indian land cessions in the interests of railroads or land companies. The territory freed of Indian title would not revert to the public domain and thus
not become subject to the land laws that frontier settlers had fought to gain
in their own interests. By means of the treaty process, one-fourth of the
lands of Kansas passed from Indian ownership to individuals, land specu-
lating companies, and railroads without ever becoming part of the public
domain or coming under congressional control. Such disposal denied settlers the benefits of the Homestead Act of 1862 and gave no voice to the
popularly elected House of Representatives, where land reform sentiment
was strongest.

For the House to get an equal voice in Indian affairs the treaty system
would have to be abolished altogether. The Senate was willing to end treaty
making if treaties already ratified were held inviolate, so the way was
cleared for the necessary legislation, which came finally in an obscure
clause in the Indian appropriation act of 1871. Added to a sentence providing funds for the Yankton Indians was the statement: "*Provided,* That hereafter no Indian nation or tribe within the territory of the United States
shall be acknowledged or recognized as an independent nation, tribe, or
power with whom the United States may contract by treaty; *Provided,* further, That nothing herein contained shall be construed to invalidate or impair the obligation of any treaty heretofore lawfully made and ratified with
any such Indian nation or tribe."

The end of treaty making created a paradox. The question of what constitutional basis the federal government had for dealing with the Indians
(aside from trade) had been answered largely by pointing to the treaty-
making power. Now Congress struck down this chief constitutional basis.
As a matter of fact, however, the old processes could not be completely
abandoned. Whether or not a group of Indians was recognized as "an independent nation, tribe, or power," dealings between it and the United States
called for formal agreements by which Indian consent was obtained. This
was especially true in land cessions. Such agreements differed from the
treaties chiefly in that they were ratified not by the Senate alone but by
both houses of Congress.

The humanitarians concerned with the Indians' rights insisted that
treaty rights of the past be respected at all costs—but to consider the Indians simultaneously both sovereign peoples and wards of the government,
as Commissioner Edward P. Smith pointed out in 1873, involved "increasing difficulties and absurdities." "So far, and as rapidly as possible," Smith

declared, "all recognition of Indians in any other relation than strictly as subjects of the Government should cease." Commissioner J. Q. Smith was even more pointed in his remarks: "There is a very general and growing opinion that observance of the strict letter of treaties with Indians is in many cases at variance both with their best interests and with sound public policy."

Yet old ways did not change as easily as the legal forms. Tribal leaders in some cases continued to exercise more authority on the reservations than the Indian agents, who were supposed to be directing the destinies of the nation's wards. Criticism of tribal authority and objections to consulting with the chiefs about government policy grew rather than diminished after the abolition of the treaty system.

CHAPTER II

Military Challenge

The period of the post–Civil War peace policy was marked, paradoxically, by continual Indian wars. Neither the philanthropists on the Board of Indian Commissioners nor the agents appointed by the churches were able to reverse conditions that led to Indian resistance, and the civilian men who dominated the Indian Office did not succeed in eliminating the need for military action. The promoters of the peace policy, in fact, developed a modus vivendi with the army, a fragile balance between the Indian Office and the War Department. Commissioner of Indian Affairs Ely S. Parker in the early days of the peace policy spoke of "a perfect understanding" between the officers of the two departments. He summarized the policy of the government in the following terms: "that they [the Indians] should be secured their legal rights; located, where practicable, upon reservations; assisted in agricultural pursuits and the arts of civilized life; and that Indians who should fail or refuse to come in and locate in permanent abodes provided for them, would be subject wholly to the control and supervision of military authorities, to be treated as friendly or hostile as circumstances might justify."

Francis A. Walker, Parker's successor, likewise saw no inconsistency in making use of soldiers when Indians needed chastisement, while at the same time pursuing the peace policy on the reservations. Walker had little patience with recalcitrant Indians and little sympathy for their situation, and he had no qualms about using military men to restrain refractory tribesmen. He insisted that such action was neither an abandonment of the peace policy nor disparagement of it. The reservation policy from the beginning, he said, demanded "that the Indians should be made as comfortable on, and as uncomfortable off, their reservations as it was in the power of the Government to make them," and he saw the use of military force not as war but as discipline.

The limited use of military police power that Walker envisaged in 1872, however, gave way to all-out war. The military encounters of the 1860s with the Apaches and Navajos in the Southwest, with the Cheyennes and Arapahos in the central plains, and with the Sioux in the Powder River valley along the Bozeman Trail turned out to be, not the final examples of Indian wars cut short by the peace policy, but the beginning of a decade or more of desperate fighting in the West.

On the southern plains the Kiowas and Comanches, for whom raiding had become a way of life, would not stay confined to the reservation assigned to them by the Treaty of Medicine Lodge Creek. Led by aggressive leaders like Satanta and Satank, these Indians left the reservation time and again to raid across the Red River into Texas. Lawrie Tatum, the Iowa Quaker farmer who had been sent to the Kiowas as agent in 1869 under the peace policy, tried desperately to make a nonviolent policy work. He seemed for a while to make some headway; but he resorted to withholding rations to force the chiefs to return white captives taken on the raids, and ultimately, when such coercion proved insufficient to restrain the Indians, he called for military assistance.

Periodic promises of peace on the part of the Indians, interspersed with murderous raids off the reservation, kept the Red River frontier in a state of turmoil. The Cheyennes, too, joined in the depredations and in June 1874 an attack by Kiowas, Comanches, and Cheyennes on a trading establishment at Adobe Walls in the Texas panhandle signaled the beginning of a full-scale war. Strong columns of troops were sent into the western part of the Indian Territory and into the Staked Plains of northwestern Texas to corral and subdue the Indians and force them to the reservations. But not until June 1875 were the last of the hostiles rounded up, the Red River War brought to a close, and the Indian prisoners of war sent to Fort Marion, Florida. With the defeat of the three tribes peace finally came to the southern plains.

The peace policy was severely tried also by the Modoc War, a flaring up of hostilities along the Oregon-California border in 1872–1873 that grew out of Indian resistance to white pressures on their homelands. The Modocs lived around Tule Lake, which stretched across the border, and they included in their lands along the southern edge of the lake a forbidding region of lava beds, a remarkable stronghold against attacking forces. The Modocs were little affected by the mining frontier, but their grasslands attracted ranchers, who soon clamored to have the Indians out of the way. In 1864, in response to these white cries, the United States government negotiated a treaty with the Indians by which they were moved to a reservation twenty-five miles to the north. They were to share the reservation with the Klamath tribe; and the Modocs, on alien ground and outnumbered by the Klamaths, were restless and unhappy. One of the Modoc leaders, called Captain Jack by the whites, soon led his followers back to their old homes along Lost River.

When Grant became president in 1869, he appointed as superintendent of Indian affairs for Oregon a faithful Republican named Alfred B. Meacham, an ardent temperance man moved by deep reforming instincts. Meacham was a staunch supporter of the peace policy and undertook to carry out its reform principles. He talked Captain Jack into returning to the reservation, but pressures from the Klamath Indians and the Indian agent drove Captain Jack again to Lost River in April 1870. The use of army troops in an attempt to force the Modocs back to the reserve led in 1872 to armed conflict. The Indians holed up in the lava beds, from which the army without enthusiasm and without success sought to dislodge them, even though General Edward R. S. Canby, commanding the Department of the Columbia, himself assumed direction of the campaign.

To overcome this expensive and embarrassing impasse, a peace commission, headed by Meacham, was appointed on January 29, 1873, but negotiations made little progress. The Modocs themselves were divided, and the army tightened the pressure on the area held by the Indians. Captain Jack, his hand forced by more desperate members of his band, at length agreed to the treacherous murder of General Canby and the peace commissioners when they came unarmed to the next council. On Good Friday, April 11, 1873, the deed was done. At a signal from Captain Jack the Indians rose up armed, and Jack himself, drawing a pistol he had concealed under his coat, shot General Canby at pointblank range. The Reverend Eleasar Thomas, a member of the peace commission, was quickly killed, too. Meacham, who started to flee when the trouble broke out, was grazed by bullets and fell unconscious. He was partially scalped when a cry that soldiers were coming drove off his assailant, and he was found still alive when the rescuers arrived and eventually recovered.

The disaster shocked the nation. Much of the sympathy that had supported the Modocs was destroyed, and cries for vengeance against the murderers resounded. The army intensified its drive until at last, giving up before hopeless odds, the Indians surrendered. Some of the criminals were granted amnesty for aiding in the capture of Captain Jack, but six of the Modocs were sentenced to death by a military commission at Fort Klamath. On October 3, Captain Jack and three of his companions were executed at Fort Klamath; two lesser participants had their sentences commuted by President Grant to life imprisonment at Alcatraz.

The Modoc murders touched off a nationwide attack on Grant's peace policy. Western opposition was intense, and even supporters of the policy were stunned by the murder of the commissioners and agreed that stiff punishment was in order. It did not take long, however, for the peace advocates to renew their insistent urging that the peace policy be continued, and they spoke strongly against recurring white attacks upon the Indians— which, they charged, deserved as strict an accounting as that meted out to the Modocs. Meacham himself held no grudge against the Indians and devoted the rest of his life to Indian reform. He toured the lecture circuit with talks about his Modoc adventure, founded *The Council Fire,* a journal devoted to Indian matters, and served the government on special commissions.

After the sentences of the military tribunal had been executed, the remaining 153 Modocs were moved to the Indian Territory and placed in care of the Quapaw Agency. "The Indian is greatly attached to his tribal organization," Secretary Delano asserted, "and it is believed that this example of extinguishing their so-called national existence and merging their members into other tribes, while in reality a humane punishment, will be esteemed by them as the severest penalty that could have been inflicted, and tend by its example to deter hostile Indians in future from serious and flagrant insurrection." The Modocs lived quietly and productively as farmers in the Indian Territory until in 1909 those who were left were allowed to return to the Klamath reservation in Oregon.

In Arizona and New Mexico the Apaches carried on a continual guerrilla war with the troops sent to subdue them. Attempts to isolate friendly groups from those who continued depredations led to strong criticisms from local whites, who feared that the "feeding stations" were merely refuges for marauding Indians. On April 30, 1871, a force of Tucson citizens attacked the unsuspecting Apaches at Camp Grant, murdered and mutilated them, and carried off children into slavery. The Camp Grant Massacre speeded up attempts to apply the peace policy in Arizona, and in July 1871 Vincent Colyer, secretary of the Board of Indian Commissioners, was dispatched there to make peace with the Apaches and establish them on reservations.

The outraged Arizonans ridiculed Colyer's attempts, but a good many Apaches gathered at temporary reservations set up at military posts, and General O. O. Howard, following in Colyer's path, made peace with the Chiricahua chief Cochise and induced more Indians to come in to the agencies. A system of reservations was established, and a sizable number of Indians gathered at them. Still the raiding continued, and in 1872–1873 General George Crook mounted a successful offensive against the bands. More Apaches settled on the reservations, and for several years peace was maintained in Arizona. The peace, however, did not end the raids into Mexico carried on from both Arizona and New Mexico. Under Victorio, a Warm

Springs Apache, the frontier was again terrorized until the chief was killed in 1880. And then new leaders, of whom Geronimo became the best known, continued the guerrilla warfare until they too were tracked down. Geronimo finally surrendered in 1886.

Another challenge to civilian control of the Indians came in the conflicts with the Sioux. The Treaty of Fort Laramie in 1868 had left unceded lands in the Powder River country as hunting lands of the Sioux, but it had also set aside the Great Sioux Reserve west of the Missouri River in Dakota, and the chiefs had agreed to settle at the agencies and accept reservation life. Many of the Indians, lured by the government's rations, went to the agencies, but some, like Sitting Bull, remained on the unceded lands and refused to settle down. The nonreservation Indians were considered "hostile," for they occasionally raided Montana settlements and fought the advancing railroad surveyors who entered their lands. The Sioux were irritated, too, by the invasion of the Black Hills by a military expedition under George Armstrong Custer in 1874 that confirmed the rumors that gold was there and stimulated the miners to invade the forbidden hills.

As long as the Indians were able to subsist by hunting in the Powder River valley, it was impossible to control them fully. Only on the reservations would they be completely dependent upon the United States, and in December 1875 runners were sent to the Sioux to announce that all who were not at the agencies by January 31, 1876, would be hunted down by the army and brought in by military force. The midwinter deadline made compliance impossible, but in any event the Indians did not intend to obey. On February 1, 1876, the secretary of the interior declared that all Indians not on the reservations were to be considered hostile and asked the secretary of war to take appropriate action. General Phil Sheridan, now in command of the Division of the Missouri, wanted a winter campaign, but delays prevented a full-scale attack until April and May, when three columns moved in toward the Sioux and their Cheyenne allies. One column headed eastward from Fort Ellis in Montana, a second moved north along the old Bozeman Trail from Fort Fetterman, and a third, comprising part of the Seventh Cavalry under Custer, traveled west from Fort Abraham Lincoln on the Missouri. Seriously underestimating the size of the opposing Indian force, Custer launched a premature attack on the Indian camp on the Little Bighorn on June 25, and he and his entire force were annihilated.

News of the disaster on the Little Bighorn arrived in the East just as the centennial of the signing of the Declaration of Independence was being celebrated. The report stunned the nation, and heavy army reinforcements were sent into Montana to hunt down the bands of Sioux and Cheyenne who had scattered after the fight. Such pressure was more than the Indians could withstand, and little by little during the fall and winter the bands surrendered at the agencies. Even the most recalcitrant at length came in. Crazy Horse with a band of more than a thousand surrendered at Camp Robinson, Nebraska, on May 6, 1877. Sitting Bull with his adherents fled into Canada determined never to submit to reservation life, but finally he, too, came back and gave up in July 1881. The Sioux war had accomplished what the peace policy had been unable to; it had forced the Indians to abandon their hunting grounds and accept government control on the reservations.

The defeat of the Sioux did not end all military action in the north, however. The traditionally peaceful Nez Perces in 1877 startled the nation with a new military conflict. When the Nez Perce Reservation had been reduced in 1863, some of the Indians, mostly those who had resisted the attempts to convert them to Christianity, refused to accept the treaty. Chief Joseph was among these "nontreaty" Indians, and he and his band continued to live in their beloved Wallowa Valley in eastern Oregon. Increasing white encroachments there laid the groundwork for trouble, and the United States was eager to persuade these tribesmen to join their relatives on the Lapwai Reservation in Idaho. General Howard was given responsibility for the peace, and in a series of meetings with Chief Joseph he finally won the Indians' consent to move to Lapwai.

Before the movement could be accomplished, hostilities broke out. In June 1877 young men of the band, avenging the murder of an Indian by whites, killed a party of settlers. General Howard's troops were ordered in, and war began. The Indians' choice was flight. By skillful maneuvers, Joseph and the military leaders of the band moved east through the Lolo Pass into the Bitterroot Valley of Montana, down into Yellowstone Park, and then north, seeking to reach asylum in Canada. Pursued by Howard's soldiers and with occasional military encounters, the fleeing Indians executed one of the great military movements in history. They had almost reached their objective when they were cut off by troops from Fort Keogh under General Nelson A. Miles. With many warriors dead and the rest exhausted and the women and children cold and starving, Chief Joseph surrendered at the Bear Paw Mountains on October 5.

In 1878 and 1879, Bannocks, Shoshones, and Paiutes in Idaho, Nevada, and eastern Oregon, upset by increasing white pressures on their lands, rose up in minor wars against the whites. Military expeditions directed by General Howard tracked down the hostiles through the rugged country of the Rockies and Great Basin and forced them back to their reservations.

In neighboring Colorado, the Utes faced similar encroachment. By a treaty of 1868 they had been guaranteed a reservation in the western quarter of Colorado. The expanding mining frontier in Colorado soon encroached upon the reserved lands, however, and a United States commission succeeded in gaining from the Indians in 1873 a large cession of land in the southern part of the reservation. The Utes remained at peace and under Chief Ouray exhibited loyalty and friendship to the United States. But white pressures upon their lands did not let up; and after Colorado became a state in 1876 they became incessant, as the state's inhabitants, its government, and the press shouted in ever louder chorus, "The Utes must go!"

A violent outbreak might have been avoided but for a change in agents at the White River Agency in 1878. In that year, Agent H. E. Danforth, a nominee of the Unitarians under the peace policy, was replaced by Nathan C. Meeker. Meeker, a visionary who had been converted to the agrarian socialism of Fourier and lived for several years in a phalanx in Ohio, hoped to apply his agricultural principles as a solution to the Indian problem. He moved the agency downriver to a spot more suitable for his agricultural plans and began to plow, fence, and irrigate the meadows favored by the Indians as grazing grounds for their ponies. He met adamant opposition from some members of the tribe, who had no interest in farming and who objected to Meeker's plowing up their lands. When the agent realized their growing antagonism, he called for military support, and troops under Major Thomas T. Thornburgh were dispatched to strengthen his position. Thornburgh's troops were attacked as they entered the reservation, and the major and eleven of his soldiers were killed. At the same time, the agency was assaulted; Meeker and eight others were killed, and Meeker's wife and daughters were taken captive.

Although the uprising, the work of a small group of Indians, was quickly quieted through the good offices of Ouray and the concentration of additional troops in the area, the effect upon the Coloradans was electrifying. It was just the occasion they sought to demand a war of extermination against the Utes. Secretary of the Interior Carl Schurz moved at once to prevent an expensive and destructive war, which he was sure would come if the situation of the Utes in Colorado could not be radically changed. He sent a special agent to get back the captives and then to obtain the surrender of the guilty Indians. Schurz was chiefly interested in a plan for long-range settlement of the difficulties, a plan he expressed in succinct terms: "settlement of the Utes in severalty, so as to promote the civilization of the Indians, and to open the main part of the Ute reservation to development by white citizens, thus removing a source of constant irritation between the latter and the Utes." An agreement was signed in Washington on March 6, 1880, by representatives of the Ute tribe that provided for removal of the White River Utes to the Uintah Reservation in Utah and for the band of Uncompahgre and Southern Utes to settle on lands on the Grand and La Plata rivers.

THE ARMY AND THE INDIANS

The Indian wars made the army an agent of the United States government in the control and management of the Indians that was on a par, or at least almost so, with the Indian Office. And the ultimate goal of the two services was the same: to locate the Indians on reservations with set boundaries, where they could be educated and trained for American citizenship. It was in methods and the nature of their tasks that the Interior Department and the War Department differed.

The post–Civil War army, composed of officers and men who stayed with the army as a career at the end of the sectional struggle, entered a period of rapid professionalization. The commanding officers had their eyes set on European models of what an up-to-date army preparing for conventional warfare should be. The schools and the manuals and theorists like Emory Upton sought to change the American military forces into a thoroughly modern and professional organization.

But the actual work of the postwar army was Indian fighting, a highly unorthodox warfare, which the army somehow considered not its primary mission but only a passing phase. So the military men were not well geared to meet the enemy they actually confronted, an enemy with quite unconventional characteristics. To begin with, the Indians could not readily be classified as hostile or friendly, so the enemy was seldom clearly identified. Who was friend and who was foe was never absolutely resolved, for the lines of division shifted rapidly, and the Indians wore no sharply distinguishing uniforms and did not draw up in organized array.

Moreover, the army did not develop a sharp ideological stand of hostility toward its Indian foes. Although the soldiers and their officers saw the horrors of savage warfare, they could also view the Indians through eyes that recognized the fraud, corruption, and injustice heaped upon the tribes. "Ambivalence, therefore," the historian Robert Utley has noted, "marked military attitudes toward the Indians—fear, distrust, loathing, contempt, and condescension, on the one hand; curiosity, admiration, sympathy, and even friendship, on the other." Humanitarians in the East, harping on Sand Creek (which was not a work of the regular army) or the Piegan Massacre and picking up exasperated statements of General Sherman and General Sheridan about refractory bands of Indians, charged that the army's policy was one of extermination. Such accusations were wide of the mark, for the impulse to civilize the Indians was as strong in the army as it was among humanitarian reformers and government officials. Some military men, notably General George Crook, were known for their sincere concern for the Indians and their welfare.

The work of troops in the West was more that of a police force than of a conventional army, as Commissioner Walker had discerned: not war, but discipline. The basic unconventionality was that Indian warfare was guerrilla warfare—stealth, cunning, and ambush in small parties were the rule. The Indians refused to engage in long-drawn battles and often faded away before a white force rather than engage it, and this quality won the admiration of the army. A sympathetic General Nelson A. Miles wrote: "The art of war among the white race is called strategy, or tactics; when practised by the Indians it is called treachery. They employed the art of deceiving, misleading, decoying, and surprising the enemy with great cleverness. The celerity and secrecy of their movements were never excelled by the warriors of any country. They had courage, skill, sagacity, endurance, fortitude, and self-sacrifice of a high order."

To carry out its mission against such an enemy, with inadequate numbers stretched out thinly over an extensive frontier, the army built small military posts all over the West, tiny outposts housing a company or two of soldiers, as a warning to the Indians and as stations from which forays of detachments could march out when occasion demanded. In the 1860s and 1870s the trans-Mississippi West was dotted with scores of these forts, each established in response to some military problem or the clamor of settlers for protection.

The problem with this strategy was that the army was not large enough to man a fort at every critical spot. Yet the alternative, concentration of troops at a few strategic locations from which soldiers could be dispatched in strength to trouble spots, was impossible, both politically (because settlers wanted soldiers close at hand for protection and as a market for their produce) and practically (because the army did not have the means of rapid deployment). Even from the dispersed posts, the army usually moved only after the Indians had struck, dispersed, and disappeared. The army in the first decades after the Civil War was unable to solve its logistical problems.

In an attempt to overcome its deficiences, the army used surprise attacks on Indian villages, and sometimes it resorted to campaigns during the winter, when the Indians were accustomed to curtail their operations and were often ill-prepared to beat back an attacker. Such tactics were "total war," for the women and children were nearly always intermingled with the fighting men and often took part in the fighting. The inability to distinguish between combatants and noncombatants raised questions that greatly disturbed the humanitarians and many military leaders as well. Another tactic was to employ Indians against other Indians, a common occurrence in all the Indian wars. Tribal rivalries and enmity made it possible to use Crows and Pawnees, for example, against the Sioux.

Military leaders, unable to set aside planning and organization of the army for future possible wars with conventional enemies, stumbled along in their campaigns against their unconventional Indian foes, whom they were trying more to control than to destroy. The punishment they meted out often fell on the innocent as well as on the guilty, for the two were difficult to distinguish, and this destruction blackened the record of the army. Yet neither in theory nor in fact was the result extermination or genocide. It is impossible to establish an accurate record of Indian deaths in the post–Civil War Indian wars, but the casualties on both sides from armed conflict were in total small. The tragedy was in the destruction of the Indians' traditional way of life, which was the conscious goal of both military and civilian officials.

THE TRANSFER ISSUE

Military actions against hostile Indians led to agitation for transferring the Indian Office to the War Department. This was a serious challenge to civilian control of Indian affairs, for the proposals called for placing the Indians into the hands of army men on active military duty.

As the peace policy progressed and the Indian agencies were handed over to representatives of the religious denominations, the opponents of civilian control found a rich field for criticism. Each failure of the peace policy, each act of Indian hostility, could be used to show that the humanitarians from the East, who had little contact with the wild Indians of the West, were unfit to formulate and carry out a practical Indian policy. Instances of failure by peaceful methods were taken to be automatic proof that Indian affairs belonged in the hands of the military.

Strong support of the army came from the West, where frontier governors, legislators, and newspaper editors called for aggressive military action against the Indians. Nor did transfer lack support in the East. After the Fetterman disaster the *Nation* recommended transfer as the "primal remedy for our evils." Lamenting the *divisum imperium* that marked Indian management, it supported sole military control. What could the troops do if they had sole responsibility? the editor asked. "The answer is," he declared, "the troops could *corral* the Indians; they could keep them away from the emigrant routes; could establish a healthful state of non-intercourse; could remove the temptations to plunder by forcing the Indians away from certain prescribed regions. In this way they would effectually police the 'short route' to Montana and the Pacific."

The failure of Congress to pass a transfer measure, despite incessant agitation on the part of military supporters, was due to the desperate struggle to maintain civilian control—and with it the peace policy—that came from the humanitarian Christian reformers. The peace policy had been launched in fear of military control of Indian affairs and developed in an atmosphere of constant threat that army dominance would be reasserted. Such insecurity kept the reformers alert to the least wind blowing in the direction of army control; their outbursts against the army made the arguments of the advocates of transfer seem moderate and mild-mannered by comparison.

At first everything seemed promising. The Peace Commission after a careful analysis of conditions in the West, decided against transfer in its initial report of January 7, 1868. "If we intend to have war with them [the Indians] the bureau should go to the Secretary of war," it declared. "If we intend to have peace it should be in the civil department." The commission felt that the chief tasks of the Indian Office were to educate and instruct the Indians in peaceful arts. "The military arm of the government," it flatly asserted, "is not the most admirably adapted to the discharge of duties of this character." Not one army man in a thousand, the commissioners thought, would like to teach Indian children to read and write or Indian men to farm. But renewal of war in the West in the summer led to reversal of the commission's stand in October.

To counteract this change of mind on the part of such a distinguished group, which would threaten the hopeful goals of the reformers, Commissioner of Indian Affairs Taylor, who as president of the Peace Commission had refused to vote for transfer when the commission as a whole reversed its position, issued a powerful report. His indictment of military control of Indian matters, issued as part of his annual report on November 12, 1868, exhausted the arguments of the civilian reformers. He argued that transfer would mean the maintenance of a large standing army in peacetime, an expensive undertaking and one contrary to the republican principles of the nation. Previous military management of the Indians, he charged, had been a failure and must "in the very nature of things, always prove a failure," for soldiers were trained for war and were not competent to teach the arts of civilization. "Will you send professional soldiers, sword in one hand, musket in the other, and tactics on the brain," he asked, "to teach the wards of the nation agriculture, the mechanic arts, theology and peace? You would civilize the Indian! Will you send him the sword? You would inspire him with the peaceful principles of Christianity! Is the bayonet their symbol? You would invite him to the sanctuary! Will you herald his approach with the clangor of arms and the thunder of artillery?"

The Board of Indian Commissioners made a great stir about the question of economy, providing comparative figures to show that costs had been greater under the War Department than under the Interior Department. But it did not want such practical issues to crowd out the main issue. "In all our dealings with the Indians, in all our legislation for them," it declared, "their civilization and ultimate citizenship should be the one purpose steadily pursued. That is the only aim worthy of us as a great Christian nation. And the attainment of this end will hardly be possible by military means."

Indians, too, opposed transfer to military control. Delegates of the Five Civilized Tribes, for example, met in Washington on February 12, 1878, to oppose a new transfer bill and addressed a long memorial to Congress in which they praised the peace policy inaugurated under Grant and echoed the reformers' pleas for keeping the Indians out of the hands of the military. "Do you desire to save from further destruction your Indian population?" they asked Congress. "Is it your purpose to civilize and christianize them, so as to prepare them eventually for citizenship? Then in the name of civilization, christianity, and humanity, we earnestly ask you to make no change in the present general management unless it be to create an independent Indian department."

The opposing sides were careful to seek supporting evidence from their friends. The Board of Indian Commissioners sent a questionnaire in 1875 to the civilian agents, who were part of the Interior Department structure and who would have been eliminated under the army's proposals. No wonder the respondents were almost unanimous in asserting that what was needed was civilian effort to educate and civilize the Indians. The House Committee on Military Affairs in 1876, on the other hand, seeking advice on the expediency of transferring the Indian service to military control, sent a questionnaire to sixty high-ranking army officers, all but two of whom recommended the transfer as a measure of "expediency, wisdom, and economy." Not until 1878 was there an attempt by an investigating group to get both sides of the story, and then the report was a four-to-four split.

When the campaign for transfer was renewed in Congress in 1878, the Senate succeeded once more in stopping a transfer amendment added to the Indian appropriation bill. A joint committee appointed to investigate the subject, after exhaustive testimony that repeated endlessly all the old arguments on both sides, could not overcome its partisan differences and submitted two reports—the Democrats urging transfer and the Republicans opposing it. By that time the issue had lost much of its urgency, and later congressional action was half-hearted and indecisive.

Much of the credit for the victory against transfer belongs to Carl Schurz, whose reform of the Indian Office weakened one of the main lines of attack by military men against Interior Department control. Schurz publicly stood up to the generals who criticized civilian administrators. On the other side, in 1876, just at a crucial point when military advocates seemed to be winning, the impeachment of Secretary of War William Belknap for malfeasance in office and his subsequent resignation gave the opponents of the War Department control a new argument. Did the nation, they asked, want Indian affairs turned over to such a corrupt office?

The transfer issue was the greatest challenge that the peace program of the Christian Indian reformers had to meet. The persistent advocacy of military management of Indian affairs was an explicit denial that civilian methods, on which the peace policy depended, could succeed. The contest kept the air filled with charges and countercharges, forced the reformers to defend their policy both in theory and by practical accomplishments, and kept the public agitated over the Indian question. Scraping by with the narrowest of victories in Congress, the reformers stuck to their position until the succession of crises passed and they were able to begin anew with an aggressive humanitarian program for turning the Indians into standardized Americans.

THE END OF THE MILITARY PHASE

The military phase of Indian relations had practically ended by the early 1880s, at the same time that the church-appointed agency program of the peace policy collapsed. General Sherman, in his final report as general of the army, October 27, 1883, noted the changed situation:

> I now regard the Indians as substantially eliminated from the problem of the Army. There may be spasmodic and temporary alarms, but such Indian wars as have hitherto disturbed the public peace and tranquillity are not probable. The Army has been a large factor in producing this result, but it is not the only one. Immigration and the occupation by industrious farmers and miners of land vacated by the aborigines have been largely instrumental to that end, but the *railroad* which used to follow in the rear now goes forward with the picket-line in the great battle for civilization with barbarism, and has become the *greater* cause.

Four great transcontinental lines cut across the West, and branch lines and lesser railroads crisscrossed the country that had once been the sole domain of the Indians. The logistical problems that had hampered the army's supply in the trans-Mississippi West and made the mobile Indians more than an even match were solved by the railroads. The rapid extension of the lines made it possible to transport troops and supplies quickly to areas where they were needed.

The railroads also speeded the destruction of the buffalo on the plains and thereby destroyed the Indians' independence and ability to wage war. At the end of the Civil War, great herds of buffalo had blackened the landscape. By the mid-1870s the buffalo were largely gone in Kansas, and after

1883, the year of the last large kill, nearly all the herds vanished. New tanning methods and cheap transportation increased the market for buffalo hides, and hunters with their high-powered rifles covered the plains, slaughtering the huge beasts by the thousands and leaving the flesh to rot and the bones to whiten in the sun.

The slaughter of the buffalo was applauded by both the civilian and the military officers of the government concerned with the Indians, for the disappearance of the Indians' means of subsistence would force them into the dependent condition that was to be the first step toward their transformation into hard-working, self-supporting farmers. Secretary of the Interior Delano wrote as early as 1874: "The buffalo are disappearing rapidly, but not faster than I desire. I regard the destruction of such game . . . as facilitating the policy of the Government, of destroying their hunting habits, coercing them on reservations, and compelling them to begin to adopt the habits of civilization." In the same year General Sheridan suggested that the Texas legislature award medals to the buffalo hunters in gratitude. "These men have done more in the last two years, and will do more in the next year, to settle the vexed Indian question," he said, "than the entire regular army has done in the last thirty years. They are destroying the Indian's commissary." The end of the buffalo meant the end of the life that the plains Indians had known and was a fundamental condition for establishing the reservation system for the once-nomadic Indians.

CHAPTER 12

Indian Reservations

The post–Civil War Indian Office and the Indian reformers inherited a reservation policy that had developed gradually during the previous decades, and the concentration of Indians on reservations was the underpinning of Grant's peace policy. When Commissioner of Indian Affairs Ely S. Parker asked the new Board of Indian Commissioners whether the Indians should be placed on reservations, he received a strong affirmative answer. The board declared in its first report:

> The policy of collecting the Indian tribes upon small reservations contiguous to each other, and within the limits of a large reservation, eventually to become a State of the Union, and of which the small reservations will probably be the counties, seems to be the best that can be devised. Many tribes may thus be collected in the present Indian territory. The larger the number that can be thus concentrated the better for the success of the plan; care being taken to separate hereditary enemies from each other. When upon the reservation they should be taught as soon as possible the advantage of individual ownership of property; and should be given land in severalty as soon as it is desired by any of them, and the tribal relation should be discouraged.

CONSOLIDATION OF RESERVATIONS

The views of the Board of Indian Commissioners accorded well with those of responsible men in Grant's administration. Secretary of the Interior Jacob D. Cox looked not to a new reservation policy but to "an enlarged and more enlightened application of the general principles of the old one."

He saw two objects in the policy: "First, the location of the Indians upon fixed reservations, so that the pioneers and settlers may be freed from the terrors of wandering hostile tribes, and second, an earnest effort at their civilization, so that they may themselves be elevated in the scale of humanity, and our obligation to them as fellowmen be discharged." Cox believed that larger concentration would obviate many of the evils that arose when small reservations were surrounded by the unscrupulous frontier whites, and he hoped that moving less advanced tribes into contact with more civilized ones would have a beneficial result.

With Columbus Delano, Cox's successor, consolidation of tribes in the Indian Territory became almost an obsession, and he began to play a numbers game, trying to fit all the Indians into one large reservation. He counted 172,600 Indians outside the Indian Territory, occupying 96,155,785 acres—558 acres per capita. Inside the Indian Territory he found only one person to every 630 acres. "Could the entire Indian population of the country, excluding Alaska and those scattered among the States . . . be located in the Indian Territory," he decided, "there would be 180 acres of land, *per capita*, for the entire number, showing that there is ample area of land to afford them all comfortable homes." At the same time he candidly admitted that the acres given up by the assembling tribes could be thrown open to white settlement and cultivation. He wanted the Indians to realize that if they did not cooperate in this scheme to preserve them in the consolidated reservation, they would inevitably be inundated or crushed by the rapidly growing tide of white emigration.

It might be suspected that men like Delano, whose record was none too clean, were more interested in freeing Indian lands for white exploitation than in Indian welfare, but they no doubt honestly believed that the Indians had to be moved from their present situations if they were to survive and advance. It was the almost universal opinion of the age and a doctrine that went back as far as Thomas Jefferson. Views like Delano's on Indian consolidation were accepted as part of the humanitarians' package of Indian reform. "Since the inauguration of the present Indian policy," the Board of Indian Commissioners declared in 1876, "this board has not ceased to recommend the consolidation of agencies where it can be effected without infringing existing treaties. The time has now arrived when the Government must, if it would see an impulse given to the work of Indian civilization, take decided ground and prompt action upon this important subject." Tribes that occupied small reservations and had made little progress, if moved to large reservations, would profit from the encouragement of their more advanced brethren and would learn by daily observation "that thrift, enterprise, and energy do always produce their legitimate fruits of civilization and self-dependence." Moreover, a system of law could be more easily introduced, early allotment of land could be provided, and tribal relations could be broken up. Such action, the board concluded, would "go far toward the successful solution of the Indian problem, which has so long perplexed our nation, puzzled our statesmen, and disturbed our philanthropists."

INDIAN RESISTANCE TO REMOVAL

The theorists who elaborated schemes for consolidating all the Indians in one big reservation reckoned too little with the Indians, whom they were so willing to move around like pieces on a chessboard. The Indians were deeply attached to their homelands, and the topographical and climatic conditions were psychologically if not physically of tremendous importance to their well-being. Sioux, long acclimated to the northern plains, foresaw only misery and disaster if they had to move to the actually better lands in the Indian Territory. In the 1870s, while government officials and humanitarians were concocting fine schemes to remove the Indians to a few large reservations in order to save money and at the same time speed the civilization process, three disastrous removals propelled the issue into the public consciousness.

The most famous removal was that of the Ponca Indians from their reservation along the Missouri River to the Indian Territory. It was, in fact, the spark that ignited a new flame of concern for the rights of the Indians. The cause was just, the propaganda arising from it was spectacular, and the interest of eastern philanthropists in the Indians burned with a new intensity.

The Poncas, a small peaceful Siouan tribe, in 1865 had been guaranteed a reservation of 96,000 acres along the Missouri north of the Niobrara River. Three years later, however, the United States in the Fort Laramie treaty with the Sioux—without consulting the Poncas—ceded the entire Ponca reservation to the Sioux, the Poncas' traditional enemies. Although the United States admitted that the transfer had been a mistake, the government's resolution of the problem was not to restore the lands, which might have irritated the Sioux, but to remove the Poncas to the Indian Territory. Over their objections, the Indians in 1877 were escorted south by federal troops and settled on the Quapaw reserve.

The hardships of the journey and the change in climate brought great misery and many deaths to the Poncas, and even after they had found a new and more favorable location within the Indian Territory, they remained restless and unhappy and longed to return to their old home in the north. One of the chiefs, Standing Bear, could endure the situation no longer. With a small portion of the tribe, he started out in January 1879 to return north, reached Nebraska early in the spring, and settled down for the time being with the Omaha Indians. The plight of Standing Bear and his followers had by this time become a public issue, and a group of citizens of Omaha, encouraged by General George Crook, took up their case. When federal troops arrived to arrest the runaways and return them to the Indian Territory, prominent lawyers of the city drew up a writ of habeas corpus to prevent the chief's return, and on April 30 the matter was brought before Judge Elmer S. Dundy of the United States District Court. In the celebrated case of *Standing Bear* v. *Crook*, Judge Dundy ruled that "an Indian is a 'person' within the meaning of the laws of the United States, and has, therefore, the right to sue out a writ of habeas corpus in a federal court." Since he could find no authority for forcing the Poncas back to the Indian Territory, Dundy ordered their release.

The Ponca affair had important repercussions on Indian reform, for an assistant editor of the *Omaha Herald*, Thomas Henry Tibbles, soon mounted a campaign in the East to stir up public support for the Poncas. Accompanied by Standing Bear and Susette La Flesche, an Omaha Indian girl known as Bright Eyes, Tibbles appeared in Chicago and in several eastern cities to relate the wrongs of the Poncas, condemn the government for its actions, and appeal for support of the Indians' cause.

His greatest success was in Boston, where a group of prominent men (including John D. Long, governor of Massachusetts, and Frederick O. Prince, mayor of Boston) organized the Boston Indian Citizenship Committee to fight for the rights of the Poncas and other Indians. The principal thrust of the group's program was to demand respect for the Indians' rights, including the return to their original reservation, and to denounce the federal government for its part in the Ponca removal. Tibbles fitted well into the program and spoke to enthusiastic audiences in Boston. Bright Eyes and Standing Bear, appearing on stage in Indian dress, added a strong personal touch to the proceedings.

The bête noire of Tibbles and the Boston reformers was Secretary of the Interior Carl Schurz, who had assumed his duties just as the actual movement of the Poncas to the Indian Territory got under way. In public speeches and published letters, the Boston committee and its supporters on one side and Secretary Schurz on the other engaged in acrimonious debate. Schurz was also engaged in a public exchange with Helen Hunt Jackson, who had heard Tibbles and Bright Eyes in Boston in November 1879 and became a zealous convert to the cause of Indian reform. Schurz quashed an attempt to carry the Standing Bear case to the Supreme Court, and he urged Jackson and her friends, who were collecting funds for further legal action on Indian rights, to use the money for Indian education rather than pour it into the pockets of attorneys in futile cases.

The verbal combat between the reformers and the secretary of the interior did not prevent the working out of a solution to the Ponca problem, although nearly every move of the administration was subject to critical attack. There were conflicting reports about the condition of the Indians and about the willingness of those in the Indian Territory to remain there. But at length Congress in 1881 appropriated $165,000 to enable the secretary of the interior "to indemnify the Ponca tribe of Indians for losses sustained by them in consequence of their removal to the Indian Territory, to secure to them land in severalty on either the old or new reservation, in accordance with their wishes, and to settle all matters of difference with these Indians."

The controversy over the Poncas between Schurz and the reformers, although it kept the country much alive to Indian problems, was unfortunate, for it obscured the fundamental agreement of both sides in their desire to promote justice for the Indians. In large part, no doubt, the attacks on Schurz by the evangelical reformers reflected the fundamental differences of the two parties. Schurz was a severely practical and unsentimental man. His program was one of "policy," not of religious motivation. A man more different in background and outlook from the general run of Indian reformers can hardly be imagined, yet Schurz's Indian policy—attack upon corruption and inefficiency in the Indian Office, support of civilian as opposed to military control of Indian affairs, allotment of land in severalty and sale of "surplus" lands, and an aggressive educational program for Indians—were all in line with what the friends of the Indian came to espouse so ardently later in the 1880s.

Another celebrated case that illustrated the weakness of the consolidation policy was the flight of a band of Northern Cheyennes from the Indian Territory in 1878. Following military action on the northern plains after Custer's defeat, a part of these Indians had been placed on the reservation of the Southern Cheyennes and Arapahos near Fort Reno. The Indians suffered greatly in their new home, and the subsistence supplied by the government was inadequate. On September 9, 1878, about three hundred of them led by chiefs Dull Knife and Little Wolf fled the reservation and headed north to join their friends the Sioux. When troops of the United States army were sent to stop the Indians and return them to the Indian Territory, the flight became a running fight, and the Cheyennes killed a number of settlers in their passage through Kansas.

When the Indians reached the Platte, they separated into two groups. One of them under Dull Knife moved westward toward Fort Robinson; the party surrendered on October 23 and was imprisoned at the fort. The post commandant received orders to transport the Indians back to the Indian Territory, but they steadfastly refused to go, and the officer attempted to freeze and starve them into submission. Able to endure the torture no longer and frightened by the seizure of one of their leaders, the Indians broke out of their quarters on the night of January 9. Weakened by the ordeal of their imprisonment, they were easy prey for the soldiers who pursued them, and fifty or sixty men, women, and children were killed in flight. Some were captured and returned to the south, while Dull Knife and others escaped to the Sioux. The other group, led by Little Wolf, had continued north, hoping to reach Montana. They were induced to surrender on March 25, 1879, and were taken to Fort Keogh, where they were allowed to remain.

Commissioner Ezra Hayt blamed the affair upon unwarranted dissatisfaction on the part of the Indians and asserted that Dull Knife's band contained "the evilest and most dangerous element of their tribe." With elaborate statistics he attempted to prove that the Indians had not been maltreated or underfed in the Indian Territory. But a select committee of the Senate appointed to investigate the case returned a critical report in June 1880 based on testimony taken at Fort Reno and on interviews with Indians imprisoned in Kansas. Its findings sharply contradicted Hayt's report and described the government's lack of compliance with treaty agreements and the disastrous conditions that resulted from the shortage of supplies. The committee noted, too, that the band had left the reservation not as a marauding party but simply with the intention of escaping to their former homes, and that they had begun to fight only when attacked by the army. The handling of Dull Knife's band at Fort Robinson was severely condemned.

The committee's conclusion was decisive: there was no hope of civilizing Indians and making them self-supporting in a location where they were discontented. Unless they were living in a place they could look upon as home, it was unlikely that they would ever gain the independence of feeling that would lead them to work for their own living. "If they are compelled to accept a prison as a home," the report said, "they will naturally prefer to compel the keepers to feed and clothe them. They will remain pensioners upon our humanity, having lost all pride of character and all care of anything except to live."

Still another example of the impossibility of forcing northern Indians into the Indian Territory was the case of Chief Joseph's band of Nez Perces. When these Indians surrendered to General Miles in northern Montana in October 1877, Miles had promised that they could return to Idaho in the spring to settle down peacefully on the reservation. General Sherman overruled this humane decision. Declaring that the Indians were prisoners of war and that they should not be allowed to return to the Northwest, Sherman directed that the Nez Perces be imprisoned at Fort Leavenworth until they could be turned over to the Indian Office for disposition. Transported down the Yellowstone and the Missouri to Fort Leavenworth, the miserable Indians were encamped in unhealthy lowlands along the river, where, ill provided for and pining for the clear mountain streams of their homeland, they succumbed to sickness, and many died.

The Nez Perces at Fort Leavenworth were turned over by the army to agents of the Indian Office, and on July 21, 1878, they headed south to be settled on a section of the Quapaw Reservation. It was hoped that there, under the guidance of the Quaker agent, the desolate Indians would soon become self-supporting, as the Modocs had done in the same location. But the Indians did not recover, and more of the band sickened and died. Chief Joseph insisted that he had been promised by Generals Miles and Howard that he would be allowed to return to Idaho and that he had surrendered under that condition, and he complained about the quality of the region selected for his people in the Indian Territory. Movement to a new area in the Indian Territory brought some relief, but the basic dissatisfaction remained.

Finally in 1883 arrangements were made for the return of thirty-three women and children to Idaho. Philanthropists, encouraged no doubt by this break in the government's position, carried on a campaign to return the rest of the Nez Perces to the Pacific Northwest, and numerous memorials were sent to Congress for that purpose. Congress then authorized the secretary of the interior to remove the Nez Perces from the Indian Territory if he judged proper. In May 1885, 118 of the band settled on the Lapwai Reservation in Idaho, where they were warmly received by friends and relatives. The remaining 150, because of continuing threats from Idaho citizens against them, were sent on to the Colville Reservation in Washington. Chief Joseph's eternal hope that he might eventually return to the Wallowa Valley was never fulfilled.

The cases of the Poncas, Cheyennes, and Nez Perces uncovered evils in forced removals that policy makers could not ignore, whatever theoretical advantages there might have been in moving small tribes to large reservations and consolidating the agencies. Carl Schurz noted in 1880 that when he had taken charge of the Department of the Interior three and a half years earlier, the prevailing opinion seemed to be that it was best for the Indians to be gathered together where they could be kept out of contact with the whites and where their peaceful conduct could be ensured by a few strong military posts. He had accepted that view himself, but as he learned more from experience he realized that it was a "mistaken policy." In his new wisdom, he argued that it was more in accordance with justice as well as experience to respect the home attachments of the Indians and to introduce them to agricultural and pastoral pursuits in the lands they occupied, provided the lands were capable of sustaining the tribe. Moreover, he began to see that large reservations would become impracticable as the pressure of white settlement increased. "The policy of changing, shifting, and consolidating reservations," he declared, ". . . was therefore abandoned."

But if consolidation of reservations was given up as a realizable ideal,

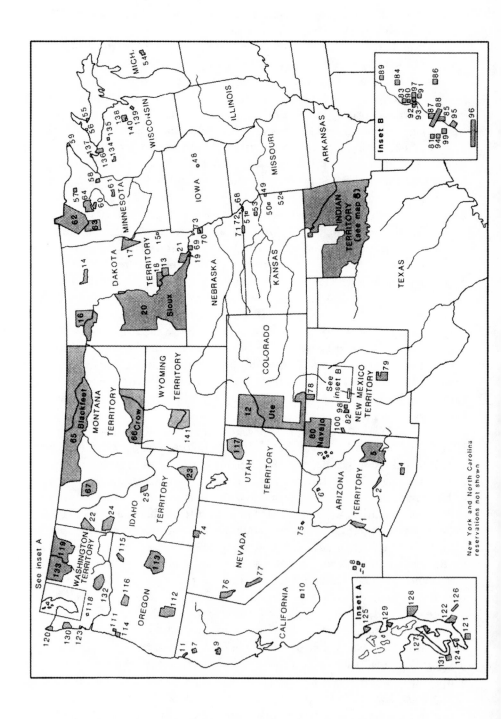

New York and North Carolina
reservations not shown

MAP 6: Indian Reservations, 1880

ARIZONA TERRITORY
1. Colorado River
2. Gila River
3. Moqui Pueblo
4. Papago
5. White Mountain
6. Suppai

CALIFORNIA
7. Hoopa Valley
8. Mission
9. Round Valley
10. Tule River
11. Klamath River

COLORADO
12. Ute

DAKOTA TERRITORY
13. Crow Creek
14. Devils Lake
15. Flandreau
16. Ft. Berthold
17. Lake Traverse
18. Old Winnebago
19. Ponca
20. Sioux
21. Yankton

IDAHO TERRITORY
22. Coeur d'Alene
23. Ft. Hall
24. Lapwai
25. Lemhi

INDIAN TERRITORY
26. Arapaho and
    Cheyenne
27. Cherokee
28. Chickasaw
29. Choctaw
30. Creek
31. Kansas
32. Kiowa and
    Comanche
33. Modoc
34. Nez Perce
35. Osage
36. Ottawa
37. Pawnee
38. Peoria
39. Ponca
40. Potawatomi
41. Quapaw
42. Sac and Fox
43. Seminole
44. Seneca
45. Shawnee
46. Wichita
47. Wyandot

IOWA
48. Sac and Fox

KANSAS
49. Black Bob
50. Chippewa and
    Munsee
51. Kickapoo
52. Miami
53. Potawatomi

MICHIGAN
54. Isabella
55. L'Anse
56. Ontonagon

MINNESOTA
57. Bois Forte
58. Fond du Lac
59. Grand Portage
60. Leech Lake
61. Mille Lac
62. Red Lake
63. White Earth
64. Winnebagoshish

MONTANA TERRITORY
65. Blackfeet
66. Crow
67. Jocko

NEBRASKA
68. Iowa
69. Niobrara
70. Omaha
71. Oto
72. Sac and Fox
73. Winnebago

NEVADA
74. Duck Valley
75. Moapa Valley
76. Pyramid Lake
77. Walker River

NEW MEXICO TERRITORY
78. Jicarilla Apache
79. Mescalero Apache
80. Navajo

Pueblos
81. Jemez
82. Acoma
83. San Juan
84. Picuris
85. San Felipe
86. Pecos
87. Cochiti
88. Santo Domingo
89. Taos
90. Santa Clara
91. Tesuque
92. San Ildefonso
93. Pojoaque
94. Zia
95. Sandia
96. Isleta
97. Nambe
98. Laguna
99. Santa Ana
100. Zuni

NEW YORK
101. Allegany
102. Cattaraugus
103. Oil Spring
104. Oneida
105. Onandaga
106. St. Regis
107. Tonawanda
108. Tuscarora

NORTH CAROLINA
109. Cheoah Boundary
110. Qualla Boundary

OREGON
111. Grande Ronde
112. Klamath
113. Malheur
114. Siletz
115. Umatilla
116. Warm Springs

UTAH TERRITORY
117. Uinta Valley

WASHINGTON TERRITORY
118. Chehalis
119. Colville
120. Makah
121. Nisqually
122. Puyallup
123. Shoalwater
124. Squaxin Island
125. Lummi
126. Muckleshoot
127. Port Madison
128. Snohomish or Tulalip
129. Swinomish
130. Quinaielt
131. Skokomish
132. Yakima
133. Columbia

WISCONSIN
134. Lac Court Oreilles
135. Lac du Flambeau
136. La Point (Bad River)
137. Red Cliff
138. Menominee
139. Oneida
140. Stockbridge

WYOMING TERRITORY
141. Wind River

Source: Annual Report
of the Commissioner of
Indian Affairs, 1880.

reduction of the existing reservations continued to be strongly pushed. Secretary of the Interior Henry M. Teller in 1881 admitted the necessity of the reservations but did not think their size should be disproportionate to the needs of the Indians. "Very many of the reservations," he noted, "contain large areas of valuable land that cannot be cultivated by the Indians, even though they were as energetic and laborious as the best class of white agriculturists. All such reservations ought to be reduced in size and the surplus not needed ought to be bought by the government and opened to the operation of the homestead law, and it would then soon be settled by industrious whites, who, as neighbors, would become valuable auxiliaries in the work of civilizing the Indians residing on the remainder of the reservation." The reduced lands should be vested in the tribe in fee simple.

The reformers continued to see great advantages in such a program. The pressure of the whites on Indian lands would be lessened if not entirely removed, the land left in Indian hands could be given a sure title, proceeds from the sale of the excess lands could replace direct appropriations for Indian subsistence and welfare, and the Indians would be driven closer to an agricultural pattern.

THE INDIAN SERVICE

The Indian service, upon which rested much of the responsibility for solving the "Indian problem" of the post–Civil War decades, was itself a large part of the problem, for it was a primary example of the corruption that tainted Grant's administration. To protect and aid the Indians without at the same time curtailing the expansion of white population in the West created a problem of major dimensions, which would have taxed the abilities of wise and competent men. Yet, somehow, in spite of all the experiments with philanthropic advisers and church-related agents, the men who ran the Indian service, although they promoted the civilization programs that had become a standard element of Indian policy, left much to be desired.

In the first decade and a half after the Civil War, ten men held the office of commissioner of Indian affairs. This was an average tenure of about a year and a half, a very short time given the reform ferment and the frontier turmoil of the time. Commissioner Dennis Cooley, who directed the crucial work of dealing with the Indian nations in the Indian Territory after the war, was appalled by the waste and corruption of the Indian service, but Congress was too busy with other matters to pay attention to the call for reform. Cooley's successor, Lewis Vital Bogy, a flexible Missouri politician, failed to win confirmation from the Senate, which accused him of fraudulent contracts for Indian goods. More significant in directing Indian affairs was Nathaniel G. Taylor, the Methodist minister and Tennessee politician

whose humanitarian sentiments put a strong stamp of Christian philanthropy on Indian Office documents and activities, but whose convictions
on Indian perfectibility often got in the way of his grasp of the present situation. Ely S. Parker, the Seneca, who formally began the peace policy of
Grant, resigned under a cloud in 1871, just as the program was getting
under way.

The peace policy was then directed by a group of commissioners with
strong views about Indian policy and the civilization of their charges. The
first of these, Francis A. Walker, was an anomaly. A brilliant economist and
statistician who had directed the Ninth Census, Walker was appointed to
the Indian Office to keep him on the government payroll when census salary appropriations were cut. Although he had no previous Indian experience, he quickly grasped the situation and the needs of the office. He had a
philosophy of firmness in settling Indians on definite reservations and a
strong commitment to protecting their rights once they arrived there. A
practical man with little trace of the sentimentality that marked Christian
reformers like Nathaniel Taylor, Walker nevertheless had strong humanitarian instincts and deep concern for fair treatment of the Indians.

Edward P. Smith, who succeeded Walker, was the epitome of a peace policy commissioner. An ordained Congregational minister who worked with
the United States Christian Commission during the Civil War, he served as
Indian agent to the Chippewas in Minnesota under the peace policy (nominated by the American Missionary Association). He was strongly recommended for the position of commissioner of Indian affairs by Secretary Delano and by the Board of Indian Commissioners and was appointed to that
office in March 1873, bringing with him a commitment to the reforms
urged by the Christian humanitarians. He held no brief with Indians as
sovereign tribes and promoted incessantly the movement toward individual
allotment of land, American law for the Indians, and progress toward self-
support. Ironically, Smith fell victim himself to the demand for reform, for
his actions as Chippewa agent in regard to timber sales led to a formal investigation. Although he was cleared of any wrongdoing in the Chippewa
affair, he was attacked again during an investigation of charges of fraud
against the Red Cloud agent in 1875, and in December of that year he
resigned.

John Q. Smith, who followed, continued the reform principles of his
predecessors, but he left no strong mark on the office or on Indian affairs.
His term, from December 1875 to September 1877, was a high point for
charges of fraud against the Indian service, and although he himself escaped any charges of personal corruption, he was removed from office soon
after Carl Schurz became secretary of the interior.

Smith's successor was Ezra A. Hayt, a businessman from New Jersey with close ties to the Board of Foreign Missions of the Reformed Church, which had secured his appointment on the Board of Indian Commissioners in 1874. Schurz, seeking a man of high integrity to replace Smith as commissioner of Indian affairs, appointed Hayt to the position. Hayt carried out his duties with energy and aggressive promotion of a civilization program for the Indians. But when evidence of irregularities at the San Carlos Agency were uncovered that incriminated him, Hayt became a liability in Schurz's campaign of reform, and the secretary removed him from office at the end of January 1880.

These commissioners, including two ordained Protestant ministers and other upright Christian gentlemen of close church affiliation, were unable to stem the abuses that plagued the Indian service, for they faced conditions that stimulated fraud and corruption in official Indian-white relations. As land cessions multiplied and the money and other goods due the Indians increased, the chances for unscrupulous whites to cash in on the payments grew almost without bounds. Disposition of such resources as timber from Indian reservations offered still other opportunities for robbing the Indians through fraudulent contracts. Not only was this a matter of plain injustice to the nation's wards, but cheating the Indians of their rightful due frequently led to reprisals. Supplying goods to the Indians—a multimillion-dollar business by the 1870s—was the chief arena for illegal and unjust economic gain at the expense of the government and the Indians. There seemed to be endless ways of cheating by the supply of inferior or insufficient goods for full or inflated prices, and the huge transportation costs of moving masses of goods from eastern markets to the far distant and often isolated agencies offered still other prizes. Although it was never possible to put one's finger on them precisely, "Indian rings"— some sort of conspiratorial aggregation of suppliers and Indian service personnel and sometimes corrupt Indians leaders—seemed to be everywhere.

The creation of the Board of Indian Commissioners was one attempt to correct the evils by having an independent, disinterested group of high-minded businessmen supervise the purchase of Indian goods. The purchasing committee of the board performed valuable and to some extent effective service by checking the bids and inspecting the goods supplied. Yet no matter how much the board may have helped, its failure to break through entrenched corruption meant that it was not the solution to the problem. Nor did the church nomination of agency personnel provide a satisfactory answer by furnishing presumably honest men to deal with the Indians, for evils continued to crop up, and even Christian gentlemen in the office of commissioner of Indian affairs were forced from office because tainted by corrupt practices for which they may or may not have been personally responsible.

One special remedy that was used to ease the problem of corruption was a corps of inspectors to keep tab on operations in the field and to give the central headquarters closer supervision over the activities of the agents and other personnel on the reservations. By a law of February 14, 1873, Congress authorized five inspectors, with power not only to inspect all records but to suspend superintendents, agents, and agency employees and appoint others in their places, subject to the president's approval. The Indian inspectors were hardly a panacea, but they provided an instrument that, with the right personnel and the right use, could facilitate reform and a tighter and more formal organization of the service. Inspections had of course been carried on before by special agents or commissioners appointed for particular one-time duties, but the inspectors authorized in 1873 were a new element between the agencies and the Washington office—men who, unlike the superintendents, viewed headquarters rather than the agents as the object of their first loyalty.

The inspectors performed a great variety of tasks, although their primary function was to monitor the activities of the agents and make sure that laws and regulations were obeyed. They were used frequently to investigate specific complaints lodged against agents, often by whites in the neighborhood who charged discrimination against their economic interests. They aided in the removal of tribes (for example, the Ponca removal of 1877). They helped in problems resulting from the dissolution of the superintendencies, negotiated with tribes for railroad rights of way through the reservations, and made recommendations about transfers of personnel.

POLICIES AND PROGRAMS

As they struggled to control and improve the administration of Indian affairs, the commissioners, despite their diversity of background and short tenures, nevertheless had a uniform policy. All of them, in varying degrees, continued the promotion of Indian civilization that was the corollary of the reservation system, believing that the expansion of the white population across the nation had forever doomed the Indians' traditional way of life.

The movement of railroads westward and the climactic event of the completion of the Union Pacific transcontinental line in 1869 greatly speeded the process. "The completion of one of the great lines of railway to the Pacific coast has totally changed the conditions under which the civilized population of the country come in contact with the wild tribes," Secretary Jacob D. Cox noted in that year. "Instead of a slowly advancing tide of migration, making its gradual inroads upon the circumference of the great interior wilderness, the very center of the desert has been pierced. Every station upon the railway has become a nucleus for a civilized settlement, and a base from which lines of exploration for both mineral and agricultural wealth are pushed in every direction." The inevitability of the advance was taken for granted; the westward course of white population could not—and should not—be stopped or delayed by the Indians. Francis Walker lectured the humanitarian reformers in 1872 that they should exert themselves "not feebly and futilely to attempt to stay this tide, whose depth and strength can hardly be measured, but to snatch the remnants of the Indian race from destruction before it."

The first step in saving the Indians from destruction had been the reservation system, which sought to remove the Indians from the path of the onrushing whites; by 1880 the pattern of reservations was set, although some of them would later be reduced again in size. But once that measure was accomplished, proposals for how to treat the Indians now confined to the reservations became the important elements of United States Indian policy. The Indians, having lost the independence and freedom that marked their aboriginal existence, now became in fact the wards and dependents of a paternal government, and the officials of the Department of the Interior and the Indian Office accepted that fact. They saw it as their responsibility to provide the means for the Indians to move from their traditional life to the white man's civilization—and to force this change upon the Indians for their own good.

A list of priorities in Indian policy emerged during the 1870s that the secretaries of the interior and the commissioners of Indian affairs, aided and abetted by reform sentiment, all espoused. They were set forth in excellent summary form by Schurz in 1879:

1. To set the Indians to work as agriculturists or herders, thus to break up their habits of savage life and to make them self-supporting.

2. To educate their youth of both sexes, so as to introduce to the growing generation civilized ideas, wants, and aspirations.

3. To allot parcels of land to Indians in severalty and to give them individual title to their farms in fee, inalienable for a certain period, thus to foster the pride of individual ownership of property instead of their former dependence upon the tribe, with its territory held in common.

4. When settlement in severalty with individual title is accomplished, to dispose, with their consent, of those lands on their reservations which are not settled and used by them, the proceeds to form a fund for their benefit, which will gradually relieve the government of the expenses at present provided for by annual appropriations.

5. When this is accomplished, to treat the Indians like other inhabitants of the United States, under the laws of the land.

To Schurz these elements of an Indian policy would solve the problems without injustice to the Indians or hindrance to the development of white settlement. The Indians would be raised to a high level of civilization because of the stimulus of individual ownership of property. The policy would not deprive them by force of what belonged to them but would induce them to part with, for a just compensation, lands they did not need and did not cultivate, which could then be opened to progress and improvement.

LAW AND ORDER

Much of the program of civilization, Christianization, and education, of course, was no more than a continuation and intensification of ideas long promoted by officials and others interested in Indian affairs. A newer element was the emphasis on law for the Indians. It had been an assumption of United States Indian policy that the tribes were political entities within which law and order were maintained by Indian custom or law. But the traumatic changes brought by reservation life and the stepped-up attacks on Indian tribalism and Indian ways that were part of the reform movement brought with them a general disorganization and disintegration of Indian societies. "A serious detriment to the progress of the partially civilized Indians," the Board of Indian Commissioners declared in 1871, "is found in the fact that they are not brought under the domination of law, so far as regards crimes committed against each other." The board admitted that Indian tribes differed greatly among themselves and that all were not yet suited to white legal norms. "But when they have adopted civilized costume and civilized modes of subsistence," it said, "we owe it to them, and to ourselves, to teach them the majesty of civilized law, and to extend to them its protection against the lawless among themselves."

A new agency of law that developed in the 1870s, which became a regular element on the reservations, was an Indian police force, quasi-military units under the command of the agents that emerged as substitutes for the authority of the chiefs or for military control of the reservations. Some sort of police force was necessary in the best-ordered societies, it was argued, and to think that the Indian reservations, whose traditional tribal governments were weakened by the white reformers' attacks, could get along without law enforcers was absurd. It was all very well to condemn military management of Indian affairs, but if army troops were not on hand, the agent had to find some other way to back up his decisions.

The idea of a constabulary force of Indian policemen arose spontaneously on several reservations. Indians enrolled by the army as scouts had
performed well, and it was not a difficult step to conceive of Indians as a
temporary or even a permanent civilian corps. The Apache police force established by John P. Clum, the agent at the San Carlos Reservation, was the
best example. Two days after his arrival in August 1874, Clum held a big
talk with the Apaches and explained his plans. "I then told them that I
intended to appoint some Indians as police-men," he later wrote; "that we
would establish a supreme court for the trial of offenders; that I would pre-
side as chief justice, and four or five Apache chiefs would serve as assistant
justices; that Indians would be called as witnesses at the trials. Under this
system, all Apache offenders would be arrested by Apache police, brought
before an Apache court, with Apaches as witnesses, and, if convicted, sentenced by Apache judges, and finally delivered into the custody of Apache
guards." The self-government plan worked, and Clum controlled the volatile Apaches without the aid of the army.

In 1877 Commissioner Hayt urged the creation of a general system of
Indian police. He noted the successes where such police had already been
tried and the practice of using police in Canada. The police system, he said,
would relieve the army from police duty on Indian reservations, would save
lives and property, and would "materially aid in placing the entire Indian
population of the country on the road to civilization." But Congress, where
supporters of military control of the reservations were numerous and influential, held back. Finally, on May 27, 1878, Congress authorized $30,000 to
pay for 430 privates at $5 a month and fifty officers at $8 a month, "to be
employed in maintaining order and prohibiting illegal traffic in liquor on
the several Indian reservations." By the end of the year, the commissioner
reported success at the thirty agencies where police forces had been organized, and in 1879 Congress doubled the number of policemen authorized.
By 1880 there were police at forty agencies and a decade later at fifty-nine.

The police were immediately useful to the agents as an extension of
their authority, but the tasks they performed were in many cases hardly
police duties at all. An Indian policeman was the "reservation handyman."
The police served as couriers and messengers, slaughtered cattle for the
beef ration, kept accounts of births and deaths in the tribe, and took cen-
suses for the agent; and they augmented the labor force of the agency by
building roads, clearing out irrigation ditches, and doing other chores. In
all this they contributed substantially to the smooth operation of the
agency.

Routine labor, however, did not obscure the enforcement of order, which
had been foremost on the minds of advocates of the police system. The Indian police were armed and often mounted, at the beck and call of the agent

when disorder threatened or force was needed to see that rules and regulations on the reservation were properly observed. The police arrested or turned back intruders on the Indian lands and tore out the squatters' stakes, arrested horse thieves, escorted surveying parties, and served as scouts. They acted as guards at annuity payments, preserved order at ration issues, protected agency buildings and other property, and returned truant children to school. They searched for and returned lost or stolen goods, prevented depredations in timber, and brought whiskey sellers to trial. They arrested Indians for disorderly conduct, drunkenness, wife beating, and theft, and reported the comings and goings of strangers on the reservation.

The reformers soon became aware, if they had not been from the start, that these duties and responsibilities of the Indian police were means to an end of greater worth than day-to-day good order on the reservations. The police were to become important chiefly for their moral influence. The police force on a reservation impressed the Indians with the supremacy of law; it discouraged the traditional practice of personal revenge; it imbued a sense of duty and personal responsibility, subjected the policemen themselves to strict discipline and self-control, and inspired them with a pride of good conduct; it taught respect for the personal and property rights of others; by strengthening the authority of the government agent against that of the chiefs, it prepared the Indians for the dissolution of their tribal relations and pushed them forward toward incorporation into American society. The Indian police taught by good example as well as by the enforcement of precepts. They were expected to have only one wife and to dress in the accepted white man's costume, with short hair and unpainted faces. The police force, Commissioner Hiram Price commented in 1881, was "a perpetual educator."

All in all, the Indian police worked remarkably well in fulfilling the reformers' designs. The success rested to a large extent on the fact that the police forces often paralleled or replaced similar institutions within the tribes themselves. The soldier societies that had regulated much of tribal life had performed functions not unlike those assigned to the Indian police, and wittingly or unwittingly, agents drew their policemen from the membership of such societies.

There were, of course, some critics who argued that the Indian police gave too much power to the agent. There was no doubt that an obedient police force in the hands of an authoritarian or unscrupulous agent would be a dangerous thing. But isolated examples of dangerous behavior did not outweigh the overwhelmingly favorable impression made by the Indian police on white observers.

CHAPTER 13

The New Christian Reformers

The drive to acculturate and assimilate the American Indians culminated in the last two decades of the nineteenth century. The policies that statesmen and reformers had advocated through the previous decades now came to fruition. The military struggles were over except for isolated conflicts, and the programs for Americanizing the Indians were pushed with new energy and enthusiasm.

The method to accomplish this ultimate reform was no longer direct participation by laymen in Indian administration, for the early attempts of the Board of Indian Commissioners and the assignment of Indian agencies to missionary groups had proved unworkable. The movement turned now in another direction. By arousing and channeling public sentiment, humanitarians forced through Congress a program of reform that was considered the final answer to "the Indian problem." Uniting reformers in voluntary associations, flooding the nation with press reports and pamphlet propaganda, lobbying in Washington for specific measures, investigating the actual conditions of the Indians in the West, fighting for Indian rights in particular cases—these became the means of revolutionizing the relations of the Indians with the rest of the nation.

A concerted drive on the part of earnest men and women who unabashedly called themselves "the Friends of the Indians" made Congress listen at last. The reformers and their sympathetic friends in government had great confidence in the righteousness of their cause. Convinced of the superiority of the Christian civilization they enjoyed, they were determined to do away with Indianness and tribal relations and to turn the individual Indian into a patriotic American citizen, indistinguishable from his white brothers.

Here was a high point of paternalism, although the Great Father image had largely faded from the rhetoric. The reformers knew what was best for the wards of the government. Lacking all appreciation of the Indian cultures, they were intent on forcing upon the natives the qualities that they themselves embodied. It was an ethnocentrism of frightening intensity, and it set a pattern that was not easily eradicated.

REFORM ORGANIZATIONS

The reformers, in traditional American fashion, worked principally through voluntary associations or societies. Initiated by concerned individuals who often continued to energize the whole, the organizations united likeminded persons in a needed and noble work. By means of branches and auxiliaries they could boast a national membership and bring pressure to bear from all sections of the country. Eastern philanthropists and humanitarians, chiefly from Boston and Philadelphia, led the fight, but they elicited a sympathetic response across the land and brought a unity to the movement that was a primary basis for success.

New organizations devoted to Indian affairs seemed to spring up spontaneously and to attract enough membership and money to keep them viable. The first of these was the Boston Indian Citizenship Committee, which grew out of the furor created by the Ponca affair in the late 1870s. Although it spent much energy at first in its controversy with Secretary of the Interior Carl Schurz over the Ponca tragedy, the Boston Indian Citizenship Committee continued to keep interest alive in Indian welfare. Some of its members played a continuing role among the Indian reformers, emphasizing the need to secure for the Indians their political and civil rights.

At the same time that the Boston group began its work, a similar organization was established in Philadelphia. The work began in the spring of 1879 in an informal fashion; but under the amazing organizational ability of Amelia S. Quinton, the dominant force in the group, the eager women soon developed into a national body. Like the Boston businessmen, they had been aroused by injustices to the Indians and hoped to stir up the God-fearing people of the United States to demand reform in Indian affairs. In October 1883 the organization took the name the Women's National Indian Association.

The work of the association was manifold. Its most cherished projects at the beginning were petitions sent to the president and to Congress, the first of which, with thirteen thousand signatures condemning the invasion of the Indian Territory by white settlers, was sent to Washington in February 1880. Two years later a mammoth petition, claiming to represent no fewer than one hundred thousand persons, was delivered to President Arthur by a committee of the association. It was presented in the Senate on February 21, 1882, by Senator Henry L. Dawes of Massachusetts, who warmly supported the petitioners and their pleas. The petition asked four things: the maintenance of all treaties "with scrupulous fidelity" until they were abrogated or modified with the free consent of the Indian involved; provision of common schools on the reservations "sufficient for the education of every child of every tribe" and of industrial schools as well; allotment of land in severalty (160 acres in fee simple, inalienable for twenty years) to all Indians who desired it; and full rights under the law for the Indians, making them amenable to the laws of the United States, granting full religious liberty, and encouraging them in industry and trade.

A second work of the Women's National Indian Association was the circulation of literature. The women distributed copies of their annual reports and thousands of copies of leaflets on Indian topics printed by the association, as well as the pamphlets printed by the Indian Rights Association. It made efforts also to gain wide circulation for books that agreed with its positions on the Indian question, and it furnished information on the Indian question to the press. The local branches secured the publication in both religious and secular papers of articles on Indian education, on national duty to the Indians, and on missionary work, together with extracts of pamphlets and books. Finally, the women presented their cause at public meetings, often with the cooperation of church groups. Mrs. Quinton herself in 1884 traveled more than ten thousand miles in promoting the work of the association and addressed more than one hundred meetings in the East and Middle West.

The success of the petitions and the other work of the association depended on the active support of branches organized throughout the country. By 1886 there were eighty-three such branches, and contributions rose rapidly. Some of the branches, like those of Connecticut and Massachusetts, became important in their own right. In order to have a medium of communication between the national headquarters and the branches, the association in 1888 began to publish a monthly paper called *The Indian's Friend*, which recorded current legislation concerning Indians, made appeals for help in the association's work, and chronicled the efforts being made by other reform groups.

As the years passed, however, the Women's National Indian Association reduced its interest in propagandizing for Indian reform. The women's group cooperated with other reform-minded groups, but it more and more devoted its energies to direct missionary activity. One of its projects was providing aid to young Indian couples in building homes, and the association established a special Indian Home Building Department.

The most important of the reform organizations was the Indian Rights

Association. It was founded in December 1882 in Philadelphia, a direct outgrowth of a visit of two young Philadelphians, Henry S. Pancoast and Herbert Welsh, to the Great Sioux Reserve in Dakota during the previous summer. "This visit," Welsh later recorded, "resulted in a revolution of many preconceived opinions and in fixing in our minds clearly and firmly two important truths:—1st. That the Indians were capable of civilization, and 2d. That it was largely due to the injustice or inefficiency of the government's dealings with him that the Indian had attained to civilization so imperfectly." Welsh and his companion were struck by the solid accomplishments of the missionaries whose work they inspected, which pointed to a humane solution to the Indian problem, but they were disturbed that so few of the general public were aware of what they themselves had witnessed. "The Indian must have just and faithful friends," Welsh decided, "who will plead his cause with the people, who will represent him in the East and at Washington, until his rights are accorded, and his days of tutelage are over."

Back in Philadelphia, these young humanitarians determined to establish an organization to promote their views. In December, at a meeting in Welsh's home, the Indian Rights Association was founded, and it quickly became a dominant force in Indian affairs. Welsh became the secretary and for all practical purposes the guiding genius of the organization.

While not denying or denigrating the good accomplished in the past by missionaries, teachers, and government agents, the association turned its attention primarily to the question of vital legislation. "No man in these United States to-day," it asserted, "can be rightly termed civilized, nor can his position be considered a safe one, who is removed from both the protection and the punishment of law, who is denied a protected title to land and the right of holding it as an individual, or who is deprived of the blessings of a practical education." Since these conditions did not obtain for the Indians, the Indian Rights Association believed its program was necessary, and it claimed moral and financial support from the general public.

Branch associations were organized in principal cities, which kept in close contact with the central headquarters, receiving information on questions of concern to the association. Representatives were sent out to the Indian reservations in order to get complete, independent, and accurate information on which to base recommendations. Here lay much of the reason for the association's success, for it soon became evident to reasonable men that the Indian Rights Association, although often aggressively promoting its own point of view, had abundant facts behind its arguments. When it investigated an alleged evil or some unjust treatment of the Indians, it could not easily be dismissed as a group of unthinking sentimentalists who did not know what they were talking about.

To place its information and its program before the public, the association embarked on an extensive publication program. It circulated in pamphlet form the reports of its own members' trips of investigation, and it reprinted and spread abroad newspaper articles, speeches, and other materials to further its program. Moreover, Welsh and his associates lectured frequently to interested groups, spelling out their ideas and eliciting support. In the first years of the organization, Welsh alone averaged more than forty talks a year, usually before church groups or local Indian reform associations.

Even more important was the direct and effective lobbying in Washington done by the Indian Rights Association's full-time representative in the capital, Charles C. Painter. Painter followed the progress of legislation on Indian matters, brought information to the attention of the members of the Indian committees of Congress and other legislators, and pressed for measures deemed beneficial to the Indians while opposing those considered injurious. In his work he kept in close touch with Welsh in Philadelphia and as much as possible with branches of the association. To gain firsthand information to aid him in his work, Painter made frequent visits to the Indian country.

The work of the various reform groups came to a focus in a conference held each autumn at a resort hotel on Lake Mohonk, near New Paltz, New York. There men and women interested in Indian affairs met to discuss Indian reform, to hear speakers on matters of concern, and to formulate resolutions that could be broadcast to the public and used to lobby for specific goals in Congress. The instigator of these Lake Mohonk Conferences of Friends of the Indian and a continuing presence behind them was a Quaker schoolteacher, Albert K. Smiley, who with his brother Alfred had purchased the Lake Mohonk property in 1869 and developed it into a summer resort that quickly gained popularity with a substantial religious-minded clientele. Smiley, who had been appointed a member of the Board of Indian Commissioners in 1879, found the meetings of the board in Washington too short to allow time for adequate consideration of Indian matters, so he determined to invite the members of the board and other interested individuals to Lake Mohonk each fall.

The first group assembled in October 1883. It was a small gathering, but as the idea took hold, the yearly conferences grew in size until they averaged in the later 1880s and early 1890s more than 150 persons. The format of the meetings was set, yet relaxed. The mornings were devoted to formal sessions in the spacious parlors of the hotel. A president of the conference was designated (regularly a member of the Board of Indian Commissioners), a resolutions and platform committee chosen, the group welcomed by Smiley, and opening remarks made by the president as the conference got under way. Prepared papers on Indian matters by a variety of experts served as the focus for discussion. The afternoons were free for informal conversations, often on walks through the well-kept grounds of the resort, and the evenings were devoted again to formal sessions.

The Lake Mohonk Conference had no official status other than as a loose extension of the Board of Indian Commissioners. Its work, instead, was the deliberate focusing of public opinion behind specific measures of Indian policy and the aggressive propagandizing of these measures in the press and in the halls of government. The aim, as Smiley expressed it, was "to unite the best minds interested in Indian affairs, so that all should act together and be in harmony, and so that the prominent persons connected with Indian affairs should act as one body and create a public sentiment in favor of the Indians." The group was in fact closely knit. Although it appeared on the surface that the net had been thrown wide to bring in the members in attendance, the large numbers were deceiving, for a small core of dedicated men gave direction to the movement.

CHRISTIAN HUMANITARIANISM

The harmony that marked the Lake Mohonk Conferences was based on a common religious outlook. The Women's National Indian Association, which had been established under Baptist auspices, assumed a nondenominational stance, but it consciously drew on support from the evangelical churches. Its executive board in 1884 comprised members from eight Protestant denominations, and the support of Christian congregations throughout the country was essential for its reform crusade. The Indian Rights Association, too, acknowledged the Christian motivation of its work. Herbert Welsh asserted that the Indian needed to be "taught to labor, to live in civilized ways, and to serve God." He remarked further that "the best Christian sentiment of the country is needed to redeem the Indian, to stimulate and guide the constantly changing functionaries of the government who are charged with the task of his civilization."

The atmosphere of deep religiosity in which the reformers worked was most noticeable at the Lake Mohonk Conferences. The meetings began with an invocation, and the discussions were full of religious spirit and religious terminology. Part of this was due, no doubt, to the influence of the Quaker host; part, also, to the heavy clerical participation in the gatherings. Of the names listed in the membership roster, 1883–1900, more than a fourth were ministers, their wives, and representatives of religious groups, and a great many more were prominent lay leaders in their churches. The editors of the leading religious journals and papers, too, were regularly on hand. All had strong religious motivation for their work in Indians affairs. The president of the conference, Merrill E. Gates, declared in 1891: "This is essentially a philanthropic and Christian reform. Whatever may be our views, our slight differences of view or differences that may seem to us profound, we all gather here believing that, ever since God himself became incarnate, for a man to see God truly, he must learn to see something of God in his fellow-man, and to work for his fellow-men. We come in the spirit of service."

The word *Christian* dropped unselfconsciously from the lips of the reformers as they set about to do God's will, to guide the Indian "from the night of barbarism into the fair dawn of Christian civilization," as Herbert Welsh expressed it in 1886. The only hope for a solution to the Indian problem, Gates declared at the end of nearly two decades of organized humanitarian effort, would be to bring the Indians "under the sway of Christian thought and Christian life, and into touch with the people of this Christian nation under the laws and institutions which govern the life of our States and Territories."

The decades at the end of the century in which Indian reform flourished were marked by an intensification of the desire on the part of zealous evangelicals to create a "righteous empire" in America, and the Indians were caught up in that thrust. The coincidence of an ultimate crisis in Indian affairs, brought about by the overwhelming pressure of expanding white civilization upon the Indians and their reservations, and the intensified religious drive for a unified American society provided the momentum for the new program of Indian policy reform.

The distinguishing mark of American evangelicalism was its insistence on individual salvation: conversion and reformation of individuals was the means to correct evils or wrongs in society. The Indian reformers eventually realized the fundamental conflict between this principle and the communal life and customs of the Indians. Rather than approach the Indian problem in Indian terms, the reformers insisted adamantly on the individualization of the Indians and their acculturation as individuals freed from bondage to the tribe. "The philosophy of the present [Indian] policy," Senator Dawes said in January 1884, "is to treat him as an individual, and not as an insoluble substance that the civilization of this country has been unable, hitherto, to digest, but to take him as an individual, a human being, and treat him as you find him."

The fight for individualization was carried on on many fronts by the evangelical reformers and sympathetic Indian Office officials. They intended to break up tribal ownership of land and substitute allotment of Indian lands in severalty. They wished to end tribal jurisdiction and to treat the Indians as individual citizens before the law. Their individualism, moreover, was tied closely to the Puritan work ethic. Hard work and thrift were virtues that seemed to be at the very basis of individual salvation.

No transformation for the Indians that did not include self-support could be conceived in the reformers' minds. Annuities to the tribes and rations to subsist the Indians were imposing blocks that prevented realization of the ideal; until these were abolished and the Indians made to labor to support themselves and their families, there would be no solution to the Indian problem. Allotment of land in severalty to the Indians was insisted upon because the reformers believed that without the personal labor needed to maintain the private homestead the virtue of hard work could never be inculcated. It was common for the reformers to see in labor a fulfillment of an essential command of God, as Gates did in 1885, when he criticized past efforts to aid the Indians. "Above all else we have utterly neglected to teach them the value of honest labor," he said. "Nay, by rations dealt out whether needed or not, we have interfered to suspend the efficient teaching by which God leads men to love and honor labor. We have taken from them the compelling inspiration that grows out of His law, 'if a man will not work, neither shall he eat!'"

Individual development and the stimulation of honest labor, in the evangelical Protestant worldview, were possible only in the perspective of the family. Glorification of hearth and home was an essential element in their program for Christian living, for the Christian purity and virtues that they extolled could take root and be nurtured to full maturity only within the Christian family. What the reformers saw of Indian life, therefore, seriously offended their sensibilities. Not understanding a culture and a family life that differed so markedly from their own experience, the humanitarians saw only heathen practices, which they felt it their duty to stamp out as quickly and as thoroughly as possible. Polygamy was a special abomination, and the whole tribal arrangement was thought to create and perpetuate un-Christian modes of life.

The goals envisaged for the Indians were deemed possible because the humanitarians believed in the unity of mankind. If the Indians were basically no different from other human beings—except for the conditioning that came from their environment—then there could be no real obstacle to their assimilation. "Let us forget once and forever the word 'Indian' and all that it has signified in the past," Charles C. Painter told the Lake Mohonk Conference in 1889, "and remember only that we are dealing with so many children of a common Father." The doctrine of the brotherhood of man was a cardinal principle of the reformers, who wanted to erase all lines of distinction that separated the Indians from the rest of the nation. Commissioner of Indian Affairs Thomas J. Morgan, speaking of Indian children, stressed first of all "their kinship with us." He observed that "they, too, are human and endowed with all the faculties of human nature, made in the image of God, bearing the likeness of their Creator, and having the same possibilities of growth and development that are possessed by any other class of children."

The reformers accepted the traditional view that mankind had passed through distinct stages of society in the advance from savagery to civilization, and their goal, like that of so many before them, was to speed up the process by educational and other civilizing programs. They quietly ignored scientific studies that pointed to the slowness of change or the racial inferiority of the Indians, and they ridiculed those who challenged their convictions.

AMERICANIZATION

What especially marked the last decades of the nineteenth century in the development of evangelical Protestantism and gave it its peculiar flavor was the subtle transformation that brought about an almost complete identification of Protestantism and Americanism, the culmination of a movement that had extended through the century. The amalgamation of Protestantism and Americanism was not simply an acceptance of evangelical religion by the officials of the state. It came increasingly to be a complacent defense of the social and economic status quo by the churches. Despite warnings of the necessity of separation of church and state, the churches gave a religious endorsement to the American way of life. The perceptive English observer Lord Bryce noted in 1885: "Christianity is in fact understood to be, though not the legally established religion, yet the national religion."

As the nineteenth century drew to a close, two tendencies or forces intensified the union between Protestantism and Americanism. One was the weakening of traditional theological interest, so that the principles of Americanism became in large part the religious creed. The other was the growing threat to the dominance of the "righteous empire" by new forces in the United States, principally the influx of millions of European immigrants, many of whom did not fit the Anglo-Saxon Protestant pattern of America, as well as the growing industrialization and urbanization of the nation, which upset the foundations of the traditional rural Protestant outlook. Afraid that the unity of America was being weakened, the churches sought to strengthen union and conformity.

The Indians were engulfed in this flood of Americanism. Their Americanization, indeed, became the all-embracing goal of the reformers in the last two decades of the century. The reformers were convinced of the divine approbation of the spread of American culture; and the development of the West as an indication of that progress was part of the Protestant mission. There was no intention among the friends of the Indian to protect tribal rights that would obstruct the fruitful exploitation of the nation's domain. "Three hundred thousand people have no right to hold a continent and keep at bay a race able to people it and provide the happy homes of civilization," Lyman Abbott told his colleagues at Lake Mohonk. "We do owe the

Indians sacred rights and obligations, but one of those duties is not the right to let them hold forever the land they did not occupy, and which they were not making fruitful for themselves or others." The Indian reservations should be abolished, letting the full blast of civilization rush in upon the Indians. "Christianity is not merely a thing of churches and school-houses," Abbott insisted. "The post-office is a Christianizing institution; the railroad, with all its corruptions, is a Christianizing power, and will do more to teach the people punctuality than schoolmaster or preacher can."

The Christian reformers who promoted the Americanization of the Indians were not a small, peripheral group of men and women, who by clever machinations and unjustified propaganda foisted a program upon Congress and the Indian service, as they have sometimes been depicted. Rather, they represented or reflected a powerful and predominant segment of Protestant church membership, and thereby of late-nineteenth-century American society. When they spoke, they spoke for a large majority of the nation, expressing views that were widely held, consciously or unconsciously. They were the chief channel through which this Americanism came to bear upon the Indians. It was the fate of the Indians that the solution of the "Indian problem," which had troubled the conscience of many Americans throughout the nineteenth century, should have been formulated at the end of the century, when such a group was in command. The friends of the Indian set about with good intentions to stamp out Indianness altogether and to substitute for it a uniform Americanness, to destroy all remnants of corporate existence or tribalism and to replace them with an absolute rugged individualism that was foreign to the traditions and to the hearts of the Indian peoples.

OTHER VOICES

A singular voice in Indian reform was that of Helen Hunt Jackson, whose memory stimulated the reformers represented at Lake Mohonk. Born Helen Maria Fiske in Amherst, Massachusetts, in 1830, she married an army engineer, Edward B. Hunt, in 1852. When he died accidentally in 1863, she returned to New England and began a literary career. She wrote articles for *The Independent* and other journals, published travel pieces, and in 1870 brought out a book of poetry. While passing the winter of 1873–1874 in Colorado Springs she met a Quaker businessman, William Sharpless Jackson, whom she married in 1875. Making Colorado Springs her home, she continued writing, producing a series of novels and short stories.

By chance, Mrs. Jackson was in Boston in the winter of 1879–1880, when the great furor over Ponca removal was at its height. In November 1879 she heard Chief Standing Bear and Bright Eyes lecture on the wrongs done to the Indians. She had never been noticeably interested in Indians before, but she was suddenly fired by a tremendous indignation and threw herself headlong into the controversy raging over the Ponca affair.

To confirm her position that the government was to blame for the Indians' troubles, she undertook extensive research in the Astor Library in New York City; as she came across evidence of broken treaties or unjust treatment, she wrote up and published her findings. In a whirlwind of activity, she became a veritable one-person reform movement, circulating petitions and tracts, rebuking editors, army officers, clergymen, college presidents, and congressmen, and filling the press with stinging letters. The material she had gathered she incorporated into her famous volume *A Century of Dishonor: A Sketch of the United States Government's Dealings with Some of the Indian Tribes*, published in 1881.

A Century of Dishonor was a strange book, a disorganized, cluttered compilation of fragments, which told the story of the government's relations with seven tribes. It was a polemic, not balanced history, and everywhere evidenced the haste with which it had been put together. The intention was to awaken the conscience of America to the flagrant wrongs that had been perpetrated upon the Indians. Once the people were aroused, the author was convinced that they would demand that Congress right the wrongs. She also took care to see that the members of Congress got her message directly, sending a copy of the book to every one of them at her own expense. "What an opportunity for the Congress of 1880," she exclaimed, "to cover itself with a lustre of glory, as the first to cut short our nation's record of cruelties and perjuries! the first to attempt to redeem the name of the United States from the stain of a century of dishonor!"

The book was a sentimental overdramatization of a complex problem, and it was of little help to the statesmen who had to wrestle with practical solutions to Indian questions. But there is no doubt that its author touched sympathetic chords among the reformers and much of the public. Her writings brought her fame; and her later concern for the Mission Indians in California helped their cause. Her fictionalized treatment of the California Indian story in *Ramona*, published in 1884, enjoyed more popular success than *A Century of Dishonor*, although it never quite fulfilled its author's hope that it would be another *Uncle Tom's Cabin* in the drive for racial justice. But the strain of her crusade was too much, and she died in Colorado Springs in August 1885, concerned for the Indians to the very last.

The humanitarian Indian reformers enjoyed a near unanimity. The notable exception was Dr. Thomas A. Bland, who began his reform career as the associate of Alfred B. Meacham in the 1870s. Meacham and Bland in the early pages of their publication *The Council Fire* did not depart materially from the programs that were so enthusiastically promoted by the new reform organizations. Even when Bland succeeded to full control of the journal on Meacham's death early in 1882, he did not appear to be in opposition to the main currents of Indian reform. The *Council Fire* reported favorably on the 1882 petition of the Women's National Indian Association and welcomed the formation of the Indian Rights Association and other reform organizations. The allotment of land in severalty, a key proposal of the reformers, was agreed to in principle, provided that Indian consent be obtained.

But Bland soon parted company with the rest of the reformers. In November 1885 he organized the National Indian Defence Association and gathered supporters in the East, who preferred to conserve Indians ways, and among the chiefs and squawmen on the reservations, who held fast to the old ways that benefited them. The National Indian Defence Association hoped to slow down if not stop the movement for land in severalty and for citizenship. It argued that the immediate dissolution of tribal relations would be an impediment to the civilization of the Indians, that individual allotments would motivate the Indians to part with their holdings, and that although education might help the next generation, it could not solve the problems of the present one. Bland and his friends actively promoted their views in Washington and in the national press and appeared to have some influence in high places.

The Indian Rights Association fought strongly against that influence, insisting upon the view of Indian policy espoused by the Lake Mohonk reformers. In a long letter printed in the *Boston Herald* on December 27, 1886, and then circulated in pamphlet form, Herbert Welsh analyzed the "irreconcilable difference of opinion" that separated Dr. Bland and his association from Senator Dawes and "other prominent defenders of Indian rights":

> Dr. Bland's efforts have been directed toward keeping the Indian as he is, his tribal relations untouched, his reservations intact; and in opposing the sale of his unused lands, upon no matter how equitable conditions, for white settlement. . . . Senator Dawes and the Indian Rights Association, on the other hand, believe that such a theory is prejudicial to the best interests of the Indians, and even were it not so that it is wholly impracticable, that the settlement of the Indian question, in view of the uncontrollable pressure of white civilization upon the reservations, can only be reached through a careful, wise and equitable adjustment of the rights and needs of the white man and of the Indian; that under fair conditions the Indian should be persuaded to sell unused and unneeded land, upon which the white should be permitted to enter for *bona fide* settlement.

Bland's attempts to defeat the severalty bill and his threat to challenge it in the courts were met by accusations that he was in the pay of the chiefs who opposed reforms. Bland's views if not his methods, however, look better in the perspective of time than many of those of the united humanitarian reformers, who in the 1880s regarded criticism from the National Indian Defence Association as little more than the nipping of a dog at their heels. "Vituperation from that source," Senator Dawes declared in 1887, "is considered by all acquainted with it as a certificate of fidelity to public trust."

CHAPTER 14

The Reservations
and Reform

When the new Christian reformers came on the scene about 1880, the reservation system was firmly established and had become the foundation of United States Indian policy. The reformers at first accepted the reservations and worked within the system, seeking to protect the land rights of the Indians, although they did not hesitate to promote the reduction of reservations in order to speed the Indians' acceptance of an individualized agricultural existence. They supported the reservations, too, as protected enclaves in which the programs of civilization and Americanization could move forward. Yet in the end the reservations became an abomination, for they symbolized the great separation between the Indians and the rest of American society, a separation that precluded the absolute Americanization that was the ultimate goal of the reform organizations and their friends in the government.

DISMANTLING THE GREAT SIOUX RESERVE

Division of the Great Sioux Reserve was the most blatant example of reduction of a large reservation as a humanitarian measure in order to force the Indians into an economic and social pattern acceptable to the whites. Driven by the fear that if the Indians did not agree to give up some of their holdings for fair compensation they were likely to lose them all without recompense, the reformers led the movement to cut down the reservation held by the Teton Sioux in Dakota.

The Great Sioux Reserve, stretching from the Missouri River to the western boundary of Dakota, had been set off for the Indians by the Treaty of Fort Laramie in 1868. Although they were allowed to use the Powder

River country as hunting grounds, the Sioux chiefs who signed the treaty agreed to settle on the new reserve, and the treaty was full of provisions for promoting civilization. With the Sioux boundaries clearly set, the government in article 12 of the treaty assured the Indians that no future cession of any part of the reservation would be valid until approved by at least three-fourths of the adult male Indians occupying or interested in it.

It was not long before the discovery of gold in the Black Hills in the southwestern portion of the Sioux reserve upset the 1868 arrangements. Whites swarmed into the area, eager for gold, and the government found it difficult to live up to its pledge to guarantee the reservation for the Sioux. The familiar tactics of attempting to persuade the Indians to cede the coveted section soon began. A commission headed by Senator William B. Allison of Iowa was appointed on June 18, 1875, to treat with the Sioux for the relinquishing of the Black Hills, but its meetings with the Indians accomplished nothing, and its report ended with the recommendation that Congress should simply fix a fair price for the Black Hills and present the matter to the Indians "as a finality."

After the defeat of Custer, while the army was still engaged against the hostiles, Congress decided on such an ultimatum. On August 15, 1876, it directed that the Indians were to receive no further subsistence unless they relinquished all claims to land outside the 1868 reserve and all of that reservation lying west of the 103d meridian (an area including the Black Hills). The president appointed a commission to carry this word to the Sioux. The commission—headed by George W. Manypenny, former commissioner of Indian affairs, and including among others Newton Edmunds, onetime governor of Dakota Territory, and Bishop Henry B. Whipple, the old reformer—met with the Indians at the Red Cloud Agency in early September. There Manypenny laid down the government's terms, and other commissioners lectured the Indians about the paths to civilization. Although it seems clear from the speeches of the Indians at the signing that they did not fully understand the import of the agreement, the chiefs marked their Xs and the scene was repeated at each of the agencies. "We finished our labors in the Indian country," the commissioners said, "with our hearts full of gratitude to God, who had guarded and protected us, and had directed our labors to a successful issue." They had won the cession of the Black Hills, but only by ignoring article 12 of the treaty of 1868. They had settled for the signatures of the chiefs and headmen only of each tribe, but this seemed not to trouble the good men on the commission, who concluded their report with a fine-sounding plea for good faith and justice.

The land hunger of the whites was not sated by the large bite into the Sioux homelands made by the agreement of 1876. By the early 1880s, new pressures had built up along the borders of the reservation that were all but irresistible. The Chicago and Northwestern Railroad had reached Pierre, and the Chicago, Milwaukee, and St. Paul had built as far as Chamberlain, one hundred miles south on the Missouri. Here they were stopped in their drive to reach the Black Hills beyond. It seemed to Dakota promoters that civilization had come to a halt, blocked by the Great Sioux Reserve to the west.

In 1882 a new commission, headed by Newton Edmunds, approached the Sioux with a new agreement, which called for the cession of reservation lands between the White and Cheyenne rivers and for the lands north of the Cheyenne and west of the 102d meridian—altogether some eleven million acres, including a wide corridor from the Missouri River to the Black Hills. What was left was divided into five separate reservations, one for each of the agencies: Standing Rock, Cheyenne River, Lower Brule, Rosebud, and Pine Ridge. In return, each head of a family was to be allowed to choose a 320-acre tract, plus 80 acres for each minor child. By cajolery and threats the commission gathered the signatures of a number of chiefs and headmen and, disregarding the need for approval of three-fourths of the adult males, submitted the agreement as an accomplished fact.

Outcries of protest arose immediately from the Indians, who claimed with good cause that they had been victimized, and from the Indian Rights Association and other humanitarian friends of the Indians, who pointed to the failure to obtain the necessary consent of the Sioux. Senator Dawes was able to block the measure, and the commission was sent back for more signatures. The second round was little more successful than the first, and Congress rejected the agreement.

When the Senate refused to approve the Edmunds commission agreement, it appointed a select committee with Dawes as chairman to investigate the Sioux reservation situation. Dawes's committee visited all the Sioux agencies, interviewed Indians and agency personnel, and interrogated the Edmunds commission as well. It condemned the work of the commission, but Dawes much favored cutting up the large reservation and opening part of it to white settlement if it could be done without violating treaty stipulations. He hoped to convert what he considered the useless and unnecessary Indian lands into a permanent fund, the annual income of which could be devoted to "the civilization, education, and advancement in agriculture and other self-supporting pursuits" of the Sioux.

Dawes submitted with the report of his select committee a bill that incorporated the changes he advocated. The main point was the establishment of a permanent fund for the Sioux. The fund was to total $1 million and be held in the Treasury of the United States to the credit of the Indians at 5 percent interest, one half of the income to be used for the promotion of "industrial and other suitable education" and the other half in whatever way the secretary of the interior would judge best for the advancement of the Indians "in civilization and self-support." All the land acquired by the bill was to be disposed of under existing homestead acts, but the settler would pay fifty cents an acre, in four equal annual payments. The money thus received would reimburse the government for the permanent fund, for the purchase of stock for the Indians to encourage them in herding, and for government expenses in administering the act. The bill provided explicitly that the law would be null and void without the consent of three-fourths of the Indian men.

The passage of this bill, known as Senator Dawes's Sioux Bill, became one of the primary objectives of the reform groups. The bill passed easily in the Senate, but it had trouble in the House, where it was joined with the general land in severalty bill and a bill to provide relief for the Mission Indians as the essential package of legislation demanded by the humanitarians. Although the severalty bill finally passed early in 1887, the other two measures were put off again. The reformers continued their efforts, for they were convinced of the rightness of their cause. "The waves of an importunate civilization that cannot long be either staid or stopped, at the bidding of any man," Herbert Welsh wrote, "are breaking incessantly upon the border of the Great Reservation. It is the deep conviction of the Indian Rights Association that sound policy now demands the opening of a lawful channel for the advance of this mighty tide. Hesitation at the present critical time invites a possible catastrophe."

The House at last bowed to the pressure. On April 30, 1888, Dawes's measure became law, and Secretary of the Interior William F. Vilas appointed a commission led by Richard Henry Pratt, head of the Carlisle Indian School, to submit the act to the various bands of Sioux to get their consent. There was to be no negotiation; the commissioners were to inform the Indians that Congress had drawn up the agreement with care and that the president after wise scrutiny had approved it and that it embodied "the desire and purpose of the Government of the United States for the advancement and civilization" of the Sioux. The commissioners, moreover, were to impress upon the Indians the fact that new conditions made the old reservation no longer viable and that if they did not accept the "generous and beneficent" arrangements now proposed by Congress, their future would be "problematical and uncertain."

The Pratt commission made little headway against the intransigence of the Indians, who united in opposition to the new agreement. Having been severely burned before, the Sioux were now careful to stay far away from the fire. Even when Little Wound, American Horse, and other tribal leaders were called to Washington for new talks, no progress was made.

The supporters of the program were not yet ready to give up, for the

MAP 7: The Sioux Reservations, 1890

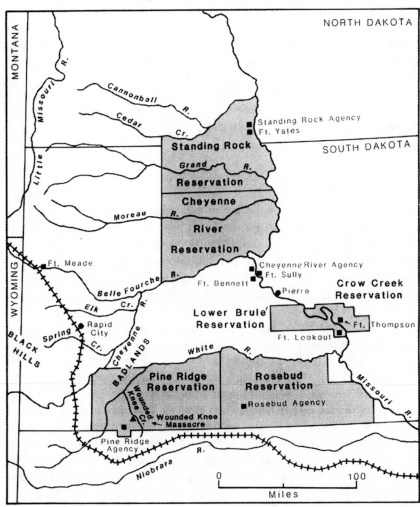

urgency of the need had increased with the passage of the Omnibus Bill in February 1889 providing for the admission to statehood of North and South Dakota in November. On March 3, 1889, Congress authorized a new commission to negotiate for the reduction and division of the Sioux reservation. A separate act approved the same day set forth a new and decidedly more generous agreement, which the commission proposed to the Indians for their consent.

The new commission was dominated by Major General George Crook, who used his long experience and his knowledge of Indian temperament and customs to succeed where previous commissions had failed. The com-

mission put on feasts for the Indians, permitted tribal dances that had long
been proscribed, and in general put the Sioux at ease, until little by little
the Indians' will to resist was broken. But Crook also spoke bluntly to the
Indians: "Last year when you refused to accept that bill, Congress came
very near opening this reservation anyhow. It is certain that you will never
get any better terms than are offered in this bill, and the chances are that
you will not get so good. And it strikes me that instead of complaining of
the past, you had better provide for the future." In the end, out of 5,678
eligible to vote, 4,463 signified their approval.

MISSION INDIANS OF CALIFORNIA

While the Indian Rights Association and other humanitarian reformers
were carrying on their fight for the Sioux bill, they paid special attention
also to the Mission Indians of California, "a singularly helpless race in a
singularly anomalous position." Left unprotected by federal policy in California because of the failure to ratify treaties with them, these Indians and
the loss of their lands became renewed concerns as reform sentiment grew
after the Civil War.

In January 1883 Helen Hunt Jackson was appointed to investigate their
condition and to make recommendations for correcting injustices. With
the aid of Abbot Kinney, a Californian of sympathetic views, she submitted
a report on July 13, 1883. Declaring that, with such long neglect and multiplication of wrongs, it was no longer possible to render the Indians a full
measure of justice and that what was possible was only some measure of
atonement, Jackson and Kinney recommended confirmation of land titles
to the Indians, appointment of lawyers to safeguard the Indians' rights,
more schools, and agricultural and other assistance. The recommendations
were incorporated into a bill by the Indian Office and submitted to Congress, where it passed the Senate but was not acted upon by the House.

Reform pressure brought some action on the part of the Indian Office,
which did what it could to remove intruders from lands on which the Indians lived. Then, finally, in January 1891 Congress directed that the secretary of the interior appoint three disinterested persons as commissioners
to arrange a just and satisfactory settlement. The commissioners were to
select reservations for the Indians to be held in trust by the government for
twenty-five years. White settlers were to be removed and compensated for
their improvements and allotments provided for individuals judged to be
"so advanced in civilization as to be capable of owning and managing land
in severalty." The allotments would be granted in fee simple after a twenty-
five-year trust period.

The law fitted perfectly into the patterns of land tenure that the humanitarian reformers had decided upon for the Indians, emphasizing individual holdings in fee simple but with restrictions against alienation for a term of years. The Mission Indians were no more successful in attaining the great benefits envisaged than were the majority of American Indians, who soon lost most of the land that reformers had hoped to guarantee them forever. But with the passage of the law, the reformers rejoiced that they had accomplished their goal, and concern for the Mission Indians ceased to be a major element in Indian reform.

PROMOTION OF CIVILIZATION

The reservations segregated the Indians from the whites in order to prevent violent conflict, but the reformers initially gave them enthusiastic support also as hothouses in which the seedlings of civilization could get a protected start. Because the reservations were to serve this purpose, humanitarians had always had an interest in agency affairs, and the government accepted their help.

As the nineteenth century waned and the Indians were forced to accept reservations and were then squeezed ever more tightly together on reduced holdings, the reservations became of greater and greater critical importance. They were the means to transform the Indians into American citizens, for the segregation and isolation they provided allowed the civilization process to proceed unhindered by outside forces. The reservations were a controlled society in which, the sooner the better, tribal ways would fall before the ways of the dominant white society.

The inhabitants of the reservation, however, were not a homogeneous group in their reaction to the purposes the government and the reformers had in mind. Most reservations, in fact, were split into two factions, designated by the reformers as "progressives" and "nonprogressives." Herbert Welsh in 1891 described the divisions among the Sioux in typical terms:

> There are two great and sharply defined parties among the Sioux Indians to-day, either of which is the creation and representation of an idea. These ideas are antagonistic and irreconcilable.
>
> First. There is the old pagan and non-progressive party. Inspired by sentiments of hostility to the Government and to white civilization, it believes in what is Indian, and hates what belongs to the white man. It delights in the past, and its dream is that the past shall come back again—the illimitable prairie, with vast herds of the vanished buffalo, the deer, the antelope, all the excitement of the chase, and

the still fiercer thrill of bloody struggles with rival savage men. Consider what has been the education of the men who form this party— eating Government rations paid them in lieu of ceded lands, idleness, visits to distant relatives and friends, constant feasts and dances, with oft-repeated recitals from the older men of their own deeds of valor and the achievements of their ancestors. . . .

Second. A new, progressive, and what may properly be termed Christian party, whose life was begotten, nourished, and trained by missionary enterprise and devotion. . . . In these Christian Indians is to be found abundant food for a study of the germs and first awakenings of civilized life rich in variety and suggestion. They present all possible differences of age, condition, and of moral and mental attainments. . . . And yet in all this diversity to be found in the progressive party among the Sioux is clearly shown one controlling principle— an awakened moral purpose, newborn, or well-developed, the stirring of an enlightened conscience, and of a long-dormant intellect.

It was the reformers' mission to encourage the progressives and to stamp out the nonprogressives, to support men and measures that promoted the former and restricted or crushed the latter.

The key figure in the process was the Indian agent. The regulations for the Indian service promulgated by the Indian Office said bluntly: "The chief duty of an agent is to induce his Indians to labor in civilized pursuits. To attain this end every possible influence should be brought to bear, and in proportion as it is attained, other things being equal, an agent's administration is successful or unsuccessful." If the agent was a man of strength and integrity who could control the conservative chiefs and who would aggressively foster the civilization programs, he won the commendation of the humanitarians and their support against attack. Other agency personnel were considered instruments for carrying out the civilization program of the agent. Thus the licensed traders were to provide good example by their lives and honest dealings, and the agency physicians were not only to care for the sick but were to counteract the work of the Indian medicine men.

Preeminent supporters of the agent were the Indian police, who in the 1880s were joined by a complementary institution, the courts of Indian offenses. The instigator of the courts was Secretary of the Interior Henry M. Teller, who in December 1882 called attention to "a great hindrance to the civilization of the Indians, viz, the continuance of the old heathenish dances, such as the sun-dance, scalp-dance, etc." Such practices, he insisted, led to a war spirit and demoralized the young. He objected further to the practice of polygamy among the Indians, which could not be afforded when the Indians supported themselves by the chase but which now seemed to flourish when the government furnished rations. A third hindrance to the advancement of the Indians he found in the influence of the medicine men, who kept children from attending school and promoted heathenish customs. Nor could he abide the practice among the Indians of giving away or destroying the property of a man who died. "It will be extremely difficult to accomplish much towards the civilization of the Indians," Teller concluded, "while these adverse influences are allowed to exist."

Following the secretary's orders, Commissioner Hiram Price on April 10, 1883, directed the establishment of courts. The judges were to be "intelligent, honest, and upright and of undoubted integrity," and could not practice polygamy. The courts were to meet twice a month and rule upon all questions presented to them for consideration by the agent. Specific jurisdiction was granted over the dances objected to by Teller, polygamous marriages, interference of the medicine men with the civilization program, thefts and destruction of property, intoxication and the liquor traffic, and misdemeanors. Punishments were usually in the form of a fine, although imprisonment also could be ordered. All the decrees of the court were subject to the approval or disapproval of the agent, and appeal could be made to the commissioner of Indian affairs, but there was no intention that the courts should handle major crimes.

The legal basis on which the courts of Indian offenses rested was extremely vague, but everyone spoke favorably of the work of the courts. Teller was enthusiastic from the beginning, and Price after a year's experience with the system noted that the decisions of the judges had been quietly accepted and peaceably enforced and that at some agencies the courts had been instrumental in abolishing "many of the most barbarous and pernicious customs that have existed among the Indians from time immemorial."

The Indian Office and its humanitarian supporters waged an incessant war, which they never quite won, against intruders and other discordant elements on the reservations. The treaties and executive orders by which the reservations were established uniformly prohibited the entrance of whites who were not official agency personnel or licensed for some special purpose. Casual intruders were expelled by the agents and their police forces, and in serious cases, of which the infiltrations into the Indian Territory were most notorious, a call was made upon the troops of the United States army. Two groups, however, caused special trouble.

The first of these were squawmen, white men who had married Indian women and lived as members of the tribe. These men sometimes exploited the Indians by using without charge large portions of the reservation for grazing or agricultural purposes, but often they merely lived off the tribe with little work. Everywhere they were a discordant element, backed the chiefs in their resistance to change, and earned the enmity of the reformers.

A second serious challenge to the isolation of the reservations came from the intrusion of white cattlemen and their herds upon the Indian lands. The reservation of the Cheyennes and Arapahos in the Indian Territory was an especially attractive target, for the sparse population left vast acres of grassland lying vacant. In 1883 enterprising men entered into agreements with certain Indians within this reservation at minimal fees and began to exploit the lands; of 4,297,771 acres in the reservation, only 465,651 were left in Indian hands. Similar leases were made on other reservations. The members of the Lake Mohonk Conference in 1883 considered the leasing of Indian lands for grazing as "inexpedient"; they wanted the Indians themselves to become herders on these lands and suggested that Congress appropriate money to buy herds to get the Indians started.

The government, unfortunately, was caught without a policy. The Indian Office declined to approve the leases because it doubted its legal authority to do so, but it permitted the Indians to make them under the pretense that they were merely licenses granted by the Indians to the whites to enter the reservations. The average annual rental price, however, ran to about two cents an acre, which government officials considered altogether too low. The leases of the Cheyennes and Arapahos, moreover, caused great dissension among the Indians themselves. Powerful traditionalist groups within the reservation fought against the presence of the cattlemen and their herds, and the factionalism threatened to result in open conflict. President Cleveland issued a proclamation on July 23, 1885, declaring the leases null and void and calling for the removal of the whites and their cattle from the Indian lands. By the end of the year the cattlemen and their herds were gone.

On the Kiowa, Comanche, and Apache reservation, lying south of the Cheyennes and Arapahos along the Texas border, the encroachment of cattlemen was less successfully resisted. Texas cattlemen moved across the Red River with large herds, and leases signed with influential chiefs gave a color of legality to their operations. The Indian Office, unsure of its ground, let the leases stand. The cattlemen here formed a powerful lobby supporting the Indians in opposition to the allotment of their lands in severalty and the opening of the surplus to white settlement, but their presence was in many ways harmful to the Indians. The money they poured into the pockets of the Indians corrupted the leaders, contributed to tribal factionalism, and did little to stimulate personal economic effort on the part of the tribesmen.

The problem of white cattlemen on the reservations was never satisfactorily faced because of the ambivalence of the government and the reformers toward the matter. Vast areas of the reservations were lying empty—a condition abhorrent to men imbued with the exploitative sentiment of the day. If the lands were not profitably used by the Indians, should they not be utilized by others who would pay for the use and provide funds for the benefit of the Indians? And could not the Indians learn by observing the profit-making enterprise of the whites in their midst? Would not such benefits outweigh the evils of white infiltration? No final answers were forthcoming. The solution instead was to eliminate the questions by cutting down the holdings of the Indians as they were moved toward accepting land in severalty, and making the surplus lands directly accessible to the whites.

In one notable case the progress toward the civilization on the reservations was impeded by continued warfare, a last holdout of hostile Indians who rejected reservation life and the restrictions it entailed. The Apaches of the Southwest, led finally by the Chiricahua chief Geronimo, had been placed on reservations in Arizona and New Mexico, but they remained restless, and inefficient administration brought disorder rather than calm. The intermixture of Apache bands, moreover, increased the tensions. All the while, expanding white population in the region intensified the likelihood of Indian-white conflicts.

As Indian bands left the reservations to renew their raiding, in Mexico as well as in the United States, new military campaigns were organized to subdue them and return them to the reservations. It was a long and weary conflict, for the guerrilla warfare of the Indians was more than a match for the United States regulars. Not until September 1886 did Geronimo and the last of the hostile Apaches finally surrender. No chances could be taken that surrendered Indians would break loose again to terrify the countryside. This time the hostile Indians, and neutral Indians as well, were loaded into railroad cars and sent into exile in Florida.

The forced removal of the Apaches from their homeland, although it undoubtedly ended the Apache dangers in Arizona and New Mexico, caused great concern among the reformers in the East, who took up the exiled Indians as one of their causes. Many Indians died in Florida; and the Indian warriors at first were separated from their families. The families were united in 1887 and moved to a more healthful location at Mount Vernon Barracks in Alabama. In 1894 they were moved once more, this time to Fort Sill, Oklahoma. There Geronimo died in 1909, having become a sort of celebrity. Some of the Apaches were transferred in 1913 to the Mescalero Reservation in New Mexico, but others remained at Fort Sill.

OPPOSITION TO RESERVATIONS

The reformers were more successful in enacting programs for "elevating" the Indians than they were in providing for the basic human needs of the Indians in the process. The plains tribes, who got most of the attention, had been self-sufficient in their hunting culture. With the buffalo gone, these Indians were supposed to become self-sustaining agriculturalists almost immediately. For a short period the government was willing to provide subsistence—either through annuity arrangements or as gratuities— and it publicly proclaimed that it was cheaper to feed the Indians than to fight them. The rations in many cases, however, had to continue indefinitely, for the conversion to agriculture came slowly if at all, and large numbers of the formerly energetic and aggressive warriors became enervated and dispirited recipients of the dole.

In such an unanticipated circumstance, it was perhaps understandable that the rations supplied were insufficient and often poor in quality. Conditions of starvation and near starvation were prevalent, and the reformers and the Indian Office again and again had to make special appeals to stir Congress into making the necessary appropriations to prevent disaster. Cattle supplied for the purpose of starting a grazing economy among the Indians frequently disappeared to assuage hunger before they could begin to thrive. Other goods—clothing and farming implements, for example— were of bad quality and not plentiful enough to answer the Indians' needs.

Such circumstances made the reservations appear to be mammoth poorhouses rather than nurseries of civilization, and they seriously undercut the positive efforts made to convert the Indians into American citizens. The reformers had looked with optimism to the reservations as halfway houses in which the native Americans could make a more or less speedy transition from their traditional ways to full acculturation. The change was to be made from the nomadic life of a buffalo hunter to the sedentary life of a small farmer, from communal patterns to fiercely individualistic ones, from native religious ceremonials to Christian practices, from Indian languages and oral traditions to spoken and written English. For most of the reservation Indians the changes were a shattering experience, demoralizing rather than uplifting. The self-reliance and self-support that underlay the hopes of reformers for the Indians were little in evidence.

The realization that the Indians were not changing as the reformers had so confidently believed they would led to an outright condemnation of the reservations as an unmitigated evil to be destroyed. The strongest voice was that of Lyman Abbott, the vigorous proponent of so many reforms. Abbott admitted that his knowledge of the Indians was limited, that he had never visited an Indian reservation and had never known more than ten Indians, but his convictions about what was best for the Indians were absolute. The solution to the Indian problem, he believed, lay "in the annihilation of the reservation system root and branch." It soon became clear, however, that Abbott's views were too radical to suit the rest of the reformers, for he argued that treaties made with the Indians should be unilaterally abrogated by the United States if they stood in the way of abolishing the reservation system. Herbert Welsh took it upon himself to head off "the crude and radical views" of Abbott, speaking against them to his colleagues and writing to Dawes to enlist his support. At Lake Mohonk Dawes spoke eloquently against Abbott's position, insisting that the treaties with the Indians were inviolable and could not in justice be overthrown.

Abbott was not easily put down and spoke his mind forcefully at the conference. "If we have made a bad contract," he said, "it is better broken than kept. . . . It is not right to do a wrong thing, and if you have agreed to do a wrong thing, that agreement does not make it right." He continued:

> I declare my conviction then that the reservation system is hopelessly wrong; that it cannot be amended or modified; that it can only be uprooted, root, trunk, branch, and leaf, and a new system put in its place. We evangelical ministers believe in immediate repentance. I hold to immediate repentance as a national duty. Cease to do evil, cease instantly, abruptly, immediately. I hold that the reservation barriers should be cast down and the land given to the Indians in severalty; that every Indian should be protected in his right to his home, and in his right to free intercourse and free trade, whether the rest of the tribe wish him so protected or not; that these are his individual, personal rights, which no tribe has the right to take from him, and no nation the right to sanction the robbery of.

Most of his listeners were not quite ready for immediate repentance, for they were strongly committed to maintaining the formal treaty rights of the Indians. Although Abbott served on the resolutions committee at the conference, he was unable to swing the gathering completely to his way of thinking. The platform adopted was a compromise. It agreed to the principle of allotting the lands of the reservations in severalty, and it urged that negotiations be undertaken to modify existing treaties and that "these negotiations should be pressed in every honorable way until the consent of the Indians be obtained." But it rejected the proposal to abrogate the treaties or to force severalty upon the Indians.

There could be little doubt, however, that the powerful drive then under way for general allotment of land in severalty and for extending United States law over the Indians was intended ultimately to destroy the reservation system.

CHAPTER 15

Severalty, Law, and

Education

No panacea for the Indian problem was more persistently proposed than allotment of land to the Indians in severalty. It was an article of faith with the reformers that civilization was impossible without the incentive to work that came only from individual ownership of a piece of property. The upsurge of humanitarian concern for Indian reform in the post–Civil War era gave a new impetus to the severalty principle, which was almost universally accepted and aggressively promoted, until Congress finally passed a general allotment law. Allotment of land in severalty, however, was part of the drive to individualize the Indian that became the obsession of the late-nineteenth-century Christian reformers and did not stand by itself. The breakup of tribalism, a major goal of this Indian policy, had been moved forward by the abolition of the treaty system and would be carried on by a government educational system and by the extension of American law over the Indian communities. Yet for many years the dissolution of communal lands by allotment, together with the citizenship attached to private land-owning, was the central issue.

A GENERAL ALLOTMENT LAW (DAWES ACT)

The advocates of change wanted general legislation that would permit or require the allotment of lands in severalty for all the Indians on reservations. Early in 1879, Commissioner of Indian Affairs Ezra Hayt drew up a draft of such legislation. He criticized past allotment provisions for failure to protect the Indian allotments adequately from imprudent alienation, and his own proposal prohibited alienation for a period of twenty-five years. The inefficiency of the old system of common title and of the treaties that granted land in severalty with a title in fee had been demonstrated, he thought, and he believed that his plan with delayed title would solve the problem. By such a measure, he was convinced that "the race can be led in a few years to a condition where they may be clothed with citizenship and left to their own resources to maintain themselves as citizens of the republic."

The measure was considered by Congress in the form of a bill drawn up by Senator Richard Coke of Texas, which had tremendous support from many sides, most importantly, perhaps, from Carl Schurz, who again and again urged its passage. Schurz spoke of the Coke bill as "the most essential step in the solution of the Indian problem," and his statement of the advantages that would accrue summed up the views of the reformers generally:

It will inspire the Indians with a feeling of assurance as to the permanency of their ownership of the lands they occupy and cultivate; it will give them a clear and legal standing as landed proprietors in the courts of law; it will secure to them for the first time fixed homes under the protection of the same law under which white men own theirs; it will eventually open to settlement by white men the large tracts of land now belonging to the reservations, but not used by the Indians. It will thus put the relations between the Indians and their white neighbors in the Western country upon a new basis, by gradually doing away with the system of large reservations, which has so frequently provoked those encroachments which in the past have led to so much cruel injustice and so many disastrous collisions. It will also by the sale, with their consent, of reservation lands not used by the Indians, create for the benefit of the Indians a fund, which will gradually relieve the government of those expenditures which have now to be provided for by appropriations. It will be the most effective measure to place the Indians and white men upon an equal footing as to the protection and restraints of law common to both.

There were, to be sure, some who spoke out against allotment and who criticized the humanitarians' arguments. By far the strongest of these was Senator Teller, who criticized the reformers' desire for a universal and uniform measure, which did not take into account the tremendous diversity among the Indian tribes, and he flatly denied the claims of the advocates of severalty that the Indians were clamoring for allotments in fee simple. In Teller's view, the friends of severalty had the whole matter turned around, mistaking the end for the means. Once the Indians were civilized and Christianized and knew the value of property and the value of a home, then give them an allotment of their own, he argued. But do not expect the allotment to civilize and Christianize and transform the Indians.

Early attempts to pass the bill failed in the House, and when the severalty bill came up again in December 1885, it was introduced by Senator Henry L. Dawes, now chairman of the Committee on Indian Affairs. His name stuck to the final act, although he had been relatively late in climbing on the allotment bandwagon, and Senator Coke was soon forgotten. Dawes, perhaps because he despaired of any other answer, became one of the most active supporters of the individualization of the Indian through private property, answering questions in public meetings about the details of the proposal and ultimately pushing the measure through Congress. His bill became law on February 8, 1887.

The Dawes Act dealt primarily with ownership of the land. It authorized but did not require the president to survey the reservations or selected parts of them and to allot the land to individual Indians. The amounts to be allotted reflected the strong tradition of a quarter-section homestead for the yeoman farmer. One-quarter of a section (160 acres) was to be allotted to each head of family and smaller parcels to single persons and minors. In cases where lands were suitable only for grazing, the allotments would be doubled, and if prior treaty provisions specified larger allotments, the treaty would govern. If anyone entitled to an allotment did not make the selection within four years after the president had directed allotment, the law authorized the secretary of the interior to order the agent of the tribe or a special agent to make such selection.

When the secretary of the interior approved the allotments, he would issue to each Indian a patent, which declared that the United States would hold the allotted lands in trust for twenty-five years for the Indian and for his sole benefit or that of his heirs. At the expiration of the trust period, the Indian would receive the land in fee simple. Any conveyance or contract touching the land during the trust period was null and void, and the president at his discretion could extend the period. Once an Indian had received his allotment, he would become a citizen of the United States.

After the lands had been allotted on a reservation, or sooner if the president thought it was in the best interests of the tribe, the secretary of the interior could negotiate with the tribe for the purchase of the remaining or surplus lands, the purchase to be ratified by Congress before becoming effective. The money paid to the Indians for the surplus lands was to be held in the Treasury for the sole use of the tribes to whom the reservation belonged, and the funds were subject to appropriation by Congress for the education and civilization of the Indians concerned. Excluded from the provisions of the act were the Five Civilized Tribes, the Osages, Miamis, Peorias, and Sacs and Foxes in the Indian Territory, the Seneca Indians in New York, and the strip of Sioux lands in Nebraska.

The Dawes Act, as one historian of the measure observed, was "an act of faith." It was an act pushed through Congress, not by western interests greedy for Indian lands, but by eastern humanitarians who deeply believed that communal landholding was an obstacle to the civilization they wanted the Indians to acquire and who were convinced that they had the history of human experience on their side.

The passage of the Dawes Act caused great exultation among the reformers who had fought so persistently for the proposal. "In securing the passage of this law the Indian Rights Association achieved the greatest success in its history," the executive committee of the association declared, "and its enactment was the most important step forward ever taken by the national Government in its methods of dealing with the Indians." Secretary of the Interior L. Q. C. Lamar described it as "the most important measure of legislation ever enacted in this country affecting our Indian affairs . . . [and] practically a general naturalization law for the American Indians." It was to his mind "the only escape open to these people from the dire alternative of impending extirpation." Merrill E. Gates, president of the Lake Mohonk Conference, said in 1900 that the act was "a mighty pulverizing engine for breaking up the tribal mass."

Year by year the process of allotment moved ahead, and the surplus lands were rapidly transferred to the whites. The Indians held 155,632,312 acres in 1881; by 1890 they had 104,314,349, and by 1900 only 77,865,373, of which 5,409,530 had been allotted. So successful did the process seem that the reformers looked forward to the day when government supervision over the Indians would disappear entirely and the Indians would all be absorbed into American society.

Dissatisfaction with the Dawes Act soon arose, however, when it was realized that the allotment of a homestead to an Indian did not automatically turn him into a practical farmer. The provisions of the act that prohibited the leasing or other such conveyance of the allotments—wisely intended to protect the Indian holdings for an extended period—actually seemed to work a hardship on many Indians. Women and children and Indians who were in some way disabled could not reap the benefits of the allotments because they were unable to farm them. Moreover, lands belonging to students who were away at school lay fallow or were used illegally by whites with no benefit to the Indians. If leasing were allowed for these needy persons, an income from the land could be provided for them. Other Indians, it turned out, did not have the work animals or agricultural implements indispensable for effective use of their allotments. If a portion of their land could be rented, the income could be used to provide the tools needed to farm the rest.

There was in addition the question of advancing the Indians toward full participation in American society by letting them assume the full responsibility for their own property. To hedge their ownership around with all kinds of restrictions in its use hardly was conducive to Indian growth in maturity, and the interspersing of white farmers among the Indians, it was argued, would furnish object lessons of great value in teaching the Indians how to farm.

It is strange how readily the reformers accepted these arguments—the same men and women who had championed allotment in severalty as the way to move the Indians from idleness to hard work on their own land. Only a few voices were raised against the proposals to make leasing legal under set conditions, and the opposition was too slight to stem the movement.

By a law of February 28, 1891, Congress made leasing possible. It allowed Indians who "by reason of age or other disability" were personally unable to occupy and improve their allotments to lease their lands for set periods, subject to the approval of the secretary of the interior. Although the Indian Office moved slowly at first in applying the leasing law, the program soon gained a momentum that swept away the restrictions the advocates had intended, and the wording of the law was loosened in 1894 by adding "inability" to age and disability as a reason for leasing allotments and by extending the period of lease. The number of leases climbed steadily.

There is no doubt that the leasing policy ate deeply into the goals envisaged by reformers for the allotment policy, for many Indians came to look upon the land as a source of revenue from the labor of a tenant, not as a homestead to be worked personally by an independent small farmer. The leasing, furthermore, was a step toward complete alienation of the allotments by sale, a process that soon began to appear as a break in the dike of protection erected around the allotments.

LAW AND CITIZENSHIP

Paralleling the drive for allotment in severalty was strong agitation to make the Indians amenable to white law. The reformers attacked this problem with their usual gusto, and some of them offered law as a new panacea.

The historical starting point was clear enough. The Indian tribes had been treated as "nations," and although John Marshall had characterized them as "domestic" and "dependent" in order to distinguish them from foreign states, the internal independence of the Indian group was assumed. The reformers after the Civil War, however, discovered weaknesses in this traditional arrangement, and various elements in their program eventually so changed the status of the Indians that the problem of law for the Indians acquired new and threatening dimensions. "A serious detriment to the

progress of the partially civilized Indians," the Board of Indian Commissioners declared in 1871, "is found in the fact that they are not brought
under the domination of law, so far as regards crimes committed against
each other." The board admitted that Indian tribes differed greatly among
themselves and that all were not yet suited to white legal norms. "But
when they have adopted civilized costume and civilized modes of subsistence," it said, "we owe it to them, and to ourselves, to teach them the majesty of civilized law, and to extend to them its protection against the lawless among themselves."

By 1882 well-worked-out arguments began to appear with regularity. Although punishment for crimes committed by Indians on other Indians was
not lost sight of, the dominant concern came to be the protection of the
individual Indian in his personal and property rights. "That law is the solution of the Indian problem would seem to be a self-evident proposition,"
declared a writer in the *North American Review* in March 1882. Everything that was sought for the Indians—inducements to make them labor,
educational facilities, and land in severalty—rested, he argued, upon adequate protection of law. To declare that the Indian is "a *person* before the
law" was the first and all-important thing. "When his possessions are secure," the writer concluded, "his labor will be both profitable and attractive; when he feels himself a man, he will desire his own and his children's
education; when he can be protected by law, the granting of land to him in
severalty will be something more than a pretentious form."

While concern for general Indian rights and recognition of the individual
Indian's manhood was thus an essential part of the reform program, the
question of a criminal code for the reservations came again to the forefront
in the case of the Sioux Indian Crow Dog, who had been sentenced to death
by the territorial court of Dakota for murdering Chief Spotted Tail. In the
case of *ex parte Crow Dog*, decided on December 17, 1883, the United
States Supreme Court ordered Crow Dog's immediate release because the
United States had no jurisdiction over crimes committed by one Indian
against another. Since Congress had provided no national jurisdiction over
Indian crimes, even a murderer could not be punished, and the chief was
permitted to return to his tribe. The decision caused great consternation,
for such a state of lawlessness could not be tolerated in the republic.

To meet the problem Congress in March 1885 extended federal criminal
jurisdiction over the Indians for seven major crimes (murder, manslaughter,
rape, assault with intent to kill, arson, burglary, and larceny). Restricted
though it was, this legislation was revolutionary. For the first time the
United States asserted its jurisdiction over strictly internal crimes of Indians against Indians, a major blow at the integrity of the Indian tribes
and a fundamental readjustment in relations between the Indians and the

United States government. When the Supreme Court in *United States v. Kagama* on May 10, 1886, upheld the right of Congress to take this step, the way was open for unlimited interference by the federal government in the affairs of the Indians.

For a while the efforts to bring further legal reforms, measures that would extend civil as well as criminal law over the Indians, were diverted by interest in the land in severalty bills that resulted in the Dawes Act. There was no doubt in the reformers' minds that the Dawes Act was a major step in the direction they aimed to go in making the Indians individually indistinguishable from other Americans. Senator Dawes and many others felt that this act answered all the needs of the Indians for legal protection and equality.

But for men interested primarily in the Indians' legal status, the Dawes Act was too slow. Its legal provisions and opportunities for citizenship did not immediately embrace all the Indians, and in the long transition period until the act had taken effect everywhere, some further legislation, they felt, was absolutely necessary. The man most eager for this to happen and most earnest and articulate in its promotion was a learned and highly respected professor in the Harvard Law School, James Bradley Thayer. Thayer considered the Dawes Act merely "one great step to be followed by others."

Thayer and his friends drew up a bill to accomplish what they had in mind for the Indians, but they were unable to force the legislation through Congress, primarily because of conflict within the ranks of the reformers themselves. The chief opponent of the measure was Dawes, who had qualms about the constitutionality of Thayer's proposal and who, more fundamentally, pinned his hopes for Indian salvation on the severalty measure he had sponsored. As the allotment went forward and the Indians became citizens and subject to state and territorial laws, there would be no need for Thayer's measure.

Although the question of law for the Indians and Indian citizenship were intimately related, advocates of a system of law did not equate the two. Yet the question of citizenship for the Indians could not be kept down. To make the Indians into acceptable American citizens was the great goal of the humanitarian reformers and of the Indian Office. But the niceties of the precise legal formulation and how and when legal citizenship should be acquired by the red men were all matters of divided opinion. The immediate granting of citizenship, unlike most of the reforms proposed at the end of the nineteenth century for the Indians, was not universally accepted as a panacea. The anomalous legal status of the Indians was the major difficulty. As long as the Indians were members of tribes or nations, which treated with the United States as quasi-independent political units, they could not be considered American citizens.

The status of the Indians came into question with the adoption of the Fourteenth Amendment to the Constitution in 1868. That Reconstruction measure provided in section 1: "All persons born or naturalized in the United States, and subject to the jurisdiction thereof, are citizens of the United States and of the State wherein they reside." Although the amendment was aimed at the recently emancipated slaves, the Indians did not escape attention when the amendment was being debated in Congress.

In December 1870 the Senate Committee on the Judiciary declared that the tribal Indians did not become citizens because they were not subject to the jurisdiction of the United States in the sense meant by the amendment, but what was still not clear was the citizenship status of Indians who voluntarily severed their connections with their tribes and took up the ways of white society. Did they, by such an act, automatically receive citizenship?

A definite answer to that question came in the Supreme Court decision in the case of *Elk* v. *Wilkins*, November 3, 1884. John Elk, an Indian who had separated from his tribe, was refused permission to register to vote in a local election in Omaha, Nebraska, and when he later appeared at the polls he was again refused the right to vote. Elk met the residence and other requirements of the state of Nebraska and of the city of Omaha, but he was turned back because it was alleged that as an Indian he was not a citizen. The majority of the court held against the plaintiff, declaring that an Indian who was born a member of an Indian tribe, although he voluntarily separated himself from the tribe and took up residence among white citizens, was not thereby a citizen of the United States. Some specific act of Congress was necessary to naturalize him.

Granted the necessity, then, of some sort of congressional action to make Indians citizens, would such an enactment be wise and in the best interests of the Indians and of the United States? It was on this question that disagreement prevailed. Was citizenship a reward to be conferred when an Indian had demonstrated his desire and his competence to live among the whites, or was citizenship to be a means whereby the Indian would advance on the road to civilization? At first the reformers seemed to agree that preparation was necessary for citizenship and that Indians should not all suddenly be made citizens in a mass. But by the end of 1884 a reversal had occurred on this point, and the Board of Indian Commissioners could assert: "The solution of the Indian problem is citizenship, and we believe that the time has come to declare by an act of Congress that every Indian born within the territorial limits of the United States is a citizen of the United States and subject to the jurisdiction thereof."

There were more cautious voices, however, especially that of Senator Dawes, the towering figure in Indian reform legislation. He persisted in his opinion that indiscriminate granting of citizenship to all Indians would be bad and held to the position that citizenship should be tied to taking land in severalty.

The final provisions on citizenship in the Dawes Act were a compromise: Every Indian to whom an allotment was made and every Indian who separated himself from his tribe and adopted the ways of civilized life was declared to be a citizen of the United States, without, however, impairing the Indian's right to tribal or other property. As a compromise, it did not fully satisfy either faction. Dawes complained that the act provided citizenship for others than allottees under the severalty provisions of the bill. Advocates of immediate citizenship for all Indians were disappointed because tribal Indians on reservations were still excluded.

The Indians frequently did not welcome federal citizenship, and the effects of citizenship in the end were meager, for the actual situation of the Indians was changed very little. Citizenship did not impair tribal law or affect tribal existence. It was not considered incompatible with federal powers of guardianship, nor was it inconsistent with restriction on the right to alienate property. The great drive to make American citizens out of the Indians in the late 1880s and the 1890s through a system of national Indian schools was not a matter of legal citizenship but of cultural amalgamation of the Indians into the mass of white citizens, a much more comprehensive matter.

PROMOTION OF INDIAN SCHOOLS

Education of the Indians was the ultimate reform. The Lake Mohonk Conference declared in 1884: "The Indian must have a knowledge of the English language, that he may associate with his white neighbors and transact business as they do. He must have practical industrial training to fit him to compete with others in the struggle for life. He must have a Christian education to enable him to perform the duties of the family, the State, and the Church." Despite the intense agitation for land in severalty and equality under the law for the Indians, there was fundamental agreement that neither homesteads nor legal citizenship would benefit the Indians if they were not properly educated to appreciate the responsibilities as well as the benefits of both.

Indian education, of course, was not new. After the Civil War, when the nation faced the great mass of new Indians who had come within the immediate scope of American Indian policy and needed "civilizing," government officials had looked to Indian education with a new urgency. The same principles and programs that had been promoted so ardently in the

1840s for the Shawnees, the Potawatomis, and the Cherokees were advocated with renewed vigor in the 1870s and 1880s for the Sioux, the Cheyennes, and the Comanches. Commissioner Edward P. Smith argued in 1873 that "any plan for civilization which does not provide for training the young, even though at a largely increased expenditure, is short-sighted and expensive." He thought that with proper facilities half the Indian children then growing up in barbarism could be put into schools.

The primary concern in all Indian education schemes was to make the Indian self-supporting—not only as a means of advancing the individual's manhood but, quite practically, to end the enormous governmental outlays needed to maintain large numbers of Indians who had lost their old means of subsistence and had not taken up any new ones. To this end, training in agriculture or the common trades for the boys and in the domestic tasks of white households for the girls was considered indispensable. Despite the heavier costs of providing such schools—equipping them with stock, wagons, farming implements, and tools—they were proposed as the only economical policy in the long run.

These manual labor schools had to be boarding schools. Although day schools were provided on the reservations and were an important means of bringing the first lessons of civilization to the young, they were not satisfactory for accomplishing the complete transformation of the Indian children that the reformers had in mind. As Commissioner Ezra Hayt remarked in 1877, "the exposure of children who attend only day-schools to the demoralization and degradation of an Indian home neutralized the efforts of the schoolteacher, especially those efforts which are directed to advancement in morality and civilization." How could the Indian child become properly acculturated, the reformers asked, if he were not removed from the Indian life and language of his home? What was needed was a substitute home, and this the boarding school provided.

The cultural imperialism of the reformers was exhibited sharply in the demand that Indian languages be prohibited and only English allowed in the Indian schools. The principle was stated clearly by Carl Schurz: "If Indian children are to be civilized they must learn the language of civilization. They will become far more accessible to civilized ideas and ways of thinking when they are enabled to receive those ideas and ways of thinking through the most direct channel of expression." Schurz dismissed efforts to draw up Indian grammars and to instruct the Indians in their native languages as "certainly very interesting and meritorious philological work" but of little use to the Indians. The policy of teaching English in the government schools was praised by the Board of Indian Commissioners as "eminently wise," for if the Indians were to become useful American citizens, they had to know the common language of the country.

Considerable progress was made in the system of Indian education in the quarter-century following the Civil War, even though the enthusiastic proclamations made periodically by officials in Washington have to be accepted with caution. In 1887 Secretary Lamar presented data for the previous decade. At the beginning of the decade, in 1878, there had been 137 Indian schools of all kinds provided by the government, with an average attendance of about thirty-five hundred, maintained at a total cost of nearly $196,000. In 1887 there were 231 schools, with over ten thousand students, at a cost of almost $1,200,000. Lamar considered this "a gratifying improvement," which showed how interest in education was growing among the Indians.

The figures surely indicated substantial growth, but the surface had been little more than scratched. Ten thousand pupils out of an Indian population estimated at one-third of a million could hardly be considered satisfactory. The fact, of course, did not escape the proponents of Indian education, and the commissioners of Indian affairs kept pounding on the doors of Congress for additional funds needed to establish a reasonably inclusive system for the Indian children.

Since the appropriations, although they were increasing, were by no means equal to the task, the government continued to rely on missionary effort for many schools. By means of so-called contract schools, the government gave financial aid on a per capita basis to religious groups that set up schools on the reservations. The religious groups responded generously, putting more money into Indian school buildings than did the government. The increase in enrollment between 1887 and 1888, for example, was substantially greater in the contract schools than in the government schools because the contract schools had increased their accommodations more. The Christian interest in Indian matters explicitly acknowledged by government officials made such an arrangement seem unexceptionable.

CARLISLE INDIAN INDUSTRIAL SCHOOL

A showpiece of Indian education, which some reformers considered a model of what could be done to transform the Indians, was the Indian school at Carlisle, Pennsylvania. It was the work of a remarkable young army officer named Richard Henry Pratt, whose appearance on the scene in the mid-1870s gave a new impetus and, in a sense, a new direction to Indian schooling. Pratt, born in New York State in 1840, served in the Civil War as a cavalry officer and after the war reentered the army as a second lieutenant. He saw considerable action on the southern plains against hostile Indians in 1868–1869 and in the Red River War of 1874–1875. As commander of

Indian scouts, he gained firsthand knowledge of the Indian's character and capabilities.

When the fighting ended, Pratt was detailed to take a group of seventy-two Indian prisoners to Fort Marion at St. Augustine, Florida. As he cared for the prisoners there, he began a program of education that was to make him a national figure. He got permission to release the Indians from close confinement, replaced their guards with some of the Indian prisoners themselves, instituted classes for them, and found useful work for them in the St. Augustine area. He interested white benefactors in his cause and persuaded his army superiors to assign him to the work of Indian education, where he could promote and expand the approach to Indian assimilation that he had begun so dramatically at Fort Marion.

When the Indians' imprisonment came to an end, Pratt was assigned to Hampton Normal and Agricultural Institute in Virginia, and he took with him twenty-two of his Indian students. But Pratt was unhappy at Hampton, which had been founded to educate black students, and he feared that popular prejudices against the blacks would rub off on his Indians, whom he wished to see associate and mix fully with whites. He proposed, therefore, to set up an industrial training school solely for Indians, where he could carry out his educational principles unhampered. He importuned his superiors in the army and the officials of the Interior Department for a chance to prove the value of his program, and by a series of bureaucratic maneuvers he got permission to use the abandoned military barracks at Carlisle for his work.

Pratt went west in the summer of 1879 to recruit students for his school. At the Rosebud Agency, he persuaded Spotted Tail to send his children to Carlisle, and other Sioux there and at Pine Ridge followed the chief's example. Eighty-two children, who were in a sense hostages for the good behavior of their parents, made a dramatic entry into Carlisle on October 6, 1879, still wearing their tribal costumes, and the Carlisle Indian Industrial School began its influential history. The Sioux were soon joined by fifty-five students from tribes in the Indian Territory, and on November 1, 1879, the school was officially opened. Enrollment steadily increased as facilities grew and the fame of the school spread, until it reached about a thousand students.

Pratt's views on Indian matters were simple. He insisted upon complete integration of the Indians into white society, and his whole program was geared to that goal. Anything that tended to isolate or segregate the Indians was to him anathema. Reservations he considered an unmitigated evil and tribal status a preservation of outmoded ways and attitudes; he condemned what he called "this whole segregating and reservating process." He was only half jesting when he noted that there were about 260,000 Indians in

236   *Severalty, Law, and Education*

the United States and twenty-seven hundred counties and suggested that
the Indians be divided up and sprinkled, nine to a county, across the nation.
There were no twilight zones in Pratt's mind; his principle shone as a brilliant light, and he wavered not an inch from the path it marked out.

Pratt firmly believed that human beings were products of their environment. "There is no resistless clog placed upon us by birth," he insisted.
"We are not born with language, nor are we born with ideas of either civilization or savagery. Language, savagery and civilization are forced upon us
entirely by our environment after birth." If the Indians were kept in tribal
surroundings on the reservation, he said, the nation would "not lack material for Wild West shows which the gaping throngs of our great cities may
scoff at and the crowned heads of Europe patronize, for centuries to come."
He repeatedly pointed to the example of the blacks, who had learned the
white man's language and his customs by associating with him, and to Europeans, who had immigrated in large numbers but were being rapidly integrated, while the Indians still remained Indians.

The Carlisle Indian Industrial School was to be but the beginning, the
prototype of a system of similar schools that would eventually provide all
Indian youth with training for assimilation. Pratt wanted the results to be
so convincing that other off-reservation schools would follow until the universal training he envisaged would obtain, and he used his considerable
promotional skills to make sure that the story of Carlisle was widely
known. He himself lectured widely, he invited influential men and women
to visit the school, and he gave the Carlisle band full exposure at parades
and other public gatherings. In this he was much helped by the discovery in
the 1890s that the Indians at Carlisle could play great football, holding
their own on the gridiron with the best of the Ivy League schools.

The athletic association with Harvard and Cornell and Pennsylvania
was a grossly inaccurate indication of the academic level that Carlisle was
able to achieve, for its level of instruction was basically that of a grammar
school. Indian students came to Carlisle with little or no schooling, and
some of them had to learn English after they arrived. Not until 1889, a decade after its opening, did Carlisle graduate its first class. Ultimately the
course was extended to include the first two years of high school and some
teacher training.

The prominence of Carlisle in the public eye and the unmistakable
achievements of many of the students were convincing proof to many former skeptics that Indians were indeed educable and could take their places
in white society. Still, few of the reformers or the officials in the Indian
Office wanted to go down Pratt's single track. After the initial years of enthusiastic support and rich praise, Pratt's doctrine ran into opposition, and
alternative programs were projected that ultimately won the day.

A problem that bothered Pratt's critics was the eventual status of the alumni of the eastern industrial training schools. Were they, in fact, absorbed into white society as Pratt hoped? Or did they return to the reservation, and if so, did their eastern off-reservation schooling fit them for the lives they actually led? The advocates of Hampton and Carlisle published careful reports to show that few graduates reverted to their old ways when they returned to their reservations. But there were serious problems of adjustment, and the solution seemed to be to raise the general level of education on the reservations so that there would be less disparity between the returned students and those they had left behind. To attain this goal, emphasis would have to be placed on reservation schools. Planting a school on a reservation, it was argued, would bring the older members of the tribe within the school's sphere of influence.

As the movement for reservation schools grew, Pratt struck back at his opponents. He attacked the missionaries for fostering Indian ways and the Indian Rights Association because it openly supported day schools and other schools on the reservations. Ethnologists, too, were victims of his tirades, and he accused them of persuading the Indians to remain in their old ways and teaching them to be proud of their race. Pratt saved his strongest denunciations, however, for the Office of Indian Affairs because of its educational policy and because it dealt with tribes and thought in terms of reservations. His intemperate remarks and cantankerous attitude were finally too much for Washington officialdom, and in 1904 Pratt was dismissed from his post at Carlisle.

Pratt's goal was never attained, and the system on which he had placed his hope was rejected. His basic assumption that it was possible to eradicate completely the culture of the Indians and assimilate them as European immigrants were assimilated into American society was a questionable one and could not have been accomplished without great human cost. His importance lies not in promoting this impossible dream, but in his part in awakening public opinion to the capabilities of the Indians and in mobilizing forces to promote their education.

THOMAS JEFFERSON MORGAN AND INDIAN SCHOOLS

The early efforts to create an Indian school system look anemic compared with the earnest drive for Indian education that came after the passage of the Dawes Act in 1887. The Lake Mohonk Conference of 1888, with a fearful sense of urgency, turned most of its attention to Indian education, and it soon had the powerful aid of Thomas Jefferson Morgan, commissioner of Indian affairs from 1889 to 1893 and the most significant national figure in

Indian education in the nineteenth century. Not only was Morgan a professional educator, but he epitomized important intellectual trends of his age. His ardent and aggressive Americanism, his unquestioning belief in the public school system, his professional Protestantism (with its corollary of anti-Catholicism), and his deep humanitarianism brought together strands of American thought that had been slowly but steadily intertwining in the preceding decades. With him the United States government embarked upon a comprehensive system of Indian education that had enduring effects for the Indians and for the nation.

After service as an officer in the Civil War and then ordination as a Baptist minister, Morgan devoted his life to public education, serving as head of state normal schools in Nebraska, New York, and Rhode Island. He gained attention in the educational world through his writings and public addresses, and he at first hoped to be appointed United States commissioner of education. When that office went to another, he eagerly accepted the post of commissioner of Indian affairs instead.

In October 1889 Morgan outlined his general position on Indian affairs—a position clearly in accord with the views advanced by the Board of Indian Commissioners, the Lake Mohonk Conference, and other associated Indian reform groups. Morgan pointed out that the education of the Indians was a responsibility of the national government that could not safely be shirked or delegated to any other party. And he insisted that the government of the United States, "now one of the richest on the face of the earth, with an overflowing treasury," could undertake the work without finding it a burden.

To accomplish the work he set forth a series of stipulations. The schools should accommodate all the Indian children and be completely systematized. The common schools on the reservations, the agency boarding schools, and the great national industrial schools like Carlisle should be properly related to form one whole. There should be a uniform course of study, similar methods of instruction, and standard textbooks, so that the Indian schools would conform to the public school system of the states. Although Morgan placed special stress on industrial training that would fit the Indian to earn an honest living, he asked for provision as well for "that general literary culture which the experience of the white race has shown to be the very essence of education." To this end command of the English language was necessary, and Morgan proposed that in schools supported wholly or in part by the government only English-speaking teachers be employed and that no language but English be allowed in the schools.

"The Indian youth," he said, "should be instructed in their rights, privileges and duties as American citizens; should be taught to love the American flag; should be imbued with genuine patriotism, and made to feel that the United States, and not some paltry reservation, is their home." He urged those responsible for educating the Indians to waken in them "a sense of independence, self-reliance, and self-respect." He concluded: "Education should seek the disintegration of the tribes, and not their segregation. They should be educated, not as Indians, but as Americans. In short, public schools should do for them what they are so successfully doing for all the other races in this country,—assimilate them."

Coeducation was another part of Morgan's plan. It was the surest way, he thought, to lift Indian women out of their position of "servility and degradation" up to a plane where they would be treated with "the same gallantry and respect which is accorded to their more favored white sisters." Still another was patriotic training for the Indian pupils, for love of America was the keystone in Morgan's arch of American citizenship. "The Indian heroes of the camp-fire need not be disparaged," he said, "but gradually and unobtrusively the heroes of American homes and history may be substituted as models and ideals." The students were to be taught that the highest privilege that could be conferred on them was American citizenship.

Morgan realized that persuasion alone would not succeed in making his theoretically wonderful system work. The depth of his conviction that it must succeed can be seen in his ultimate willingness to resort to force. The Indian Office, he told the secretary of the interior in 1892, "has argued with the Indians; has pleaded with them; has offered every inducement in its power to cause them voluntarily to put their children into school; has, wherever it seemed wise, resorted to mild punishment by the withholding of rations or supplies, and, where necessary, has directed Agents to use their Indian police as truant officers in compelling attendance."

Indian parents, not appreciating the value of the schools, and medicine men, who feared the enlightenment of the people, Morgan charged, threw themselves against the new movement, but he remained convinced that the great work of making acceptable citizens through education must go on. "I would not needlessly nor lightly interfere with the rights of Indian parents," he wrote. "But I do not believe that Indians like the Bannacks and Shoshones at Fort Hall, the Southern Utes in Colorado, the Apaches, or the Navajoes of Arizona,—people who, for the most part, speak no English, live in squalor and degradation, make little progress from year to year, who are a perpetual source of expense to the Government and a constant menace to thousands of their white neighbors, a hindrance to civilization and a clog on our progress—have any right to forcibly keep their children out of school to grow up like themselves, a race of barbarians and semi-savages. We owe it to those children to prevent, forcibly if need be, so great and appalling a calamity from befalling them."

Morgan had expressed similar views publicly at the Lake Mohonk Conference in October 1892 and had won the support of the meeting. The platform adopted at the conference read in part: "In cases where parents, without good reason, refuse to educate their children, we believe that the government is justified, as a last resort, in using power to compel attendance. We do not think it desirable to rear another generation of savages."

Opposition from Indian parents was not the only obstacle Morgan faced in his drive for a universal public school system of Indian education, for his plan was challenged by the system of schools run by Catholic missionaries. The conflict was in large part an outgrowth of Catholic-Protestant antagonism that arose during the peace policy in the decade after the Civil War. Catholics were aggrieved by the assignment of so few agencies to them, and their determination to have a bigger role in Indian affairs gradually gained momentum under the direction of the Bureau of Catholic Indian Missions, established in 1874. As Catholic population steadily increased in the United States, a vigorous and growing church stepped up its mission work, and Catholic mission schools came to receive the great bulk of contract school money.

This resurgence was not lost on the Protestant formulators of American Indian policy, who warned of an aggressive "Romanist" influence in Indian matters that threatened the traditional Protestant hegemony. And when the Lake Mohonk Conference in 1888 began its serious promotion of a comprehensive government school system for Indians, it did so in the context of the mission school controversy, which played a large part in the discussion.

The appointment of Morgan as commissioner of Indian affairs and of Daniel Dorchester, a Methodist minister, as superintendent of Indian schools brought great relief to the Protestant reformers at Lake Mohonk, and they expected these men to reverse the dangerous trend toward Catholic dominance. They were not disappointed, for Morgan from the first made clear his unconditional opposition to the contract school concept, although he did not intend suddenly to kill the schools already in operation. To the Catholic missionaries, on the other hand, the appointment of Morgan and Dorchester spelled disaster. Both men had a record of public anti-Catholic statements, and Morgan's opposition to government support of mission schools and his dismissal of Catholics from the Indian service led to a concerted effort on the part of Catholics to unseat him. Throughout his term Morgan fought with the Catholics, and charges and countercharges exacerbated the conflict.

In the presidential election of 1892 Catholic promoters used the contract school question to attack President Benjamin Harrison and the Republicans, charging Morgan with anti-Catholic bigotry that rubbed off on the whole administration. It was a sorry spectacle. Yet the defeat of the Republicans and the election of Grover Cleveland did not bring the support of their schools that the Catholics had hoped for. The new administration was no more sympathetic than Morgan had been, and Congress in the 1890s, influenced by the strong nativist and anti-Catholic movement of that decade represented by the American Protective Association (APA), little by little whittled away the money appropriated for contract schools. Morgan's national school system for the Indians had won the day.

CHAPTER 16

The Indian Service

The reform program of the late nineteenth century aimed to solve the Indian problem by helping the Indians disappear into white American society as independent landowners and United States citizens. When the process was complete there would be no more need for an Indian Office to manage the government's relations with the Indians, for there would be no more identifiable Indians. Little by little, many believed, the Indian service would wither away. What happened instead was that the Indian Office was formalized as an institution—and its bureaucracy grew tremendously. Thus while the Lake Mohonk reformers, intent on the substantive elements in their program for the Indians, pushed for allotment, law, and citizenship and persuaded the federal government to establish a government Indian school system, they did not lose sight of the need to improve the administration of Indian affairs.

GROWTH OF THE INDIAN SERVICE

As the Indians were individualized and as the federal government took increasing responsibility for them as individual citizens, the work and size of the Indian Office multiplied. In 1881 there were 2,102 employees in the field service; in 1897 there were 3,917. With the increase in numbers came striking shifts in personnel occasioned by new programs. The institution of the Indian police forces at the agencies and the subsequent organization of courts of Indian offenses placed a considerable number of Indians on the agency payrolls, even though the remuneration allowed them was small. Much more significant was the concentration of agency employees in school work. In 1875 educational employees made up about 16.5 percent of the total personnel in the field; by 1895 they were nearly one-half of the work force, and they continued to dominate the rolls.

Such growth depended, of course, upon the willingness of Congress to provide increased funds for the Indian service, and the annual augmentation was increasingly for education. While the total expenditures for the Indian service doubled between 1874–1875 and 1894–1895, school funds increased almost ten times.

The increasing detail in the work of the Indian Office required systematization within the office itself, and the movement toward differentiation of function and the regularization of the work in the field that had begun in mid-century was continued and amplified. Circulars containing directions on administration were sent to the agents, school superintendents, and other agency personnel to govern their activities, sometimes in minute detail, and from time to time cumulations of directives were published.

The publications reflected the increasing concern of the Indian Office for civilization and education as it instructed the agents in their responsibilities. The following extracts from the *Instructions to Indian Agents* of 1880 set the tone.

Sec. 231. The chief duty of an agent is to induce his Indians to labor in civilized pursuits. To attain this end every possible influence should be brought to bear, and in proportion as it is attained, other things being equal, an agent's administration is successful or unsuccessful.

Sec. 232. No Indian should be idle for want of an opportunity to labor or of instructions as to how to go to work, and, if farm work is not extensive enough to employ all idle hands, some other occupation should be introduced. No work must be given white men which can be done by Indians, and it is expected that hereafter no payments will be made to white laborers for cutting hay or wood, splitting rails, or gathering crops. Plowing and fencing should also be done by Indians.

Sec. 233. An agency farm should be used as a school where Indians shall be taught to labor, not by watching others, but by taking hold themselves. It is believed, however, that the best and most permanent results will be realized where the agency farm is *abandoned*, and all the time and effort of agency employes are expended in persuading Indians to cultivate small patches or farms of their own, and in directing and aiding such individual effort, even though the manner of farming be rude and the crops much smaller than a model agency farm would have produced. A well-ordered agency farm and "establishment" is far less creditable to an agent than a large number of comparatively unprofitably managed Indian farms, which will awaken in their Indian owners a sense of proprietorship, and will serve as beginnings in the direction of self-support.

In addition the instructions noted the agent's duty in enforcing the prohibitions against liquor and his responsibility to provide and supervise English education and industrial training for his charges in the agency school. The publication directed the agent to allow the Indians to leave the reservation only with a permit (to be granted to worthy Indians as a reward for meritorious conduct) and to prohibit the custom of visiting between reservations for the purpose of giving or receiving presents of ponies or other property.

The increased centralization of administration indicated by the directives increased the work of the headquarters office. The total staff in Washington increased from 70 in 1881 to 129 in 1901, and in addition there were inspectors and special agents, as well as allotting agents, who worked in the field but were responsible to headquarters.

The management of the growing and varied activities came to depend largely on the bureaucracy of clerks, for the commissioners of Indian affairs came and went with the changes in presidential administrations. Yet in the last two decades of the century the Indian Office was better served than usual in the commissioners appointed, for they did not let their political appointment becloud all the reform goals that dominated the period. Hiram Price, who was appointed in 1881 by his former congressional colleague President James A. Garfield, was a good example of a "peace policy" official. Not only did he advocate the measures deemed vital to the transformation of the Indians, but he brought a moralistic sense to his office that rivaled that of Nathaniel Taylor a dozen years before. He supported and encouraged the new reform organizations that came into national prominence during his term of office.

Price was followed by John DeWitt Clinton Atkins, a Tennessee Democrat who left the House of Representatives at the time of the Civil War and served as a general in the Confederate army and as a member of the Confederate Congress. Returned to Congress after the war in 1873, he gained bipartisan support, and his appointment as commissioner in 1885 was well received. Atkins stood for all the right reform measures, and during his term of office significant changes in Indian policy occurred: improvements in Indian education, the beginning of a federal judicial system for the reservations, and the culmination of the severalty movement in the Dawes Act of 1887. But Atkins was a politician, and he lost the support of the reform groups by his patronage appointments in the Indian service.

John Oberly, who was appointed to succeed Atkins in October 1888, was of a different breed. He was one of the few commissioners who were chosen for competence rather than for political considerations. A newspaperman from Illinois, Oberly had served effectively as superintendent of Indian education, and President Cleveland had named him to the civil service commission. He was just the kind of person the reformers wanted, but before he had completed a month of service as commissioner of Indian affairs, Cleveland was defeated at the polls and Republican Benjamin Harrison elected to the presidency.

Thomas Jefferson Morgan, who followed Oberly, was without doubt one of the most important commissioners in the nation's history. His absolute and unwavering conviction that the Indians must all be completely Americanized made him a key figure in strengthening and completing the reforms that marked the closing decades of the century. Although, like most others, he was not an Indian expert, he was an education specialist, and he represented and in large measure directed the change that made Indian education the dominant activity of the Indian Office. His successor, Daniel M. Browning, who served as commissioner from 1893 to 1897, by contrast, left no mark on Indian policy or on the Indian Office. A faithful judge and party worker from Illinois, Browning had hoped to use the commissioner's office to reward his political friends, but he found few openings to fill, and in the daily work of the office he seems to have succumbed to the influence of the entrenched bureaucracy.

CIVIL SERVICE REFORM

The growth of personnel in the Indian service and the increasing importance of the agent in the civilization and education programs highlighted a continuing problem of serious dimensions: the appointment of the Indian agents and other agency personnel under a political patronage system. The Indian reformers realized that their programs and policies for Indian betterment depended upon the quality of the men who administered them. Without honest and competent men in the Indian service—especially in the office of agent—the best-laid plans would amount to little. Although Carl Schurz's attack on corruption in the Indian service had brought a temporary calm, by the end of the 1880s a cry was again raised against the politicization of the Indian service and the degradation that followed in its wake. For the better part of a decade, a sustained drive to bring civil service reform to the Indian Office vied with education and a system of law for the Indians as the major concern of the Indian reformers.

Several converging developments gave impetus to this movement for reform in Indian administration. For one thing, the changes in political parties in the executive branch of the government that occurred with four-year regularity between 1884 and 1896 brought the spoils system into new prominence. The Democrats, capturing the presidency for the first time since the Civil War with the election of Grover Cleveland in 1884, had a hunger for the fruits of victory that could not be denied, and the house that had been cleaned out by Schurz began again to show unmistakably the messy accumulations of partisan favors under Commissioner Atkins.

A second factor was the Indian reform movement itself. In 1887, just as the worst evils of partisan appointments were beginning to be noticed, the humanitarians won a great victory with the Dawes Act. The allotment and citizenship provisions of that measure and the plans for a federal Indian school system marked the successful completion of the legislative program that the reformers had advocated. What remained to be achieved, then, was not new legislation but careful and competent carrying out of the laws already enacted.

The third element was the national movement for civil service reform, which provided ready-made principles and rules to govern the Indian reformers in purifying the Indian service. The Pendleton Act of 1883 supplied the necessary structure for reform, and the humanitarian friends of the Indian soon began a campaign to have the whole Indian service classified under the reform legislation.

The driving force behind the growing demand that civil service rules be applied to the Indian service was the Indian Rights Association and most particularly its secretary, Herbert Welsh, who made the reform his principal goal for more than a decade. At first it seemed that no headway was possible, but persistence in calling attention to the need and the support of other reforming groups began to tell. William F. Vilas, who became secretary of the interior in January 1888, was willing to listen to the pleas of the reformers, and his approval of Oberly as commissioner of Indian affairs met the high standards set by the Indian Rights Association.

When the change of presidents spelled Oberly's doom, Welsh determined to meet the danger by campaigning to retain him as commissioner under the new administration. If he could succeed in this, he would strike a blow at the spoils system, set a precedent for future times, and provide an opportunity for an upright commissioner to retain and to appoint qualified men in the service. Welsh was unable to break such a sturdy barrier, however, and he had to be satisfied with his second choice, Thomas J. Morgan, who saw pretty much eye to eye with the reformers and was determined in his own way to improve the quality and efficiency of the Indian service. Morgan's initial report gave Welsh and his friends considerable satisfaction, for the new commissioner declared, "The chief thing to be considered in the administration of this office is the character of the men and women employed to carry out the designs of the Government." He favored integrity, justice, patience, and good sense, and said that dishonesty, injustice, favoritism, and incompetency had no place in the Indian service.

THE LESSON OF WOUNDED KNEE

The disastrous outbreak of the Sioux in 1890, shortly after Morgan had taken office, provided substantial fuel for the fires of the civil service reformers. The reservation life for the Sioux had brought degradation rather than the revitalization that its promoters envisaged. The Indians had many grievances, and the reduction of their large reserve in 1889, instead of moving them more rapidly toward acculturation, had been a great disaster.

Then came news of a messiah. Far to the west in a remote corner of Nevada a Paiute shaman named Wovoka was preaching a wonderful message, compounded of Christian doctrines and Indian mysticism, which promised the Indians a new paradise if they would remain at peace, live honest and industrious lives, and perform a ghost dance that God had taught to the messiah. The Sioux, like many other tribes, sent a delegation to Wovoka to investigate the new religion. The emissaries, returning to the reservation in March 1890, told remarkable tales of the messiah.

The Sioux, however, modified the nonviolent peace message of Wovoka and made it into one of antagonism toward the whites, who were held responsible for the present misery of the tribes. At first little disturbance was caused, and the Indian agents did not take the ghost dance religion seriously. But the specter of hunger still rode over the Dakota reservations, for rations were short and the promising crops of early summer were destroyed by the scorching heat of midsummer. Under such conditions other grievances assumed mountainous proportions. New boundary lines between reservations upset traditional tribal ties, and the taking of a census presaged in the minds of the Indians still another ration cut. The restlessness of the Indians led to movements of troops into uncomfortably close proximity to the reservations.

The troubles and misery of the summer furnished an occasion for conservative chiefs to assert their leadership in opposition to government policies with a reasonable hope of gaining adherents. Sitting Bull at Standing Rock Agency, Hump and Big Foot at Cheyenne River, Red Cloud at Pine Ridge, and a group at Rosebud began to take courage that the old ways might yet be saved. The deep distress of the Sioux offered a favorable climate for their efforts, and when the most aggressive of the ghost dance apostles, Kicking Bear, returned in midsummer from a visit to the Arapahos and told of the regeneration of that tribe through Wovoka's religion, he gained important converts. Ghost dances multiplied among the Sioux, the dancers garbed in ghost shirts supposed to be invested with magic qualities that made the wearers invulnerable to bullets. Trances were common, with visions of earth regenerated and repeopled by the Indians. In alarm, as the movement spread, the Indian agents warned of its dangers and attempted with little success to suppress it with the agency police. Hump and Big Foot enthusiastically espoused the new religion at Cheyenne River Agency; and at Standing Rock, Sitting Bull became its apostle.

To meet this growing challenge to government authority, there were new and ineffectual agents, spawned by the spoils system. James McLaughlin at Standing Rock was a man of experience and ability, although he was faced with troubles enough in handling the shrewd Sitting Bull. At Cheyenne River a Republican without experience, Perain P. Palmer, was cast in the difficult role of dealing with Kicking Bear, Hump, and Big Foot. But the greatest crisis of leadership came at Pine Ridge, where the powerful agent Valentine McGillycuddy had fallen victim to the system and been replaced in 1886 by the well-meaning but weak Democrat Hugh Gallagher. In October 1890 Gallagher in turn was dismissed to make room for the patronage appointment of a South Dakota Republican, Daniel F. Royer, whom the Indians in derision called Young-Man-Afraid-of-Indians. Royer soon lost all control of the situation as the dancers openly defied him. Army troops sent to the reservation excited the ghost dancers and united them in armed defiance of the government. The disaffected Pine Ridge and Rosebud Indians massed in the Bad Lands in the northwest corner of the Pine Ridge Reservation and threw themselves into a continuous frenzy of dancing.

To end the troubles, government officials proposed to arrest the ghost dance leaders. High on the government's list was Sitting Bull at Standing Rock. Efforts of Indian police to arrest the chief, however, led to a shooting match between the chief's supporters and the police in which Sitting Bull was killed, along with seven of his Indians and six of the police. At Cheyenne River, Hump unexpectedly gave up without trouble, but Big Foot, befriending refugees from Sitting Bull's followers, was treated as an outlaw, and with his people he fled south from the reservation.

Meanwhile the hostiles in the Bad Lands, pressed by troops to the north and west and suffering from cold and weariness, moved in toward the Pine Ridge Agency to surrender. When Big Foot approached the Bad Lands, they had already moved out, and Big Foot and his band were intercepted by troops of the Seventh Cavalry, who led the band to a spot on Wounded Knee Creek, northeast of the agency, where they were surrounded by more troops under Colonel James W. Forsyth, the regimental commander.

On the following day, December 29, Forsyth prepared to disarm the Indians. The situation was tense, and when one of the Indians discharged a concealed gun, the troops surrounding the camp interpreted it as an out-

break and opened fire on the encampment. Both sides fought in fury. Hotch-
kiss guns mounted on the overlooking hill raked the camp with murderous
fire, catching many of the women and children. Fleeing Indians were shot
down by the soldiers without discrimination of age or sex. A total of 146
Indians was buried on the battlefield, 84 men and boys, 44 women, and 18
children, many of them frozen in distraught postures by the blizzard that
swept down upon the scene after the massacre. Seven more Indians of the
51 wounded died later; how many more were carried away by the Indians is
not known. The whites lost 25 killed and 39 wounded.

The reaction to Wounded Knee was polarized at two extremes in the
press. Some papers saw the battle as a victorious triumph of the soldiers
over treacherous Indians. Others condemned the action as a brutal revenge
for Custer's defeat (the soldiers were of the same regiment), in which wom-
en and children were wantonly butchered. Neither position was right, for
neither side in the conflict had planned or foreseen the tragedy that occurred. Big Foot and his people sought peace, but they were afraid and suspicious, and when the shooting started they reacted violently. The soldiers
fought back savagely against what they considered Indian treachery. "It is
time that Wounded Knee be viewed for what it was," historian Robert Utley
concludes, "—a regrettable, tragic accident of war that neither side intended, and that called forth behavior for which some individuals on both
sides, in unemotional retrospect, may be judged culpable, but for which
neither side as a whole may be properly condemned."

SUCCESSFUL REFORMS

The Sioux troubles that led to Wounded Knee in 1890 convinced the advocates of reform more than ever that they were right. Herbert Welsh and his
friends declared that the troubles could have been prevented had not the
spoils system operated to weaken the administrative control so necessary
at Pine Ridge. The event gave new impetus to the movement for civil service reform.

There was some success, for on April 13, 1891, the president extended
the civil service rules to cover all physicians, superintendents of schools,
assistant superintendents, teachers, and matrons in the Indian service. It
was a substantial beginning, and the reformers rejoiced, but the success
only whetted their appetite for more. Their goal was to bring the rest of the
agency employees under the classified service and then, if possible, make
sure that the agents, too, were freed from the political rotation that interrupted the smooth continuation of policy. If rules could not formally be
extended, the reformers pleaded that at least the spirit of the law be fol-

lowed. If the Indians were to be fitted for citizenship, the spoils system would have to be abandoned entirely.

For employees below the level of agent, the civil service reformers won their case. By direction of President Cleveland, the Department of the Interior on March 30, 1896, amended the classification of the Indian service to include all physicians, school superintendents, assistant superintendents, supervisors of schools, day school inspectors, school teachers, assistant teachers, industrial teachers, teachers of industries, disciplinarians, kindergarten teachers, matrons, assistant matrons, farmers, seamstresses, and nurses. All of these, without regard to salary level, were made subject to competitive examination for appointment. Another order of the same date included all clerks, assistant clerks, issue clerks, property clerks, and other clerical positions and storekeepers at Indian agencies and Indian schools. Furthermore, on May 6, 1896, the scope of the classified service was enlarged still more to include all officers and employees, of whatever designation, except persons employed merely as laborers or workmen and persons nominated for confirmation by the Senate. These regulations, however, did not apply to Indians themselves, who in increasing numbers were employed at the agencies, usually in positions of lower rank.

This extension of the civil service system still left the key men, the agents, under the spoils system. Until the political pressures that kept them there could be dissipated, other expedients were tried. One of these—remarkable as it may seem after the controversy that raged over the transfer issue in the 1870s—was the assignment of army officers as Indian agents. A law of July 13, 1892, provided that thereafter when any vacancies occurred, the president was to detail army officers to fill them, although he could appoint civilians if the good of the service would be better promoted thereby. The military men were to act under the orders and direction of the secretary of the interior in their duties as agents. By the end of 1893, twenty-seven out of fifty-seven agencies were under the charge of army officers.

A more radical and ultimately more satisfactory expedient was to eliminate the position of agent altogether. Commissioner Morgan made such a suggestion in his annual report of 1892, declaring that it was "entirely feasible and very desirable to modify the agency system and prepare the way for its complete abolition by placing the agency affairs, in certain cases, in the hands of school superintendents." An act of March 3, 1893, authorized the commissioner to assign the agent's duties to the superintendent at any agency where he felt the superintendent was qualified for the job. The agent's position at the Eastern Cherokee Agency in North Carolina, in fact, was abolished by the same law and the duties turned over to the school superintendent, but no other such assignments seem to have been made until after 1900.

The millennium, clearly, had not yet arrived, and the advent of William McKinley's administration brought forebodings to the Indian reformers. The Indian Rights Association feared that a plan was afloat for getting rid of a number of the army officers who served as agents in order to make room for civilian appointees, who were more likely than the officers to serve local or personal interests at the cost of the Indians. And in fact the number of army officers in the service greatly declined. The McKinley administration got low marks in general from the Indian Rights Association, which asserted in 1898 that the advances made in the two previous administrations had been negated and that affairs were worse than ever.

The Board of Indian Commissioners, too, continued its agitation for including the agents in the classified civil service and for a strict application of the existing laws to correct abuses on the reservations. At the end of the century it repeated its conviction, "never more deeply felt, that *Indian agents should be appointed solely for merit and fitness for the work,* and *should be retained in the service when they prove themselves to be efficient and helpful by their* character and moral influence, as well as by their experience." The evils that remained in the Indian service it attributed to "the partisan and political influences which still surround the appointment and removal of Indian agents."

The advent of Theodore Roosevelt, soon after the turn of the century, brought the culmination of the movement. Roosevelt had been a civil service crusader and member of the civil service commission, and during his presidency the remaining agents were replaced by school superintendents. The president considered the matter significant enough to note in his final annual message to Congress on December 8, 1908. He spoke of the agency system as "gradually falling to pieces from natural or purely evolutionary causes" and as "decaying slowly in its later stages." Now was the time, he asserted, to bring about its final extinction "so that ground can be cleared for larger constructive work on behalf of the Indians, preparatory to their induction into the full measure of responsible citizenship."

Like views about most panaceas, the reformers' insistence that the civil service would solve the problems of Indian administration was too simple. Bureaucratic personnel, securely protected by civil service rules, were not necessarily enlightened in their administration of Indian affairs, nor would perfection in administration alone have been able to solve the Indian problem. Once again the Indian reformers, seizing upon a remedy that was important in the general reform atmosphere of the day, mistakenly thought they had found the answer.

CHAPTER 17

The Indian Territory

The dreams of the Indian reformers for the Americanization of all the Indians and the desire of western settlers for Indian lands that lay unused were long frustrated by the Indian Territory. Here were the Five Civilized Tribes—Cherokee, Creek, Choctaw, Chickasaw, and Seminole—who had advanced the farthest along the white man's road and who seemed most apt for final absorption into American society as individualized, land-owning citizens. Here too were rich acres only partially used by the Indians, which were coveted by white farmers as the surrounding states of Arkansas, Texas, and Kansas grew rapidly in population, and rich mineral resources that beckoned developers. The transformation seemed almost inevitable.

The situation in the Indian Territory was complex and confused. Indians, seeking economic well-being within their autonomous nations, private white corporations driven by the spirit of enterprise and profit, and the United States government, hoping both to protect the Indians and to encourage "progress," all contributed to the political and economic cauldron. Development of the region pitted corporations against the tribal governments, which in the long run were no match for the economic monsters. The Indian Territory stood across the lines of commerce, north and south and east and west, and agitation for railroad lines through the territory developed soon after the Civil War. Hopes for profit intrigued the Indians as well as the whites, and tremendous pressures, only partially resisted, came to bear on the tribal governments and the federal government to promote the railroad interests. Then coal resources became the goal of corporate developers, and finally the new riches of oil and gas. And always there was the magnet of valuable lands for grazing cattle and ultimately for agricultural homesteaders.

The drive to open the Indian Territory to these economic forces filled much of the period between the Civil War and the end of the century. As the invasion proceeded, the independence of the tribes declined in almost direct proportion. Although the Indians skillfully postponed the day of destruction, in the end the demand for progress and conformity won out. It is an instructive story of the force of the reforming spirit, which, blocked time and again in its efforts to eradicate this last great obstacle to the fulfillment of its promise, by the end of the century here too had triumphed.

THE DRIVE FOR TERRITORIAL ORGANIZATION

The ultimate goal was to bring the Indian Territory into the regular political structure of the United States, beginning with territorial status that would lead to statehood. There seemed no hope for full economic development until the region could be open to all citizens of the United States on an equal footing. That goal fitted perfectly with the program of Americanization espoused by the humanitarian reformers. As early as the end of the Civil War, the plans of the federal government for the Indian Territory, in addition to the emancipation of the slaves and the reduction of territory as a punishment for joining the Confederacy, included a determination to replace the independent tribal governments with a consolidated or confederated government that would be a regular territory of the United States. At the heart of the matter was the conviction that there were too few Indians on too much land, that if the Indians could be forced to work 160-acre homesteads of their own, they would find their salvation and the rest of the land could be put into profitable production by whites.

Aside from the purported advantages to the Indians from territorial government, American citizenship, and land in severalty, the advocates of territorial organization were deeply concerned about lawlessness in the Indian Territory. They saw ineffective governments, inadequate courts, and no protection of the rights of whites and freedmen. Severely complicating the matter was the growing number of whites within the Five Civilized Tribes. Some of these had intermarried into the tribes or been adopted as tribal citizens and caused no special problem. A few others were simply intruders, who infiltrated into the territory unbidden and unwanted. The great majority, however, were farmers or other laborers who had been invited in by the Indians. Although the Five Civilized Tribes all prohibited the leasing of Indian lands, contracts or permits were given to whites to open up farms in return for a share of the crops. By such means ambitious Indians or mixed-bloods were able to establish large holdings not greatly different from antebellum plantations. Railroad and mineral development augmented still more the number of whites within the Indian nations. Because the tribal governments pertained to Indians alone, the demand arose for an adequate means to protect the personal and property rights of the whites.

The agitation for changes in the Indian Territory in the 1870s bore no fruit. Bill after bill was introduced in Congress, but all failed, for opponents of territorial organization were able to hold off the threat of radical change. Among these opponents the Indians themselves were foremost. The Five Civilized Tribes had astute and articulate spokesmen, who countered each congressional move toward territorial status with forceful memorials protesting the action. Many of the memorials were drawn up and presented by the national delegates maintained in Washington to look after tribal interests and to oppose changes in the political status or in the land tenure system. Other protests came from intertribal councils or from the principal chiefs of the various nations.

The Indians' first defense was to rely upon the treaties that had guaranteed them self-government without white interference, and their statements and memorials skillfully marshaled the historical evidence in support of their stand. They argued that the establishment of a territorial government over them would "work our ruin and speedy extinction, by subjecting us to the absolute rule of a people foreign to us in blood, language, customs, traditions, and interest, who would speedily possess themselves of our homes, degrade us in our own estimation, and leave us prey to the politician and land speculator, thus destroying the unity of our race, and producing national disintegration." They denied, moreover, the condition of lawlessness, which was the foundation for so much of the proterritorial argument, and they lectured Congress that it should not be misled by "mischievous falsehoods."

A basic fear of the Indians was that proposed changes would mean the ultimate loss of their lands. Especially disturbing were conditional land grants that Congress had made to railroad companies. The Indians charged that territorial organization and the end of tribal independence would fulfill the conditions and that the land would then fall to the railroads. Most of the Indian protests adverted to the danger inherent in the railroad grants, and there was strong sympathy for the Indian position. Bills proposed for territorial organization at the end of the 1870s, in fact, added sections specifically repealing the earlier conditional grants.

The Indians, of course, did not lack support. Cattlemen who benefited from leasing Indian lands fought for the maintenance of the status quo, and many persons agreed with the Indians' analysis of their treaty rights. A strong minority report from the House Committee on Territories was lodged against one of the proposed territory bills on the grounds that the bill would contravene treaty agreements and that the movement for territorial organization came from the railroads. In 1879 the committee reported unfavorably on a bill to organize the Indian Territory and divide the land in severalty, arguing that the measure would conflict with treaty agreements, that there was no need to invalidate the treaties, and that past experience had shown that allotment of land in severalty and granting of citizenship to Indians had had uniformly bad results. The report, of course, was lauded by the Indian delegates.

INVASION OF THE INDIAN TERRITORY

White agitation for changes in the Indian Territory intensified in the 1880s as new elements came to the fore. Westerners' desire for land, played upon by railroad interests, caused a decade of increasing pressure to open parts of the Territory to homesteaders, and federal officials supported by the humanitarian reformers found new arguments for dividing the Indians' land and absorbing the Indians as citizens of the United States.

The business interests were tireless advocates. Aided by Elias Cornelius Boudinot, of the prominent Ridge faction of the Cherokees, they fostered a group of professional promoters called "boomers," who by propaganda and direct action determined to force open the lands in the territory. Boudinot had wholeheartedly accepted the white vision of the future of the Five Civilized Tribes that called for citizenship and allotment of land. Now he claimed that fourteen million acres of land in the Indian Territory were in fact already in the public domain and subject to homestead entry. Such activities, together with a tremendous flood of boomer literature, led to organized Oklahoma colonies on the borders of the Indian Territory in Kansas and Texas that claimed the right to homestead in the territory and made forays into the territory and established incipient communities before they were driven out by federal troops.

The illegal invasions of the Indian Territory stirred new support for the Indians among humanitarians concerned with Indian rights, but the pressure was too great to withstand. Carl Schurz told the Indians in 1879 that "the difficulties of protecting the integrity of the Territory might in the course of time increase beyond control," and he urged them to meet the emergency by dividing their lands and obtaining individual titles in fee, which could be defended against attack.

Little by little the government gave way. Congressional friends of the boomers regularly introduced bills for opening lands in the territory for homesteading, and in 1889 they succeeded. On March 2 of that year, Congress authorized homesteading in the Oklahoma District, and President Benjamin Harrison proclaimed the lands open to settlement at noon on

April 22, 1889. Fifty thousand homeseekers lined the area waiting for the signal to advance, and when the blast of the bugle sounded, the first of the dramatic Oklahoma "runs" was under way.

For a year the new inhabitants were forced to maintain their own communities, for Congress had failed to provide government for the region. Then on May 2, 1890, with the Oklahoma Organic Act, a formal territorial government was established for the Oklahoma District and for "No Man's Land" (the Oklahoma panhandle), which was joined to it. This was a far cry from the organization of the whole Indian Territory that had been advocated so strenuously; but white settlers had at last broken the barrier and begun their legal invasion of the once sacrosanct region.

Meanwhile, the attack on the independent status of the Five Civilized Tribes went on. Commissioner Atkins was especially vehement. He asserted in 1885 that the idea of Indian nationality was fast melting away and that the tribal relations would sooner or later have to be broken up. When the Indians had taken their lands in severalty and become citizens, they would be prepared to dispose of their surplus lands to their own advantage and for the public good.

Atkins made much of the recurring argument used by the proponents of forced change that the nations were controlled by aristocratic leaders who had built up huge land monopolies. He pointed to large holdings within the nations controlled by certain important men who had acquired land that belonged to all in common. "What a baronial estate!" he exclaimed about one such holding. "In theory the lands are held in common under the tribal relation, and are equally owned by each member of the tribe, but in point of fact they are simply held in the grasping hand of moneyed monopolists and powerful and influential leaders and politicians, who pay no rental to the other members of the tribe." Such a situation, the commissioner insisted, needed radical reformation.

DEFEAT OF THE FIVE CIVILIZED TRIBES

The humanitarian reformers who aimed to turn the Indians into land-owning, civilized, Christian citizens of the United States wanted the Five Civilized Tribes to be the model for the rest of the Indian tribes. Not only would the incorporation of these Indians into the American system solve the problems that beset the Indian Territory, but it would provide encouragement for other Indians to follow suit. Because of the insistent opposition of the Five Civilized Tribes to proposed land in severalty and citizenship legislation, however, Congress excluded them from the Dawes Act of 1887. Thus the very tribes that might have been the first to whom the

Dawes Act could be applied and who had been a prime target of such proposals for two decades slipped out of the net.

Although the reformers lost this battle, they had not yet lost the war. The acquisition of lands for homesteading was accomplished by direct negotiation with the Cherokees for sale of the Cherokee Outlet and with other tribes residing west of the Five Civilized Tribes for cession of their surplus lands. This work was undertaken by the so-called Cherokee Commission, authorized on March 2, 1889. Much opposition came from the Indians, but the persistence of the commissioners resulted finally in eleven agreements with plains Indians and Indians who had moved to the Indian Territory from the Old Northwest, by which the tribes gave up more than fifteen million acres. The common pattern provided for a 160-acre allotment in severalty to each man, woman, and child on the tribal rolls. The remainder of the land was declared surplus and bought by the government for homesteading. As the areas were opened to white settlers, new counties were organized and incorporated into Oklahoma Territory. The Cherokee Outlet was the largest transfer of land. When it was opened to homesteaders in September 1893, the greatest of the Oklahoma land runs occurred with a hundred thousand persons rushing in to locate homes on the new land.

A second line of attack on the problems of the Indian Territory was the extension of the federal judicial system over the region. Criminal cases in the territory involving white citizens of the United States had been handled by the United States District Court at Fort Smith, Arkansas, but the distance and expense involved in bringing cases before the court were so great that only important ones were brought in. There were no courts to take care of civil cases. Then in 1889 a United States court was established at Muskogee, with jurisdiction in civil cases affecting citizens of the United States if the amount involved was more than one hundred dollars, and the court was given criminal jurisdiction over cases in which the offense was not punishable by death or imprisonment at hard labor. But the more serious cases still had to go to Fort Smith or to the United States District Court at Paris, Texas, which had been designated for criminal cases arising in the Choctaw and Chickasaw nations.

On March 1, 1895, Congress created two new United States courts for the Indian Territory and ended the jurisdiction of the courts in the neighboring states, and the system was gradually expanded. The dissolution of the Indian governments was thus rapidly advanced. In 1897 Congress provided that after January 1, 1898, all civil and criminal cases should be tried in the United States courts. The Curtis Act of June 28, 1898, abolished tribal laws and tribal courts and brought all persons in the Indian Territory, regardless of race, under United States authority. The law, entitled "an act for the protection of the people of the Indian Territory," was unilateral action by the United States that signaled the end of the tribal governments; it was practically an organic act for the establishment of the long-sought territorial government.

Paralleling this dissolution of the tribal governments, and in fact a strong force in their destruction, was the work of the Commission to the Five Civilized Tribes (usually known as the Dawes Commission), which accomplished the allotment of land that had been the goal of the government and of the reformers for nearly three decades. The commission was directed to negotiate with the Five Civilized Tribes for the extinguishment of the national or tribal title to their lands and for consent to measures that would be "requisite and suitable to enable the ultimate creation of a State or States of the Union" out of the Indian Territory. It is significant that President Grover Cleveland chose Henry L. Dawes, who had retired from the Senate in 1893, to head the commission. Dawes's strong views as to the future of the Indians and the necessity of incorporation into white society through allotment of lands and citizenship made him a fit instrument to carry out the mandate of Congress. There is no doubt of his conviction that the goal was the proper one.

The reformers, who had long been agitated by conditions in the Indian Territory, soon had strong supporting evidence for their position. A Senate committee headed by Senator Henry M. Teller investigated the Indian Territory early in 1894 and submitted a report in May. This report, as well as the report of the Dawes Commission submitted in November 1894, emphasized the crisis resulting from the great influx of whites into the territory and from the monopolization of land by a few individuals. The whites were estimated to number 250,000 or more, and they had for the most part been invited in by the Indians themselves, despite provision in the treaties that the lands were to be for the exclusive use of the Indians.

It had been the theory, the reports noted, that when the government made over title to the lands to the Indian nations, the lands would be held in trust for all the Indians. Instead, Teller reported, a few enterprising citizens of the tribe, frequently Indian not by blood but by intermarriage, had become the practical owners of the largest and best part of the lands, even though the title still remained in the tribe. The monopoly was so great that in one tribe a hundred persons were reported to have appropriated fully one-half of the best land. The trust had been broken, nor would it ever be properly executed, Teller thought, if left to the Indians.

The Dawes Commission, too, faced the question of the duty of the government of the United States with reference to the trust. "These tribal governments," it asserted, "have wholly perverted their high trust, and it is the plain duty of the United States to enforce the trust it has so created and recover for its original uses the domain and all the gains derived from the perversion of the trust or discharge the trustee." Noted too were the inequities in the condition of the freedmen—despite the clear provisions of the 1866 treaties—and "corruption of the grossest kind, openly and unblushingly practiced" in all branches of the tribal governments. It was apparent to these official observers that the existing system could not continue.

The reformers at Lake Mohonk placed themselves firmly on the side of the Dawes Commission. Their platform for 1895 included this forthright statement:

> The nation possesses a supreme sovereignty over every foot of soil within its boundaries. Its legislative authority over its people it has neither right nor power to alienate. Its attempt to do so by Indian treaties in the past does not relieve it from the responsibility for the condition of government in the reservations and in the Indian Territory; and, despite those treaties, it is under a sacred obligation to exercise its sovereignty extending over the three hundred thousand whites and fifty thousand so-called Indians in the Indian Territory the same restraints and protection of government which other parts of the country enjoy.

Congress heeded the message. A law of June 10, 1896, directed the Dawes Commission to make out rolls of Indian citizens in preparation for allotment and stated: "It is hereby declared to be the duty of the United States to establish a government in the Indian Territory which will rectify the many inequalities and discriminations now existing in said Territory and afford needful protection to the lives and property of all citizens and residents thereof." Under these new mandates, the commission moved rapidly ahead toward the dissolution of the Five Civilized Tribes.

The Indian Rights Association, like the Lake Mohonk Conference, was on Dawes's side. In an analysis of the question of the Five Civilized Tribes in 1896, the association spokesmen opted for a middle course between "a purely sentimental policy which considered the present situation of the five civilized tribes an autonomous one" and urged that the Indians be left alone, and a change overriding all rights of the Indians, forced by outside interests, not by friends of the Indians—between "land-grabbing and spoliation on the one side; a sentimentalism which takes no account of facts on the other." But ultimately the Indian Rights Association was "quite content to let the tribe go." It noted that all recent Indian legislation had contemplated the extinction of the tribes and that the great majority of Indian reformers were agreed on that policy. The association wanted to do all that could be done wisely "to save and guard the individual Indian."

The tribes finally saw the futility of further resistance and gave in. On April 23, 1897, the Dawes Commission negotiated the Atoka Agreement with the Choctaws and Chickasaws, which determined the fundamental formula for allotment in those nations. An agreement was reached with the Seminoles in 1898, with the Creeks in 1901, and with the Cherokees finally in 1902. Meanwhile the Curtis Act authorized the Dawes Commission to proceed with the allotment of lands as soon as the tribal rolls were completed.

The work of the Dawes Commission was exacting. The lands had to be surveyed, not only for extent but also for quality of land, since the agreements specified that allotments would be based on the value of the land, not simply on acreage. In addition the commission had to determine the eligibility of allottees, a tremendous job, for more than 300,000 persons claimed membership in the Five Civilized Tribes. Beginning in 1898 and continuing until the rolls were closed in 1907, the commission entered 101,506 persons on the rolls.

The size of the allotments varied from tribe to tribe. Choctaws and Chickasaws received 320 acres each, Cherokees 110 acres, Creeks 160 acres, and Seminoles 120 acres. Freedmen among the Cherokees, Creeks, and Seminoles shared equally with the Indians; those among the Chickasaws and Choctaws received 40-acre allotments. Some part of each allotment was designated a homestead and made inalienable for a period of years. Altogether 19,526,966 acres were surveyed in the Five Civilized Tribes, of which 15,794,400 were allotted to persons on the tribal rolls. The rest comprised land for townsites, schools, and other public purposes, and coal and mineral lands held for tribal benefit. There were few surplus lands within the Five Civilized Tribes to be opened to whites.

These moves meant that members of the Five Civilized Tribes were to lose their tribal citizenship and become citizens of the United States. Congress in 1890, in fact, had provided that individuals could apply at the federal court at Muskogee for United States citizenship, and the allotment agreements drawn up by the Dawes Commission provided for a switch in citizenship. Finally, in 1901, Congress made every Indian in the Indian Territory a citizen of the United States.

Thus ended the campaign to destroy the exclusiveness of the Indians in the Indian Territory. For more than three decades after the Civil War the Indian nations struggled to preserve their national existence, but the odds were too great. There was the continual tension between traditional tribal independence on one side and economic development on the other, for the two in practice seemed to be contradictory. As railroad or mining corporations gained power, tribal self-determination was weakened, and often even the moves of the federal government to protect the Indians' welfare were made in a paternalistic spirit independently of the tribal governments and thus were another wound to Indian sovereignty.

More damaging, perhaps, was the factionalism that developed within the Indian tribes themselves over the question of economic exploitation of their resources. There were strong elements among the Indians—Elias Cornelius Boudinot is but a striking example—who on principle or for personal gain were on the side of the white corporations. These advocates of change were for the most part mixed-bloods, whereas the full-bloods in the more isolated country regions clung to the old ways. Events moved too rapidly for the federal government to develop a firm and consistent policy in regard to leasing and other elements of economic development; and the tribes, too, had to make decisions—often irrevocable—before they fully grasped the significance of their actions. Hesitation on the part of the government and informal permissions allowed business interests to get a vested interest in the Indian Territory, and they then influenced the circumstances under which formal policy decisions were made.

The tribal governments were allowed to continue until their property was liquidated, and national councils were allowed to meet, but their acts were all subject to approval by the president of the United States. Indian nations had succumbed to the pressures of the whites, who could brook no alien economic or political enclaves within their completely Americanized society.

OKLAHOMA STATEHOOD

Strong agitation for Oklahoma statehood developed at the end of the century, and the growing population in both Oklahoma Territory and the Indian Territory fully justified it; but there was delay because of the question of what should be included in the new state or states. Some wanted the immediate admission of Oklahoma Territory, leaving the status of the Indian Territory undecided; others wanted the admission of Oklahoma Territory and the Indian Territory as separate states; still others wanted the admission of the two territories as a single state.

The leaders of the Five Civilized Tribes made a valiant attempt to preserve their identity within the federal system by promoting separate statehood for the Indian Territory. On November 28, 1902, at Eufaula in the Creek Nation, officials of the Creeks, Cherokees, and Choctaws (supported by the Chickasaws as well) adopted a statement against union with Oklahoma Territory. The individual tribes also made separate protests. But the movement seemed to have little effect at the time in persuading a majority of the citizens or the federal officials to accept the Indians' view.

In the summer of 1905 new agitation for a separate state developed, and strong arguments were presented. The Indian Territory had a population as large as that of Maine; its resources for economic development surpassed those of Oklahoma Territory, and it had numerous railroads and incorporated towns. Union with Oklahoma, moreover, would bring together two political entities with different histories and different current problems. A convention, meeting at Muskogee in August, drew up a constitution for a proposed state of Sequoyah, and in an election on November 7 the document was ratified by a vote of fifty-six thousand to nine thousand (though not more than half of the qualified voters went to the polls).

This seeming success was blocked in Congress. Although bills for admission of the separate state were introduced in both houses, no action was taken, and the whole movement died. President Theodore Roosevelt recommended joint statehood in his annual message on December 4, 1905, and Congress proceeded with its plans to unite the two territories. Under an enabling act passed on June 16, 1906, a constitutional convention was held and a constitution drawn up, which was ratified by an overwhelming majority on September 17, 1907. A month later President Roosevelt issued a proclamation declaring that Oklahoma was a state of the Union. According to a special census of 1907, the population of the new state stood at 1,414,177, slightly less than half of which was in the former Indian Territory. Of this total, there were 101,228 persons in the Five Civilized Tribes, including intermarried whites and the freedmen, and 15,603 other Indians.

The Indians of Oklahoma were an anomaly in Indian-white relations. Many had long been acculturated to the white man's ways and took an active part in the formation of the new state and in its economic and political life. Yet they maintained an identity as Indians and for many years far surpassed the Indian population of other states. There are no Indian reservations in Oklahoma, however, and the reservation experience that was fundamental for most Indian groups in the twentieth century was not part of Oklahoma Indian history.

CHAPTER 18

The Nation's Wards

The individualization and Americanization of the Indians that was the goal of the Christian reformers in the last two decades of the nineteenth century were worked out in practice in the first three decades of the twentieth. The theory embodied in the Dawes Act, with its allotment of land in severalty and its provisions for citizenship, and the establishment of a national school system for the Indians that had been the dream of Thomas Jefferson Morgan and his Lake Mohonk supporters were refined and implemented after 1900. The policy had been set; now the administration of the policy became the crucial matter.

Perhaps because the period was devoid of striking policy changes, historians have neglected it, jumping for the most part from the Dawes Act of 1887 to its antithesis, the Indian Reorganization Act of 1934. Yet it was in the intervening years that the nineteenth-century policy was tested in the fire of experience. It was in these years that the Indian Office came face to face with the problems of dealing with the Indians, not as a relatively few tribal units, but as thousands upon thousands of individual wards of the federal government. Under these conditions the paternalism of the federal government, which was supposed to end when the individual Indians disappeared into the dominant American society, increased instead of diminished, until the bureaucracy of the Indian Service dominated every aspect of the Indians' lives.

Although the basic philosophy of assimilation continued to be the foundation of the government's relations with the Indians, there were important changes in outlook or in emphasis after 1900. Most noticeable was a change from the nineteenth-century Christian faith that the individualization and Christianization of the Indians would abruptly and dramatically transform them and result in a rapid disappearance of the "Indian problem," to a pragmatic, practical approach, with the emphasis on efficiency and businesslike management that marked the Progressive Era. The key words in the new age were *self-support* and *self-reliance*. The Indian must be turned into an efficient worker who could care for himself and his family and no longer be dependent upon the government. Even those who needed long-term protection and guardianship would eventually reach this ultimate state with improved education and proper guidance.

PROGRESSIVES IN THE INDIAN OFFICE

The Indian Office in the Progressive Era was directed by men of ability and personal integrity, and they brought a period of continuity and stability in Indian affairs. In the thirty-two years between the beginning of Commissioner William A. Jones's administration in 1897 and the resignation of Charles H. Burke in 1929, only five men held the office of commissioner of Indian affairs. These men took seriously their charge as guardians of the Indians, and although they were subject to considerable just criticism, they were free of fraud and corruption, misguided as their policies might seem to later generations.

Jones, from Mineral Point, Wisconsin, came into office while the Christian reform sentiment was strong. He reflected its principles in his handling of Indian affairs, but he also moved away from strict adherence to those theories when changed conditions or a better understanding of them demanded modifications. He was a transition figure, carrying on the Christian reform he inherited but bringing to the office, too, a keen interest in administrative efficiency to meet modern needs.

One example of the older tradition that Jones exemplified was his notorious "short hair" order to agents and superintendents in late December 1901 and early January 1902. Jones directed attention to "a few customs among the Indians which, it is believed, should be modified or discontinued." The first was the wearing of long hair by the men, which was "not in keeping with the advancement they are making, or will soon be expected to make, in civilization." If Indians who were employed by the Indian service or drawing rations refused to comply, they could be discharged and their supplies stopped. If they became obstreperous, "a short confinement in the guard-house at hard labor, with shorn locks, should furnish a cure." He also directed action against painting of the face and against dances and Indian feasts, which were "simply subterfuges to cover degrading acts and to disguise immoral purposes."

The reaction in the press was immediate and widespread in criticism of the order. Jones himself saw in the press's reporting good-natured bantering rather than serious criticism, and he affirmed the purpose of the order, calling attention to Secretary Henry M. Teller's previous action and the courts of Indian offenses that had resulted. He thought it quite proper to enforce the order against employees of the Indian service and against returned students, who had been the recipients of "bounteous favors."

Of more substance was Jones's strong promotion of all measures that would lead to Indian self-support, which became a kind of leitmotif of his administration. His annual report of 1900 began with a long section entitled "Obstacles to Self-Support," in which he lashed out at distribution of rations and annuities to the Indians and the practice of leasing allotments. To these, in the following year, he added the educational system, which coddled the Indians in boarding schools. "Whatever the condition of the Indian may be," he wrote, "he should be removed from a state of dependence to one of independence. And the only way to do this is to take away those things that encourage him to lead an idle life, and, after giving him a fair start, leave him to take care of himself." Jones in 1901 instructed the agents to cut from the ration rolls all able-bodied Indians who were self-supporting and those who could work but refused to do so.

Jones was optimistic about Indian progress because he saw the inferiority of the Indian not as an inherent quality but as a "husk of savagery and barbarism" to be taken away by "the gradual evolution of educational processes." He admired the Indian's love of freedom, his pride of ancestry, and his intense and fervent love of his children. "Such a race," he asserted, "is worthy of all the time, money, and labor expended on it by a generous Congress and people."

Francis E. Leupp, who succeeded Jones on January 1, 1905, came with a remarkably extensive background of interest in the Indians, a tremendous commitment to efficiency and economy, and a self-confidence that his detractors considered sheer arrogance. He was, moreover, a longtime personal friend of Theodore Roosevelt, with whom he worked directly on Indian affairs, largely bypassing the secretary of the interior.

Leupp parted company with earlier reformers and asserted that the Indians had qualities and a heritage of art and music that should be preserved and cultivated, not eradicated. "The Indian is a natural warrior, a natural logician, a natural artist," he insisted. "We have room for all three in our highly organized social system. Let us not make the mistake, in the process of absorbing them, of washing out of them whatever is distinctly Indian. Our aboriginal brother brings, as his contribution to the common store of character, a great deal which is admirable, and which needs only to be developed along the right line. Our proper work with him is improvement, not transformation."

But his general refusal to assume that the Indian was "simply a white man with a red skin" did not stop Leupp from energetically promoting programs to improve the Indians, and what he considered "improvement" differed little from "transformation." Like Jones, he felt that the chief need was to turn the Indian into a self-reliant, independent worker, individualized both as to his land and his money, and "an active factor in the upbuilding of the community in which he is going to live."

Leupp's forthright handling of Indian affairs according to his own positive views soon brought him into conflict with the Indian Rights Association, which still considered its independent concern for Indian rights a necessary influence on Indian policy and its voice one to be listened to. Leupp was irritated by what he thought was meddling in official matters, and he ended his career as commissioner in a storm of controversy with Herbert Welsh and the association.

Leupp picked his own successor, Robert G. Valentine, who had taken office with him as his personal secretary and moved into the position of assistant commissioner. A native of Massachusetts and a graduate of Harvard, Valentine was only thirty-six years old when Taft appointed him commissioner on June 19, 1909. Valentine was a solid Progressive, committed to economy and efficiency, who energetically continued the policies of his mentor. He gave high priority in his administration to the crucial problems of Indian health, promoted the industrial education program of the Indian Office, and developed its forestry program. In all he did he sought to advance the professional and businesslike performance of the Indian service, noting on one occasion. "The only things I care for . . . [are] speed, economy and efficiency."

Cato Sells, whom President Wilson appointed commissioner, carried on the tradition of Leupp and Valentine. He combined a deep concern for Indians who needed the help of the government with a ruthless determination to rid the government of responsibility for those Indians whom he judged able to manage fully their own affairs. It was his "fixed purpose to bring about the speedy individualizing of the Indians," he said early in his administration, and the removal from guardianship of those individualized Indians who presumably could stand on their own.

Sells's administration of Indian affairs was seriously interrupted by World War I, which called for new efforts in Indian agriculture, stock raising, and forestry to support the war effort, while at the same time it decimated Indian service personnel. The commissioner met the challenge with characteristic energy and enthusiasm, and he found in the wartime experiences of the Indians a great and positive advance toward the ultimate goal of American citizenship.

The Indians increased food production, supported the relief work of the Red Cross, and contributed money to the war bond drives. More significantly, a large number of Indians entered military service: in 1918 Sells estimated that there were eight thousand in training or on active duty in some branch of the army and navy and that six thousand of them had enlisted, and he later spoke of ten thousand in the services. Sells, however, refused to sanction separate Indian military units, which some persons proposed, as "not in harmony with our plans for developing the Indian's citizenship." The Indian, he said, should fight shoulder to shoulder with the white man in a common cause and go into the war "as the equal and comrade of every man who assails autocracy and ancient might, and to come home with a new light in his face and a clearer conception of the democracy in which he may participate and prosper."

The war affected positively the drive for Indian citizenship. By an act of November 6, 1919, Congress provided that any Indian who received an honorable discharge from military service during World War I could, if he desired it, apply for citizenship and be granted it by a competent court without affecting rights to tribal property. Sells greeted the legislation enthusiastically as a "just and fitting tribute to the intelligence, patriotism, and courage of the young men of a virile and enduring race."

THE DECLINE OF THE CHRISTIAN REFORMERS

Protestant Christian reformers had dominated the formulation of Indian policy in the late nineteenth century, operating effectively through the Board of Indian Commissioners and such voluntary organizations as the Indian Rights Association and the Lake Mohonk Conference. They looked upon themselves as the guardians of the Indians and the watchdogs and arbiters of national Indian policy. They saw themselves, not unrealistically, as the effective force in moving the Indians into an individualized, Americanized society (which meant to them a Protestant Christian nation). In the dozen or so years after the turn of the century their position of dominance was severely shaken, if not indeed shattered, and the privileged place of their organizations and the strongly religious orientation of the programs had faded away.

In the first place, the old reformers were no longer able to control the legislative formulation of Indian policy. Their ineffectiveness could be seen in the Burke Act of 1906, which postponed citizenship for the Indians until the end of the trust period, thus reversing, or at least slowing down, the individualizing, Americanizing process of the Dawes Act. The act was severely criticized and strongly opposed by the reformers' groups, but to no avail. A second law in which the reform groups failed to obtain their goals was the Lacey Act of 1907, which dealt with the allotment of money held in trust for the Indians in the United States Treasury. It was intended, in the minds of the reformers who initiated it, to break up the Indian trust funds (held in common by each tribe) exactly as the Dawes Act had broken up the reservation lands. But when the act finally passed in Congress, it was merely permissive, and it required an Indian to apply for his allotment before any action could be taken. The Lacey Act was, to the reformers, no more than a "makeshift substitute."

Second, the reformers lost their decisive influence with the commissioner of Indian affairs and the executive branch in general. The reform groups, with their investigative trips, their yearly conferences at Lake Mohonk, and their effective lobbying, had been a force to be reckoned with. They had spoken out fearlessly and had become accustomed to being listened to. Then they ran into Commissioner Leupp. To their dismay, they learned that Leupp, despite the fact that he had once been one of their number, had a mind of his own and that he intended to run his office without their advice and in fact sometimes in sharp opposition to them.

One celebrated case concerned the Crow Agency in Montana, where the Indian Rights Association sought an investigation into alleged violations of Indian rights by the stockmen and the Indian agent. The Washington representative of the association was turned away when he went to Montana to investigate, and the secretary of the association was arrested by agency personnel when he appeared for the same purpose. The Indian Rights Association fought unsuccessfully to defeat Senate confirmation of a special inspector sent out to look into the charges. A second case involved eight Navajo Indian outlaws, led by Bai-a-lil-le, who were arrested in 1907 and confined without specific charges and without trial. The Indian Rights Association insisted that the Indians be released; Leupp countered that he would do what he thought necessary to protect the peaceful Indians, "law or no law." Although in the end Leupp's opponents won their case, the affair showed the strong opposition of views between the commissioner and the Indian Rights Association and Leupp's strong and independent action.

The Indian Rights Association was delighted when Leupp resigned. "It is a cause of congratulations," the president of the association wrote, "that a commissioner whose egotism had made it impossible for him to catch other people's point of view, should give place to one of a more open mind and less assured infallibility."

The Board of Indian Commissioners fared little better than the Indian Rights Association, and under Secretary of the Interior Ethan Allen Hitchcock it had to defend its authority, if not its very existence. Although the board survived through the 1920s and was used from time to time by the Indian Office, its position as an independent force in Indian administration was not strong. The Lake Mohonk Conference also lost influence in Indian affairs. To begin with, after 1900 it broadened its activities to include the peoples in the territories acquired after the Spanish American War. It changed its name in fact to Friends of the Indian and Other Dependent Peoples. Then its founder and guiding light, Albert K. Smiley, grew old, moved to California, and died in 1912. The year 1916 marked the last in the regular series of historic Lake Mohonk Conferences.

The attempts of the reform organizations to use the courts to promote their ends were no more successful than their attempts to influence the legislative and executive branches. The Indian Rights Association undertook two cases that went to the Supreme Court, in which it supported Indian litigants against the federal government. In both instances the court ruled against the Indian Rights Association and its clients.

The first case, *Lone Wolf* v. *Hitchcock*, was a landmark decision that in significance went far beyond the question of reform influence. Under the provisions of the Treaty of Medicine Lodge Creek of 1867, no part of the reservation set up for the Kiowas and Comanches could be ceded without the approval of three-fourths of the adult males. Nevertheless, the Cherokee Commission on October 6, 1892, concluded an agreement with the Indians for the allotment of their lands and the disposition of the surplus to the United States to be opened to settlement, without obtaining the three-fourths approval. When Congress, by an act of June 6, 1900, accepted and confirmed the agreement, Lone Wolf, a prominent Kiowa, brought suit to prevent implemention of the act. With the aid of the Indian Rights Association, the case went to the Supreme Court of the United States, which on January 5, 1903, rendered its decision against Lone Wolf. The court, in rejecting the arguments of the Indians' attorneys, asserted the plenary authority of Congress over Indian relations and its power to pass laws abrogating treaty stipulations.

A second case was *Quick Bear* v. *Leupp*, in which the Indian Rights Association, in the name of certain Rosebud Sioux Indians, sought an injunction against the use of Indian trust and treaty funds for support of Catholic Indian mission schools. This was the culmination of a renewed attack upon Catholic mission interests by Protestant forces and a resounding defeat for the influence that those forces had enjoyed in national Indian affairs, for the Supreme Court decided that the money used belonged to the Indians and was not a gratuitous appropriation by Congress. The court found no violation of the First Amendment's principle of separation of church and state in the sectarian use of the funds.

The Catholic contract schools, thus saved by the *Quick Bear* decision, could not of course provide education for all Indian children of Catholic faith. Those who were forced to attend government schools, the Catholic missionaries charged, were subjected to undue Protestant influence in common religious services, Sunday school lessons, the work of the YMCA and YWCA, and even in singing from the popular Protestant hymnal, *Gospel Hymns*. The Bureau of Catholic Indian Missions campaigned to protect the religious rights of the Catholic pupils, and despite the cries of Protestant missionary groups, who had been willing to curtail their own Indian schools because the government schools served them so well, the Indian Office prescribed equal religious rights for the Catholic Indian students in government schools and eliminated many of the positive Protestant elements in the schools.

The Catholic victories in these matters were evidence of the breakdown of evangelical Protestant domination that came with the advent of large numbers of Catholics through the new immigration. The loss of Protestant influence came also from the increasing secularization of American society, an inchoative spirit that burst full-blown in the 1920s. It could be seen in the importance attached to efficient administration on the part of Progressive government officials, which was a sort of secular force.

LIQUOR AND PEYOTE

The old-time reformers, however, saw a continuation of their policies in the renewed determination to prevent the deleterious effects of liquor among the Indians and in a new fight against another presumed evil, peyote.

All the past efforts to end intoxication among Indians had failed to achieve complete success, and recognition of the liquor problem was sharpened as the drive for self-support gained momentum in the first decades of the twentieth century. A serious obstacle to these efforts, however, came in the decision of the United States Supreme Court on April 10, 1905, in *Matter of Heff*, which struck down a conviction against a man who had sold liquor to an allotted Indian. The United States, the court said,

> is under no constitutional obligation to perpetually continue the relationship of guardian and ward. It may at any time abandon its guardianship and leave the ward to assume and be subject to all the privileges and burdens of one *sui juris*. . . . We are of the opinion that when the United States grants the privileges of citizenship to an Indian, gives to him the benefit of and requires him to be subject to the laws, both civil and criminal, of the State, it places him outside the reach of police regulations on the part of Congress.

The Indian Office, however, maintained that as long as the United States held the allotments in trust it could prevent the taking of liquor into allotted lands, and it persevered in the drive to crack down on the traffic. The

Burke Act of 1906 met the challenge of the court's ruling by postponing citizenship for Indian allottees until the end of the twenty-five-year trust period. The Indian Office was materially aided, too, by the appropriation of funds to enforce prohibitions against the liquor traffic.

The times, of course, were auspicious. In 1916 the Supreme Court in *United States* v. *Nice* expressly overruled the Heff decision, declaring that "citizenship is not incompatible with tribal existence or continued guardianship, and so may be conferred without completely emancipating the Indians or placing them beyond the reach of congressional regulations adopted for their protection." More significantly, the demand for national prohibition was gaining strength, and as states with Indian populations went "dry," the alcohol problem was lessened. Congress, too, helped the Indian Office with special legislation that made the mere possession of intoxicating liquor within the Indian country illegal. Then, with the ratification of the Eighteenth Amendment on January 16, 1919, to take effect one year later, it became much more difficult for the Indians to obtain liquor.

Meanwhile, a new danger appeared in the form of peyote, a drug obtained from a cactus that was alleged to be a narcotic with serious harmful effects. The use of peyote by Indians in the southern parts of the nation went back into the nineteenth century and beyond, but aside from some localized cases it had not attracted the attention of the Indian Office. By the end of the first decade of the twentieth century, however, a cry arose against the drug, and federal officials attempted to proscribe it.

The concern of the Indian Office was supported and no doubt to a large extent stimulated by the frenzy against peyote that developed among the humanitarian reformers. The Board of Indian Commissioners in 1912 voted formally to condemn all use of the drug, and the Lake Mohonk Conference in 1914 and 1915 urged its prohibition. The Indian Rights Association in 1916 entered a section on "The Ravages of Peyote" in its annual report, which described the harmful effects of peyote and ridiculed the Indians' claim that the religious use of the drug demanded protection under the Constitution.

Yet repeated attempts to obtain legislation to prohibit the use of peyote got nowhere. The reason for the failure was clear enough, for evidence of the narcotic and addictive effects of peyote was not convincing, and counterevidence cast doubts on the justice of prohibiting the drug. Ironically, one of the arguments in favor of peyote was that it curbed intoxication from liquor. In addition, the ceremonial religious use of peyote made it difficult to proscribe use of the drug universally, especially after the organization and spread of the Native American Church. The changed atmosphere of the 1920s, with strong voices speaking out in favor of Indian customs and religious rites, doomed to failure the crusade for the national prohibition of peyote. At the end of the decade there had not yet been convincing demonstration that peyote was an evil.

THE 1920S: CONTINUITY AND DEVELOPMENT

The decade of the 1920s was a difficult period for the administration of Indian policy. The federal officials in charge of Indian programs were committed to the assimilationist policy they had inherited and were concerned about the progressive development of education and health care for those Indians who remained wards of the government and about the protection and utilization of Indian lands and other resources. The decade, thus, must be viewed first of all as a continuation and culmination of the Indian program begun in the late 1880s with the Dawes Act and the national Indian school system of Commissioner Morgan. Yet it was a time, also, of widespread and bitter criticism of the Indian Office, its officials, and the program they promoted. The cry for reform was in the air and it grew in volume as the decade passed, but the period was not a period of reform. There were no significant changes in policy, but rather defense of existing ways on the part of the Indian Office and its supporters. It was a time of unrest and questioning, however, in which the ground was prepared and the seeds planted in the public mind for the radical change that came in the 1930s.

The direction of federal Indian policy fell to Charles H. Burke, who succeeded Cato Sells as commissioner of Indian affairs in 1921. Burke had served as a representative from South Dakota from 1899 to 1901 and again from 1909 to 1915 and was a man of long official contact with Indian affairs. But he was no innovator and continued with some modifications the programs in education, health, and land ownership of his predecessors.

It was Burke's lot to be the target of the growing dissatisfaction with the old approach to Indian affairs. During his long term the Indian Office was attacked from many sides, and the criticism came to be leveled at him personally. One factor contributing to the uproar experienced by Burke was the inflation that followed World War I and the new administration's attempt to counter it with a policy of retrenchment. At a time when Indian health and education programs needed massive increases in funding if they were to accomplish their goals, the Indian Office was expected to economize instead. Burke was willing to follow the new philosophy, and the harmful effects of such a policy on Indian welfare haunted Burke through his whole term.

Burke saw the culmination of the movement for Indian citizenship. Through the Dawes Act and the Burke Act, the blanket grants of citizenship to such groups as the Five Civilized Tribes, and the provisions made for citizenship for veterans of World War I, a majority of the Indians—some estimates put the figure at two-thirds—had achieved citizenship. But the patriotic fervor that persisted after the war seemed to call for a measure to complete the circle. It came in 1924, in a law that declared all Indians to be citizens of the United States. The effect of the act, however, was nebulous. Like earlier Indian citizenship measures, it specified that the granting of citizenship would not "in any manner impair or otherwise affect the right of any Indian to tribal or other property." So the complete transition from tribal status to individualized citizenship that the Dawes Act reformers had had in mind when they talked about citizenship did not occur. The Indians were both citizens of the United States and persons with tribal relations. Nor did citizenship necessarily signify withdrawal from the protective guardianship of the United States government.

While the Indians were being pushed willy-nilly into citizenship, the Indian Office continued to be a honeycomb of offices and programs, all dedicated to the administration of affairs for Indian citizens who were still wards of the government. It was a bureaucracy of great size and complexity, which made a mockery of the earlier pronouncements that it was soon to go out of business. In the best of times, the supervision of such machinery would require high administrative ability, yet the maintenance and operation of the structure was always hindered by the lack of sufficient money to turn the organization into a first-class enterprise.

THE BUREAU UNDER SIEGE

The Office of Indian Affairs, generally referred to as the "Indian Bureau" by its critics, came under heavy attack in the 1920s, and its work was carried on in an atmosphere of tension. New groups arose to challenge the very principles upon which federal policy was based and to demand reform. Burke and his supporters fought back, denying the legitimacy of the most extreme criticism but showing a willingness to listen and to compromise where they judged benefits would come to the Indians. It was a question of whose vision for the Indian future was the right one, and the issue was in doubt throughout the decade. Would the existing system be overturned, or would there be gradual change and reform from within?

The lines of the conflict were drawn over the question of land rights of the Pueblo Indians in New Mexico. These Indians, with territorial grants going back to Spanish times, had come within the limits of the United States in 1848 by the Treaty of Guadalupe Hidalgo, which specified that all Mexican citizens in the cession would enjoy the full rights and privileges of citizens of the United States. Because the Pueblos had been considered citizens by Mexico, the federal government treated them differently from other Indians, although some provisions were made for their welfare. Laws protecting Indian lands and prohibiting the encroachment of whites were not enforced against Anglo-Americans and Mexicans who settled on the Pueblo grants, for the territorial courts denied the applicability of the intercourse law of 1834 to the Pueblos, and that position was upheld by the United States Supreme Court in 1876 in *United States* v. *Joseph.*

There was a change, however, when New Mexico became a state, and the lines between state authority and federal authority over the Indians became sharply drawn. The enabling act for the state of New Mexico specifically provided that "the terms 'Indian' and 'Indian country' shall include the Pueblo Indians of New Mexico and the lands now owned or occupied by them." This extension of federal control over the Pueblos was upheld by the Supreme Court in 1913 in *United States* v. *Sandoval,* which reversed the decision of the *Joseph* case.

The *Sandoval* decision called into question the titles of non-Indians who had settled on lands claimed by the Pueblos, titles in many cases acquired in good faith. New Mexicans, of course, were deeply interested in the matter, and Albert J. Fall, as senator from the state and then as secretary of the interior, represented their interests. In order to settle the controversy over the land claims, Holm O. Bursum, who had taken Fall's seat in the Senate, introduced a bill on July 20, 1922, "to quiet title to lands within Pueblo Indian land grants." At first sight the bill seemed to resolve the problem, and it passed the Senate without much stir. But more careful study showed that the Bursum bill strongly favored the non-Indian claimants and placed the burden of proving title not on the claimants but on the Pueblos.

The Pueblos were not without friends, and a tremendous protest arose that changed the course of American Indian affairs. The leadership devolved upon John Collier, a one-time social worker in New York City, who had been introduced to the Pueblos in 1920. Collier found in the Pueblo communal and ceremonial life an answer to the problems of human society, and he eagerly joined with others in organizing opposition to the Bursum bill. They used the pages of *Survey,* a progressive journal staffed by reformers, and the liberal *Sunset* to take their case to the American people. A statement entitled "Shall the Pueblo Indians of New Mexico Be Destroyed?" was widely circulated and sent to members of Congress.

When Burke supported the bill as an administration measure, the open conflict between Collier's forces and the Indian Office began. An All Pueblo Council (organized and run to a large extent by the Indians' white friends) denounced the bill, and Collier led delegates of Indians to Chicago, New York, and Washington to demonstrate against it. He was backed by the venerable Indian Rights Association and by the Eastern Association on Indian

Affairs and the New Mexico Association on Indian Affairs, new white reform groups that had come into being in response to the Pueblo crisis. In
May 1923 Collier organized the American Indian Defense Association,
which soon became the chief vehicle for promoting his reforms. Collier
served as its executive secretary from 1923 until 1933.

Before congressional committees conducting hearings on the Pueblo
bills and in a muckraking barrage, Collier and his friends pounded home
their defense of the Indians' rights. The propaganda of the Collier camp
was roundly condemned, of course, by supporters of the administration.
The House Committee on Indian Affairs, reporting favorably on the Bursum bill, called the propaganda "insidious, untruthful, and malicious" and
charged that some of it was "nothing more nor less than criminal libel."
But official defense of the bill and condemnation of the propaganda tech-
niques of its opponents could not save it from defeat. Then a battle raged
over proposed alternatives to the Bursum bill.

Finally, on June 7, 1924, the Pueblo Lands Act, a measure that seemed to
satisfy both sides, became law. It established a Pueblo land board, which
was to determine the boundaries of the Pueblo land grants and then fix the
status of lands within those limits. Under the law, the process of examining claims and evicting settlers proceeded slowly until by 1938 the Pueblo
land question was generally settled.

Although defense of Pueblo land rights could engage the support of a
broad range of Indian welfare organizations and the Indian Office as well,
despite controversy over the precise method of protecting Indian rights in
the face of counter-claims by non-Indians, a second challenge to the Indian
Office by Collier and his supporters created a sharp split into two irreconcilable camps. This was the issue of Indian dances and other Indian
customs.

From the beginning of the decade the Indian Rights Association and
missionaries among the Indians had complained to the Indian Office about
Indian dances, which they argued were inconsistent with the Indians' progress, and in April 1921 Burke issued a special circular on dances, in which
he asserted: "The dance *per se* is not condemned. It is recognized as a
manifestation of something inherent in human nature, widely evidenced
by both sacred and profane history, and as a medium through which elevated minds may happily unite art, refinement, and healthful exercise."
But he then called attention to dances that involved "acts of self-torture,
immoral relations between the sexes, the sacrificial destruction of clothing
or other useful articles, the reckless giving away of property, the use of injurious drugs or intoxicants, and frequent or prolonged periods of celebration
which bring the Indians together from remote points to the neglect of their
crops, livestock, and home interest." In such cases the regulations that prohibited "Indian offenses" were to be enforced.

Two years later Burke issued a supplement to his 1921 circular, urging the superintendents to "persistently encourage and emphasize the Indian's attention to those practical, useful, thrifty, and orderly activities that are indispensable to his well-being and underlie the preservation of his race in the midst of complex and highly competitive conditions." With the supplement Burke sent a "Message to All Indians," in which he appealed to the Indians to stop the dances and celebrations that interfered with their making a living and to do so of their own free will.

It was clear from the reports of the superintendents, the humanitarian criticism of the dances, and Burke's circulars and message to the Indians that the initial concern was about interruptions in the work of earning a livelihood that were caused by the dances, not the isolated examples of behavior that was considered immoral. As the controversy over the dances developed, however, the focus of criticism came to be placed on alleged sexual excesses in the religious dances among the Indians of the Southwest (the Hopi snake dance was a favorite example). There was repeated talk about "the most depraved and immoral practices" and fear that young returned students were being drawn into the evil practices. The Indian Rights Association kept a file of testimony ("of an unprintable nature") about the immoral character of the dances, which it invited people to look at in its office.

This attack upon Indian culture, much of it aimed specifically at the Indians of the Southwest, infuriated John Collier. It was further proof to him of the bureau's disregard of Indian rights, and he mounted a campaign in support of religious liberty for the Indians. Whereas Burke saw immorality and degradation in the dances, Collier saw beauty and mystical experience. He accused the government of destroying Indian culture in its striving to Americanize and civilize the Indians, and he defended the dances in a pamphlet published by the American Indian Defense Association in July 1924, called *The Indian and Religious Freedom*. The Eastern Association on Indian Affairs issued a special bulletin entitled "Concerning Indian Dances," in which it objected to the "slander of a noble and disappearing race" and printed letters from ethnologists and anthropologists refuting the charges of immorality made against the dances.

The battle was spirited and enduring. Each attempt of the Indian Office to enforce its sanctions against the dances or to prevent the withdrawal of Indian children from school so they could be trained in the religious ceremonies brought new cries from defenders of the Indians' rights. The Indians themselves, however, were divided, and Protestant Indians passed resolutions condemning the domination of the Indian priests, who forced them to retain pagan customs. Such evidence led the Indian Rights Association to charge violation of individual religious liberty by "the oligarchy of caciques" who controlled the pueblos.

Pueblo lands and Indian religious liberty were by no means the only basis of attack upon Burke and the Indian Office, for all aspects of Indian administration came under the critical gaze of Collier and the American Indian Defense Association. The failures in the Indian schools, the deplorable state of Indian health, and the loss of Indian lands through allotment and fee patents furnished material for a constant chorus of complaint. The question of Indian rights to oil reserves in executive order reservations, the use of Indian funds on a reimbursable basis to construct improvements alleged to be of more use to whites than to Indians, and the part played by Burke in handling the estate of a rich Oklahoma Indian, Jackson Barnett, furnished more rich grist for the critics' mill.

Pervading all the controversy on particular issues was the charge that the Indian Office ignored the Indians themselves and their views and rode roughshod over their rights. The assimilationist policy was wrong, Collier charged, and must be replaced by one that respected the Indians as human beings with a dignity and culture of their own. In a forceful statement at the beginning of his crusade for Indian policy reform, he wrote:

The policy of denying to the Indian a group existence, and at the same time of denying him personal option in matters of property, of parental authority, of amusement, and even of religion—this policy which is sanctioned by the belief that the Indian as a race must perish from the earth in order that, naked of memories, homeless, inferior and fugitive, some creatures with Amerindian blood in their veins may rush to the arms of Civilization: this policy, historically so natural but now so inhuman and un-American, is still the policy of the guardian before whose command all Indians must bow down.

Collier now called for an end to "monopolistic and autocratic control over person and property by a single bureau of the Federal Government" and for protection of Indian property rights, for respect of "elementary rights guaranteed to other Americans by the Constitution or long-established tradition," and for the use of cultural pride and "native social endowments and institutions" in the education of the Indians.

INVESTIGATIONS AND REPORTS

It was inevitable that so much outspoken criticism would generate demands for a thorough study of the situation of the Indians and the activities of the Indian Office. Secretary of the Interior Hubert Work slowly began to see the wisdom, if not the necessity, of a broad independent study from outside the normal course of government operations.

His first attempt, shortly after he took office and in response to the crusade of the Collier forces in the Pueblo lands question, was the establishment of an Advisory Council on Indian Affairs, more generally known as the Committee of One Hundred. In the spring of 1923 Work appointed about one hundred men and women to the committee "for the purpose of discussion and recommendation on the Government's Indian policy," and a meeting was called for December 12 and 13. The membership represented all the groups concerned with Indian affairs: Collier and his associates, members of the Indian Rights Association and the Board of Indian Commissioners, anthropologists and missionaries, political figures and educators, journalists and military men, and a sizable group of educated Indians.

Although Work called the council "a landmark in the history of the Government's effort to handle the Indian question," in fact the Committee of One Hundred accomplished little or nothing. John Collier called it "the most representative conference on Indian affairs ever held" and spoke of the goodwill and spirit of mutuality exhibited, but he concluded: "Preconference politics and the absence of fundamental concepts held in common by the members defeated the results." The conference was clearly not the critical appraisal of Indian affairs that the reformers had called for.

As the critics stepped up their attacks, Secretary Work took more constructive action. In 1926 he engaged the independent Institute for Government Research to make a comprehensive survey of Indian affairs, "in a thoroughly impartial and scientific spirit with the object of making the result of its work a constructive contribution in this difficult field of government administration." With financial support from John D. Rockefeller, Jr., the work quickly got under way.

The person chosen to direct the survey was Lewis Meriam, a permanent staff member of the Institute for Government Research with long experience in technical study of government operations and a man who epitomized the concern of the institute with efficiency and expertise in government administration. To aid Meriam there was a staff of nine technical specialists in the fields of law, economic conditions, health, education, agriculture, family life, and the conditions of Indians in urban communities, and one "Indian adviser." In seven months of fieldwork the members of the staff visited ninety-five reservations, agencies, hospitals, and schools, as well as many communities of Indians who had moved from the reservations; they made a remarkably thorough investigation of all aspects of government work touching the Indians. The report was submitted on February 21, 1928, and published under the title *The Problem of Indian Administration*.

The survey team reported deplorable conditions in health, education, and economic welfare and incompetent and inefficient personnel, for almost nothing that it found met its progressive standards. The recommendations were in line with the findings and the outlook of the experts: generous appropriations to improve the administration of the Indian service in health care, education, and economic development and the establishment of a Division of Planning and Development in the Indian Office that would consist of a group of experts with time free for research and planning of Indian programs.

The Meriam Report was not a radical innovative document seeking to overturn existing policy. It was seeking, in fact, what commissioners of Indian affairs had been asking for since the beginning of the century: more money at once so that the process of preparing the Indian wards to enter American society as self-supporting, independent citizens could be efficiently speeded up and the Indian problem of the federal government dissolved.

The moderate tone and scientific impartiality of the Meriam Report almost guaranteed a favorable acceptance. Secretary Work and Commissioner Burke accepted the criticism with equanimity and set about to study the report in detail, and reform groups appreciated both the confirmation of their charges that all was not well and the recommendations for betterment.

While the Meriam Report was in preparation, the secretary of the interior instituted a companion investigation. Because the Meriam survey team lacked specialists in the important and complex problems related to Indian irrigation projects, a separate study was undertaken. For this task Work appointed two irrigation experts—Porter J. Preston, an engineer from the Bureau of Reclamation, and Charles A. Engle, supervising engineer from the Office of Indian Affairs—to make a critical study of irrigation projects. Their report, submitted on June 8, 1928, was a severe indictment of the government's irrigation program on Indian reservations.

The enemies of Burke's administration in the end were not satisfied with the moderate tone of the Meriam Report. Even before the survey team had turned in its finding, Collier aggressively supported a move in the Senate for a full-scale congressional investigation of the administration of Indian affairs. Burke insisted that the forthcoming Meriam Report would obviate any need for a Senate investigation, but Collier argued the necessity, and the Senate passed the authorizing resolution on February 2, 1928. Thus began a series of hearings and investigations that ran from November 1928 to August 1943 and resulted in 23,069 printed pages of reports in forty-one parts.

With this general survey of events and policies from 1900 to 1929 in mind, we can now look in more detail, in the next two chapters, at the government's programs for Indian education, health, and land.

CHAPTER 19

Education and
Health

No means was more important than education in leading the Indians toward the goal of self-support. Thus Estelle Reel, superintendent of Indian schools, declared at the end of 1900: "We are aiming at the unification of the Indian school system in all that tends to the formation of self-supporting, God-fearing Indian men and women." The emphasis in education continued to be heavily on practical work. "A civilization without the elements of labor in it rests on a foundation of sand," Reel said. "Labor is the basis of all lasting civilization and the most potent influence for good in the world. Whenever any race, of its own volition, begins to labor its future is assured." The developing school system for the Indians was intended to make this possible and to fit Indian youth for the world into which they were to be absorbed.

THE INDIAN SCHOOL SYSTEM

The aggressive promotion of Indian schools that began with Thomas J. Morgan in 1889 had accomplished much by the end of the century. Commissioner William A. Jones in 1900 reported impressive statistics. There were twenty-five off-reservation industrial schools with a total enrollment of 7,430. The largest (with over 1,000 pupils) was Carlisle, with Phoenix and Haskell (600–700 pupils) next in order. Eighteen of the schools had been established since 1890. There were eighty-one boarding schools on the reservations, which made the necessary modifications in the elaborate industrial training that the better-equipped off-reservation schools could offer but pursued the same policy; in addition they stood "as object lessons among the homes of the Indians" to present them with "ideals for emulation." These schools were smaller—rarely with a capacity as large as 200—and the total enrollment was 9,600. Next was a collection of government day schools with 30–40 pupils each, located in remote parts of the reservations and conducted by a single teacher and a housekeeper, if possible a man and wife team. These schools totaled 147 and enrolled about 5,000 pupils. There were also some 250 students in twenty-two public schools, the modest seeds of a program that would soon blossom forth with larger and larger proportions of the Indian students, and Jones counted thirty-two contract schools with an enrollment of 2,800 and twenty-two mission schools with 1,275 students.

Although Jones spoke with pride of the increase in the number of off-reservation boarding schools during the previous decade, in fact a strong movement against such schools had already begun—and Jones was one of the leaders. Those schools, of which the Carlisle Indian Industrial School was the first and prime example, had represented Richard Henry Pratt's strong insistence on "bringing the Indian to civilization and keeping him there," immersing the Indian children in white ways far away from the traditional influences of camp life on the reservations. By means of such schools, the rising generation would be abruptly and completely inducted into white society, where Pratt expected them to remain. But hard reality quickly punctured the dream.

In the first place, it was difficult to fill the schools with suitable pupils, as Carlisle itself experienced, and the pressures to "collect students" (as the saying went) in order to keep the off-reservation institutions at an efficient capacity led to abuses and tensions with the teachers and superintendents on the reservations, to say nothing of the Indian parents. In the second place, it was soon apparent that the graduates of such schools did not stay to take their places in white society but drifted back to their homes, and the problem of these "returned students" and their readjustment to reservation life attracted much attention. The interest and hope that had once been pinned on the off-reservation schools was diverted to the schools on the reservations. There schools could be better adapted to the actual life the students would live when they left school, and the educational center could widen its immediate influence to include parents and the whole Indian community.

Jones began his attack in 1901. "Analysis of the data obtained by this office," he said, "indicates that the methods of education which have been pursued for the past generation have not produced the results anticipated." He concluded that the number of off-reservation schools could be materially reduced and the remainder, without increasing their capacity, could be refined and developed, and he said flatly, "More reservation boarding schools and less nonreservation institutions are required." He predicted that in an-

282 Education and Health

other generation, as graduates of the reservation boarding schools learned to live by the sweat of their brow, the boarding schools, too, could be phased out and replaced by day schools.

The movement away from off-reservation schools was carried a step further by Francis E. Leupp. He intended to enlarge the system of day schools as opposed to any increase in boarding schools and to prefer reservation boarding schools to those off the reservation. It was a question, he said, of "whether we are to carry civilization to the Indian or carry the Indian to civilization, and the former seems to me infinitely the wiser plan." In 1906 Leupp reported with pleasure an increase of day schools, which he considered "the greatest general civilizing agency of any through which we try to operate upon the rising generation." He saw the boarding schools as an anomaly, "simply educational almshouses" he called them, in which everything was provided for the Indians and nothing won by hard work. He noted, too, that education of an Indian in a day school cost only one-fourth or one-fifth of the amount needed in a boarding school.

Leupp could not get Congress to cut appropriations for well-established off-reservation schools that had popular support—like Carlisle and Hampton—so he undertook to turn them into specialized institutions. Gradually the off-reservation schools that persisted came to be thought of as "advanced" schools (that is, of upper grades and eventually some high school courses) in which students who had completed the limited courses at day schools and reservation boarding schools might transfer to further their education. But in order to keep enrollment up, most off-reservation schools continued to offer primary and elementary education as well.

The final goal in revamping the Indian school system was to disband the strictly Indian schools and let the Indians enroll in the public schools of the states. The germ of this idea had been planted in Commissioner Morgan's time. "Indeed," he had said, "it is reasonable to expect that at no distant day, when the Indians shall have all taken up their lands in severalty and have become American citizens, there will cease to be any necessity for Indian schools maintained by the government." The time was more distant than Morgan had hoped, but little by little the balance began to swing toward public schools as white settlements multiplied in the West and the opened reservations stimulated the establishment of district schools in the neighborhoods of allotted Indians.

In 1912 Commissioner Valentine noted that a larger number of Indian pupils were in public schools than ever before. It was, he said, the "final step" and the "way out" for Indian education. The advance in enrollment in public schools was so rapid that two years later almost as many Indian pupils were in these schools as in all the Indians schools under government control. Commissioner Cato Sells rejoiced in this development, which he himself studiously encouraged. He praised what he saw on the allotted reservations, where white settlers were moving in and organizing district public schools, which the Indian children, too, could attend. "This process of disintegration of the Indian reservations," Sells claimed, "is a splendid example of the elimination of the Indian as a distinct problem for the Federal or the State governments. The most distinctive element aiding in this growth is the public school."

The flow of Indian children into the public schools continued. In 1923 Commissioner Burke called it "unprecedented." Five years later there were 34,103 Indians in public schools, compared with 25,174 in government schools and 7,621 in mission and private schools. In areas where there were few public schools and where the Indians continued as wards of the government, however, the federal Indian schools were absolutely necessary, and Congress during the 1920s year by year appropriated more money for these schools, until in 1928 the total appropriation stood at $5,923,000. Both Sells and Burke were especially concerned about the large number of Indians in the Southwest, notably the Navajos, who lagged behind in school facilities and school enrollment.

The federal government paid tuition for the Indian children attending public schools because many Indians were not taxed, and the additional burden of instruction could not well be borne by the states. Congress in 1914 provided $20,000 for such tuition; in 1917 the sum was raised to $200,000, and in 1924 it reached $350,000. Yet the increases did not meet the demand, and many applications were refused for lack of funds. The appropriation of $375,000 for fiscal year 1929 was exhausted before the year ran out.

The enthusiastic promotion of public schools for Indians and the favorable reports about snowballing enrollment, however, covered over some disturbing facts. "Enrollment" did not necessarily mean regular attendance, and as the numbers in district schools multiplied, so did a realization that the solution of the Indian school problem was not yet in sight. The irregularity of attendance had several causes. Indian children were often ridiculed by their white classmates and would then refuse to return to class. The poverty of Indian families also affected attendance, and in some areas whites opposed the admission of Indians. But the principal cause was that Indian pupils were simply not competent enough in English to mix in classes with white children their own age, and older Indian boys and girls were ashamed and uncomfortable sitting in classes with younger white children. The movement toward public schools, which had looked so promising to government officials, continued, and increasing percentages of Indians were cared for in the public schools, but the Indian school system put together after 1880 did not wither away. Government schools remained a permanent fixture on the reservation landscape.

The Indian schools were grammar schools, for Thomas J. Morgan's plan for a graded hierarchy of primary schools, grammar schools, and high schools was never fully realized. At the beginning of the twentieth century, in fact, the goal was explicitly more modest, as Commissioner Jones noted in 1900:

> The Indian school system aims to provide a training which will prepare the Indian boy or girl for the everyday life of the average American citizen. It does not contemplate, as some have supposed on a superficial examination, an elaborate preparation for a collegiate course through an extended high-school curriculum. The course of instruction in these schools is limited to that usually taught in the common schools of the country. . . . It is not considered the province of the Government to provide either its wards or citizens with what is known as "higher education."

Character building and moral uplift were always in the minds of the educators, for education was equated with civilization. And the only means to that end for the Indian children was industrial education aimed at self-support.

The content of Indian education was set forth in explicit terms in a new *Course of Study* promulgated on August 10, 1901. Under it one-half of the day was devoted to the academic classroom work, the other half to the industrial and domestic arts (much of which was simply performing the work necessary to keep the boarding schools operating economically). Most of the "industrial training" at all the schools was agricultural in a broad sense, to enable the average Indian man, as Jones candidly expressed it in 1903, "to wring an existence from the too-frequently ungenerous soils the white man has allowed him to retain." It was accepted that "nature, environment, and necessity will and should make at least nine-tenths of the Indian youth tillers of the soil and breeders of stock."

A new course of study was adopted in 1916, which reflected a conscious move toward what had come to be called "vocational training." The Indian Office followed the current educational modes of the day, in which *vocational* education became a highly publicized development, giving a new name and new impetus to what had earlier been called *industrial* education. Although the goal of the national movement was aimed at preparing youth for a technological society and looked toward problems that were different from those facing the Indian schools, the Indian Office could not help but be influenced by the agitation.

Sells in fact noted in 1916: "For many years the general country has recognized a vital deficiency in its system of education. There has been a chasm, often impassable, between the completion of a course in school and the selection of a vocation in life. The Indian Service has recognized a similar deficiency, although partially overcome in its system. The new vocational course of study for Indian schools is believed to provide a safe and substantial passage from school life to success in real life."

Sells's course was soon modified to keep up with changing times, and Commissioner Burke prepared a new course of study promulgated in 1922. It divided the vocational phase into two stages: junior vocational (corresponding to seventh and eighth grades) and senior vocational (which contemplated a four-year course above the eighth grade to correspond to a regular high school course). It added work on gas engines and auto mechanics, for example, to meet the new demands of the times, and it revised the time allotment in the primary grades to call for full days instead of only half-days devoted to academic work. But the fundamentals had not changed.

All the courses of study, of course, depended upon having the children in the schools, and to accomplish that it was necessary to resort to compulsion. In February 1920 Congress authorized the secretary of the interior to compel attendance, and Cato Sells, a year later, promulgated appropriate regulations with elaborate procedures for hearings before special boards in cases where parents refused to send a child to school. If the board decided against the parents, the child was to be sent to the designated school, "with escort if necessary." The regulations ended with the admonition: "All existing school facilities for Indians, whether Government, public, or otherwise, must be utilized to the fullest extent."

Although the Indian schools may have kept pace with the times in the matter of industrial training, they fared badly in comparison with the white public school system in regard to level of instruction. At the end of four decades following Morgan's initial drive for an Indian school system in 1889, the government schools were almost universally still only primary and elementary schools. A high school course was added to one school in 1921, and three more appeared in 1925 and one each in 1926 and 1927, so that at the end of Burke's administration there were only six schools maintained by the federal government where an Indian could received a high school education, and in all of them the high school course was appended to elementary and junior high school programs. "The enrollment in the public high schools in the United States is approximately 1 to every 6 pupils of school age," Burke ruefully reported in 1928, "while among Indians it is only 1 to every 20. The aggregate number of Indians in institutions of higher learning or who are pursuing extension courses is negligible."

SUCCESS AND FAILURE IN INDIAN EDUCATION

Evaluation of the Indian school system in the first three decades of the twentieth century depends upon the viewpoint of the judge. The teachers and administrators in the Indian service considered the schools a primary tool in the improvement and transformation of the Indians—and that meant knowledge of English and of white American culture and the skills necessary to make one's way in the white-dominated world. And these teachers and administrators could point to considerable success. Commissioner Sells presented a very favorable picture at the end of World War I:

> The pressing demand of the war period for all kinds of efficient labor found a fully proportionate supply from the output of our Indian schools. A large force of young men entered the Government shipbuilding service with excellent results. Many young women entered hospital service, quite a number going abroad as trained nurses. Scores of others were accepted as stenographers and typists and fully evidenced their ability. Nothing has equaled the power of the school in producing the large percentage of Indians who today attend church, live in well arranged houses, are English-speaking citizens and voters, efficient artisans, successful in business, in the learned professions, in literature, and in legislative assemblies.

Sells's point of view was shared by Commissioner Burke, who in 1925 declared of the school program: "Its results are now unmistakable and the best argument for its continuance through some years to come. It has enabled the Indians to make greater progress than any other pagan race in a like period of which there is any written record. Of the 347,000 Indians in the United States, approximately two-thirds speak English and nearly 150,000 can read and write that language."

The favorable—at times even exuberant—reports about progress in Indian education, however, were strongly contradicted by two serious national studies that occurred at the end of the 1920s: the Meriam Report (1928) and the report of the National Advisory Committee on Education (1931).

The Meriam Report, in its general findings and recommendations, was blunt: "The survey staff finds itself obliged to say frankly and unequivocally that the provisions for the care of the Indian children in boarding schools are grossly inadequate." The "outstanding deficiency" was the children's diet, but then came overcrowding in dormitories, below-standard medical service, too much labor on the part of the students (without much distinction between work to maintain the schools and vocational training), a teaching staff that could not meet "the standards set by reasonably progressive white communities," restrictive rather than "developmental" school discipline, and an obsolete industrial curriculum. The fundamental need, the report declared, was for a change in point of view. The Indian schools still operated on the theory that it was necessary to remove the Indian children from their home environment instead of adopting the "modern point of view in education and social work," which stressed education in the natural setting of home and family. The Indian educational system, it said, needed to be less concerned with a conventional school system and more with the understanding of human beings. The minimum standards applied to education should be directed not toward courses and examinations, but to the qualifications of the personnel, and here the Indian school service fared badly. The fault lay of course in lack of sufficient appropriations to pay adequate salaries. "From the point of view of education," it concluded, "the Indian service is almost literally a 'starved' service."

The Meriam Report argued that boarding schools should be deemphasized; day schools were especially recommended as "the best opportunity available at present to furnish schooling to Indian children and at the same time build up a needed home and community education." In the end, it was the public schools, however, that appeared to be the solution. "Any policy for Indians based on the notion that they can or should be kept permanently isolated from other Americans is bound to fail," the report said; "mingling is inevitable, and Indian children brought up in public schools with white children have the advantage of early contacts with whites while still retaining their connection with their own Indian family and home."

The general tone and criticism of the Meriam Report was repeated in the report of the National Advisory Committee on Education. Organized by Secretary of the Interior Ray Lyman Wilbur at President Herbert Hoover's instigation in May 1929, the committee and its staff undertook extensive fieldwork and elicited the cooperation of numerous public and private organizations interested in education. The committee concluded that the government's educational policy for Indians was "a tragic failure." It considered the transfer of the ordinary American elementary school to the Indian reservations a mistake, and, like the Meriam Report, it condemned centralization in the school system, the inadequacy of the existing vocational training, and the failure to attract competent teachers and other staff.

These critical surveys of Indian education were not revolutionary, and even in their emphasis on orientation of the educational system to meet the needs of Indian children rather than to match some conventional, traditional types of school system, they did not depart greatly from the ultimate goals and principles long enunciated by the educational leaders of the Indian service. The kernel of the criticism was that what had been attempted had not been well done, and again and again a finger was pointed at the incompetence of the teachers and other personnel who made up the Indian school service.

The criticisms of the time did not touch what became a central point later in the twentieth century: the intent of the Indian schools to transfer Indian children from their own culture into white civilization. Despite some feeble attempts to include elements of Indian culture, the curriculum ignored the Indian heritage of the students and followed as closely as possible the curriculum in the public schools of the state in which each school was located. Though it might lament the sacrifice of traditional customs "as a picturesque factor in the national life," the Indian Office was convinced that the ancient laws and customs that did not coincide with national laws must inevitably give way. There can be little doubt that failures in educating the Indians throughout the decades stemmed in part from the unwillingness of the educators to consider the Indians' cultural heritage and its persistence in spite of the efforts to eradicate it.

THE CONDITION OF INDIAN HEALTH

Education for self-support was inextricably intertwined with the health of the Indians. Here a strange paradox appeared. As more and more Indian children were enrolled in school, where they could be observed and examined, awareness of the prevalence of serious diseases was immeasurably sharpened. Even more troublesome was the realization that the very conditions of the schools under which the pupils lived aggravated, if indeed they did not cause, the shocking status of morbidity among the Indians. As the twentieth century advanced, the Indian Office devoted increasing attention to the problems of health, until that topic became one of the major areas of the federal government's paternalistic activity in regard to its Indian wards. It was unfortunately the case, however, that both the realization of the magnitude of the problem and the programs adopted to combat it came much too slowly.

By 1900 deficiencies in Indian health could no longer be overlooked or pushed aside, and charges were leveled against the Indian Office for its negligence. The strongest critic, who fearlessly exposed the shocking conditions in Indian schools and on the reservations, was one of the Interior Department's Indian inspectors, William J. McConnell, who spent his four-year term from 1897 to 1901 as a stinging gadfly. As he made his inspection rounds, McConnell was astounded by the health conditions he found. He railed especially against the policy of filling the schools at all costs and pointed to the common acceptance of diseased children in order to keep the enrollment high, as the schools were repeatedly urged to do by the Indian Office.

Everywhere McConnell found unconscionable overcrowding in the schools. He told the secretary of the interior that of one group of fifteen boys sent to Carlisle from the Shoshone Agency "11 died there or returned home to die" and that out of two groups sent to boarding schools in Nebraska the mortality rate was nearly as great. "The word murder is a fearful word," he wrote, "but yet the transfer of pupils and subjecting them to such fearful mortality is little less." He told the secretary when he wrote from the Yakima Agency in 1899: "The United States declared war against Spain, our people being impelled to this course largely by the abuses imposed upon the Cubans by the Spaniards. Yet I venture to say that upon every one of our Indian Reservations in the Northwest there are conditions as bad or worse than any which were exposed in Cuba."

A large part of the problem, which the inspector immediately pinpointed, was the sad state of the medical service of the Indian Office. Because of low pay, the personnel were often ill-trained, uninterested, and generally incompetent. The physicians had to get along without adequate equipment and medicines and with little chance to improve their knowledge either through professional associations or by reading the latest journals, and esprit de corps was almost entirely lacking.

The Indian Office at last began to move. Commissioner Jones, realizing at last that the demand for increasing enrollment in the Indian schools led to overcrowding and to the admission of students with contagious diseases, directed the agents and school superintendents to admit only sound and healthy children and to avoid overcrowding in the dormitories. Then in the summer of 1903 he ordered a comprehensive survey of health conditions in the Indian schools and on the reservations.

The report of the survey should have shocked the Indian Office out of any complacency. It showed that tuberculosis was more widespread among the Indians than among an equal number of whites—even though many Indians lived in healthful climates. The causes were clear: poor sanitation, lack of cleanliness, and specifically failure to destroy tubercular sputum; improper and poorly prepared food; overcrowding in dormitories; and lack of proper medical attention after infection. The report referred, too, to such general causes as use of alcohol, the change of children from camp life to confinement in school, and general weakening of the Indians by intermarriage, as well as Indian cultural patterns and the "ignorance and superstitions [which] often make it impossible to institute many of the procedures deemed advisable."

CAMPAIGNS AGAINST DISEASE

Much of Jones's administration was marked by a business-as-usual approach to the problems of contagion. More intense action began under Commissioner Leupp. Tuberculosis was the first item on the agenda, for its fatal nature threatened to decimate the tribes. What sparked Leupp's interest was the Sixth International Congress on Tuberculosis, held in Washington in 1908. The Indian Office and the Smithsonian Institution cooperated in preparing material dealing with the Indians for the congress. Leupp was caught up in the movement, and he himself gave an address at the congress, in which he admitted that tuberculosis was "the greatest single menace to the Indian race."

One important action of Leupp was the appointment in 1908 of Dr. Joseph A. Murphy as medical supervisor for the Indian service. Murphy was an outstanding choice, for he was an expert in the treatment of tuberculosis and an intelligent and energetic medical leader. Until he resigned at the end of World War I, he gave forceful direction to the health campaigns of the Indian Office, although he operated against great odds. Murphy was an able promoter of the cause. He spoke to the assembly at Lake Mohonk in 1909; testified at congressional appropriation hearings; developed formal lectures on disease, which he gave at Indian schools; and prepared a *Manual on Tuberculosis: Its Cause, Prevention, and Treatment* for distribution to Indian service employees, Indian students, and adult Indians who could read.

Following close upon tuberculosis as a malady of serious proportions was trachoma, an eye disease that for undetermined reasons struck especially hard at the Indian schools and reservations. An investigation of trachoma turned up a heavy incidence of the disease, and the seriousness of the situation could not be denied. Congress began to make separate appropriations "to relieve distress among the Indians and to provide for their care and for the prevention and treatment of tuberculosis, trachoma, smallpox, and other contagious and infectious diseases." The first appropriation, for fiscal year 1911, was $40,000, but the sums were rapidly increased as more information was received about the tragic prevalence of disease among the Indians.

Not trusting the statistics of the Indian Office, Congress in 1912 authorized $10,000 to enable the United States Public Health Service "to make a thorough examination as to the prevalence of tuberculosis, trachoma, smallpox, and other contagious and infectious diseases among the Indians of the United States." The findings substantiated the earlier reports: 22.7 percent of the Indians examined had trachoma (29.86 percent of children in the boarding schools), and the incidence of tuberculosis ranged from a high of 32.6 percent among the Pyramid Lake Paiutes to a low of 2.33 percent among the Indians of Michigan. The prevalence of tuberculosis was "very greatly in excess of that among the white race" and "so serious as to require the prosecution of vigorous measures for its relief." Trachoma was more prevalent in the schools than on the reservations, and the survey concluded that the infection was frequently picked up at the boarding schools and then spread to the reservations when the students returned home.

The survey noted the highly unsanitary conditions on the reservations: overcrowded homes, uncleanliness, and poor food. And it found the schools generally overcrowded, with diseased children mingling among the others. Insufficient measures were taken to prevent the spread of disease through towels and by means of flies. The status of the physicians in the medical service was declared unsatisfactory from the standpoint of compensation, organization, and esprit de corps, and record keeping ("the foundation of public-health work") was indefinite and fragmentary. The general conclusion was inevitable: "It was found that the curative efforts of the physicians of the Office of Indian Affairs were largely nullified by the conditions under which work is attempted and by the indifference and ignorance of the primitive Indians. The important problem is not so much the medical treatment of the Indians for disease as the improvement of insanitary conditions causing such diseases."

With new congressional appropriations, Commissioner Cato Sells enthusiastically continued the fight to protect and improve the condition of the Indians. He built new hospitals, appointed ophthalmologists to special districts of the Indian country, stressed educational measures to prevent disease, promoted lectures (illustrated with stereopticon slides and motion pictures) at the schools and on the reservations, and pushed the standard remedies of better sanitary conditions in Indian homes, better ventilation, and sufficient nourishing food. He fought especially the high infant mortality rate among the Indians, and he promoted a "Swat the Fly" campaign, for it was generally agreed that flies were responsible for the spread of disease, especially tuberculosis and trachoma.

It is impossible to judge what might have been the results of the steadily increasing appropriations for Indian health and the strenuous campaigns directed by Sells if they had continued unabated. The fight, unfortunately, was obstructed, cut back, and in some cases halted by World War I and the postwar inflation and government retrenchment. The wartime demands for personnel made a shambles of the Indian medical service. Nearly 40 percent of the positions for regular physicians were vacant in 1918, and similar cuts had been made among the nurses.

Added to this already dismal picture was the devastating influenza epidemic of 1918–1919, which struck some Indian reservations with even more terrifying force than it did the army units and the general public. Indian Office statistics showed that between October 1, 1918, and March 31, 1919, out of a total Indian population of 304,854, there were 73,651 cases of influenza and 6,270 deaths. Thus more than 2 percent of the Indians died from the epidemic, with the mortality especially high in Colorado, Utah, and New Mexico. The death rate for Indians far exceeded that of the white population in the same period.

The attacks on the Indian Office by the rising tide of reformers in the 1920s shocked the administration into new efforts, but the concentration on curing diseases among the Indians was open to serious criticism, for in the long run preventive measures promised the only effective control of disease. That would have entailed an emphasis on public health measures, which the Indian Office seemed unable or unwilling to undertake. The ineffectiveness of the Indian medical service in this matter was strikingly revealed by a report prepared in the early 1920s by Florence Patterson, a Red Cross public health nurse with extensive experience in America and Europe during and after World War I. Patterson spent nine months in the field, visiting thirteen superintendencies and examining some forty thousand Indians. What she reported was not of much consolation to the Indian Office, for she still found rampant disease. Worse still, she reported extremely spotty and ineffective record keeping and an indifference, if not outright hostility, toward preventive medicine, which was the foundation of a public health approach.

Although Burke had suggested that such a report could be used as leverage upon Congress for increased appropriations, he in fact suppressed the report when he received it in June 1924. He asked the Red Cross not to make the report public and buried his copy in the files, for he feared that John Collier and others of his critics might seize the evidence it presented and make capital of it in their fight against the Indian Office.

Yet, despite such criticism as that in Patterson's report, there were advances in the medical service in the 1920s. The Classification Act of 1923, with its extension to field positions in 1924, redefined positions in the civil service system and upgraded salaries for the Indian service, including those of physicians. The pay of the doctors still did not equal that of other government physicians, but the move was in the right direction. And, although Burke in his concern for economy eliminated positions in the Indian service as a whole, the appropriations and numbers for the medical service slowly increased.

A large share of the increased appropriations that came from time to time went into hospitals, which were classified as sanatoriums, primarily for the treatment of tuberculosis (there were eleven in 1925), general and agency hospitals, and school hospitals for treatment of children in the boarding schools. In addition, the government had built an insane asylum for Indians at Canton, South Dakota, which admitted its first patients in 1903 and gradually expanded its capacity; in 1915 the asylum had about fifty patients, in 1925 one hundred.

CRITICS OF INDIAN HEALTH CARE

The Indian Office worked within an atmosphere of growing criticism from John Collier and the American Indian Defense Association. The ineffectiveness of the health programs for Indians that was revealed in the surveys and the continuing high morbidity statistics led critics to recommend transfer of the responsibility for Indian health to the Public Health Service, which was directed by the surgeon general within the Treasury Department. Because the Public Health Service was highly respected, whereas the Indian medical service seemed unable to accomplish effectively what was needed in Indian health care, such a transfer won many supporters. The Indian Office, however, strongly opposed such a move, which it called "a proposition so extraordinary and so radically at variance with administration procedures." The main argument was that medical problems could not be separated from "the educational, social, and industrial problems that concern a race that is in the critical transformation period of evolution from one social plane to another." The surgeon general also opposed transfer, for he claimed that he was already overwhelmed with caring for disabled veterans.

Naturally enough, the commissioner of Indian affairs and the secretary of the interior were defensive in the face of attacks on their Indian health policies and programs, and they prepared statements that pointed to the advances made, while admitting that serious problems still remained. Their ultimate refuge was the insufficiency of the appropriations made by Congress for Indian health.

If the commissioner and the secretary were well pleased because they had accomplished so much for Indian health, the Meriam survey staff was appalled that they had accomplished so little. "Taken as a whole," the Meriam Report stated, "practically every activity undertaken by the national government for the promotion of the health of the Indians is below a reasonable standard of efficiency." The cause it saw was lack of sufficient money to set salaries high enough to hire really competent people and to provide facilities for health care that met even minimum standards from a scientific standpoint. More telling was the criticism that "lack of vision and real understanding have precluded the establishment in the Indian service of a real program of preventive medicine," and the report ridiculed the attempts to prevent trachoma as consisting "mainly in providing separate towels in boarding schools, displaying posters in Indian communities, and in a small amount of rather ineffective segregating of cases in schools." The position of the Meriam staff was that an effective public health program—with public health nurses in place of matrons and physicians who were "public health men"—would have to be substituted for the existing system, which was largely relief of the sick, not the prevention and eradication of disease.

The Meriam Report furnished a stimulus and a guide for bettering the care of Indian health, but health conditions improved very slowly and never kept pace with the advances made by the general society of the United States.

CHAPTER 20

The Indians' Land

The key to Indian self-support was the ability to make a living from the land. The Dawes Act of 1887 was the fruit of the philosophy that individual pieces of property—homesteads—would not only protect the Indians' title to the land but would be the paramount means of turning them into hardworking farmers. Although allotment began almost at once after the Dawes Act was passed, the great period of allotment was the first decade of the twentieth century, as the machinery shifted into high gear and as the pressure from white farmers for the opening of the reservations grew.

CONTINUING ALLOTMENT

Year by year the number of allotted acres was totaled up as a sign of progress. In 1900 there were 55,996 allotments, covering 6,736,504 acres; by 1910 these figures had swelled to 190,401 allotments covering 31,093,647 acres. In 1911 Commissioner Valentine reported that roughly two-thirds of the Indians had been allotted. After that the process slowed down, for most of the land in reservations that were amenable to allotment had been allotted, and what was left was in areas, especially in the Southwest, where division of the lands was not immediately feasible. By 1920 the number of allotments on reservations had advanced to only 217,572 and the acres allotted to 35,897,069.

The allotment of Indian reservation lands was accompanied by the disposal of the "surplus" land to white settlers. The Dawes Act had specified negotiation with the Indians for the sale of lands remaining after allotment, and agreements had been made with the tribes and approved by Congress. After the Supreme Court in *Lone Wolf* v. *Hitchcock* in 1903 declared that Congress had power to dispose of Indian lands without Indian consent, the process was speeded up.

The opening of a part of the Rosebud Reservation in South Dakota in 1904 set the pattern. In order to avoid appropriations for buying Indian lands, Congress proposed that instead of the outright purchase of surplus lands to add to the public domain, the actual settlers on those lands should be required to pay the Indians directly. The House Committee on Indian Affairs, in favorably reporting the new measure, relied upon the Lone Wolf decision in asserting the power of Congress to act without consulting the Indians, and it quoted at length testimony before the committee given by Commissioner Jones:

> If you depend upon the consent of the Indians as to the disposition of the land where they have the fee to the land, you will have diffi- culty in getting it, and I think the decision in the Lone Wolf case, that Congress can do as it sees fit with the property of the Indians will enable you to dispose of that land without the consent of the Indians. If you wait for their consent in these matters, it will be fifty years before you can do away with the reservations.

Both the committee and the commissioner, in accepting the authority to act without Indian consent, asserted the responsibility of the govern- ment to act in good faith in the Indians' best interests. These statements, however, did not satisfy the watchdogs of Indian rights, and there was soon harsh criticism of the proposed Rosebud bill from the Indian Rights Asso- ciation and other Indian advocates. The association condemned the three dollars an acre that the Rosebud bill proposed as completely inadequate. Marshaling evidence from the Indians and from others about the substan- tially greater value of the lands in question, it petitioned Congress to set at least five dollars an acre as the price (a compromise, it said, that the In- dians were willing to accept). Although it broadcast its plea through news- paper articles and a special pamphlet, the association was unable to pre- vent the passage of the measure and could not persuade the president to veto it, and the bill became law on April 23, 1904. Congress, with the con- tinued support of Commissioner Jones, similarly revised an earlier agree- ment with the Crow Indians and provided for opening their lands in the pattern of the Rosebud legislation, and other measures followed suit.

Although allotment of Indian lands moved forward rapidly, much com- munal property still existed in the form of trust funds of the various tribes in the Treasury of the United States. In 1900 these funds amounted to $34,317,955. If allotment of land was necessary for the civilization of the Indians and their disappearance into the dominant American society, so too was it necessary to divide the tribal moneys among the individual Indians.

A drive for "segregation" of these funds—at least dividing them into separate accounts for the individual Indians entitled to them, if not actually paying them out to the Indians—gained momentum in the twentieth century.

The movement to divide the trust funds ran into trouble. A bill was introduced by Representative John F. Lacey of Iowa on January 5, 1905, which would have been a counterpart of the Dawes Act by authorizing the president to order the distribution and payment of their tribal funds to the tribal members. But before the bill reached the floor of the House, its contents were replaced by a proposal that emasculated the original measure by directing that the segregation of funds would apply only to those Indians who personally requested it. In that form the bill became law as the Lacey Act on March 2, 1907. The absolute faith of the Indian Rights Association and similar humanitarian reformers in the immediate civilizing power of a division of tribal property—be it land or money—was not held by Congress, for the experience of allotment of land under the Dawes Act indicated that not all Indians were ready for sudden immersion into the white man's economic world.

MODIFICATIONS OF THE DAWES ACT

Under the Dawes Act land allotments were to be held in trust by the United States government for twenty-five years, during which time the land would be completely inalienable. When, at the end of the period, the Indians received fee simple patents to the land and could do with it as they pleased, it was judged that they would have become competent to deal with the pressures that surrounded them. But modifications were soon made in the original act.

A serious problem with the allotment machinery arose with the death of Indians who held trust patents to allotments. Because most Indians died intestate, the interests in these allotments were divided equally among the heirs. Many of the heirs already held allotments in their own names, which they were not farming themselves, and they lacked the incentive or capital needed to utilize the inherited lands. Moreover, in many cases the lands could not be divided in any useful way, and the leasing of small parcels was often impracticable. The solution seemed to be to sell the inherited lands and divide the proceeds among the Indians. In 1902 Congress authorized such sale, with the approval of the secretary of the interior.

In 1910 Congress provided for the making of wills by Indians, but this did not solve the heirship problem, which became increasingly serious as allotments were divided and subdivided on the death of heirs. The fractionalization of the land made a mockery of the concern to turn the Indians into landowning farmers by means of individual allotments, for generation by generation the division of inherited land broke down a single allotment into a multitude of tiny pieces that were economically unmanageable. On the other hand, a single Indian might be heir to a number of allotments, with an interest in each so small as to be infinitesimal. There was no way he could gather these pieces together into a usable parcel, so leasing and sale were the only alternatives, and outright sale often seemed the better choice because leasing income was received in very small amounts.

A major change in allotment policy came with the Burke Act of May 8, 1906. It was the result of growing dissatisfaction with the trust and citizenship provisions of the law. The original legislation provided that with the acceptance of an allotment (even though it was to be held in trust for twenty-five years) the Indian became a citizen. The paradoxical situation of granting citizenship to a person who at the same time was declared incompetent to manage his property was not unnoticed, but the change in the law came from more practical considerations.

The particular event that brought the issue to the fore was the Supreme Court's decision *Matter of Heff* in 1905, which declared that an Indian who was a citizen was no longer a ward of the nation and was not subject to the liquor restriction laws. To solve that problem, the Burke Act declared that Indians allotted land in the future would not become citizens until the end of the trust period and receipt of a fee patent to their land. To remove any doubt about the Indians in trust status, the law provided that they should be "subject to the exclusive jurisdiction of the United States" until they received their fee simple patents. The act also authorized the president to extend the trust status of Indians beyond the twenty-five-year period if conditions warranted.

But if some Indians were not yet ready for citizenship, others were competent to manage their own land; for them a twenty-five-year trust period seemed unnecessary and unwise. The Burke Act, therefore, authorized the secretary of the interior to issue a fee patent to any Indian deemed "competent and capable of managing his or her affairs" before the end of the trust period.

The Board of Indian Commissioners, still strongly imbued with the Dawes Act mentality, objected vigorously to postponing citizenship. The Burke Act took away the presumption in favor of citizenship, the board complained, and threw the presumption *against* it, placing on the individual Indian the burden of proving his competence in order to become a citizen before the trust period expired. The real difficulty with the law, however, was that it opened the door to early alienation of allotments. Although it was the intention of the legislators that great care should be taken by the secretary of the interior in determining competency, in practice the safeguards were often neglected. No doubt some Indians kept their allotments and profited from them, but for most the patent in fee was soon followed by sale of the land.

The leasing of Indian lands, probating of estates, determination of heirs, adjustment in the size of allotments, declaration of competency, and issuance of patents, to say nothing of the management of forestry operations and irrigation projects, required new legislation, a flood of regulations and circulars, and the multiplication of official correspondence, as the Indian Office had to deal more and more with individual cases. In order to refine and clarify procedures in many of these activities, Congress on June 25, 1910, passed an "omnibus bill," which gathered together a variety of measures.

The law of 1910 indicated a realization that allotment could not apply uniformly to all Indian communities—a realization that was long in coming. As irrigation projects were promoted, it became clear that the across-the-board allotment of 80 acres of farming land or 160 acres of grazing land was not suitable in many regions. Congress partially met the need by authorizing allotments of irrigable land "in such areas [quantities] as may be for their best interest not to exceed, however, forty acres to any one Indian." The rest of an Indian's entitlement to allotted land was to be filled from nonirrigable land. The omnibus bill also authorized the issuance of patents for village lots to Indians in the state of Washington whose livelihood came from the sea and for whom agricultural plots made no sense. The patents, however, restricted alienation of the lots to other members of the tribe.

COMPETENCY AND FEE PATENTS

The radical switch from emphasis on protection of the Indian allotments toward provisions for alienation of the Indian landholdings reached it height in the period 1913–1920, under the leadership of Secretary of the Interior Franklin K. Lane and Commissioner Cato Sells, with whom the issuance of fee patents to competent Indians became a high priority.

Both Lane and Sells were obsessed with the idea that land and other natural resources should be fully utilized, and they applied this principle to Indian lands, which they were committed to making as productive as possible. "The Indian's rich agricultural lands, his vast acres of grass land, his great forests should be so utilized as to become a powerful instrument for his civilization," Sells told the superintendents in 1914. "I hold it to be an economic and social crime, in this age and under modern conditions, to permit thousands of acres of fertile land belonging to the Indians and capable of great industrial development to lie in unproductive idleness." Additional farmers were employed to teach the Indians farming methods, and stock-raising programs were instituted. Moreover, leasing was encouraged and approved, and the sale of allotted land continued.

Another guiding principle of policy in the Wilson administration, perhaps the dominant one, was to free "competent" Indians from wardship status and set them and their land loose from federal supervision. Here was a zenith in the drive that began in the late nineteenth century to let the Indians take their places, on their own, in American society. Lane and Sells pursued this termination principle with a vengeance. By eliminating Indians who did not need government care from the responsibility of the Indian Office, attention could then be concentrated on those wards who still needed help.

Sells proceeded enthusiastically, using declarations of competency and the issuance of fee simple patents authorized by the Burke Act of 1906. But the task of determining competent Indians was a job of frightening magnitude if the decisions had to be made carefully one by one. To speed up the granting of the patents, the government resorted to a "competency commission."

In 1915 Lane appointed a commission or board to move from reservation to reservation and, in conjunction with the local superintendent, determine the "qualification of each Indian who may apply for a severance of tribal relations, or who, in its judgment, has arrived at the degree of business competency that he should assume the duties of citizenship." The following year the original commission was split into two, and then a third one was created. Effectiveness was at once demonstrated. During fiscal year 1916, on the recommendation of the commission, 576 fee patents were issued. These were added to the 949 approved through other channels for a total of 1,525 fee patents for the year, covering about 220,490 acres.

Despite abuses in the patenting program, Sells was pleased with the program of freeing the Indians from wardship, and he was determined not to let the momentum be lost. Accordingly, on April 17, 1917, he issued a "Declaration of Policy in the Administration of Indian Affairs." He pointed to the successful activities under way in regard to health, vocational training, suppression of the liquor traffic, and protection of Indian property and said that he was ready to take "the next step." He declared: "Broadly speaking, a policy of greater liberalism will henceforth prevail in Indian administration to the end that every Indian, as soon as he has been determined to be as competent to transact his own business as the average white man, shall be given full control of his property and have all his lands and moneys turned over to him, after which he will no longer be a ward of the Government."

The guidelines issued in the new policy set blood quantum as a norm. Patents in fee, as a general rule, would be issued to Indians who had less than one-half Indian blood, as well as to those with more than half Indian blood if they were found to be competent. Moreover, Indians over twenty-one years of age who had received diplomas from government Indian schools, if they demonstrated competence, would be so declared. In addition, the sale of inherited Indian lands and the sale of lands of incompetent Indians who were old and feeble and needed the proceeds for support would be done under a "liberal ruling." The use of individual Indian moneys, too, would be unrestricted for competent Indians, and pro rata shares of tribal moneys would be set aside for them "as speedily as possible."

Although it was evident almost immediately that on some reservations a very high percentage of the patentees quickly sold or mortgaged their land and wasted the proceeds, Sells was not deterred. He and many of the superintendents who saw the evils firsthand argued that sooner or later the Indians would have to face the world without government protection, and that although some would fail, many would rise to meet the challenge. They would realize, at last, that work was necessary if they were to be saved.

The policy of hastening the patenting of Indian allottees took place during the war years, in which the need for foodstuffs demanded full use of the agricultural resources of the Indian reservations. The national food campaign was strongly supported by the Indian Office, which sought to arouse the Indians' interest in more production and to increase the amount of Indian land under cultivation, whether by the Indians themselves or by white lessees, thus accelerating the process of assimilating the Indians into the nation's economic life. The Indian Office eagerly promoted the leasing of unused Indian lands, both for agricultural production and for mineral resources, and approved the sale of land if that move would expedite its productive use.

Before Sells left office a critical reaction had set in against his "liberal" policy, for its disastrous effects in loss of Indian lands were becoming evident to many. A sharp change in policy came when Secretary Lane resigned in early 1920 and President Wilson appointed John Barton Payne to replace him. Payne saw no need to rush the Indians into full citizenship status. "It may take the Indians a very long, long time to become really competent," he told Sells; "but we should be patient and not permit ourselves to be hurried. . . . For a long time yet the Indians must continue the wards of the nation, and the nation must take care of them." The new secretary ended the policy of blanket issuance of patents and returned to the policy of examining each case for competency on its merits; he rejected many of the applications forwarded by the competency commissions and then abolished the commissions altogether, turning the work of judging competence back to the superintendents. Unfortunately, the reversal came after many Indians had already lost their property.

Charles H. Burke, who replaced Sells in 1921, did not forsake the philosophy that allotment and assimilation were the proper goals of the government in dealing with the Indians. He moved much more cautiously, however, than Lane and Sells, both because he saw the evils resulting from the attempt to free the government of responsibility for Indian property and because of the whirlwind of criticism and demands for reform in Indian affairs that stirred around him in the 1920s. John Collier and his friends pointed to the loss of lands under fee patenting, and they were critical of the bureaucratic control that the Indian Office exerted over the lives and property of the Indians. For Collier, the basic wrong lay in the allotment policy, which had dominated Indian life for thirty or forty years, much to the detriment of the Indians.

In the 1920s, as in previous decades, there was a great deal of pressure for leasing Indian lands. Burke acknowledged the long-held government policy of giving each Indian "a tract of land that he could call his own and from the cultivation of which he might gain a livelihood, and at the same time acquire the arts of civilization." He directed the superintendents to encourage the Indians "to go upon their allotments and establish homes and work their lands, either themselves or by hired help, rather than to depend upon the small rents received." But if an Indian could not or would not make productive use of his land, Burke permitted leasing, even though he knew it subverted the intention of the allotment policy of turning the Indians into hardworking citizens.

In regard to issuing fee patents to Indians, Burke took a cautious stand. He objected to any automatic determination of competency—such as blood quantum or amount of schooling—and was determined to protect noncompetent Indians. He was critical of the free and easy policy of Lane and Sells and attempted to undo some of the damage that had resulted under the "liberal policy" by promoting cancellation of patents issued to Indians who had not applied for them or against their will. Such attempts to save Indian lands and Indian rights, however, were piecemeal solutions. The demand for a complete rejection of allotment and its corollaries did not die.

FORESTRY AND IRRIGATION

Two economic developments closely related to the land and its use were the management of Indian forests and the building of irrigation projects on the reservations. Although concern for these matters began in the late nineteenth century, it was only in the twentieth that they became consuming interests and heavy administrative duties of the Indian Office. In both there was a fundamental question of safeguarding Indian interests while promoting utilization and development of the nation's natural resources.

Because many tribal lands were covered in part by forests, the question
of Indian rights to the timber arose early. Most Indian tribes were accorded
only a right of occupancy in their reservations while the fee remained in
the United States, and it was a common opinion that Indian rights did not
extend to the timber except where the timber was cut off arable lands in the
process of making them available for cultivation. From time to time Congress passed special acts authorizing disposition of the timber on Indian
lands, but there was no general legislation until February 16, 1889, when
Congress permitted the sale of dead and down timber only, under presidential regulations. Then gradually the principle developed that the establishment of a reservation for use and occupancy of the Indians conveyed to
the Indians a title in the timber that was comparable to their title in the
land and that the disposition of the timber was subject to congressional legislation. The omnibus act of 1910 expressly recognized the theory and provided that the forests could contribute to the support and advancement of
the Indians through the sale of timber.

Administrative structures were established to survey and protect the Indian forests, to prevent what the Board of Indian Commissioners in 1908
called the "wholesale slaughter of forests" on Indian reservations. Beginning in 1910, Congress authorized $100,000 annually to enable the Indian
Service to manage the forests on the reservations, and the funds made it
possible to organize a Forestry Section in 1910 and then in 1926 a full Forestry Division.

Of greater investment but ultimately of less benefit to the Indians were
the irrigation projects initiated by the government on Indian reservations.
Much of the land of the reservations was arid or semi-arid and could support the Indian communities only if intensive agriculture under irrigation
were undertaken, and in 1884 Congress began the practice of appropriating
a general irrigation fund to be spent at the discretion of the secretary of the
interior. Most appropriations, however, were specified for particular projects, of which the most important were on the Blackfeet, Colorado River,
Crow, Flathead, Fort Belknap, Fort Hall, Fort Peck, San Carlos, Uintah,
Wind River, and Yakima reservations.

The projects at first were under control of the agents or superintendents,
whose primary interest in irrigation was affording employment for the Indians. But the haphazard approach of the early years was gradually replaced, as the nation as a whole took up interest in reclamation of the arid
lands in the West and as irrigation became increasingly essential on both
allotted and unallotted Indian lands. National demands for efficient utilization of the land and Indian needs for economic subsistence resulted in a
continually more regulated approach.

As the costs of irrigation projects increased, they came to be charged against the Indian tribes themselves in the form of reimbursable funds. It was next to impossible to collect the money, and little attempt was made to do so until Congress in 1920 directed the secretary of the interior to enforce at least partial reimbursement. The Meriam Report of 1928 urged the canceling of reimbursable debts if the money had been originally given as a gratuity, and in 1932 Congress canceled all outstanding debts due on construction of irrigation projects.

The primary concern of the federal irrigation program administrators seemed to be the construction of reservoirs and ditches and their maintenance. A more important matter, the protection of the water rights of Indians so that there would be a continuing adequate supply of water for the projects, was slighted. In 1908 the Supreme Court, in the landmark case of *Winters* v. *United States*, decreed that where land was reserved by treaty to an Indian tribe, there was an implied reservation of water necessary for the irrigation of their lands, and the Indian Office tended to rely on this decision, without taking other action to protect the water rights of the Indians.

The overriding question in the end, however, was whether and to what extent the irrigation projects in fact benefited the Indians. Were the Indians actually using the lands for successful irrigated agriculture? The answer was no. It became increasingly clear through the 1920s that irrigation projects were authorized for Indian reservations, not with the primary intent of aiding Indian advance toward self-sufficiency, but to develop the arid West for the benefit of white interests. The conclusion was inescapable from the special report on Indian irrigation projects submitted in June 1928 by Porter J. Preston and Charles A. Engle. The statistics in the report pretty much tell the story. As of June 30, 1927, government projects had prepared 692,057 acres for irrigation on reservations, at a total expenditure since the first appropriation of 1867 of $35,967,925.72. Of these acres 70 percent were owned by the Indians and 30 percent by whites. Only 52 percent of the total acreage susceptible of irrigation, however, was actually being irrigated, and of this 32 percent was farmed by Indians and the rest by whites. On the large projects studied by Preston and Engle (which accounted for 91 percent of the acreage), the Indians irrigated only 23 percent.

APPRAISAL OF THE ALLOTMENT POLICY

The allotment policy, begun and carried out by federal officials imbued with the philosophy of individualizing the Indians, failed miserably. The paternalistic concern to transform the Indians into independent farmers and stockmen did not take sufficiently into consideration the nature of traditional Indian ways or the geographical conditions of the area in which the allotted Indians were supposed to work out their destiny.

Allotment did not perform its primary function: to turn the Indians generally into agriculturalists. Many Indians had farmed successfully under their communal land patterns, with individuals and families using designated sections of tribal land for their cultivation, and as allotment began it was hoped that more and more Indians would become self-sufficient through the land. Yet in fact, under allotment, the amount of Indian farming declined rather than grew.

A primary cause of this decline, of course, was the loss of Indian lands in the allotment period. When John Collier testified before a congressional committee in 1934 on legislation to reverse allotment, he declared that "two thirds of the Indians in two thirds of the Indian country for many years have been drifting toward complete impoverishment." He asserted that Indian lands had been cut from 138 million acres in 1887 to 48 million (actually 52 million) in 1934, and that of the residual lands nearly one-half were desert or semi-desert. About one hundred thousand Indians, he said, were "totally landless as a result of allotment."

Thus the grand dream of Henry Dawes and his friends and followers came to naught. However one looks at allotment, it was disappointing and damaging. A principal goal of Collier and the reform movement he inaugurated was to correct the evils that had come with the individualizing of Indian economic activity, the subdivision of the lands into economically unsound parcels, and the loss of so much of the Indian landed estate.

THE INDIANS OF OKLAHOMA

The Five Civilized Tribes had unique relations with the federal government. The Dawes Act and many other measures that embodied federal Indian policy specifically exempted the Five Tribes—and sometimes all the Indians of Oklahoma. Yet until the census of 1950 Oklahoma was the most populous Indian state (it was overtaken in that year by Arizona), and in the first decades of the twentieth century Oklahoma Indians comprised about one-third of the Indian population in the United States.

The Dawes Commission, appointed in 1893 to work for the allotment of Indian lands and the dissolution of tribal government, the Curtis Act of 1898, which gave legislative sanction to the commission's work, and the agreements made by the commission with the separate tribes were the foundation upon which the new political relations with the Five Civilized Tribes rested. But the transformation from tribal governments to an aggregate of individualized American citizens did not happen instantaneously. It was a long and complicated process, and it engaged much of the time and energy of the Indian Office.

In March 1901, by an amendment to the Dawes Act, Congress conferred

United States citizenship on all the Indians in the Indian Territory. Skeletal tribal administrations were still maintained as a necessary means to expedite the disposition of tribal property, but the act "to provide for the final disposition of the affairs of the Five Civilized Tribes in the Indian Territory" of April 26, 1906, indicated that the continuing tribal governments were puppet regimes controlled by the federal government.

There was no regret in Washington about the end of the once-flourishing Indian governments. Secretary Lane expressed the general attitude in 1914:

> On the 1st of last July the Cherokee Nation ceased to exist. This act was the culmination of a treaty promise made over 80 years ago, extended by statute, and at last placed within administrative discretion. The word of the white man has been made good. These native and aspiring people have been lifted as American citizens into full fellowship with their civilized conquerors. The Cherokee Nation, with its senate and house, governor and officers, laws, property, and authority exists no longer. Surely there is something fine in this slight bit of history. It takes hold upon the imagination and the memory, arouses dreams of the day when the Indian shall be wholly blended into our life, and at the same time draws the mind backward over the stumbling story of our relationship with him.

The American citizenship of the Indians and the dissolution of their tribal governments, however, did not end the federal government's business with them. Citizenship, in fact, had little effect upon the paternalistic directing of the individual Indians from Washington. Even statehood for Oklahoma in 1907 did not materially affect this condition, for in the enabling act Congress had set the provision that the constitution of a new state could not be construed to limit the rights of the Indians or affect the authority of the government of the United States in dealing with them.

When the rolls were closed, 101,506 persons had been enrolled in the Five Civilized Tribes, including 2,582 whites married into the tribes and 23,405 freedmen. Out of the 19,525,966 acres of land embraced within these five nations, 15,794,351 were allotted to the enrolled members. Unlike allotments made under the Dawes Act, the patents for Oklahoma allotments were granted by the tribes, but with exemptions from taxation and specific restrictions against alienation. In general, a set portion—usually forty acres—of the allotment was designated a homestead and made inalienable for twenty-one years; the rest was called "surplus lands."

To the whites, who comprised the great majority of the Oklahoma population, the restricted, nontaxable lands in the hands of the Indians appeared as an obstacle to economic development, and pressures soon mounted for a removal of restrictions. In response, Congress in 1908 removed all restrictions (including those on homesteads and the lands of minors) from the allotments of intermarried whites, freedmen, and mixed-blood Indians with less than half Indian blood. In addition, all the lands, except homesteads, of mixed-blood Indians with half or more but less than three-fourths Indian blood, were freed of restrictions. By 1914, when the tribal governments ended, out of the total enrolled population of 101,209 members and freedmen of the Five Civilized Tribes, only 36,967 were in the restricted class. Then, by an order of August 6, 1919, restrictions were unconditionally removed from all allottees of one-half Indian blood, and the number of restricted Indians fell to 21,213, holding 2,683,819 acres.

The act of 1908 that removed the restrictions from the land of large numbers of Indians went a step further. It subjected minors in the Five Civilized Tribes to the jurisdiction of the probate courts of Oklahoma. This removed them from the protection of the federal government, and grafters of all sorts exploited the situation. A class of "professional guardians" arose whose sole occupation was caring for the estates of Indian minors and of adult Indians declared incompetent.

In an attempt to correct the abuses, Commissioner Sells arranged conferences with the county judges, prosecuting attorneys, and district judges in eastern Oklahoma. A set of probate procedures was adopted by the county judges, approved by the State County Judges Association, and then officially adopted and promulgated by the Supreme Court of Oklahoma. In addition, a number of special probate attorneys were appointed by the secretary of the interior to be watchdogs in probate matters. Yet the situation rapidly deteriorated. The rules of 1914 were opposed by local courts, and on April 4, 1919, the Oklahoma legislature abrogated all rules adopted by the Supreme Court and required each local court to promulgate its own rules.

In the early 1920s, conditions in Oklahoma occasioned a dramatic exposé. In a muckraking pamphlet published by the Indian Rights Association early in 1924 under the inflammatory title *Oklahoma's Poor Rich Indians: An Orgy of Graft and Exploitation of the Five Civilized Tribes— Legalized Robbery*, charges were made that the estates of members of the Five Civilized Tribes were "shamelessly and openly robbed in a scientific and ruthless manner"; that the efforts of the secretary of the interior to correct abuses had failed; that "excessive and unnecessary administrative costs, unconscionable fees and commissions" were allowed to guardians and attorneys; that "Indian guardianships are the plums to be distributed to the faithful friends of the judges as a reward for their support at the polls"; and that, when oil was found on an Indian's property, "it is usually considered prima facie evidence that he is incompetent, and in the appointment of a guardian for him his wishes in the matter are rarely considered." The bulk of the pamphlet was filled with a "bill of particulars" giving lurid details of the graft and corruption.

The Oklahoma delegation in Congress could not let such a condemnation of their state go unanswered, and a special subcommittee of the House of Representatives issued a report in 1925, which accused the Indian Rights Association of sensationalism, spoke of "ill-founded publicity," and declared that the wholesale charges against judges, attorneys, and businessmen of Oklahoma were not substantiated. Yet the report also noted the loss of lands by restricted Indians and spoke of "reprehensible and indefensible practices" by "unconscionable attorneys and persons who make it a profession to obtain appointments as guardians."

The whole affair highlighted the paradox of combining citizenship with wardship. There was a strong feeling that the Indians should be allowed to exercise responsibility for their own property as one of the rights and privileges of citizenship, and the Indians of the Five Civilized Tribes—with a long history of acculturation to the white man's ways—were thought to be particularly good cases in which to push for freedom from federal guardianship and paternalistic control of all their affairs. But in practice the Indians proved unable to protect their own interests. The only answer was to continue the protection of the United States government.

The Osage Indians presented another special case. They had been removed from Kansas in the early 1870s to a tract immediately west of the Cherokee Nation in the Outlet. Largely destitute at the time of their removal, they were located by chance on lands of tremendous riches in oil and gas resources, and they became probably the richest class of people in the world. Unfortunately, most Osages did not make good use of their riches. The chairman of the Board of Indian Commissioners reported what he had seen in 1920:

> Their wealth literally has been thrust upon them, unwittingly on their part. They are almost, if not quite, dazed by it. I have been over many of their household accounts—bills for family expenses run up with local merchants. Many of the totals are appalling. . . . These people do not know what they are doing; they have never been trained, nor have they the opportunity to learn what it all means.
>
> That the money is being largely squandered is evident. Of course, a great deal of it goes into automobiles; many Osages have several, and they are all high-priced cars. One rarely sees an Osage in a Ford. Apart from this expenditure, however, not any very valuable personal property appears to be acquired.

Some of these conditions were remedied in 1921, when Congress provided that full payments could be made only to competent Indians. In 1925 additional safeguards were provided by reasserting control of the secretary of the interior or the superintendent of the Osage Agency over many actions of the legal guardians of Osages. The secretary was also authorized to revoke certificates of competency granted to Indians of more than one-half Indian blood who were guilty of "squandering or misusing" funds.

The Indians of New York State, numbering about fifty-four hundred in 1900, were another instance of peculiar circumstances. The largest group and the one that attracted most attention was the Seneca Nation on the Allegany and Cattaraugus reserves in western New York. The unique situation of these Indians arose in part from the question of federal, state, and tribal jurisdiction over their affairs, for the United States government had paid little attention to New York, and the state government had assumed considerable authority, building and maintaining schools and highways on the reservations and exercising some control over law and order and property rights. The Indians were acculturated to white ways, and although the lands of the reserves were tribally owned, individual Indians had rights to designated parcels of land, which they cultivated and improved.

The status of Seneca land titles was seriously complicated by the confused question of the claims of the Ogden Land Company. Massachusetts, which claimed a preemptive right to lands in western New York on the basis of a royal grant, disposed of these rights in the late eighteenth century. They came to rest finally, after a number of transactions, in David A. Ogden, who had purchased the interest in Seneca lands in 1810. The rights of the Ogden Land Company, made up of heirs of Ogden and his partners, were variously interpreted to mean that the land belonged to the Seneca Nation, subject to the right of preemption of the land company, or that it belonged to the Ogden Land Company, under the grant from the crown to Massachusetts but subject to the perpetual right of occupancy by the Indians. Whatever the precise legal status of the claim, it was generally held to be an existing right, and it meant that Seneca lands could not be conveyed to anyone but the Ogden Land Company.

The Senecas, like the Five Civilized tribes, had been specifically exempted from the operation of the Dawes Act, and they were determined to maintain their tribal ownership and tribal identity. The federal government and the reformers who supported and influenced government Indian policy, on the other hand, were equally determined that the reservations be allotted and the Indians made citizens and absorbed into the general population. New York, too, was eager for this to happen, and the whites who leased lands of the Senecas wanted to obtain full title. Through much of the later nineteenth century, various commissions and individuals investigated the condition of the Senecas and the status of the Ogden claims, and attempts were repeatedly made to get federal or state legislation that would allot the Indians' lands.

The strongest agitation for allotment of the New York reservations came shortly after the turn of the century, in the form of a bill introduced in Congress in 1902 by Representative Edward B. Vreeland of New York, a man who had important economic interests in Seneca land and oil. The Christian reform organizations closed ranks behind Vreeland's bill. The Board of Indian Commissioners persistently promoted severalty for the New York Indians, and the Lake Mohonk Conference in October 1902 devoted a whole session to the subject, beginning with an address by Vreeland and continuing with long discussion by both supporters and opponents of the measure. The conference formally endorsed allotment in severalty and the Vreeland bill specifically, and in the following year reaffirmed its support. Commissioner Jones, too, was heartily in favor. His only objection to the bill was a provision that required submission of the measure to the Indians for ratification, which he wanted stricken out. "If the enforcement of the bill, should it become law, depends upon the consent of the tribe," he said, "it will be a long time before any change is seen."

Opposition from the Indians and their friends and the specter of the Ogden claims defeated the Vreeland bill. From time to time there were flutters of new interest in the status of the New York Indians, but soon attempts to allot the reservations disappeared, and attention focused instead on the critical problems of jurisdiction—federal, state, and tribal—on the reservations and the deplorable conditions that were said to arise from the confusion. No fundamental action was taken by the United States government or by the state of New York, however, and development came only in individual cases of property or other rights adjudicated by the courts.

CHAPTER 21

An Indian New Deal

The decade of the 1930s was a watershed in American Indian policy; the agitation for reform that had been building up through the previous decade now turned into substantial and, to some degree, revolutionary action.

THE HOOVER YEARS

It began during the presidency of Herbert Hoover, a transition period in the administration of Indian affairs. Hoover, known for humanitarian work during World War I, chose for his secretary of the interior a likeminded man who had assisted him with war relief, Ray Lyman Wilbur, president of Stanford University. The new secretary had more than a passing interest in Indian affairs, for he had been in contact with the Indian Rights Association since 1913 and had aided the Indian Defense Association of Central and Northern California. He had been named as a member of the Committee of One Hundred (although he did not attend the conference), and he advised Secretary Work on matters of Indian health and education. He took office with a firm conviction that he had expressed in 1924: "The government as soon as possible should get out of the position of guardian for a portion of its citizens. Indians must as speedily as possible depend upon themselves if they are ever to amount to anything except dying remnants."

To run the Indian Office, Hoover turned to two highly respected Quakers. As commissioner of Indian affairs he selected Charles J. Rhoads, a prominent Philadelphia banker who had succeeded Herbert Welsh as president of the Indian Rights Association. Rhoads initially turned down the invitation and recommended instead J. Henry Scattergood, treasurer of Haverford and Bryn Mawr colleges and another long-term member of the

Indian Rights Association. Scattergood hesitated, and in the end the two
men accepted what amounted to a joint commissionership with Rhoads as
commissioner and Scattergood as assistant commissioner but in fact a coordinated team.

Universal enthusiasm greeted the appointments. Even John Collier spoke
of "the coming of day" and noted that "each of these new men is a revolutionary type from the standpoint of the Indian Bureau old-guard." Collier
and the American Indian Defense Association expected to have a substantial part in the new regime. The officers of the association in December
1929, in fact, drew up an agenda of reform measures that they thought the
Indian Office would accept, and they hoped to be the effective right hand of
the administration in researching the topics, drawing up bills and briefs,
and lobbying for the measures in Congress. Their list comprised the following items:

1. The California Indian Plan for sharing responsibility for Indian
   affairs with the states.
2. An arts and crafts marketing corporation.
3. Amendment of allotment laws.
4. Revision of methods of handling tribal estates.
5. Cancellation of reimbursable debts owed by the Indians.
6. A special Indian claims commission.
7. Protection of Indian rights, tribal life, and culture.
8. Demobilization of Indian boarding schools.
9. Amendment of the Pueblo Lands Act, enlargement of the Navajo
   reservation, and distribution of responsibility for the New York
   Indians between the federal and state governments.
10. Protection of Indian water power sites.
11. Continuation of the Senate Indian investigation.

The new administration moved quickly to set a positive tone. Acting
upon the emergency recommendations of the Meriam Report, President
Hoover requested additional funds to supply adequate food and clothing for
pupils in the Indian schools, both through deficiency appropriations for the
remainder of fiscal year 1930 and through a $3.1-million augmentation in
the budget for 1931. Meanwhile Rhoads, with Wilbur's formal approval,
sent four letters to the committees on Indian affairs in Congress, outlining
legislation that would significantly reform the administration of Indian
affairs.

The first letter pointed to the heavy burden placed on the Indians by the
obligation to pay reimbursable loans on irrigation projects and to the serious problems with the allotment laws, by which inherited lands were sold
and the Indian landed estate inevitably lost. The second letter hit upon the
problem of the tribally held resources, the "indivisible tribal estates of the

Indians." Rhoads noted the mineral and oil deposits, power sites, timber stands, grazing lands, and unallotted agricultural lands of the southwestern Indians. Under existing law, he said, "the Government through the Interior Department, is charged with the direct and highly paternalistic administration of these properties, and unless existing law be changed it may well be that the Government 100 years from now will find itself still charged with this responsibility and still maintaining the paternalistic administration." Rhoads urged incorporation of the tribes in a way that would enable them, instead of the government, to manage the estates. A third proposal concerned tribal claims, and Rhoads recommended a special Indian claims commission that "should hear all causes, those that are human and moral as well as those that are legal and equitable." Rhoads's final letter dealt with Indian irrigation projects; he described the problems of financing them and the influx of white lessees or owners, and he suggested transferring the projects to the Bureau of Reclamation.

The proposals offered a farsighted and statesmanlike approach to problems of long standing and placed before Congress significant suggestions for study and for legislation. Collier called them "epoch making announcements concerning Indian law" and "the most adequate statement, official or unofficial, ever made, dealing with those phases of the Indian problem which are more baffling and more insistent than any others."

On many fronts, the new administrators of Indian affairs made important progress. Congress authorized added appropriations to provide adequate food and clothing for Indian students, and in time it accepted Rhoads's recommendations in regard to the reimbursable debts that were weighing so heavily upon the Indians and stifling their economic development. The most significant advance, however, was in the field of Indian education, for the Rhoads-Scattergood administration made a determined effort to change the Indian school system into one that would suit the background and needs of the Indians. The goals were clearly set forth by the commissioners in 1931: "The purpose of education for any indigenous peoples at the present day is to help these peoples, both as groups and as individuals, to adjust themselves to modern life, protecting and preserving as much of their own ways of living as possible, and capitalizing their economic and cultural resources for their own benefit and their contribution to modern civilization."

This philosophy of education reflected the influence of the man appointed director of Indian education on August 19, 1930, W. Carson Ryan, Jr. A professor of education at Swarthmore College and an ardent proponent of progressive education, Ryan had been the education specialist on the Meriam survey team, and in his deliberate manner he began slowly to implement changes that had been called for in the Meriam Report. Ryan sought a true community school system, directed toward the needs of the whole reservation population. These needs were essentially rural, and he adapted the curriculum to them. The uniform course of study that had been one of the pillars of the Indian school system, in its attempt to turn the Indians into white citizens, was discarded by Ryan. Courses that did not fit the Indian children's background and experience were gradually eliminated, and special courses adapted to Indian culture were introduced, with appropriate concern for the great diversity in these cultures from region to region. To aid in reaching these goals, decentralization of the school service was encouraged. No longer was everything to depend on the central Indian Office in Washington.

A corollary of this decentralization was the move toward state control of Indian education. More and more Indian children were enrolled in public schools, and the number of contracts with boards of education increased. Practical vocational training adapted to the localities in which the schools were situated was another abiding concern of Ryan's, and though progress was slow, he was able in 1932 to secure a position in the Indian Office for a director of vocational guidance. Ryan hoped gradually to eliminate the government boarding schools, which he considered a major obstacle to a program of local community schools.

The schools improved markedly in management, and they became less like prisons or reform schools. At the same time, the heavy labor that had made boarding school life drudgery for many students was reduced, and care was taken to see that the youngest students were not subjected to boarding school routine. Finally, sincere efforts were made to improve standards for teachers and other Indian school personnel. An academic degree was required for principals of the government schools, and salary increases enabled higher standards to be set for newly hired persons, even though the "old guard" long impeded the development of the new point of view in Indian education that Ryan fostered.

Ryan himself was a realist and did not expect to accomplish the impossible. He divided the Indians into two groups. For the first, the largely mixed-blood and acculturated Indians, he encouraged rapid commingling with the rest of the population and attendance at public schools; for them he had little hope of preserving aboriginal culture. It was with the second group, the Indians of the Southwest, that he thought opportunity lay. "Our task here," he said, "is to help the Indians to capitalize to the full their contribution and to educate the rest of the United States to an intelligent rather than a merely sentimental appreciation of the value of this contribution." This was a philosophy well in accord with John Collier's views, and in fact, when Collier became commissioner of Indian affairs in 1933, Ryan stayed on as director of Indian education for another two and a half years.

The programs for Indian health urged by the Meriam Report were advanced by Rhoads and Scattergood. Appropriations for public health purposes increased, and all the indicators (number of public health nurses, salaries for health service personnel, examinations for trachoma, hospital facilities, hospitalization for victims of tuberculosis, and live births in hospitals) showed marked improvement.

Yet the Rhoads-Scattergood administration did not bring the total reform that early expectations had indicated. One of the failures was the matter of irrigation. Although Rhoads had clearly delineated the problem in December 1929 and had suggested as a remedy the transfer of Indian irrigation projects to the Reclamation Bureau, Congress refused to take that action, and the commissioners and the secretary of the interior were willing to let things ride without a determined fight. Similarly, no significant action was taken to establish federal-state cooperation in Indian affairs, which had been an objective of Wilbur in phasing out federal domination of Indian lives.

A signal failure, especially from the standpoint of the Collier forces, was the inability or unwillingness of Rhoads and Scattergood to gain legislation to promote Indian arts and crafts. Appreciation of Indian artistic work had slowly increased from the beginning of the century, and white artists and literary figures became enamored of Indian art; government officials, too, began to see the wisdom of preserving aspects of the Indians' cultural heritage. The Committee of One Hundred in 1924 spoke favorably of incorporating into the life of the nation "the genius of the Indians in music, literature, and the decorative arts," and the Meriam Report recommended both a program to secure marketable handcrafted products and the organization of a market. The advent of the Hoover administration raised high hopes among promoters of Indian arts and crafts, and John Collier began a campaign for a comprehensive marketing plan, but Wilbur, Rhoads, and Scattergood did nothing to push the measure, and such inaction became for Collier an indication of the incompetence of the administration.

John Collier had greeted Rhoads and Scattergood with great enthusiasm. Along with Lewis Meriam and others, he had been allowed to have a hand in formulating the plans and programs of the new commissioners. In January 1930 Collier declared that the new men were accomplishing their tasks "with success visibly increasing as each month goes by." Then, less than six months later, he was back in his old role as an aggressive and vocal critic of Indian Office administration. The new day that he had discerned in 1929 had turned out to be a "false dawn." He claimed now that the old guard in Congress and in the Indian service were "devouring the new commissioners." The proof was a list of failures to act vigorously in immediately implementing the program that had earlier looked so promising. Rhoads and Scattergood had buckled too easily in the face of opposition to new programs and policy changes.

Collier's attack on Rhoads was backed up by a letter sent to Secretary

Wilbur by Haven Emerson in the name of the American Indian Defense
Association on May 6, 1930. Emerson asserted that Rhoads and Scattergood had been in office for ten months but that their accomplishment had
been practically nothing. "They have not rectified the extreme abuses in
the treatment of the Indians," Emerson charged, "nor have they put into
effect a single constructive plan." Wilbur responded to the attack in a gen-
tlemanly fashion, pointing out that the commissioners worked under serious handicaps, for they had had no part in the construction of the current
budget, had to deal with civil service employees whom they had not appointed, and were obliged to operate under legislation that was not under
their control, and he praised them for success in getting additional funds
appropriated in the new budget. But he also charged that the American Indian Defense Association was taking up the valuable time of the department with petty matters and was turning the legislators against the Indian
Office.

Wilbur's reply did nothing to ease the situation, and throughout the rest
of his administration the secretary and his Indian commissioners were subjected to a continuing barrage of criticism emanating from the Collier
forces and their friends in Congress.

The conflict was unfortunate, for it obscured the good that had been done.
Much of what the Meriam Report had recommended was accomplished or
initiated under Rhoads and Scattergood. Their work was a substantial
move in the direction of the reform Collier demanded. Yet despite the advances in education, health care, and other benefits to the Indians, there
had been failure to change things very much on two fundamental points—
allotment with its consequence and tribal incorporation—and there had
been no success in getting an Indian claims commission, an arts and crafts
board, or a law promoting state cooperation. Rhoads and Scattergood tried
hard with good intentions, but they belonged to the old school. It would
soon be up to Collier to see what he could do when he was placed in the
position of responsibility that had been held by Rhoads and Scattergood.

JOHN COLLIER, COMMISSIONER

Franklin Delano Roosevelt appointed John Collier commissioner of Indian
affairs after considerable agitation in favor of alternate candidates. The
new secretary of the interior, Harold L. Ickes, persuaded Roosevelt that
Collier was the right man, and, in reply to a critic of the appointment, he
wrote of Collier:

> I do believe . . . that no one exceeds him in knowledge of Indian mat-
> ters or his sympathy with the point of view of the Indians them-

selves. I want some one in that office who is the advocate of the Indians. The whites can take care of themselves, but the Indians need some one to protect them from exploitation. I want a man who will respect their customs and have a sympathetic point of view with reference to their culture. I want the Indians to be helped to help themselves. John Collier, with whatever faults of temperament he may have, has to a higher degree than any one available for that office, the point of view towards the Indians that I want in the Commissioner of Indian Affairs.

Collier took office on April 21, 1933. It was now his chance to bring about the revolutionary change that he had long demanded. He began with great bursts of energy and created an enthusiasm and excitement among his staff matching that generated by President Roosevelt for the New Deal as a whole. "Even after twenty-four years," William Zimmerman, Jr., Collier's assistant commissioner, wrote in 1957, "it is easy to relive the first months of the new administration. There were endless meetings, inside and outside of working hours. . . . There was zest and fun in those meetings, but also always a sense of urgency, of fighting time, of doing things now, before it should be too late; but there was always a feeling of accomplishment." Collier assembled an eager and capable staff, and he depended, too, on the expert support of anthropologists, to whom he offered a part in determining the policies and programs of his administration. In all that he did he had the active support of Secretary Ickes.

Since his days in New York City, when he had worked for the People's Institute (an organization that provided evening lectures and forums for the city's immigrant masses), Collier had sought to develop communities in which cooperation would replace individual competition and where aesthetic values would be more important than material ones. He thought he had found such a utopia among the Pueblo Indians whom he visited in the early 1920s, and he hoped that he could promote among all the Indian tribes some sort of a Red Atlantis. This would mean a restoration of Indian culture, a return to Indian political autonomy, and communal ownership of land and resources instead of the individualism of allotment.

As Collier looked back upon his commissionership, he spoke about seven basic principles that had guided his administration of Indian affairs. They were his philosophy of reform:

1. "Indian societies must and can be discovered in their continuing existence, or regenerated, or set into being *de novo* and made use of."

2. "The Indian societies, whether ancient, regenerated or created anew, must be given status, responsibility and power."

3. "The land, held, used and cherished in the way the particular Indian group desires, is fundamental in any lifesaving program."

4. "Each and all of the freedoms should be extended to Indians, and in the most convincing and dramatic manner possible." Collier asked for "proclamation and enforcement of cultural liberty, religious liberty, and unimpeded relationships of the generations."

5. Positive means must be used to ensure freedom: credit, education (of a broad and technical sort), and grants of responsibility.

6. "The experience of responsible democracy, is, of all experience, the most therapeutic, the most disciplinary, the most dynamogenic and the most productive of efficiency. In this one affirmation, we, the workers who knew so well the diversity of the Indian situation and its recalcitrancy toward monistic programs, were prepared to be unreserved, absolute, even at the risk of blunders and of turmoil."

7. "The seventh principle I would call the first and the last: That research and then more research is essential to the program, that in the ethnic field research can be made a tool of action essential to all the other tools, indeed, that it ought to be the master tool."

This was the humane vision that guided Collier. Yet, despite the high-sounding rhetoric of Indian self-determination, it was a paternalistic program for the Indians, who were expected to accept it willy-nilly.

NEW DEAL MEASURES

Collier began with a dramatic attack upon the depression conditions that engulfed the Indian reservations. Following a suggestion that had been made in the Indian Office before he had become commissioner, he worked for a separate Indian Civilian Conservation Corps (originally entitled Emergency Conservation Work). He was strongly supported by Ickes, and President Roosevelt approved an Indian CCC following Ickes's suggestions. The Indian CCC operated on its own rules, and there was great flexibility in the nature of the camps. Besides the usual boarding camps for single men, the Indian program established camps for married men with families and in some cases operated the programs by transporting the enrollees each day from their own homes. Most of the projects dealt with soil erosion control, forestation, and range development, but dozens of other projects were instituted. Collier's goal was not the improvement of the public domain, toward which the parent organization was directed, but the conservation of reservation land and the training of Indians to make good use of it. In addition, especially after 1938, an enrollee program of training in practical industrial skills was a prominent part of the Indian program, and about 50,000 individuals took part in it.

On July 2, 1942, Congress abruptly ended the whole CCC program, but the program's effect upon the Indians was considerable. The relief of economic suffering was immediate, and the conservation and other constructive work on the reservations was extensive. Equally important was the effect of the camp life and its training programs on the Indians, who made use of the experience and skills obtained there as they went into military service or entered the general work force. But the long-term results did not meet Collier's expectations of rehabilitating the reservations and training the Indians to make better use of their resources as farmers, foresters, and ranchers.

The Indians benefited also from other New Deal agencies—like the Agricultural Adjustment Administration, the Federal Emergency Relief Administration, the Civil Works Administration, the Public Works Administration, and the Works Progress Administration—and their programs helped to lift the pall of despair that had spread over many reservations. Of course there were mistakes made in the hurriedly put together programs, many of which provided short-term relief without striking deeply at the long-term problem of Indian poverty, but both Ickes and Collier were justifiably proud of their record in conservation and relief. Ickes wrote to Roosevelt in December 1935 that the president had been "a real White Father to the Indians and they appreciated it deeply." He told Roosevelt that his administration would "go down in history as the most humane and far seeing with respect to the Indians that this country ever had."

The first legislative enactments of the Indian New Deal came quickly, for the way had been prepared for them in the previous administration. On May 31, 1933, a Pueblo Relief Act was approved. This was a measure for which reformers had fought for many years, and it corrected inadequacies in the compensation allowed by the Pueblo Lands Board. The drive to share responsibility with the states for Indian programs, which had been stopped by Congress in 1930 and 1932, was now successful. The Johnson-O'Malley Act of April 16, 1934, authorized the secretary of the interior to sign contracts with states for "the education, medical attention, agricultural assistance, and social welfare, including relief of distress, of Indians," and to expend under the contracts moneys appropriated by Congress for such purposes. Other legislation extended the Navajo reservation, a project that had long been afoot to eliminate the checkerboard nature of part of the tribal domain.

It was not necessary to wait for congressional action on many aspects of reform, for executive action by the president, the secretary of the interior, or the commissioner of Indian affairs could suffice. One such move, on May 25, 1933, abolished the Board of Indian Commissioners, which in the 1920s and early 1930s had sided with Burke and then Rhoads and Scattergood against the radical reformers' attacks. The board was a conservative

body, composed mostly of Republicans, who clung fast to the assimilationist views that Collier wanted to overturn. The president justified the abolition of the board on the basis of economy and the elimination of overlapping and duplication of effort, but the action was in fact a symbol of the
changing of the guard in the management of Indian affairs.

Collier also sought to reorient Indian land policy by reversing the allotment system, and he began with partial steps that were within his administrative competence. On August 12, 1933, he directed the superintendents
to stop the sale of trust or restricted Indian land, allotted or inherited, and
ordered them not to submit certificates of competency, patents in fee, or
requests for removal of restrictions on Indian property, except "in individual cases of great distress or other emergency."

Much more controversial were Collier's executive reforms dealing with
religion and with missionary work on the reservations. By a circular of
January 3, 1934, entitled "Indian Religious Freedom and Indian Culture,"
he demanded "the fullest constitutional liberty, in all matters affecting religion, conscience, and culture" for all Indians and that the employees in the
Indian service show an "affirmative, appreciative attitude toward Indian
cultural values." He directed unequivocally: "No interference with Indian
religious life or ceremonial expression will hereafter be tolerated. The cultural liberty of Indians is in all respects to be considered equal to that of
any non-Indian group." Moreover, Indian arts and crafts were to be "prized,
nourished and honored."

Religion was a sensitive subject. Many of the missionaries who had long
used the schools as the focus of their Christianizing efforts looked upon
Collier's moves to protect religious freedom for the Indians as a direct attack upon them, and there were cries of atheism and anti-religion. If Collier had his way, his critics feared, the Indians would all return to paganism.
Criticism of Collier was widespread in Protestant circles; many Indians,
too, having firmly accepted Christianity, were offended by Collier's actions.
But Collier held his ground and refused to give up the principles of religious liberty for the Indians that he had fought for since the early 1920s. He
flatly denied that he was an infidel or an atheist or that he was hostile to
missionary effort. But he did insist that Indians be granted "the fullest constitutional liberty, in all matters affecting religion, conscience and culture." Religious liberty, he said, does not extend only to Christians.

In addition to fighting for the Indians' rights of conscience, Collier intended to relieve the Indians of numerous restrictions that had built up on
the reservations through the decades. Many of these had been reasonable
answers to specific needs when they were introduced, but they made little
sense in the 1930s, at a time when the policy was to treat Indians like other
citizens. At the instigation of the commissioner, Congress in May 1934

abolished twelve sections in the *United States Code* that, among other things, authorized military activities on the reservations, required passports of foreigners entering the Indian country, prohibited seditious messages to Indians, and gave the commissioner power to remove persons from the reservations whom he considered detrimental to the welfare of the Indians.

THE WHEELER-HOWARD (INDIAN REORGANIZATION) ACT

Collier's great goal was legislation to reverse the allotment policy, which had not only had deleterious effects upon the Indian communities but symbolized the assimilationist philosophy with which he was at odds. To achieve his goal Collier prepared a bill, which was introduced in February 1934 by Senator Burton K. Wheeler of Montana and Representative Edgar Howard of Nebraska. It was a forty-eight-page document as a printed bill, and it embodied Collier's key proposals for revolutionizing Indian policy.

The original Wheeler-Howard bill had four sections. The first granted Indians the right to organize for local self-government and for economic activities. To those who wanted to take part, the secretary of the interior would grant a charter indicating their rights and responsibilities; then the secretary would give to the new corporation the powers of government and control of funds that federal law invested in him. Congress would create a revolving credit fund to aid in the economic development of the Indian communities. The second directed the promotion of the study of Indian civilization, including arts, crafts, and traditions, and support of this policy by special appropriations. The third abolished the allotment system, restored existing "surplus" lands to the tribe, and appropriated two million dollars a year for the purchase of new lands. The most controversial parts authorized the secretary of the interior to transfer individual land interests to the tribe "if, in his opinion, such transfer is necessary for the proper consolidation of Indian lands," and directed that at the death of an allottee the restricted lands would pass not to his heirs but to the chartered community or tribe. Finally, part four created a special court of Indian affairs, to be conducted according to Indian traditions, which would serve as a court of original jurisdiction for cases involving the Indian communities or their members.

Brief hearings on the bill were held by the Senate and House committees on Indian affairs in February 1934. From the first there was strong opposition to any policy of segregation or communal ownership of property. Because of this congressional hostility, and mindful of Indian criticism, Collier moved dramatically to lessen or eliminate the Indians' misunderstandings about the bill and to gain their support when Congress took up the bills again. He organized a series of Indian congresses, attended by tribal councils and business committees, superintendents and other reservation employees, and the commissioner, the assistant commissioner, and other staff members from the Washington office, at which the Wheeler-Howard bill was openly and thoroughly discussed so that misconceptions could be dispelled.

At the congresses, most of which Collier himself attended, large numbers of the Indians supported Collier, but at all the meetings objections were raised and at some open hostility broke out. There were fears about allotments held by individuals who wanted to keep them and about the proposals for self-government, and there was frequent suspicion about any changes in Indian policy. Indians voiced objections to a revival of tribal segregation, which would mean regression from the progress they had made. And rumors that the measure was communistic or socialistic were circulated, especially among the Oklahoma Indians.

Collier also met opposition at home. Although the National Association on Indian Affairs and the American Indian Defense Association supported his measure, the Indian Rights Association broke away. An article called, "Stop, Look—and Consider," in the March 1934 issue of *Indian Truth*, issued a stern warning against the bill. "It proposes revolutionary departures in Indian policy," the writer said. "It perpetuates segregation under the guise of self-government. It jeopardizes individual Indian property rights, and shifts the incentive which the authors of the Allotment Act had in mind for individual ownership of property leading toward citizenship. The policy is a reversal of the past."

Collier faced up to the criticism and the recommendations made at the Indian congresses, and he prepared more than thirty amendments to the bill. These looked to protection of individual allotments, which could not be transferred to communal control without consent, continued division of allotments among heirs if the land so divided could be used effectively, preservation of individual title to mineral resources, protection of Indian claims, and allowance for tribes to exclude themselves from the provisions of the bill by tribal referendum. Collier in the original bill had intended not only to end allotment but, as much as possible, to undo its evil effects by returning individually owned parcels of land to tribal ownership and also to prohibit the further inheritance of lands by providing that at the death of an Indian his land interests would revert to the tribe. This was more than many Indians and most of the old-line reformers could stomach, and in the amendments Collier wisely retreated to what he thought he could get enacted.

Even with his willingness to amend the bill to meet objections, Collier faced strong opposition in Congress. He sought the president's aid against the congressional opposition, and in letters to the chairmen of the Indian committees in Congress, April 28, 1934, Roosevelt called for an end to allotment and for the extension of self-government and political liberty to the Indians. The Wheeler-Howard bill, he said, would establish "a new standard of dealing between the Federal Government and its wards" and was "a measure of justice that is long overdue." Collier also took his plea to the public. In a radio address over the National Broadcasting Company on May 7, 1934, he told the American people that "the Indian wards of our Government, supported by President Roosevelt, are pleading before Congress for a chance to live." And he pinned the responsibility on all citizens to support "this supreme effort of the Indians and their friends to win for them freedom, to win for them the right to continue to exist."

The heavily amended bill, which excluded the Indians of Oklahoma from its provisions, became law on June 18, 1934. Collier got only half his cake, but it was far better than none and was in fact a substantial piece of legislation that ranked in importance with the laws of 1834 and the Dawes Act of 1887. And he was jubilant. "One becomes a little breathless," he exclaimed, "when one realizes that the Allotment Law—the agony and ruin of the Indians—has been repealed." He noted that any one of the parts of the law alone would have been an important change in government policy.

The first sections dealt with land: further allotment was prohibited, existing trust periods and restriction on alienation for Indian land were indefinitely extended, remaining surplus lands could be restored to tribal ownership by the secretary of the interior, individual allotments could be voluntarily transferred to tribal ownership, and the secretary was authorized to acquire additional lands for reservations (with an annual appropriation not to exceed $2 million). Collier rejoiced in these provisions, although they fell short of directing the consolidation of Indian lands checkerboarded with white holdings by the allotment process.

The law granted any Indian tribe the right to organize for its common welfare and to adopt appropriate constitution and bylaws, to be ratified by a majority vote of adult members of the tribe. Such an organized tribe would have powers to employ legal counsel, to prevent the sale or other disposition of tribal assets, and to negotiate with federal, state, and local governments. Moreover, the secretary of the interior could issue a charter of incorporation to the tribe, so that it could manage its own property. A revolving fund of $10 million was provided, from which the secretary of the interior could make loans to the corporations to promote economic development. The law in addition authorized the preferential appointment of qualified Indians to positions in the Indian service without regard to civil service laws, and it provided an annual appropriation of $250,000 for loans to Indian students in vocational and trade schools. Collier saw these measures as "spiritual rehabilitation." They would help to destroy the Indians' inferiority complex brought about by fifty years of individualization and arbitrary supervision of their affairs, by which "the Indians have been robbed of initiative, their spirit has been broken, their health undermined, and their native pride ground into the dust."

The law directed that the secretary of the interior make rules and regulations to operate Indian forests on the principle of sustained yield management, to restrict the number of livestock grazed on Indian ranges, and to prevent soil erosion and other deterioration of the ranges. It protected Indian claims or suits against the United States and declared that no expenditures under the act could be considered offsets against claims. Finally, the act directed that it would not apply to any reservation where a majority of the adult Indians, voting in a special election called by the secretary of the interior within a year after the approval of the act, voted to exclude themselves from its application. There was no provision at all for a special court of Indian affairs.

The Indian Office set out at once to put the act into operation. The first step was the referendums on the reservations by which the tribes voted to accept the act or to exclude themselves from its provisions. Within the two-year period from 1934 to 1936 in which votes were eventually allowed, 181 tribes (with a population of 129,750) accepted the law and 77 tribes (86,365 Indians) voted to reject it. Fourteen more groups came under the act because they did not hold elections to exclude themselves from its operation.

A heavy blow to Collier was the rejection of the act by the Navajos, the largest of the Indian tribes, who made up about half of the Indians who voted against its application. Under the leadership of Jacob C. Morgan, there was continuing opposition to Collier and his whole program among large numbers of Navajos. An especially sore point was the stock reduction program that the commissioner had instituted in an attempt to prevent the destruction of the Navajo range by overgrazing and resulting soil erosion. Collier was adamant on the need for reducing the number of sheep on the ranges, but his move appeared to many Indians to strike at their economic basis and well-being. Opponents of Collier were able to tie together stock reduction and the Indian Reorganization Act, although Collier denied there was any relation between the two. He in fact moved ahead with the Navajo stock reduction program, setting up land management districts with the designated maximum carrying capacity for livestock.

The vote to accept the Indian Reorganization Act by itself did no more than identify the tribes to which the legislation would be applied. The next step was to organize the tribes, for their economic development as well as their self-government depended upon the drawing up of constitutions, bylaws, and corporate charters. In March 1835 Collier sent a circular to those tribes that had expressed an interest in tribal organization under the new law and an outline for a tribal constitution and bylaws that indicated the points to be included. It was clear, however, that many tribes had not the slightest idea of what was involved in the process, and to direct this basic work Collier set up an Indian Organization Division within the bureau. Field representatives, field agents, and men on special detail were appointed to work with superintendents and the Indian tribal leaders in drafting and preparing the documents, and a "systematic educational campaign" was initiated to inform the Indians and to prepare them to vote intelligently on the acceptance of the documents.

The work was slow and difficult; but within ten years, ninety-three tribes, bands, and Indian communities had adopted constitutions and bylaws and seventy-three were granted charters. This was far from total acceptance of Collier's dream, but a new period in Indian relations with the government had begun, and the tribal councils became the basis for later developments in tribal autonomy.

Rounding Out
the New Deal

The Indian Reorganization Act, even though it was a weakened version of what John Collier had originally proposed, was the heart of New Deal Indian reform. The principles on which it was based—appreciation for Indian culture, concern for Indian self-determination and self-government, and a movement toward tribal economic activity—suffused all of what the Collier administration attempted and what it accomplished.

EXTENDING COLLIER'S PROGRAM

To Collier's dismay, large groups of Indians lay outside the full benefits of the Indian Reorganization Act, notably those of Alaska and Oklahoma, and he acted to correct that situation. By the Alaska Reorganization Act of May 1, 1936, Congress extended most of the Indian Reorganization Act to Alaska, excepting only sections that were largely inapplicable to the territory. Moreover, acknowledging the unique characteristics of Alaskan native life, Congress authorized adoption of constitutions and bylaws, incorporation, and credit loans for "groups of Indians in Alaska not heretofore recognized as bands or tribes but having a common bond of occupation, or association, or residence within a well-defined neighborhood, community or rural district."

To bring the Indians of Oklahoma under the Indian New Deal umbrella was a much more difficult problem than caring for the Alaska Natives, and Collier walked a rocky road in his relations with them. When the new commissioner visited the Indian regions in March 1934 to explain the Wheeler-Howard bill, he faced strong opposition in Oklahoma, where many allotted Indians did not want to return to a condition of tribal ownership and segregation from the white community. Most support of Collier's plans came from the tribes in western Oklahoma, for the Five Civilized Tribes in the eastern part of the state seemed too deeply integrated into white society to be concerned about tribal reorganization. It is likely, however, that Collier generated enough support so that the Oklahoma Indians as a whole would not have fought the amended bill that finally became law in June 1934; but Senator Elmer Thomas, without consulting the Indians of his state, managed to exclude them from the final act.

Collier considered the Oklahoma tribes "penalized" and deeply regretted that they did not come under the law, and in October 1934 he and Senator Thomas toured Oklahoma and held a series of conferences with the Indians to get their views and to propose the New Deal programs. The meetings were often a debate between Collier, who extolled the advantages of the Indian Reorganization Act, and Thomas, who criticized the law, but they also brought forward a variety of Indian opinions, and in the end it was clear that existing legislation was not satisfactory for Oklahoma.

Early in 1935 Collier, with Senator Thomas and Representative Will Rogers, the Oklahomans who chaired the Senate and House committees on Indian affairs, drew up a bill to fit the Oklahoma tribes. After considerable further modification, this Thomas-Rogers bill became law on June 26, 1936, as the Oklahoma Indian Welfare Act.

The law made no provision for continuing restrictions on Indian property and left heirship and probate matters in the hands of the state courts. But it did enable the Oklahoma Indians to participate in self-government, corporate organization, credit, and land purchase provisions similar to those of the Indian Reorganization Act. Moreover, any ten or more Indians residing "in convenient proximity to each other" could be granted a charter as a local cooperative association and draw upon a special loan fund of $2 million. A considerable number of Oklahoma tribes took advantage of the act to adopt constitutions and charters.

A distinct legislative victory for Collier's Indian New Deal was the passage of the Indian Arts and Crafts Act of 1935. The promotion of a marketing scheme for Indian products had long been one of Collier's goals, and when the new administration began, immediate steps were taken to combat the deleterious effects of the depressed economic condition on the production and sale of handcrafted articles. A committee appointed by Collier recommended the formation of a government agency to undertake market research, provide technical assistance, coordinate the activities of private and government agencies concerned, supply management personnel, create government marks of genuineness, and establish standards of quality. A bill following these recommendations became law on August 27, 1935.

The law created an Indian Arts and Crafts Board of five members appointed by the secretary of the interior. The work of the board was directed by René d'Harnoncourt, an Austrian who had gained experience with native arts in Mexico. He chose talented staff members and soon caught the enthusiastic attention of the public with remarkable displays of Indian art at the San Francisco Golden Gate International Exposition of 1939 and at the Museum of Modern Art in New York City in 1941. Meanwhile, the board worked to establish standards for Navajo weaving, silver and turquoise jewelry, and other products, to survey Indian arts and crafts production and possibilities, and to organize production and marketing units among various groups of Indians, from a wool spinning project among the Choctaws to wood carving among the Alaska Natives and leather glove making among the Coeur d'Alenes.

Resistance in Congress to appropriations for the Arts and Crafts Board hindered development of its work and at times threatened its very existence. Then the war, which brought a large exodus from reservations, cut seriously into handcraft production, even though demand was heightened by the cutting off of foreign products and the purchases by United States servicemen in Indian areas. Yet the board survived, and after World War II its work expanded, as did congressional support. Indian arts and crafts obtained a solid and continuing acceptance by government officials and, more important, by the general public, in considerable measure because of the work of the board.

EDUCATION AND HEALTH

Education was basic to Collier's Indian New Deal, even though the Wheeler-Howard Act did not directly touch Indian education, except for its support of special vocational training for Indians. There was, however, no dramatic change in educational policy or programs when Collier entered office, for the administration of Rhoads and Scattergood had already started on the road that Collier would follow. From his appointment by Rhoads in 1930 until his resignation in 1935, W. Carson Ryan worked toward continuity in the field of education. How well Ryan fitted in with Collier's overall philosophy of Indian administration can be seen in an address he gave in late 1935.

Behind the present program of Indian administration in the United States, and particularly Indian education, there is an assumption that is new with us and I believe is still relatively infrequent in the administration of native affairs generally—namely, that native life itself has values that urgently need to be maintained. The customary assumption of white superiority is abandoned in the new program, so far as it is humanly possible to do it. It is assumed that in all efforts carried on by the Government or other outside interests in behalf of Indians the purpose is to be helpful while interfering as little as possible with existing modes of life. Indian ways of doing things are considered to be right except as they are found, by the experience of members of the tribe or others unselfishly interested in their welfare, to be positively detrimental to the Indians or harmful to the rights of others.

Ryan was replaced by Willard W. Beatty, a national leader in progressive education, who continued the education ideas of Ryan—a program of cross-cultural education in which the curriculum and methods were to be adapted to the Indians and their environment and in which the children could develop according to their individual interests and abilities. In this he had the assistance and encouragement of the anthropologists whom Collier recruited for his staff.

The boarding schools, the symbol of the old ways with their separation of the Indian children from home and community and their emphasis on training for the white man's world, were attacked by Collier as they had been by Jones and Leupp and all their successors. In his first year in office ten boarding schools were either closed or turned into community schools. But the downward trend leveled off, and in 1941 there were still forty-nine boarding schools and about 14,500 Indians attending them.

The correlative of abolishing boarding schools was the establishment of community day schools, and here there was substantial progress. Between 1933 and 1941 the number of day schools rose from 132 to 226, and in 1941 the enrollment was 15,789. A great increase in the number of day schools came with construction under the Public Works Administration, and Ryan, Beatty, and Collier all put heavy emphasis on this element in Indian education.

While the Indian Office worked to fulfill its objectives in the federal boarding schools and day schools, it continued to promote the enrollment of Indian children in the state public schools. The Johnson-O'Malley Act of 1934 laid the legislative groundwork for contracts between the federal government and the states for the education of Indians, and before World War II contracts were signed with four states: California (1934), Washington (1935), Minnesota (1937), and Arizona (1938).

As Beatty and his staff moved toward special education for the Indians, however, they began to have doubts about how well the public schools could supply the curriculum that was deemed essential for Indian students and whether the attitudes toward Indians were conducive to good learning. The bureau had little means to correct the faults detected in the public school systems, and it came to regard its own schools as superior. Although

Beatty admitted that he probably had transferred more children from federal schools to the public schools than had any other official, he questioned the wisdom of pushing the policy too far. "I am convinced," he wrote, "that there is nothing in the administration and curriculum of the average rural public school that is better for children than what is offered by a Federal school." And he claimed that teachers in the Indian service were better trained than those in many small rural public schools and that they were more carefully supervised. Many Indian parents, too, preferred the government schools, because they supplied lunches and clothing for the children.

World War II exerted a powerful influence on Indian education. The war budget dramatically cut back the appropriations for the Indian service, many of the teachers and other school employees left the Indian schools for military service or more lucrative war jobs, and thousands of Indians left school to fight or to work in industry. The war, in fact, was a great dividing line. It brought many Indians into close contact with white society for the first time and impressed upon them the need of education, which they demanded for themselves and for their children at the end of the war. And, as employment opportunities shifted during the war and postwar years, Indian schools, still under Beatty's direction, changed their emphasis from cross-cultural education and vocational training to suit the Indians' rural community needs to training young Indians for urban society and assimilation into the mainstream.

Another serious concern of the Indian New Deal was Indian health. As a critic of health conditions on Indian reservations during the 1920s and early 1930s, Collier had dramatized the tragic state of Indian health and charged the Indian Office with serious neglect. But as commissioner he found that it was not easy to find the funds needed for the reforms he had so facilely demanded before. After two years in office he praised the health service for its quality but admitted that it was "quantitatively, very much insufficient." The Indian mortality rate was 50 percent higher than that of whites, Indian morbidity rates were extremely high in various categories, and the tuberculosis rate was still seven times that of the general population.

Year by year Collier combined reports of progress with a cry that much more needed to be done. Tuberculosis rates remained far above the national average, and in 1942 the director of Indian health services declared that "tuberculosis is still the great Indian-killer." Dental facilities remained woefully short, and sanitation still needed much improvement.

The one important breakthrough came in the treatment of trachoma, which, with tuberculosis, had been the great scourge of the Indian schools and reservations. Cooperative research work carried on by Indian medical service physicians and Columbia University staff determined in 1936 that trachoma was caused by a virus, and in 1938 a report was made to the meeting of the American Medical Association on the findings and on successful treatment of the disease with sulfanilamide. The Indian service introduced sulfanilamide treatment generally in 1939, and trachoma incidence among the Indians dropped from 30 percent to 5 percent in 1943.

World War II had a deleterious effect on the Indian medical service, for it created a critical shortage of personnel. On January 1, 1944, there were 73 vacancies for full-time physicians, 27 for part-time physicians, and 188 for nurses. Employment of local persons on a temporary basis was sometimes possible, but no more than essential emergency services could be provided. After the war health conditions remained far from ideal, with scandalously high morbidity and mortality rates.

ECONOMIC DEVELOPMENT

Collier's plans for self-government and community development rested on a foundation of economic well-being for the Indians. Although the Indian Civilian Conservation Corps and other emergency relief projects eliminated much of the critical unemployment and debilitation that came with the depression, the Indian service was continuously concerned with the long-term economic development of the Indian reservations. At the end of the New Deal period these reservations comprised some fifty-six million acres of land, of which about seven million acres were agricultural, more than sixteen million acres were forests, and about thirty-two million acres were open grazing land. Because much of the Indian land was in arid or semi-arid regions, agriculture to a large extent depended upon irrigation. Thus, the administration of irrigation, forestry, and grazing formed a substantial part of Indian service activity.

Collier turned quickly to irrigation problems, moving first to cancel unjust and uncollectible reimbursable debts. Secretary Ickes made use of an act of 1932, which authorized the adjustment or elimination of reimbursable debts, to cancel more than $2 million of debt during the first year of the New Deal. Thus began a process that by 1936 had canceled over $12 million of debt, much of it for irrigation projects. Then Collier created the Irrigation Division to locate and develop supplies of water that would actually be used by the Indians themselves in the cultivation of their lands. After that came new construction on irrigation projects under the CCC and under the Public Works Administration.

The forestry activities of the Indian service were directed toward the preservation of the forests through scientific management and their utilization for maximum economic and social benefit to the Indians. Unlike forests in the public domain, which could be governed strictly by technical considerations, the Indian forests, Collier insisted, required a more flexible management, which would "take cognizance of the general Indian problem and be coordinated with the whole Indian service program of social and economic betterment."

Another major work of the Indian New Deal was proper range management, to control grazing on the Indian reservations with the corollary objective of soil conservation by controlling erosion. The work was complicated by the checkerboard pattern of many allotted reservations that made range control difficult if not impossible. By a special leasing system the Indian Office had some success in organizing solid units for range control, and the Indian CCC was instrumental in initiating much soil conservation work. The Indian service also cooperated closely with the Soil Conservation Service of the Department of Agriculture.

One ubiquitous activity on the reservations was road construction, which began in earnest with the Indian CCC and a $4 million allotment from Public Works Administration funds in August 1933. The PWA grant like the CCC work fulfilled two immediate ends, the employment of destitute Indians and the provision of badly needed roads on the reservations. The building of roads and their year-round upkeep were especially essential if the day school program of the Indian Office was to work, for transportation of the children by school buses was a necessary part of the plan. Similarly, the road system made possible increased medical service to isolated parts of the reservations. The roads, in fact, aided all manner of reservation activity, and Collier was careful to see that they were built for practical purposes of the Indians and not to satisfy tourist interests in Indians and Indian culture.

The multifarious activities of the Indian Office under the New Deal were notably different from those in previous decades in the amount of cooperation established between the bureau and other federal agencies; this brought a degree of decentralization that had never before existed. Where in the past there had been cooperation, it had been only between the bureau and the other agencies. Now some of these units—Soil Conservation Service, Farm Security Administration, Social Security Board, National Youth Administration, Public Works Administration, and Works Progress Administration—had direct contact with the Indians. Moreover, the Indian service received help from the General Land Office and the Federal Power Commission and continued to work with the Department of Agriculture and the Public Health Service. Thus, the monopoly over Indian affairs once held by the Indian Office was broken. From another viewpoint, the Indian Office now had available a great range of skills and expert knowledge that it could never have acquired as an isolated bureau. And, of course, the move-ment to transfer responsibilities to the newly formed tribal governments and corporations, and to state governments in certain areas, further decen-tralized the government's management of Indian affairs.

JOHN COLLIER'S TRAVAIL

After a period of enthusiasm and success in getting reform measures en-acted, John Collier ran into increasing opposition. The attacks on the origi-nal Wheeler-Howard bill that he had met from Indians, reform groups, and Congress forced him to curtail much of his reform plan, yet in many ways he marched bravely ahead as though nothing had happened. The goals of reasserting Indian cultural patterns, Indian self-determination, and Indian self-government, deliberately cut back by Congress in the Indian Reorgani-zation Act, remained the guiding principles of Collier's activity, which he promoted through administrative means when legislative ones failed. He thus left himself open to continuing charges that he sought a revival of tribalism, segregation of the Indians from white society, and a slowing down if not an absolute halt in the drive for assimilation.

In the first four years Collier succeeded to a large extent in overcoming opposition, and he got his program enacted, at least in amended form. But in 1935 and 1936 a case against the Collier administration slowly built up. Those who lost out in the battle over the Wheeler-Howard Act regrouped their forces and renewed the fight. Moreover, many local interests were af-fected as the new policies were put into operation, especially as land ac-quisition was pushed, and these interests joined the growing opposition. From 1937 to 1945 Collier was a man besieged.

One vocal group that kept Collier in trouble was the missionaries, who would not drop the issue of his stand on freedom of religion for the Indians. When the strong statement on promotion of Indian culture was eliminated from the Indian Reorganization Act, criticism of Collier was temporarily moderated, but it soon flared up again. In addition there was opposition from strong elements in the Indian Rights Association. Jacob C. Morgan, Collier's Navajo critic, received considerable support from the association, which took up his views against the stock reduction program and the re-organization of the tribal council.

More insistent and more aggressive in its attack on Collier and all his works was the American Indian Federation, a small but outspoken Indian group led by an Oklahoma Creek named Joseph Bruner and his dynamic lieutenant, Alice Lee Jemison, a Seneca activist. Organized in 1934, the group attracted a variety of dissidents who objected to Collier's program.

*

The platform of the federation was clear: free the Indians immediately from their status of wardship under the guardianship of the Indian Office, turn over to the states the services for Indians, remove Collier from office because he did not represent the Indian people and was an atheist and Communist, and repeal the Indian Reorganization Act, which had been drawn up by the Communist-dominated American Civil Liberties Union and which turned the Indians away from American citizenship.

Collier dismissed the federation as a very small group of Indians who spoke for nobody but themselves and who attracted all sorts of right-wing radicals and drew support from American Nazi sympathizers like the German-American Bund. Unfortunately for Collier, however, the federation's charges were given repeated and to some extent sympathetic hearing by the congressional committees on Indian affairs.

At first the attacks on Collier did little more than stir up misgivings about his competence as commissioner, but as time passed his program was seriously endangered. The appropriations authorized for land purchase and for organization were never fully provided, and in 1937 Collier suffered the first major blow to his proposals when the House refused to pass the Indian Claims Commission bill that had been passed by the Senate and favorably reported by the House Committee on Indian Affairs.

Collier suffered severely at the hands of the Senate Committee on Indian Affairs, which prepared two devastating reports, based to a large extent on the ideas of the American Indian Federation. The first of these came in connection with a bill to repeal the Indian Reorganization Act. The committee's report of August 2, 1939, charged that the Indian Office had spent large sums in promoting the Indian Reorganization Act and discriminated against Indians who opposed it, that individual rights and private property of Indians were being destroyed and the Indians forced back into a communal status, that primitive tribalism was being promoted, that the Indian Reorganization Act actually resulted in increased power for federal administrators and continued wardship status instead of moving the Indians toward full citizenship, and that Collier by administrative measures was putting into operation elements of the original Wheeler-Howard bill that had been explicitly eliminated by Congress. The committee, however, rewrote the bill so that it did not call for outright repeal of the Indian Reorganization Act but provided for the exemption of more than seventy tribes from its provisions. In this modified form it passed the Senate on February 19, 1940.

The House Committee on Indian Affairs, which held its own extensive hearing on the bill in June 1940, acted in a more balanced way and gave Collier ample opportunity to strike back. This he did, pointing especially to the Nazi connections of the American Indian Federation and accusing it of being a "fifth column" movement. The House committee submitted its own amended bill, which had Collier's approval. The House version substituted a provision to allow new tribal elections for exclusion from the operation of the Indian Reorganization Act when one-third of the adult Indians petitioned for such an election, and provisions, as well, for rescinding action on constitutions and charters. In this form it passed the House in August 1940, but the fundamental difference between the two versions made it impossible for the conference committee to come up with a compromise acceptable to both houses, and the measure died.

A second Senate report came from the investigating subcommittee, which on June 11, 1943, issued *Senate Report* no. 310. The earlier debates had to a large extent dissipated the charges of atheism and communism and discredited the radicals who had made them, but fundamental criticisms of Collier and his program remained, and they were the substance of the Senate report. They touched the basic question of whether the Indian New Deal was moving the Indians toward real self-sufficiency, which would mean the end of federal guardianship and absorption into the mass of the nation's citizenry, or whether the bureau was instead building up and perpetuating itself, continuing its guardianship as the Indians returned to tribalism and their old ways.

Collier believed that the only way the Indians could adjust to the dominant white society was through group processes, not individual ones, and that adaptation should come from free choice on the part of the Indians working within their own traditions and not be imposed from without. The Senate committee reflected quite an opposite viewpoint, and in a series of thirty-three recommendations it proposed elimination of bureau staff, cutting of funds, transfer of nearly all bureau services to other agencies or their complete elimination, the end of federal trusteeship over individual Indian lands and the end of any kind of wardship, the closing out of individual Indian money accounts, and the per capita distribution of all trust funds. To have carried out these recommendations would nearly have abolished the Office of Indian Affairs altogether.

A corollary to *Senate Report* no. 310 came from a special House investigating committee directed by Representative Karl E. Mundt of South Dakota. Although it made no radical and sweeping proposals such as those of the Senate committee, the Mundt committee offered a critical appraisal of the Indian Bureau's operations. The goal espoused by the committee for the Indian—"to take his place in the white man's community on the white man's level and with the white man's opportunity and security status"—it found to be slowed down by inadequate economic and educational opportunities, inadequate guidance for adult Indians, and lack of proper laws and regulations regarding claims, heirship lands, and the freeing of competent

Indians for full citizenship. The tone of the report was distinctly assimilationist. In terms reminiscent of Thomas Jefferson Morgan in the 1890s,
it said:

> The goal of Indian education should be to make the Indian child a
> better American rather than to equip him simply to be a better In-
> dian. The goal of our whole Indian program should be, in the opinion
> of your committee, to develop better Indian Americans rather than to
> perpetuate and develop better American Indians. The present Indian
> education program tends to operate too much in the direction of per-
> petuating the Indians as a special-status individual rather than pre-
> paring him for independent citizenship.

The Mundt report was hardly an endorsement of Collier's administration,
but it stopped far short of the radical proposal of the Senate that the bureau
be destroyed.

Collier's combat with the House and Senate committees on Indian affairs was disturbing, for it resulted from attacks upon his character and
upon the vision he had for the Indians' future, but the attacks were for the
most part driven back. But the key to the government's programs was the
appropriations made for them by Congress, and here Collier encountered
great setbacks.

The antagonism of the powerful chairman of the House Appropriations
Subcommittee on Interior Department Appropriations, Jed Johnson of
Oklahoma, was a great obstacle for Collier. Johnson was an archfoe of the
commissioner and the bureau, and he seemed to take special delight in
Collier's discomfiture. It was finally Johnson's subcommittee that triggered
Collier's resignation, for Johnson indicated that the appropriations for the
bureau would be severely cut for 1946 unless there was a new commissioner. Collier sent a letter of resignation to President Roosevelt on January
19, 1945, in time for a successor to appear at the appropriation hearings for
the new year.

THE INDIANS AND WORLD WAR II

Direct participation of Indians in the war and in wartime activities far exceeded what might have been expected. In spite of the long history of conflict between whites and Indians and of the Indians' dissatisfaction with
the treatment they had often received at the hand of the federal government, the Indian response to the war was almost uniformly positive. Even
before Pearl Harbor, many Indians became involved in the war effort. Because all Indians were citizens of the United States, they were subject to
Selective Service. They registered for the draft without any serious resis-

tance, although some thought the draft impinged upon their rights as "sovereign" nations. Large numbers of Indians volunteered for military service, and others were inducted through National Guard units. By mid-1943 there were 18,000 Indians in military service. As of April 1, 1944, there were 21,756 Indians, exclusive of officers, in the fighting forces. These men and women served in all the battle zones of the world, and the number who received battlefield citations was impressive.

Military service was only part of the Indians' role, for thousands worked in war industries, where they made use of skills acquired in the vocational training of the boarding schools or in the Indian Civilian Conservation Corps. The Indian Office in 1945 reported that more than 40,000 Indians had left the reservations for war work. Meanwhile those at home devoted their energies toward aiding the war effort. Collier noted that there was a "continual recasting of the functions of the [Indian] Service," and that much of its time and effort was devoted to problems that arose directly from the war.

The great drive that Collier had conducted for the rejuvenation of Indian culture and for Indian self-government was halted as Congress cut appropriations for nonwar activities and as the great exodus of field employees to the armed services and to war industries occurred. Educational and medical services were curtailed by the shortage of personnel, and Collier asserted in 1942 that personnel administration had suffered "the worst year, perhaps of all times." A final blow was the move of the Indian Office from Washington to Chicago in the summer of 1942 to make room in the capital for more essential war activities. Exiled from the center of government, the bureau found it difficult to keep up its coordinated efforts with other agencies of the federal government, on which services to the Indians increasingly had come to depend.

The impact of the wartime experience on the Indians was immeasurable, for the war suddenly threw thousands of reservation Indians into the midst of white society and greatly accelerated the movement toward assimilation. An anthropologist who interviewed Navajo and Pueblo veterans in the summer of 1946 asserted that the war had "exerted a great impact on the cultures of these peoples, perhaps the greatest since the arrival of the Spaniards four hundred years ago." A large part of the impact was the freedom of association and action that the Indians enjoyed in the military service, which contrasted with the regulations and discrimination they encountered when they returned home. And the higher standard of living that war incomes had brought meant that a return to old reservation ways would not satisfy many of the veterans and war industry workers.

THE LEGACY OF THE INDIAN NEW DEAL

John Collier was an effective publicist, and he wanted everyone to believe—
as no doubt he himself believed—that the Indian New Deal had been a resounding success. A harder look will reveal that Collier's dream fell short
of realization. The Indian Reorganization Act, which was the key to his
policy and programs, was not only in its very inception a truncated version
of what Collier had in mind for the regeneration of Indian communities,
but the implementation of the act was flawed. Collier's vision of a return to
communal life and government was not accepted by all the Indians; for
many of them the transition to an individualized life intermingled in white
society had progressed too far for them to turn back. Moreover, even the
Indians who voted to accept the act's provisions did not all adopt constitutions, and even fewer organized economically under corporate charters.
The goal of reestablishing the old land base was not met because of the
refusal of Congress to sanction the compulsory return of allotments or
heirship lands to communal ownership and its failure to appropriate the
large funds envisaged for the purchase of additional lands.

The most telling failures came in the organization of the Indian groups.
Collier in a sense imposed upon the Indians a *tribal* government and a
tribal economy, when traditional Indian ways often called rather for organization on a smaller basis of bands or villages. And the paraphernalia of
electoral districts, tribal councils, and majority vote all fitted better an
Anglo-Saxon conception of democratic government than the systems that
many Indians were accustomed to. Collier's overriding concern for sound
economic development of the Indian reservations demanded a total reservation and tribal approach, whereas the community development so much
talked about called for less universal conformity. Thus factionalization of
the tribes, a phenomenon long antedating white interference in Indian
matters, was seriously aggravated by the very measures that Collier intended should solidify the tribal communities. The charge was made again
and again, with some justification, that Collier was as paternalistic as any
of his predecessors—perhaps even more so—and that the Indian Bureau
had a tighter hold on Indian affairs and interfered more in them than ever
before.

Yet Collier's positive mark on Indian affairs was indelible. If nothing
else, the allotment of land was stopped, reversing a key element in previous
Indian policy. The conservation and rehabilitation of the land and other resources on the reservations was greatly forwarded by the soil erosion control programs, the sustained-yield forestry policy, and roads and irrigation
projects that flourished in the early years of the New Deal. The credit facilities of the Indian Reorganization Act had positive results, although they
were short of what Collier wanted, and the preferential hiring of In-

dians aided Indian employment and changed the composition of the Indian service.

The assimilationist movement that Collier had fought so vigorously in the 1920s and again in the last years of his tenure as commissioner and which appeared to triumph when he left office could never return to its status in the Dawes Act era. The acceptance and encouragement of Indian culture that Collier had promoted left a mark, not only in the white mind, but most especially among the Indians, in reviving a pride in their heritage and an interest in preserving and, if need be, rediscovering their culture.

The tribal councils, whatever their faults, were a fact of life. They furnished a focus for tribal dealings with the federal government and added an element to reservation life and development that was a giant step beyond the autocratic agents or superintendents with their unlimited authority, who had been targets of criticism from the late nineteenth century on. Although traditionalists among some of the tribes would come to ridicule the tribal governments established under the Indian Reorganization Act as puppets of the Bureau of Indian Affairs and deny that they truly represented the Indians, the councils and their elected tribal chairmen became a continuing and powerful force in Indian affairs. The emphasis of the Indian New Deal on tribal government made possible the perpetuation of the concept of tribal sovereignty that at a later date would play a dominant role in relations between the Indians and white society.

The Indian New Deal also, in indirect ways, stimulated pan-Indian developments. The congresses that Collier held to promote the Wheeler-Howard bill had pan-Indian overtones, and Joseph Bruner's American Indian Federation, despite its bizarre character, brought together disparate Indian individuals to combat Collier's programs. The renewed role of tribal governments created a group of Indian leaders who frequently realized their common interests in dealing with the United States government, and in 1944 a group of Indians, including many tribal leaders, organized the National Congress of American Indians, an important agency in promoting Indian interests on the national level.

It is obvious now that the great dream Collier had for regenerated Indian communities and acceptance of Indian culture as a positive contribution to American life never became a total reality. He had to compromise and fight off attacks. He was so firm in his convictions of what was right for the Indians that he sometimes imposed conformity or manipulated the Indians to behave in ways that he thought best. He fell far short of reforming the nation on the model of Indian communities. Yet, in balance, John Collier was the most important figure in the history of American Indian policy. Just as the nation could never turn back from the reforms of Roosevelt's New Deal, so Indian affairs, in subtle if not in overt ways, exist in a situation that is the legacy of Collier and the Indian New Deal.

CHAPTER 23

The Termination Era

The assimilation of Indians as individuals into the mainstream of American society, promoted so strenuously by congressional and other opponents of John Collier, had long been a dominant principle in United States Indian policy. Collier's crusade to reverse that position and stress instead group self-determination and the preservation and restoration of Indian culture was looked upon by many as an aberration. After Collier left office in 1945 and his strong supporter Harold Ickes resigned as secretary of the interior in 1946, the executive branch of the government joined the Congress in a massive drive to assimilate the Indians once and for all and thus to end the responsibility of the federal government for Indian affairs.

The rhetoric of the new age was varied. There was talk of *freeing* or *emancipating* the Indians from a status that bound them by special laws and regulations and placing them instead on an absolutely equal footing with white citizens. The other side of the coin was *withdrawal* or *termination* of federal responsibility and federal programs for Indian groups and Indian individuals. At one time the Bureau of Indian Affairs preferred the word *readjustment*, in an attempt to avoid words that had developed emotional overtones. But overall, it was *termination* that best described the movement, and the word came to be used not only of the government's responsibilities toward the Indians but of the Indians themselves. It became common, thus, to speak of terminated Indians and tribes.

Although termination came to be thought of as a single principle that lined up promoters against opponents, in fact there were many ambiguities. The repeal of discriminatory legislation was sought by Indians and their friends and was, in fact, a continuation of action inaugurated by Collier. Transfer of some services for Indians such as education, health, and welfare to other federal agencies or to the states had been an important ingredient of the Indian New Deal, as the Johnson-O'Malley Act of 1934 demonstrated. The concept of a special claims commission to handle Indian claims against the government, which was a part of Collier's program that he had failed to accomplish, became tied in with terminationist philosophy. *Freedom* and *emancipation* resonated with both Collier's policies of self-determination and the insistence of Indian New Deal critics like the American Indian Federation that the Indian Bureau be abolished. Thus there came together in the termination policy of the 1950s a good many threads of history, not only from the assimilationist era of the nineteenth and early twentieth centuries but from the reform movement of the 1920s and 1930s as well.

The years after Collier's departure from office were a period of transition to the new policy of federal withdrawal from Indian affairs. They were a time, too, of some confusion, for management of the Indian Bureau was in the hands of administrators whose actions contrasted sharply with the strong, purposeful leadership that Collier had provided. Vacillating between Collier's vision of Indian self-determination and the new principles of termination, the first two commissioners, William A. Brophy and John R. Nichols, left little mark on Indian affairs. Only when Dillon S. Myer became commissioner in 1950 did firm direction again appear, and by the end of this tenure in 1953 the bureau had been fully committed to termination.

The matter of Indian claims against the United States, however, still remained to be settled. Many tribes had grievances growing out of treaties or other contracts with the federal government, some of which were of long standing, and there was no expeditious way of coming to an equitable settlement. John Collier, as commissioner of Indian affairs, considered the claims a matter of high priority, and he and Secretary Ickes decided upon a *commission* rather than a *court*, for the former, it was believed, could solve the problems better than adversary proceedings inherent in a judicial format. Numerous bills for creating such an Indian claims commission were introduced between 1935 and 1945, but none was able to overcome the strong opposition of members of Congress, some of whom looked upon the measure as a raid upon the Treasury intended to benefit not the Indians but their lawyers. But at length, after lengthy deliberations, the Indian Claims Commission Act was approved on August 13, 1946.

The law provided for a commission of three persons (enlarged to five in 1967) to hear claims against the United States on behalf of "any Indian tribe, band, or other identifiable group of Indians residing within the territorial limits of the United States or Alaska." The classes of claims were broadly defined—from "claims in law or equity under the Constitution, laws, treaties of the United States, and Executive orders of the President," to "claims which would result if the treaties, contracts, and agreements between the claimant and the United States were revised on the grounds of fraud, duress, unconscionable consideration, mutual or unilateral mistake," and finally to "claims based upon fair and honorable dealings that are not recognized by any existing rule of law or equity."

No statute of limitations or laches would have effect, but the United States could use all other defenses, and in the determination of relief, deductions were to be made for payments made on the claims and other offsets, including "all money or property given to or funds expended gratuitously for the benefit of the claimant."

Although the filing of claims proceeded slowly at first, by the end of the five-year petition period the commission was overwhelmed. Nearly all of the 176 tribes or bands who were notified of the act filed one or more claims on old grievances; in the end there were 370 petitions, which were broken down into 617 dockets. The great majority of cases were land cases, which involved three stages: determining the claimant's title to the land (either *Indian title* based on continuous, exclusive occupation or *recognized title* based on some treaty or law), determining the value of the land and the amount of liability of the United States, and then determining gratuitous offsets to be subtracted from the government's liability. A second class of cases comprised cases concerned with fiduciary culpability on the part of the federal government in the management of Indian funds. The cases moved more slowly than the original act anticipated, and the life of the commission was repeatedly extended, until the commission finally went out of existence on September 30, 1978.

The work of the Indian Claims Commission was a mixture of positive results and substantial failure. The Indians had their day in court, and the very establishment of the commission indicated a strong willingness on the part of the United States to admit injustice toward the Indians in the past and to make amends. The total awards of more than $818 million meant a sizable injection of money into the Indian tribal economies, even though the lasting effects of the sum were not great, for many tribes insisted on per capita payments instead of investing the funds in tribal enterprises. The presentation of the cases before the commission greatly heightened the legal consciousness of the Indian communities, many of which became accustomed to hiring legal counsel for their affairs. Moreover, the heavy reliance on expert witnesses, which was necessary in determining the land cases, resulted in a new awareness of documentary sources on the Indians' past and established cooperation between anthropologists and historians that results in an extensive and continuing interest in ethnohistory.

But on a more fundamental level the Indian Claims Commission did not fulfill its purpose, for it did not bring the finality in the settlement of all claims that its framers had wanted. In some ways Indian grievances seemed to be heightened instead of diffused as the commission went about its work. The legalistic approach that developed, with rigorous appraisals of what the Indian lands were worth at the time of cession, and the concern of the United States attorneys to ferret out all gratuitous offsets, for example, often caused bitterness, and in the end the awards were smaller than the Indians had expected. Then, as the commission's work stretched out into the 1950s, it coincided with the congressional drive to terminate federal responsibility for the Indians. The settlement of claims thus appeared to be, not a bold stroke to correct all past injustices, but simply a necessary preliminary step toward termination.

Finally, the only remedy following the commission's decisions was monetary settlement, whereas more and more Indians insisted that they did not want money but the return of their lands. Indian agitation in the 1960s and 1970s—both from federally recognized tribes that had used the commission's machinery and from others, chiefly eastern tribes, that had been excluded—and the increasing number of legal cases drawn up by Indians seeking to right old wrongs made a mockery of the promise that the Indian Claims Commission would settle grievances once and for all.

Preparation for formal termination can be said to have begun with testimony of the acting commissioner of Indian affairs, William Zimmerman, Jr., on February 8, 1947, before the Senate Committee on Civil Service. Zimmerman spoke of decreasing the number of Indians to whom the expensive services of the bureau were provided, and he offered three lists of tribes. The first group, he said, could be denied federal services immediately; the second could function with minimal federal supervision within ten years; the third would need more than ten years to prepare for withdrawal of bureau support. The categories had been determined according to the degree of acculturation of the tribe, the economic condition of the tribe, its willingness to dispense with federal aid, and the willingness and ability of the state in which a tribe lived to assume the responsibilities dropped by the federal government. In addition to the lists and criteria, Zimmerman presented three specimen bills, for the Klamath, Osage, and Menominee tribes, groups that he thought would be suitable for beginning the withdrawal process.

It was not Zimmerman's aim to prepare a blueprint for termination, and he later insisted that his testimony before the committee had been "repeatedly misquoted and misinterpreted." But, whatever Zimmerman's disclaimers, the Interior Department and the Bureau of Indian Affairs came to preach a moderate form of terminationism. The bureau, in fact, took definite steps toward planning for the withdrawal of federal responsibility for the Indians.

This policy of termination and assimilation was reinforced in 1948 by

344 The Termination Era

the report of the Commission on Organization of the Executive Branch of the Government (the Hoover Commission). The commission's special task force on Indian affairs asserted in its report that "assimilation must be the dominant goal of public policy," that in fact there was no other choice. "The basis for historic Indian culture has been swept away," it said. "Traditional tribal organization was smashed a generation ago. Americans of Indian descent who are still thought of as 'Indian' are a handful of people, not three-tenths of one percent of the total population. Assimilation cannot be prevented. The only questions are: What kind of assimilation, and how fast?" The full commission picked up and endorsed the task force's position as "the keystone of the organization and of the activities of the Federal Government in the field of Indian affairs." It recommended complete integration of the Indians into the mass of the population as taxpaying citizens, and until that could occur it wanted the social programs for Indians to be transferred to the state governments, thus diminishing the activities of the Bureau of Indian Affairs. Tribal governments, it thought, should be regarded as a stage in the transition from federal tutelage to full participation in state and local government.

THE APPROACH OF TERMINATION

Dillon S. Myer, who became commissioner of Indian affairs on May 5, 1950, pushed vigorously for termination, and, although there were no laws terminating Indian tribes during his term, the movement in the direction of withdrawal of federal responsibility for Indians was pronounced. To make clear his position, Myer made a standing offer to the Indians "to work constructively with any tribe which wishes to assume either full control or a greater degree of control over its own affairs."

An important part of the planning for ultimate termination of the Indian tribes was to survey conditions existing on the various reservations. Whether Zimmerman's criteria or others were to be used, detailed information geared to answer questions about the readiness of tribes to be set free was necessary, and study and planning blossomed into a full-blown activity. Myer insisted that the programming for withdrawal be a cooperative effort with Indian leaders, but in the end he declared that the bureau must proceed even if Indian cooperation was lacking.

Myer's forthright promotion of federal withdrawal drew violent criticism from Indians and from whites sympathetic to the Indian New Deal. Fundamental differences, indeed, existed between Myer and his critics. The Association on American Indian Affairs, which was in the forefront of the attack on the new policies, sought a way out of the dilemma of freedom or protection by drawing a sharp distinction between wardship and trusteeship. *Wardship* it defined as restriction on personal freedom of action, a remnant of paternalism; *trusteeship*, on the other hand, did not touch the person of the Indian or his personal freedom as a citizen, but was a necessary means of protecting Indian property. It set up a trustee-beneficiary relation in which the trustee was the servant of the trust beneficiary. The critics of termination were adamant in demanding the continued protection of Indian property by the trusteeship provision—which the termination bills almost universally sought to end.

Myer saw that the distinction was not as sharp as his critics supposed. He asserted, "You cannot have trusteeship without paternalism and practically all the paternalism which you find in the Indian Bureau program stems directly from our trusteeship responsibilities." In his view, therefore, the only way to end the paternalism of wardship or guardianship was to eliminate the trusteeship. Thus was the issue joined.

The movement toward termination was accompanied by a reorganization of the Bureau of Indian Affairs, for the increasing work of the Washington office of the bureau called for decentralization. In September 1949 the secretary of the interior established eleven area offices, at the following cities:

Juneau, Alaska	Albuquerque, New Mexico
Phoenix, Arizona	Anadarko, Oklahoma
Window Rock, Arizona	Muskogee, Oklahoma
Sacramento, California	Portland, Oregon
Minneapolis, Minnesota	Aberdeen, South Dakota
Billings, Montana	

Under the area offices were the agencies, boarding schools, hospitals and sanatoriums, and irrigation projects. In addition to the area offices, there were ten detached field offices: Seminole Agency, Haskell Institute, Choctaw Agency, Carson Indian Agency, Western Shoshone Agency, New York Agency, Cherokee Agency, Chilocco School, Osage Agency, and Intermountain School.

The new organization, if it was to work effectively, needed firm administrative direction, and that was provided by Dillon Myer. By reducing the division directors in Washington to staff officers, he concentrated administrative decision in his own hands, and by giving substantial authority to the area directors, who would play a key role in termination activities, he strengthened the move toward withdrawal. Officials below the area level lost many of their responsibilities. The changes not only tightened the machinery of the bureau, with centralized power in the hands of the commissioner, but they eliminated to a large extent residual Collier influence among the division heads and among the field superintendents.

In all the controversies of his administration, Myer had fought back, explaining his positions to his superiors and rebutting the statements of critics in public statements of his own. But the critics had done their work too well. President Dwight D. Eisenhower, on taking office, asked for Myer's resignation, and the commissioner left office on March 20, 1953.

CONGRESSIONAL ACTION

The eight years of Eisenhower's administration were the high point of termination. Building on the policy that had evolved under President Truman and on the planning and programming of Commissioner Myer, Congress in 1953 formally endorsed the policy of termination and in succeeding years enacted laws to withdraw federal supervision from a number of small Indian groups and from two major tribes, the Menominee Indians of Wisconsin and the Klamath Indians of Oregon.

The effective drive for termination came from within Congress, but it was the work of a few men, for Indian affairs were not a major interest of the legislators. The standing committees on Indian affairs, which had played such an important role in the past, were eliminated by the Legislative Reorganization Act of 1946, and Indian matters were referred to the Committee on Public Lands (later called the Committee on Interior and Insular Affairs) in the House and in the Senate. These committees were dominated by westerners, and the subcommittees on Indian affairs pretty much had their way; what they proposed was accepted by the full committees and by the houses without much question or debate. And the subcommittees were chaired and dominated by ardent terminationists:.Senator Arthur V. Watkins of Utah and Representative E. Y. Berry of South Dakota. It was Watkins above all who directed the termination impulse.

Congress committed itself to rapid termination of the Indian tribes by House Concurrent Resolution no. 108, adopted on August 1, 1953. The measure declared that "it is the policy of Congress, as rapidly as possible, to make the Indians within the territorial limits of the United States subject to the same laws and entitled to the same privileges and responsibilities as are applicable to other citizens of the United States, to end their status as wards of the United States and to grant them all of the rights and prerogatives pertaining to American citizenship." It was the sense of Congress, it then declared, that specific Indians and Indian groups "should be freed from Federal supervision and control and from all disabilities and limitations specially applicable to Indians" at the earliest possible time: that is, Indians within the states of California, Florida, New York, and Texas; the Flathead, Klamath, Menominee, and Potawatomi tribes, and the Chippewa Indians of the Turtle Mountain Reservation. All offices of the

Bureau of Indian Affairs serving the affected states and tribes should be abolished.

While awaiting specific legislative proposals for termination, Congress moved ahead with another significant withdrawal measure, approved on August 15, 1953, which came to be known simply as Public Law 280. It provided that for all the Indian country within the states of California, Minnesota, Nebraska, Oregon, and Wisconsin (except for the Red Lake Reservation in Minnesota, the Warm Springs Reservation in Oregon, and the Menominee Reservation in Wisconsin) jurisdiction over criminal offenses and civil causes would rest with the states; the criminal laws of the state would have the same force on Indian reservations that they had elsewhere in the state. Besides specifying the five states in the act, the legislation in section 7 provided that any other state could similarly assume jurisdiction over Indian reservations by its own legislative action. This section caused great concern to Indian groups, for it raised the pertinent question of consent by Indian tribes to such state assumption of jurisdiction.

Two other measures were approved on August 15, 1953, that were part of the drive to repeal legislation setting Indians apart from other citizens. One of these ended at last the long history of prohibition against the sale of liquor to Indians off the reservations and legalized the introduction of alcoholic beverages into the Indian country by the tribes on a local option basis. The second law repealed discriminatory laws of long standing that forbade the sale of firearms or ammunition to Indians, prohibited Indians from selling or trading guns or traps, farming implements, cooking utensils, and clothing, and restricted the sale of livestock by Indians.

In response to House Concurrent Resolution no. 108 the Bureau of Indian Affairs drafted termination legislation for a number of tribes. The proposed bills had common features, which included provisions for drawing up a final tribal roll, for dividing tribal property rights among the enrolled members, and for transfer to individual Indians of their trust property. Tribes could choose to manage tribal property themselves or place it in the hands of a private trustee. The bills specified a time, from two to five years, within which final termination was to be accomplished.

The great rush to legislate termination came in 1954. The Menominees and Klamaths led the list, followed shortly by a group of small tribes in western Oregon, the Alabama-Coushatta Indians of Texas, and the Ute and Paiute Indians of Utah. Then the movement slowed, as the Democratic victories in the 1956 election changed the membership of congressional committees and as opposition mounted and deep problems in the process came to be realized. Later legislation was sporadic and touched relatively small groups without cohesive tribal organization or large land holdings (see Table 1).

TABLE I: Termination Acts

Indian Group	State	Population	Acres	Date of Act	Effective Date
Menominee	Wisconsin	3,270	233,881	June 17, 1954	1961
Klamath	Oregon	2,133	862,662	Aug. 13, 1954	1961
Western Oregon (61 tribes and bands)	Oregon	2,081	3,158	Aug. 13, 1954	1956
Alabama-Coushatta	Texas	450	3,200	Aug. 23, 1954	1955
Mixed-blood Ute	Utah	490	211,430	Aug. 27, 1954	1961
Southern Paiute	Utah	232	42,839	Sept. 1, 1954	1957
Wyandotte	Oklahoma	1,157	94	Aug. 1, 1956	1959
Peoria	Oklahoma	640	0	Aug. 2, 1956	1959
Ottawa	Oklahoma	630	0	Aug. 3, 1956	1959
California Rancherias	California	1,107	4,315	Aug. 18, 1958	1961–70
Catawba	South Carolina	631	3,388	Sept. 21, 1959	1962
Ponca	Nebraska	442	834	Sept. 5, 1962	1966
		13,263	1,365,801		

SOURCE: Data from Theodore W. Taylor, *The States and Their Indian Citizens* (Washington: Bureau of Indian Affairs, 1972), p. 180; Charles F. Wilkinson and Eric R. Biggs, "Evolution of the Termination Policy," *American Indian Law Review* 5, no. 1 (1977): 151.

The Menominee Tribe was the most noted case of termination. Its members were literate in English and appeared to be acculturated to white ways, and its forestry and lumber mill operations provided employment for a large proportion of the tribe. As an Indian tribe under federal trusteeship and exempt from taxation and federal and state regulations and licensing, the Menominees presented a picture of moderate prosperity. They were thus on all the lists of tribes to be terminated immediately.

A Menominee termination bill became law on June 17, 1954, with the effective date of termination set at December 31, 1958. Under its terms, the Menominees were directed to draw up a termination plan, which was to be submitted to the secretary of the interior by December 31, 1957. It soon became clear, however, that the tribe did not have the resources or time to accomplish the necessary planning. The state of Wisconsin created a Menominee Indian Study Committee to assist, and the tribe petitioned Congress for more time and for financial support of the planning activities.

On October 31, 1959, the Menominee tribe and the Department of the

Interior finally agreed upon a plan. A business corporation would hold title to and manage the tribe's property, and, according to an earlier tribal referendum, the reservation would be established as a separate county in Wisconsin, rather than be joined to an existing county or counties. There was one more attempt to gain a long delay in termination, but Congress granted only a four-month extension; on April 30, 1961, the property of the tribe held in trust by the federal government was transferred to a tribal corporation, Menominee Enterprises, Inc., and the individual Menominees were no longer entitled to any services provided for Indians and were subject to the laws of the state of Wisconsin.

Menominee County, the least populated and poorest of Wisconsin's seventy-two counties, was in trouble from the start, for the Indians were not prepared to accept a place in the white man's competitive world. Their cultural values differed markedly from those of their white neighbors, however much of a superficial resemblance there might be in dress, language, and education. The apparently healthy economy of the reservation depended upon props which were pulled out with federal withdrawal, and the tribal government, dominated by a small group, was not accepted by the whole tribe as a representative decision-making body. The factional opposition to the council and then to the tribal corporation obstructed effective development. No sooner was termination accomplished than agitation grew for overturning it and restoring the Menominees to reservation status.

The Klamath Indians' experience was similar to that of the Menominees. A tribe of some two thousand members living on a reservation in southern Oregon that was rich in timber resources, the Klamaths were pegged for quick termination. The tribe was sharply factionalized, however, and the division became aggravated when the federal movement toward termination began. One group sought to hold the traditional homelands together; the other urged immediate liquidation of the tribal estate and distribution of the proceeds in per capita payments. But even the anti-termination party was badgered by government officials into the conviction that a move was inevitable.

The Klamath termination act of August 13, 1954, did not satisfy either of the tribal factions, for the four years it allowed for preparation was too long a delay for one and far short of the fifteen years that the other wanted as a transition period. Many of the Indians did not understand the full import of termination and were unprepared for the social and economic shock that it would bring. Yet the government was caught in a test of its policy, and a repeal of the law would look like a reversal of the whole termination policy.

Then the conservation of the Klamath forests became a major concern. The Interior Department acknowledged that the indiscriminate sale of the

Klamath forests would result in accelerated cutting and cause "serious injury to the economy of the entire Klamath Basin"; but the original law of 1954 emphasized private property rights and omitted requirements for continued sustained-yield management of the forests. The evils that would result both to the conservation of the forests and to the local economy by the dumping of massive amounts of timber on the market were not lost upon the people of Oregon. Agitation soon began for amendment of the law and in some circles for its outright repeal. In August 1957 Congress extended the termination date to August 1960 so that the forest problems could be worked out, and a year later guaranteed that the Klamath forests would be sold as sustained-yield units and at fair market prices.

Under the termination law the individual Klamaths could vote whether to withdraw from the tribe and receive pro rata shares of the tribal assets or to remain in the tribe under a tribal management plan. In a tribal election of 1958, 1,659 tribal members voted to withdraw, whereas only 474 (either by voting to remain or not voting at all) became part of the nonwithdrawing group. Thus, about 77 percent of the Klamaths elected to receive a per capita payment (amounting to about $43,700) for their share of the tribal property, and most of the nearly one million acres of the reservation had to be sold in order to provide the money. The property of the remaining members, including about 145,000 acres of forest lands, was committed to the United States National Bank of Portland as trustee for these Indians. Most of the land sold went to the federal government for use as national forest or wildlife refuge.

The Klamath Indian Reservation was gone and the Klamath Tribe effectively destroyed. The sequel showed again the problems that termination brought to a tribe. Many of the Indians who withdrew were incompetent to manage their own assets, and arrangements were made with local banks to act as trustees, thus in effect transferring the trusteeship responsibilities from the federal government to private agencies. Others lost their money, and poverty and social disorganization resulted. The positive effects envisaged by Senator Watkins and other terminationists did not materialize.

The absolute termination of Indian tribes, which was so eagerly promoted in Congress and which seemed to have become the settled policy of the United States, slowly ground to a halt. From the very beginning, the complete withdrawal of federal responsibility for the tribes had met opposition from Indian groups and Indian welfare organizations. As termination moved into full gear and the Menominee and Klamath developments became well known, the outcry against termination became too loud to ignore. The National Congress of American Indians led the fight for the Indians, and tribal and individual Indian protests flowed into Congress. Journals of opinion were full of criticism of the talk of "liberating" the Indians.

Such sentiments were matched by new voices in Congress after 1956, as liberals began to speak out against the termination policy and to propose massive economic development for the reservations as an alternative to termination. States and localities in which the Indians lived, moreover, began to have second thoughts about the wisdom of termination and the benefits it might bring to them.

The Department of the Interior, too, pulled back. Fred A. Seaton, who was appointed secretary of the interior in June 1956, declared in a speech at Flagstaff, Arizona, on September 18, 1958: "No Indian tribe or group should end its relationship with the Federal Government unless such tribe or group has clearly demonstrated—first, that it understands the plan under which such a program would go forward, and second, that the tribe or group affected concurs in and supports the plan proposed." It was unthinkable, Seaton insisted, that a termination plan should be forced upon any Indian tribe, and he declared that it would be "incredible, even criminal" to send any tribe out into the mainstream of American life until it was properly educated to shoulder the new responsibilities.

In reality, the coercive termination policy of Senator Watkins and his supporters, with its total withdrawal of federal support, had a short life. The Indians in the terminated groups numbered 13,263 out of an estimated tribal Indian population of 400,000, or not much more than 3 percent of federally recognized Indians. The 1,365,801 acres of trust land withdrawn amounted to about 3 percent of the approximately 43,000,000 acres held in trust in 1953.

The psychological effects on all Indians, however, were enormous, for fear of termination filled the air. Opposition to the policy became a rallying point for Indian groups, and it unified Indian voices in a new and remarkable way. *Termination* became a hated word, and all government proposals on Indian matters were scrutinized with a new alertness, lest they be secret steps toward federal withdrawal.

PROGRAMS FOR INDIANS

The absolute withdrawal of federal responsibility that was the fate of the Menominees, Klamaths, and other tribes falling under Watkins's program, however, was not the whole story of the termination era, for Indian development—in education, health, and economic resources—was an abiding goal. Programs in these areas were part of a continuing story that antedated termination and extended far beyond it, and they were promoted by groups interested in Indian welfare whether they favored federal withdrawal or opposed it. Yet these programs also had strong tinges of terminationist philosophy, for by enabling Indians and Indian groups to stand more firmly on their own feet and by transferring activities away from the Bureau of Indian Affairs, the programs looked toward the elimination of the traditional federal responsibility for Indians.

In education there was continuity, for Willard Beatty stayed on as director of Indian education when Collier resigned. But Beatty faced changes that World War II had brought. Returning veterans of the armed forces and workers from war jobs carried back to the reservations a new respect and desire for education. More important, the ideal of educating to preserve Indian community patterns, which had been so strongly promoted under the New Deal, gave way now to an emphasis on preparation to succeed in the white man's world. Beatty changed with the times.

The federal Indian day school concept suffered heavily, and the movement away from boarding schools toward community day schools was stopped. A new appreciation of the boarding schools arose, both for acculturation of the young Indians and for vocational training to fit those who were approaching adulthood for jobs off the reservation. In 1946 the commissioner of Indian affairs reported an increase in boarding school attendance, both on and off the reservations, over the previous year, while day school attendance remained stationary. By 1952 there were 16,865 enrollments in federal day schools and 19,549 in boarding schools; in 1960 the comparable figures were 16,025 and 21,352.

The move toward enrollment of Indian children in the regular public schools of the state, which had begun early in the century, did not slacken. It was in fact an important part of the new drive to get the government out of the Indian business as quickly as possible, for education was a heavy part of the government's Indian responsibilities. By 1956 there were no longer any federal Indian schools in Michigan, Washington, Minnesota, Idaho, Nebraska, or Wyoming, states in which the government had once been involved.

The transfer of a large part of the Indian educational program to the states (58.6 percent attended public schools in 1956) resulted in a considerable differentiation between Indian students in the public schools and those who were in federal schools. Those in the public schools were largely mixed-bloods, whereas the reservation boarding schools and especially the day schools were heavy with full-bloods. In 1956, 83 percent of the students in the federal schools were full-blooded Indians and only 3 percent were less than half-blood. There was a close correlation between achievement on the standard tests and the degree of Indian blood, which in turn reflected the acculturation of Indian homes to the English language and white ways. A sizable number of students in the boarding schools were from broken homes or came from undesirable social and economic conditions at home.

High school education, which had barely begun for Indians in the 1920s, had by the 1950s become a recognized part of the formal school system, especially in the public schools and in off-reservation boarding schools. Whereas in 1924 only one federal Indian school offered twelve grades of instruction, in 1934 there were a dozen, and ten years later there were thirty-seven high schools. By 1956 there were 5,406 Indians in government high schools. Increasing attention now came to be paid, also, to higher education for Indians. Congress in 1957 provided seventy thousand dollars for grants to Indians in college, tribal funds were set aside, and there were special grants available from colleges and universities and from private organizations.

Health problems, like educational ones, were enduring among the Indians. The reduction of critical personnel in the Indian health services that came during World War II aggravated an already serious situation, and the government in the postwar years struggled to improve conditions. Year by year there was some progress as the morbidity and mortality rates dropped slightly and as more and more Indians made use of medical facilities. Yet these causes of optimism could not conceal radically deficient health care for the Indians. It was frequently declared that health conditions among the Indians were comparable to those among the general population half a century earlier. The great medical advances that had cut diseases and lengthened life expectancy for the white population still had not reached the Indians.

The only way to improve conditions seemed to be to transfer responsibility for Indian health out of the Bureau of Indian Affairs in the Department of the Interior to the Public Health Service in the Department of Health, Education, and Welfare. After much debate, that move was authorized by a law of August 5, 1954. All functions and responsibilities of the Bureau of Indian Affairs and the Department of the Interior relating to "the maintenance and operation of hospital and health facilities for Indians," and the conservation of the health of Indians" were given to the surgeon general of the United States Public Health Service, effective July 1, 1955. The transfer affected thirty-six hundred employees and property valued at $40 million. There were 970 buildings in thirteen states and the Territory of Alaska, including 56 hospitals, 21 health centers, and 13 boarding school infirmaries, plus numerous field clinics.

With the transfer came an increase in appropriations, which permitted hiring more staff and extending services, and statistics on the Indians continued to show both increasing use of medical facilities and a slow decline in morbidity and mortality. The Public Health Service announced in 1957: "The gains of the past two or three years may be small in relation to the ultimate objective of this program, but they are clear indications that the goals in Indian health in time will be achieved." Yet there was no sudden solution to the social and economic basis upon which ultimately the good health of the Indian population rested.

That the education, health, and general welfare of the Indians depended upon economic development was well understood, and continuing efforts were made to shore up the economic basis of Indian existence. The goal, as in the past, was to make the Indians self-supporting at a level of well-being comparable to that of the non-Indian population. But now there was a new urgency, for successful withdrawal of federal responsibility for the Indians was premised upon conditions under which they could stand on their own like other citizens without special federal aid.

The problems were many and serious. The war had obstructed development of the reservations, and some of the gains made in earlier decades were lost as irrigation projects and roads, for example, were allowed to deteriorate. Increasing Indian population aggravated the problem because it made the disparity between the number of Indians on a reservation and the economic resources available for their support greater than ever before. Yet Indian expectations, especially among those who had been relatively prosperous during the war, had risen.

In 1950 Congress authorized $88.5 million for a ten-year rehabilitation program for the Navajo and Hopi Indians, which made possible such projects as soil and water conservation, irrigation projects, development of industrial and business enterprises, off-reservation employment, relocation of Navajos and Hopis on the Colorado River Reservation, roads and communication systems, hospital and school construction, housing, and surveys of natural resources. Commissioner Glenn L. Emmons, who had replaced Myer in 1953, reported considerable economic activity on all the reservations. One of his pet schemes was industrial development in the vicinity of reservations as a solution to the economic problems of the Indians. Beginning in 1956, he persuaded some companies to open plants near reservations, and he issued encouraging reports of success, but in reality the effect upon the total problem was negligible.

New attempts at the end of the 1950s to strengthen Indian economic development by something similar to the Point 4 Programs applied to underdeveloped areas of the world ran into unsurmountable obstacles in Congress. The Eisenhower administration thus ended without the massive attack against poverty on Indian reservations that was so obviously needed.

RELOCATION

In the decade of the 1950s the federal government promoted an active policy of "relocating" Indians, that is, moving them from overcrowded reservations to urban areas, where employment possibilities might be better.

Relocation was a corollary of termination. It was directly related to the movement for better general education, more vocational training, adult education, and economic development plans, and it was another avenue for federal withdrawal from the Indian business.

Beginning with placement programs for the Navajos and Hopis in 1948 and skeletal operations in the Aberdeen, Billings, Minneapolis, Muskogee, and Portland areas in 1950, the Bureau of Indian Affairs provided staffs to facilitate off-reservation employment. The placement personnel worked with Indians and Indian organizations to stimulate interest in seeking employment, to educate Indians for adjustment to the new life, and to assist them in using established employment agencies. On the other side, it assisted employer groups and employment agencies to recruit Indian workers.

Year by year the program expanded, and the bureau shifted away from the placement activities for finding temporary jobs—work that it left to local employment agencies—to permanent relocation programs. In January 1952 the bureau initiated financial assistance to aid the resettling Indians. Bureau relocation offices opened in the major cities in which the Indians sought employment, and in 1954 the bureau assisted 2,163 Indians, including 1,649 in over four hundred family groups and 514 unattached men and women. Three hundred more left the reservations without assistance to join relatives or friends already in the cities.

The number of relocation field offices grew or declined according to employment opportunities for the Indians. The first offices were in Chicago and Los Angeles; in 1956 there were also offices in Denver and San Francisco; in 1957 San Jose and St. Louis were added; and in 1958 the number had expanded to twelve by the addition of Joliet, Waukegan, Oakland, Cincinnati, Cleveland, and Dallas. Then a decline set in as the number of jobs in some cities decreased. By 1960 only eight cities remained, four of them in California (Los Angeles, San Francisco, Oakland, and San Jose) and four others across the country (Chicago, Cleveland, Denver, and Dallas). Considering the total Indian population in cities by 1960, roughly 166,000, the 33,466 reservation Indians who took part in the government's relocation program was comparatively small.

As the work of relocation proceeded, the Bureau of Indian Affairs realized that finding employment for the Indians in the cities was only part of the problem and not the most difficult. The major concern was adjustment of the Indians to their new environment: securing housing, acquiring information about community facilities, and gaining acceptance from the urban communities into which they moved. In 1953 the bureau estimated that one-third of the Indians relocated returned to the reservations—persons who "found the adjustment to new working and living conditions more difficult than anticipated."

The problems that Indians faced in the new urban environment, with resultant unemployment, slum living, and alcoholism for many of them, led to cries of criticism and outrage against the government's relocation program, even though the program touched only a minority of Indians who migrated to cities. There is no doubt that the federal government only slowly realized the magnitude of the problem, since it saw its obligations as limited largely to Indians residing on trust or restricted lands. As the Indians moved out of the reservations, they presumably would disappear into the general population and no longer be of concern to the government. But the Indians did not so quickly adjust to their new homes. They kept their Indian identity and their place on tribal rolls, and many used the cities as only a temporary residence, still thinking of the reservations as their true home. There was a good deal of passing back and forth between reservation and city.

The Indian Bureau paid attention to the criticism, cutting back on the number of relocatees it aided in order to provide greater service over a longer period. Yet, like termination, the relocation program did not work as its promoters had hoped. The new administration that took office in 1961 would have to find new and better solutions.

CHAPTER 24

A New Day for
the Indians

Termination, for all the turmoil and fear it caused in Indian communities, was a temporary departure from the movement toward Indian self-determination that began with John Collier's principles and programs in the 1930s. The strongly assimilationist doctrine preached by the terminationists, often in the deceptively attractive rhetoric of "freedom," was not acceptable in a society that had begun to appreciate, however dimly, the values of pluralism. The two decades of the 1960s and 1970s were a period of public interest in Indian affairs and of governmental activity that rivaled in significance the era of Indian removal, the humanitarian reform movement of the late nineteenth century, and the agitation for change that Collier and his followers had sparked in the 1920s. The guilt felt by white Americans for past injustices to the Indians was a powerful stimulus to widespread support of Indian claims, both in Congress and among the general public.

TURNABOUT IN THE 1960S

The decade of the 1960s brought a reorientation of United States Indian policy. As the administration of John F. Kennedy replaced that of Eisenhower, the policy of termination was shelved although it was not formally rejected by Congress and still caused great fear among the Indians. The drive for economic betterment for the Indians received top priority, and the idea that plans and progress for Indians must be the work of the Indians themselves gained new strength.

Kennedy, campaigning for the presidency in 1960, promised the Indians "a sharp break with the policies of the Republican Party," and he specifically declared: "There would be no change in treaty or contractual relationships without the consent of the tribes concerned. No steps would be taken by the Federal Government to impair the cultural heritage of any group." When he won the election, Kennedy appointed Representative Stewart L. Udall of Arizona secretary of the interior, and Udall intended to carry out the administration's promises. He had a deep interest in Indian affairs and even considered briefly being his own commissioner of Indian affairs. He talked in terms of "maximum development," not termination.

The decade opened with three notable examples of the new mood and outlook. The first was the publication in January 1961 of the summary report of the Commission on the Rights, Liberties, and Responsibilities of the American Indian, a private study group established by the Fund for the Republic in 1957. Its report was a strongly worded statement that programs for Indians should not be imposed from above but that they should always be based on the initiative and intelligent cooperation of the Indians themselves. It condemned the termination policy and legislation of the 1950s and declared: "For the government to act out of a sense of frustration and of haste to rid itself of the vexing questions involved in administering Indian affairs is bound to ensure failure."

A second event was the American Indian Chicago Conference, held at the University of Chicago in June 1961. The conference brought together more than 450 Indian delegates from ninety tribes for a week of discussion about problems and proposals. The meeting resulted in a formal Declaration of Indian Purpose, which called for abandonment of the termination policy, for broad educational progress to remove the disabilities that prevented Indians from making use of their own resources, and for a reorganization of the Bureau of Indian Affairs with a view toward more local control. It urged economic assistance to the tribes, with full Indian participation in developing programs. It addressed, as well, specific problems of health, welfare, housing, education, and law and jurisdiction.

The third report, and the most significant because it became the basis for official policy, was the report of the Task Force on Indian Affairs. Secretary Udall, shortly after his appointment, had established the task force to study Indian affairs and make recommendations to the new administration, and the group prepared a landmark report with suggestions for programs of development—of people and of resources. "What we are attempting to do for those in the underdeveloped areas of the world," it said, "we can and must also do for the Indians here at home. Furthermore, to insure the success of our endeavor, we must solicit the collaboration of those whom we hope to benefit—the Indians themselves. To do otherwise is contrary to the American concept of democracy." Specific recommendations were made in regard to industrial development, vocational training and placement, loan funds, protection of the rights of off-reservation Indians, land problems, and educational facilities.

Secretary Udall endorsed the report and appointed one of the task force members, Philleo Nash, to be commissioner of Indian affairs. Nash was deeply concerned about Indian welfare and Indian rights, and he won the respect of Indian groups and substantially lessened their fear and antagonism toward federal activity. He stressed above all the drive for economic development and self-sufficiency, and he began at once to promote industrial development on or near the reservations, working with tribal leaders, civic organizations, and industrial groups.

The programs and plans of the Bureau of Indian Affairs were significantly augmented by the attack on poverty in the United States that was initiated by President Kennedy and enthusiastically carried forward by President Lyndon B. Johnson. Johnson, in a special message to Congress on poverty, March 16, 1964, noted the great progress the United States had made, but he said: "We still have a long way to go. The distance which remains is the measure of the great unfinished work of our society. To finish that work I have called for a national war on poverty. Our objective: total victory." The president submitted with his message a detailed draft of legislation to accomplish the goal.

The Economic Opportunity Act, approved on August 20, 1964, was very much like the bill that Johnson had submitted. It was a sort of catch-all of programs proposed earlier, but it had unifying themes in its concentration on youth and on education and training. It stressed local initiative by encouraging or requiring the poor themselves to take an active part in planning and carrying out the programs of the war. Under six titles the act provided for youth programs, community action programs, rural assistance, small loans, work experience, and VISTA (Volunteers in Service to America).

Indians were quick to take advantage of the act. Tribal governments were an efficient mechanism for community action programs, and the tribal councils frequently designated themselves as community action agency boards. By June 30, 1968, there were sixty-three community action agencies serving 129 reservations, which had a total population of 312,000. They developed a wide variety of programs to combat poverty and created a large number of jobs to administer the programs. Altogether, however, the funding from the Office of Economic Opportunity was a very small part of total federal spending for Indians. In 1968 it amounted to about $35 million out of a total Indian budget of $448,393,000 (of which Bureau of Indian Affairs funds represented $249,719,000 and Indian Health Service $103,552,000).

Commissioner Nash worked effectively with bureau personnel and with the Indians, but he got along less well with Secretary Udall and with Congress. His work for long-term goals and his realization that there could be no dramatic changes in the Indians' situation did not satisfy Udall, who hoped for more radical reforms. Although Nash was largely responsible for reestablishing a sense of trust among the Indian people—without which no program for reservation development could work—he was eased out of office in March 1966.

The new commissioner was Robert L. Bennett, an Oneida Indian from Wisconsin and the first Indian to hold the office since Ely S. Parker nearly a century before. He continued the development programs of his predecessors, but he faced a continuing fear on the part of the Indians that any federal activity might lead to termination. The policy of turning over management of their own affairs to Indian groups—an obvious corollary of the emphasis on Indian leadership and participation—seemed to carry a threat of termination by undermining the trust relationship.

One example of the apprehension felt by the Indians was their reaction to the administration's proposed Indian Resources Development Act of 1967. Secretary Udall called the measure "the most important legislation proposed for American Indians since the Wheeler-Howard Act of 1934," and he testified strongly in its favor before the congressional committees. The bill was clearly intended to increase Indian self-sufficiency by providing for a loan guarantee and insurance fund, the issuance of federal charters to Indian tribes and groups to form corporations, and authority to issue tax-exempt bonds and to mortgage trust property. Indian objections to the bill, however, were strong. The Indians disliked the fact that approval was needed from the secretary of the interior for loans over sixty thousand dollars and objected to the provision for mortgaging tribal land. But mostly they feared that the bill would lead to termination. Because of such opposition the bill did not come out of committee.

That the Indians were intended to be part of America's "Great Society" was made clear by President Johnson on March 6, 1968, in his special message to Congress on the Indians. He proposed "a new goal for our Indian programs: a goal that ends the old debate about 'termination' of Indian programs and stresses self-determination; a goal that erases old attitudes of paternalism and promotes partnership self-help." Although he noted the responsibility of the nation toward the Indians, Johnson emphasized Indian leadership and initiative in solving Indian problems, and he listed specific proposals in regard to education, health and medical care, jobs and economic development, community services, civil rights, off-reservation Indians, and Alaska Native claims. To coordinate efforts for Indians, he created a National Council on Indian Opportunity, chaired by the vice president of the United States.

Bennett was greatly encouraged by the president's message, yet he was unable to overcome the Indians' fear of termination. And he saw many problems "of longstanding duration with little prospect of immediate solution."

THE STATE OF INDIAN EDUCATION

Educational development was always linked with economic development as an essential goal of federal Indian policy, and in fact economic self-sufficiency depended upon educational improvements. Until the level of education among the Indians was raised to that of non-Indian citizens, it was unlikely that the economic level could meet the goals set in the pronouncements of the president, the secretary of the interior, and the commissioner of Indian affairs.

Progress was made possible by new programs and new legislation. Beginning in 1960 remedial programs were established during the summer, and year by year more students (although only a fraction of those in need of such additional study) were attracted to the programs. A special American Institute for Indian Art was opened in Santa Fe in 1962. Amendments to the Elementary and Secondary Education Act of 1965, passed in 1966 and 1968, provided special funds for Indian education that were effectively used for remedial programs, recreational activities, and field trips. In February 1968 Congress increased the annual authorization for adult Indian vocational training from fifteen to twenty-five million dollars. Interest in cross-cultural education was revived, and renewed emphasis was put on teaching English as a second language to Indian children.

Moreover, the increasing concern about Indians' participation in the education of their children began to bear some small fruit. In 1967 a National Indian Education Advisory Committee, which included fifteen tribal leaders, was appointed by the commissioner of Indian affairs. Indian educators themselves organized a National Indian Education Association, which held its first meeting in November 1969. The small beginning of Indian membership on school boards and in parent-teacher associations was given a boost by President Johnson, who directed the establishment of Indian school boards for federal Indian schools. By May 1969, in accordance with this directive, 174 of the bureau's 222 schools (mostly in Alaska and on the Navajo Reservation) had selected such boards. The boards, however, were advisory only and did not control the schools.

Of special significance as a sign of the new direction was the establishment in 1966 of the Rough Rock Demonstration School on the Navajo Reservation, run on contract by the Indians. Rough Rock was a widely-noted experiment in Indian community control of education, and it was highly praised; but its abundant funding by the Bureau of Indian Affairs and the Office of Economic Opportunity (nearly twice the amount per pupil as at a regular boarding school) made it difficult to duplicate. Attempts to apply traditional educational norms and standards to this nontraditional school created unusual pressures. But other such schools, which made contracts with the bureau to become locally-run community enterprises, soon appeared. A similar move was the establishment in 1968 of the Navajo Community College, the first college to be controlled and directed by Indians.

Yet all these gains, substantial as they were, could not disguise the essential weaknesses of federal Indian education, and public criticism abounded. A shocking report was made by the Senate Special Subcommittee on Indian Education on November 3, 1969. The subcommittee spent two years examining all aspects of Indian education: federal schools, state and local schools, and the mission schools. Its report was a massive indictment. "We have concluded," the committee said, "that our national policies for educating American Indians are a failure of major proportions. They have not offered Indian children—either in years past or today—an educational opportunity anywhere near equal to that offered the great bulk of American children." It compared statistics for Indian schools and Indian students with those for non-Indians, and it was struck with "the low quality of virtually every aspect of the schooling available to Indian children." The committee insisted on increased participation and control by Indians of their education, and it set forth at length a series of sixty recommendations to correct the evils.

A more balanced view of the problems of Indian education was presented in the report of another major study sponsored by the federal government, this time by the Office of Education. For two years, 1968–1970, the National Study of American Indian Education, under the direction of Robert J. Havighurst of the University of Chicago and with a large staff working out of five university centers, investigated all aspects of Indian education. Although the study admitted the unsatisfactory conditions in Indian schools and Indian programs, it sought to understand the causes of the conditions—Indian social and cultural factors, as well as weaknesses in the schools—and to suggest feasible programs for improvement. Like all those interested in Indian education in the late 1960s, the men and women involved in the National Study strongly emphasized the need to incorporate Indian planning and Indian decisions into the educational programs, and their concern for Indian participation was reflected in the number of Indians on the advisory committee and among the field workers.

The work of the Education Division of the Bureau of Indian Affairs was, in large part, overshadowed by these nonbureau studies and reports. The forces affecting Indian education came increasingly from outside the Bureau of Indian Affairs—from other agencies like the Office of Economic Opportunity, from public reports made by independent organizations, from Congress, and most of all from an awakened Indian leadership. But all these together could not suddenly change the scope or nature of Indian education.

THE CIVIL RIGHTS ACT OF 1968

A significant but controversial move toward a guarantee of Indian rights came at the end of the 1960s in special Indian titles of the Civil Rights Act signed on April 11, 1968. The existence of tribal governments and tribal courts had raised the question of the rights of individual Indians with respect to these governments. Were the constitutional rights of Indian citizens fully protected? At the same time there was increasing awareness of discrimination against Indians and of numerous violations of their civil rights.

Concern for the constitutional rights of the Indians became almost a crusade with Senator Sam J. Ervin, Jr., of North Carolina. In a time of growing agitation for protection of the rights of blacks, Ervin made it his business to look after "the first Americans, whose rights have been ignored by everyone." He wanted to correct the evils by subjecting tribal governments to the same limitations and restraints as those imposed on the federal government by the Constitution. It soon became clear from the testimony of Indian leaders and federal officials, however, that this was too sweeping a limitation. Indian tribal governments differed from the federal government; application of the full Bill of Rights to them did not make sense and would upset traditional governing practices. Especially crucial was the prohibition against the "establishment of religion," which would have obstructed the quasi-theocracies that ran some Indian communities. In the end the blanket extension of the Bill of Rights to tribal governments was replaced by a selective and specific list of individual rights that were to be protected.

Title II of the act listed ten limitations on the powers of Indian tribal governments, guaranteeing the freedoms of the Constitution that were judged to fit the Indian case, and it specifically authorized the writ of habeas corpus in federal courts for persons detained by order of an Indian tribe. Title III directed the secretary of the interior to draw up a model code for the administration of justice by courts of Indian offenses on the reservations. Title IV repealed section 7 of Public Law 280; it provided for tribal approval of the extension of state jurisdiction and authorized the retrocession of jurisdiction already assumed by a state. Title V added "assault resulting in serious bodily injury" to the offenses on reservations subject to federal jurisdiction. Title VI required the automatic approval of tribal contracts for legal counsel if the secretary of the interior did not act within ninety days.

The Indian Civil Rights Act had a mixed reception. It was clearly Senator Ervin's intention to bring the Indian tribal governments within the constitutional framework of the United States, and it was precisely on this point that the act was criticized by Indian groups and their advocates. Indians favored the amendment to Public Law 280 and the strengthening of their right to employ counsel, but they were concerned about the application of United States legal forms to their tribal governments and what this might do to self-government and tribal sovereignty.

Judicial interpretations of the Indian Civil Rights Act created tension between the congressional intent to protect the rights of individual Indians and the policy of encouraging tribal self-government. Cases were accepted by federal courts to enforce the Indian bill of rights in such matters as tribal membership, tribal elections, and selection of tribal officers, and the decisions were seen by critics of the act as intrusions upon the sovereignty of the tribes. In *Santa Clara Pueblo* v. *Martinez*, the Supreme Court on May 15, 1978, upheld the tribal objections. The court declared that suits against a tribe under the Civil Rights Act were barred by the tribe's sovereign immunity to suit, and it noted that the act had two distinct purposes: to protect individual tribal members from violation of their civil rights by the tribe, but also to promote "the well-established federal policy" of encouraging self-government.

NIXON'S INDIAN POLICY

The presidential administration of Richard M. Nixon carried forward the movement for self-determination with considerable success. In a special message on Indian affairs sent to Congress on July 8, 1970, Nixon called for self-determination without termination. He spoke of the "immense moral and legal force" of the agreements made between the tribes and the government through the decades and insisted that because the special relationship between the Indians and the United States rested on these solemn obligations it could not be terminated unilaterally. He noted, too, the harmful results of termination where it had been put into effect and the blighting effect on tribal progress caused by the fear of termination.

The proposals to Congress embodied in the message became the program for his administration. Nixon asked for nine things:

1. A "new Concurrent Resolution which would expressly renounce, repudiate and repeal the termination policy" of House Concurrent Resolution 108, a resolution that would "explicitly affirm the integrity and right to continued existence of all Indian tribes and Alaska native governments, recognizing that cultural pluralism is a source of national strength."

2. Legislation that would "empower a tribe or group of tribes or any other Indian community to take over control or operation of Federally-funded and administered programs" whenever the Indian groups voted to do so. Technical assistance to help the Indians operate the programs successfully would still be provided by the federal government.

3. Restoration to Taos Pueblo of Blue Lake and the sacred Indian lands surrounding it.

4. The right of Indians to control their own Indian schools and authorization to channel Johnson-O'Malley funds to Indian tribes and communities.

5. Economic development legislation, which would provide financing, incentives, and coordinated planning for economic development of the reservations.

6. Allocation of additional funds for improving Indian health and for training Indians for health careers.

7. Help for urban Indians by aiding them to participate in social services and government programs for the poor and disadvantaged.

8. Creation of an Indian Trust Counsel Authority, an agency independent of the Departments of the Interior and Justice, which would assure legal representation for the Indians' natural resource rights and eliminate existing conflicts of interest.

9. Creation of the position of assistant secretary for Indian and territorial affairs and "elevation of Indian affairs to their proper role within the Department of the Interior."

Congress was slow to act and did not accept the full legislative package, but large parts of the program were eventually enacted.

THE NEW INDIANS AND RED POWER

The Nixon administration's Indian policy initiatives were conceived and carried out in an atmosphere of high tension and widespread publicity of wrongs done to the Indians. Many Indians were no longer willing to accept their lot passively, and their growing activism ultimately broke out in violent confrontations. These "new Indians," who demanded attention to their needs, forced the public and the federal government to face an Indian challenge that many thought had disappeared in the nineteenth century. By the end of the decade Red Power, imitating the Black Power movement of protest and political pressure, was a force to be reckoned with in government relations with the Indians.

A number of events that received widespread publicity indicated the militancy of the Indians and the charged atmosphere in which federal relations with them were conducted. One was the Indian seizure of Alcatraz Island in San Francisco Bay on November 20, 1969. The Indians declared that they were taking the island in the name of the Indians, facetiously offered to buy it for twenty-four dollars worth of beads, and announced plans to turn the barren rock into an Indian cultural and educational center. The dramatic takeover captured the attention of the news media; there was much sympathetic support of the Indians on Alcatraz; and the federal government took no strong moves to dislodge them, although water and electricity were cut off. The occupation served as a symbol of Indian unity, and the leaders, using the designation Indians of All Tribes, issued a call for national Indian support.

The federal government moved cautiously, but it did not admit the Indian claims to Alcatraz. It deemed the Indian plans for a university and cultural center "unreasonable and unrealistic, primarily because the island does not lend itself to any high-density proposal." It offered instead to make Alcatraz a national park with an Indian theme, an Indian name, and Indian employment preference in hiring the necessary park personnel. The Indians flatly rejected the government's proposals and held firm to their original demands. They did not have the means to carry out their own plans for the island, however, and dissension on the island and steadily worsening material conditions there finally led to its abandonment. The few who remained were removed by federal marshals on June 11, 1971.

The occupation of Alcatraz was a symbolic gesture, on the periphery of government activity and concern. Not so the Trail of Broken Treaties with its attendant occupation and destruction of the headquarters building of the Bureau of Indian Affairs in Washington, D.C., that soon followed. In the fall of 1972 a caravan of Indians converged on the capital to make known their grievances and demand a righting of wrongs. The affair was dominated by members of the American Indian Movement (AIM), which had been organized in Minneapolis in 1968 to protect Indians there from harassment and which soon became the cutting edge of Indian militancy. Under the direction of such men as Russell Means (an Oglala Sioux) and Dennis Banks (a Chippewa), AIM organized groups of Indians from various parts of the nation, who gathered adherents as they moved toward Washington.

The plan for a peaceful demonstration and for serious negotiations with federal officials went awry as adequate facilities for meetings and for housing were not forthcoming and as high federal officials refused to negotiate with the Indian leaders. On November 2 the Indians occupied the Bureau of Indian Affairs building and, when forceful ejection was feared, barricaded the building. In a fit of anger and frustration, they destroyed the interior of the building and its contents before they finally gave up their occupation.

The next militant action engineered by AIM was the seizure of the hamlet of Wounded Knee on the Pine Ridge Reservation in South Dakota on February 27, 1973. The occupation was intended as a new national event to call attention to the Indians' continuing woes, but it had an added dimension that Alcatraz and the Trail of Broken Treaties lacked—an intratribal conflict at Pine Ridge. The elected tribal chairman, Richard Wilson, was condemned by AIM leader Russell Means and his followers as a puppet of the Bureau of Indian Affairs who did not truly represent the Indian tribal members.

Federal marshals and agents of the Federal Bureau of Investigation quickly sealed off the occupied village, and a stand-off developed that won world-wide news coverage. The AIM leaders were astute propagandists who fed the media their views and staged events that the television cameramen eagerly reported. For more than seventy days the impasse continued. The well-armed Indians were determined to hold out, and the government agents sought to end the occupation without a bloodbath. At length, through negotiations conducted in part with the aid of the National Council of Churches, the Indians withdrew on May 8, 1973.

The militant actions were condemned by many Indians, who declared that the activists were largely young urban Indians who did not have deep roots in the reservations, and by many whites, among whom a mild backlash developed. The dénouement of all three events showed that violent confrontation would not force the federal government to accept Indian demands and thus was ultimately ineffective and to some degree counterproductive. Yet the reality of the miserable conditions of many Indians and the deep desire of Indians to have a larger say in their own destiny were driven home to American society. The move for self-determination continued in the administration and in Congress with a new urgency because of the outbreaks.

The agitation exhibited in the public confrontations was paralleled by turmoil within the Bureau of Indian Affairs. President Nixon's appointment as commissioner of Indian affairs was Louis R. Bruce, a Mohawk–Oglala Sioux. He was a man of reason and good sense, committed to the cause of Indian self-determination, who had the misfortune to hold office during a volatile and controversial period of Indian affairs. He surrounded himself with young activist Indians, a "new team," who sought to work around the bureaucratic inertia of the old administrative setup, and Secretary of the Interior Walter J. Hickel gave him support.

The Hickel-Bruce administration, which was geared to an increased voice for Indians in the high-level management of Indian affairs, however, was soon cut short. Hickel was replaced by Rogers C. B. Morton, a man less flexible and innovative than he, who moved to tighten the administration of the bureau. When the seizure and destruction of the offices of the bureau in November 1972 brought complete disruption, Bruce and others resigned. Not until October 30, 1973, was a new commissioner appointed.

When Jimmy Carter became president in 1977, he accomplished by administrative action what Nixon had hoped but failed to achieve by legislation: elevation of the head of Indian affairs to the assistant secretary level. On July 12 he appointed a member of the Blackfeet Tribe, Forrest J. Gerard, to the new position.

RELIGIOUS FREEDOM

A key element in the Indians' advance toward self-determination and cultural freedom in the United States was freedom of religious belief and practice. From the beginning of white contact, the zeal of Christian missionaries and government officials to Christianize and civilize the Indians had
meant the denigration of aboriginal religions and an attempt to stamp
them out, replacing them with European Christianity. Not until the 1920s,
when John Collier began his crusade for reform, were there outspoken
voices in support of full religious freedom for the American Indians. As
American society became more tolerant of pluralism in religion and other
aspects of culture, Indian religions were no longer directly attacked.

There were still areas of conflict, however, for certain federal and state
laws and actions indirectly hindered the free exercise of religion for many
Indians. One problem was that of free access to sites considered sacred by
the tribes and used for religious ceremonies; traditional burying grounds,
too, had sometimes become inaccessible to the Indians. A second source of
friction was the restriction on the use of certain substances that were an
essential part of Indian rites, such as peyote (restricted as a hallucinogen)
or eagle feathers (protected under endangered species laws). A third area of
concern was occasional interference with actual ceremonies by overzeal-
ous officials or the merely curious, against which legal protection seemed
necessary.

One dramatic move to right these wrongs came in December 1970,
when the sacred Blue Lake and surrounding lands of the Taos Pueblo were
returned to the Indians. These lands had been taken from the Indians in
1906 when President Theodore Roosevelt added them to what is now Carson National Forest, thus restricting their use exclusively by Indians. After
years of Indian struggle to regain the lands and persistent rejection of the
idea of a monetary compensation for their loss, Congress authorized the
return of forty-eight thousand acres. In signing the bill President Nixon
called attention to the fact that the bill did not represent a gift to the Indians by the United States, but rather the return to them in justice of what
was rightfully theirs. "This bill," he said, "also involves respect for religion. Those of us who know something about the background of the first
Americans realize that long before any organized religion came to the
United States, for 700 years the Taos Pueblo Indians worshiped in this
place. We restore this place of worship to them for all the years to come."

A direct and broad statement of policy in regard to Indian religious freedom came in Senate Joint Resolution 102 on August 11, 1978. After noting
the American principle of freedom of religion and the infringement of that
principle in regard to Indians, Congress resolved: "That henceforth it shall

be the policy of the United States to protect and preserve for American Indians their inherent right of freedom to believe, express, and exercise the
traditional religions of the American Indian, Eskimo, Aleut, and Native
Hawaiian, including but not limited to access to sites, use and possession
of sacred objects, and the freedom to worship through ceremonials and traditional rites." The resolution directed evaluation by the various federal
departments and agencies of their policies and procedures in this regard and
appropriate changes needed to protect religious rights and practices.

Indian religious rights were further recognized in the Archaeological Resources Protection Act of 1979. The purpose of the act was to prevent the
destruction of important archaeological sites, and it required special permits for persons studying or excavating them. If such a permit might result
in harm to any religious or cultural site, the Indian tribe concerned was to
be notified before a permit was issued. The ultimate disposition of archaeological resources excavated or removed from Indian lands was subject to the
consent of the Indians or tribe.

ALASKA NATIVE CLAIMS

Another signal event in the recognition of the rights of Indians and other
native peoples was the settlement of Alaska Native claims in 1971. Alaska
Natives—Indians, Eskimos, and Aleuts—offered unique problems, for they
had never been fully encompassed in the federal policies and programs developed for the American Indians. Alaska for decades seemed remote and
out of the way; no treaties were made with the natives there, few reservations were established for them, and only small appropriations were made
for their benefit. When Russia ceded Alaska to the United States in 1867,
the treaty did not touch aboriginal rights to the land and its resources, and
the Organic Act of 1884, which established a civil government for Alaska,
merely continued the status quo.

The crisis for the Alaska Natives came with the rush for exploitation of
Alaska's tremendously rich natural resources. The arrival of white com-
mercial fishermen in the second half of the nineteenth century and gold
rushes in the late nineteenth and early twentieth centuries were harbingers
of what was to come. By mid-twentieth century the white Alaska economy—long dependent upon United States military activities—was based
on the natural resources of the territory. Exploration and development of
oil, gas, and other mineral riches and the post–World War II population influx brought an insistent demand for statehood for the territory.

Statehood, which became a reality on January 3, 1959, was an ultimate
challenge to the Alaska Natives, who formed about one-fifth of the new

state's population in 1960. Threats to their lands and to their traditional hunting and gathering economy now took on serious proportions, for Congress authorized the state to select 102.5 million acres from the "vacant, unappropriated, and unreserved" public domain, another 400,000 acres from national forests, and 400,000 acres from other public lands for disposition by the state. To meet this threatening development the natives resorted to filing protests against the state land selections, and these protests ultimately covered much of the land in the state.

The secretary of the interior froze the public lands in Alaska until Congress could settle the native claims, and the continuing freeze seriously hindered the economic development of the state. Then discovery of immense oil reserves on the North Slope and the proposal of a pipeline to transport the oil added new urgency for a quick settlement. The situation played into the hands of the Alaska Natives, for the oil companies realized that the Alaska Natives would have to be satisfied before there was any chance for the pipeline. After intense lobbying and numerous compromise suggestions Congress in December 1971 finally agreed on a measure that became law as the Alaska Native Claims Settlement Act. Though a complex compromise, it was by and large a victory for the Alaska Natives.

The law granted the Alaska Natives legal title to 40 million acres; in return all native claims in Alaska were extinguished. Compensation of $462 million was provided, plus another $500 million in revenues from mineral rights to be paid over a number of years. The law required the secretary of the interior to divide Alaska into twelve geographic regions, for each of which a regional corporation was established. All Alaska Natives would be shareholders in one of these corporations or in a thirteenth corporation for nonresident natives. In addition, native village corporations would be formed to hold the lands distributed under the act and to administer other benefits. The law itself listed more than two hundred such villages, and the secretary of the interior was empowered to add or delete villages from the list. The village corporations dealt only with surface rights; title to subsurface mineral rights was held by the regional corporations, which distributed funds to villages and at-large-stockholders according to a complex formula.

The regional corporations were organized quickly and began to invest their funds in a wide variety of economic enterprises, but the transfer of land to native title moved very slowly. One problem concerned the conservation of wilderness areas in Alaska. Persons interested in preserving wildlife refuges worried that improper native claims might affect adversely the lands within the National Wildlife Refuge System, and in any case, it would be difficult to set aside wilderness areas until the natives had chosen their 40 million acres.

The Alaska Native Claims Settlement Act of 1971 provided a revolutionary solution to a problem of long standing, but the ultimate effects were not agreed upon. Some thought that the act freed the Alaska Natives and through grants of land and money gave them a basis for political power. The native community could now take its rightful place in Alaskan society. Others argued that in exchange for money and land the natives gave up their own lifestyle and traditional mode of living. They feared that hunters and gatherers would be transformed into corporation members interested in the development of resources and dividend payments, and that the political tribe as a dominant force in native life would be replaced by the economic corporation.

MENOMINEE RESTORATION

Because deeds speak louder than words, the restoration of the terminated Menominee Indians to federal status as a tribe was one of the most significant actions of the Nixon administration. The move, supported by state and federal officials as well as by a majority of the Menominees, showed that in the new era of self-determination and Indian rights it was possible for an Indian community with determined leaders to reverse congressional action and policy.

The disastrous results of termination for the Menominees were the springboard from which the drive for restoration took off. All the economic and social indicators pointed to intolerable conditions. The sawmill operation that had employed most of the tribe before termination had to modernize to make its operations pay under the new dispensation, and many Indians lost their jobs. Federal support of schools and hospital was withdrawn, and the tax base of the new county was too small to cover the costs. Menominee Enterprises, Inc. (MEI), the trust that had taken over the tribal assets, was hard-pressed financially. When MEI decided on the necessity of selling tribal land to white developers, it created hostility among the rank and file of the tribe, who were already disturbed because of the tight control over economic and political affairs that MEI held. Termination was supposed to save the federal government money, but instead both federal and state governments were forced to pump in funds to prevent complete collapse of the Menominees.

The Menominee governing group that ran MEI, however, did not despair. It hoped by prudent development to ride out the storm, and there were many Indians who survived and prospered and who were convinced that termination could be made to work. But this group was soon vigorously attacked by a new faction that called itself Determination of Rights

and Unity for Menominee Stockholders (DRUMS). Under astute leadership furnished by Ada Deer and Jim White, DRUMS organized groups in
Chicago and Milwaukee and then in Menominee County to oust the Indians who controlled MEI and eventually—as their ultimate goal—to
bring about a reversal of termination and restore the Menominee tribe to
federal status. The new political force, through skillfully using protest tactics against MEI and the governing elite, enlisting wide public support, and
stirring up the Menominees themselves to a new determination to preserve their old ways, managed to get its members elected to controlling
offices in MEI. Then it put on a lobbying drive to get Congress to pass a
restoration bill.

In the political climate supportive of minority rights of the late 1960s
and early 1970s, the drive under Ada Deer moved forward effectively and
successfully. With support from Indian groups across the nation, who rightly
saw the symbolic significance of restoration as a final rejection of the termination policy, and with endorsement from state officials and the Department of the Interior, the Menominees won congressional approval of their
demands to be reinstated as a federally recognized tribe eligible for the federal services and benefits provided Indians. An act of December 22, 1973,
repealed the termination law of 1954 and placed the Menominee Tribe
once more under federal responsibility. It provided for the election of a
Menominee Restoration Committee, which was authorized to govern the
tribe until a constitution could be drawn up and a new government established. A new tribal roll would add members who were born since the roll
was closed in 1954.

Restoration was in the hands of its friends, and Ada Deer was chosen to
head the Menominee Restoration Committee. Reversing termination was
not a simple matter, however, for it meant disentangling public from private assets and sorting out jurisdictional responsibilities as the county became a reservation again. Finally, on April 22, 1975, Secretary of the Interior Morton and Ada Deer signed a deed conveying Menominee tribal land
back to trust status. Unfortunately, internal tribal dissension marred the
new order, and Deer and her associates in governing the tribe were soon
subjected to criticisms similar to those they had made against the old MEI.
A group of activists who called themselves the Menominee Warrior Society, in order to publicize their grievances, on New Year's Day 1975 seized
the Alexian Brothers novitiate at Gresham, Wisconsin, near the reservation. Their thirty-four-day occupancy of the building under siege became a
media event that rivaled the occupation of Wounded Knee.

Although the novitiate was evacuated and some of those who seized it
were brought to trial, the turmoil among the Menominees did not cease. It
led to considerable physical violence on the reservation, and it seriously

obstructed the necessary formation of the new tribal government. Not until November 12, 1976, did the tribe vote approval of a constitution, and then by a relatively close vote of 468 to 426. When that was accomplished, Ada Deer resigned, saying it was time for new leadership to accept responsibility.

The restoration of the Menominee Tribe was possible because those Indians had maintained a cohesive community with their own government (beset by troubles as it was) and had preserved much of their tribal land base. A similar reversal of termination was not feasible for the Klamath Indians, but some smaller groups that had been terminated in the 1950s were restored to federal status. The restoration actions effectively destroyed the termination policy, although Congress still did not formally reject House Concurrent Resolution no. 108 of 1953, which remained an irritating symbol of the hated program.

CHAPTER 25

Indian
Self-Determination

Although the return of Blue Lake, the settlement of Alaska land claims, and the reversal of Menominee termination were important links in the new chain of Indian self-determination, they affected only particular tribes or regions. The federal government in the decade of the 1970s moved forward as well in areas that affected all Indians. The government was determined to broaden Indian participation in programs that touched their lives and thus to lessen the paternalism that everyone admitted had had a deleterious effect upon the Indian communities.

PROGRAMS FOR SELF-DETERMINATION

The drive for Indian self-determination was nowhere more pronounced than in education. The responsibility of the federal government to provide educational programs was recognized and increasingly supported by congressional appropriations, but there was a new insistence on the part of both the executive branch and Congress that the programs meet the special educational and cultural needs of the Indians and that direction and control of the schools be placed in Indian hands in order to assure these goals.

The report on Indian education by the Senate Special Subcommittee on Indian Education in 1969, with its harsh criticism of the existing state of affairs, struck a responsive chord in Congress. The Education Amendments Act of 1972 provided striking advances and changes in the Indian educational scene. It directed input from Indian communities on the use of funds under the Federally Impacted Areas Act, authorized grants for special programs to improve elementary and secondary education for Indians in both public schools and federal Indian schools, and provided aid for adult education.

A dramatic departure from previous education programs was the establishment of an Office of Indian Education in the Department of Health, Education, and Welfare to administer the provisions of the act. The law also created a National Advisory Council on Indian Education, composed of fifteen Indians or Alaska Natives appointed by the president, to advise the commissioner of education, review applications for grants, evaluate programs and projects, and provide technical assistance to local educational agencies or to Indian agencies and organizations.

Thus was established a dual system of federal aid to Indian education. The Bureau of Indian Affairs continued to run its Indian schools, but now there were added as well the programs administered by the Office of Education. In fiscal year 1980, appropriations for Indian education under the Department of the Interior amounted to $270 million; those under the Department of Education (established in 1979), to $214 million. An important distinction between the two systems was the definition of those to be aided. The Bureau of Indian Affairs, by and large, provided schools for reservation Indians and some off-reservation boarding schools for special needs, and it retained responsibility for the use of Johnson-O'Malley Act funds for Indian programs in the public schools. This limitation to Indians falling under the responsibility of the Bureau of Indian Affairs was too narrow for the senators who sponsored the Indian education legislation of 1972, and the law was worded to apply not only to federally recognized tribes but broadly to *all* Indians and Alaska Natives.

One instance of the new agitation for an effective Indian voice in education was the growing concern about the dichotomy in the use of Johnson-O'Malley funds for basic support of the operating needs of the school districts, on the one hand, and for programs to meet the special needs of Indian children, on the other. Acting on the requests and recommendations of Indian groups, the Bureau of Indian Affairs in August 1974 specified that the funds were to be used for supplementary programs, defined as those "designed to meet the special needs of Indian students that may result from socio-economic conditions of the parents, or from cultural or language difference, or other factors." And it severely restricted the use of the funds for operational support of the schools. More important, the new regulations directed that the Indians concerned should, through Indian education committees, "participate in the planning, development, evaluation, and monitoring of all programs." Indian tribes themselves, furthermore, received Johnson-O'Malley contracts.

The concern for Indian rights in education extended beyond parental control of schools and their programs to the fundamental rights of the children in the schools. On September 4, 1974, the Bureau of Indian Affairs published regulations governing student rights and due process procedures for schools operated by the bureau or under contract with it. These regula-

tions were evidence of the distance education policies had come since the
days nearly half a century earlier when John Collier was railing against dic-
tatorial and repressive control in the bureau's schools, for they listed essential rights, including:

The right to freedom of religion and culture.

The right to freedom of speech and expression, including symbolic
expression, such as display of buttons, posters, choice of dress, and
length of hair, so long as the symbolic expression does not unreason-
ably and in fact disrupt the educational process or endanger the health
and safety of the student or others.

The right to freedom from discrimination.

The drive for greater control by the Indians of the education of their
children was given legislative sanction by Title II of the Indian Self-
Determination and Education Assistance Act of 1975. The law amended
the Johnson-O'Malley Act to require Indian parent advisory committees in
districts where the school boards had less than a majority of Indian members, with authority to develop new Johnson-O'Malley programs and to approve or disapprove existing contracts; and it directed the secretary of the
interior to review education plans for contracting agencies to make sure
that the special needs of Indian students were adequately cared for.

More reforms came in a special section on Indian education in the Education Amendments Act of 1978. A major innovation was the restructuring
of the Bureau of Indian Affairs educational administration required by the
legislation. Educational programs were still the ultimate responsibility of
the secretary of the interior, but the programs were placed in the hands
of the director of the bureau's Office of Indian Education Programs, who
would formulate, monitor, and evaluate education policies and programs
and would deal directly with educators in the field, bypassing the commissioner of Indian affairs, area directors, and agency superintendents. Another significant change was the removal of education personnel actions
(teacher hiring and the like) from the civil service processes, with the hope
of eliminating the "cumbersome process of recruitment" under the civil
service system.

Self-determination in the running of Indian community colleges was another element of the new educational policies. The model was the Navajo
Community College, founded in 1969, which was supported by a variety of
federal funds. With about one-third of its students in an academic course
and two-thirds in vocational training, the college enrolled Navajos of all
ages. It was intended to supplement other college opportunities and aimed
specifically at those Indians who were unwilling to leave home to enroll in
colleges or were unable to adjust to new environments.

Support of the successful Navajo institution was used as an argument for further aid to Indian community colleges, and in 1978 Congress passed the Tribally Controlled Community College Act, which provided (through grants of $4,000 per year for each full-time student) "for the operation and improvement of tribally controlled community colleges to insure continued and expanded educational opportunities for Indian students." The eligibility requirements dictated that a college must be governed by an Indian board and have a philosophy and plan of operation directed to meet the needs of Indians.

Amid all the innovations and legislative changes, the fundamental work of educating Indian children progressed, with notable increases in the number of students reached. In fiscal year 1979, Indian students numbering 221,271 received government funds for their schooling through the Bureau of Indian Affairs. The bureau itself ran 174 schools (68 boarding and 106 day) with an enrollment of 41,598 and maintained fifteen dormitories at public schools to care for 1,973 children (19.7 percent of known students). In addition, 33 schools (13 boarding and 20 day) with 6,412 students were run on contract by Indian groups (2.9 percent). Of the students in these of schools under the supervision of the bureau, 72.8 percent were full-bloods and only 6.9 percent had less than half Indian blood. In the public schools with funding under the Johnson-O'Malley Act there were 171,290 Indian children (77.7 percent).

All measures leading to increased community control of the Indian schools were limited by the inescapable fact that the financial support of the schools came from outside sources. Yet the heavy federal funding for Indian education through Bureau of Indian Affairs schools, support of special programs in public schools, and special scholarship programs for Indians was undoubtedly necessary, whatever the commitment to Indian autonomy and self-determination.

Effective self-determination depended upon a healthy Indian population, and the Indian Health Service in 1981 reported increased availability and accessibility of health services, advances in the home environment (better housing, safe water supplies, proper sewage disposal), and increased emphasis on health education.

This encouraging state of Indian health was due in large part to the increases in appropriations that came after the health programs had been transferred to the Public Health Service in 1955. In the 1970s, however, two pieces of legislation had a special impact—the Indian Self-Determination and Education Assistance Act of 1975 and the Indian Health Care Improvement Act of 1976. The first of these did for health services what it did for education and other federal Indian programs: it enabled and encouraged Indian tribes to take over and run the programs themselves. By 1980 a small but significant move had been made in this direction, and the rate of transfer was rapidly accelerating. About 10 percent of the tribes delivered all their own health services, and many others ran smaller or single elements of health programs. Almost 90 percent of eligible tribes were responsible for some part of their own health care.

The Indian Health Care Improvement Act came as a result of strong agitation to lessen or remove the gap that still existed between Indian health conditions and those of the total population. The law sought to do this by a program of incremental funding over a seven-year period rather than through a "crash" program. It established grants, scholarship programs, and continuing education allowances to aid in recruiting Indians and other persons for the Indian Health Service, authorized funds to eliminate backlogs in health care services and for the construction and renovation of hospitals and health centers, and lifted the prohibition against Medicare and Medicaid reimbursement for services performed by the Indian Health Service. Of particular significance was the provision for the establishment of urban health centers to care for the large urban Indian population.

The Indian Health Care Improvement Act did not usher in the millennium, to be sure, for many health problems facing Indian communities were not amenable to dramatic sudden solutions. And as old ones were eliminated, new ones appeared. "The scourges of yesterday such as tuberculosis and gastroenteritis," the Indian Health Service noted in 1980, "have been replaced by other more challenging problems, ones which require new ideas and new approaches. The Indians' health priorities of today— accidents, alcoholism, diabetes, mental health, suicides and homicides— stem not from organic causes, but from changes in their traditional lifestyles and values, and from deprivation." Nor did the bureaucratic operation of the Indian Health Service escape continuing criticism.

Nothing touched Indian self-determination more deeply than the problem of child custody and maintenance of Indian family life. White governmental concern for child welfare, however, had seriously eroded family rights. Indian children were taken from homes judged unsuitable or harmful to them by Bureau of Indian Affairs or state social workers and placed in foster or adoptive homes, usually non-Indian. What began as a sincere effort to protect the best interest of the child, as it was viewed by social workers, eventually was perceived more accurately as a force destructive of Indian families and Indian children. The involuntary separation of children from their parents that had marked the old boarding school experience was being continued now by child custody proceedings.

The Bureau of Indian Affairs became actively involved in the adoption of Indian children by non-Indian parents in 1958 with the establishment of an Indian Adoption Project, in which the bureau worked with the Child Welfare League of America. In 1961 the bureau provided funds to care for more than 2,300 dependent and neglected children from unstable or broken homes; and foster home placements began to grow, with bureau social workers referring homeless children to qualified adoptive agencies selected by the Child Welfare League. By the end of the decade, as state welfare agencies moved into action, the separation of Indian children from their families grew at an alarming rate.

To meet the evils, Congress passed the Child Welfare Act of 1978. The law declared that the policy of the nation was "to protect the best interests of Indian children and to promote the stability of and security of Indian tribes and families." To do this it provided for the jurisdiction of Indian tribes in child custody proceedings and the right of the tribe or Indian parents to intervene in state court proceedings. Preference in adoption was to be given to the child's extended family, other members of the child's tribe, or other Indian families. Protection was provided to make sure that the child was placed in an Indian cultural setting. The act, furthermore, authorized grants to Indian tribes and organizations for the establishment of child and family service programs on or near reservations and for the preparation and implementation of child welfare codes.

Like other legislation, however, the Indian Child Welfare Act emitted mixed signals on the issue of self-determination. Although the law clearly aimed at preserving Indian culture through stable Indian families and established tribal jurisdiction over Indian child custody cases, it on the other hand justified federal intervention in the matter on the grounds that "Congress has plenary power over Indian affairs." The grants for tribal child and family service programs were firmly in the hands of the Bureau of Indian Affairs, and the funds came from federal, not Indian, sources.

THE INDIAN SELF-DETERMINATION ACT

Although nearly every act or set of regulations in the 1970s was touched by the philosophy of self-determination, of particular significance was Title I of the Indian Self-Determination and Education Assistance Act of January 4, 1975. This was the culmination of President Nixon's intention that the tribes should be able to escape the domination of the Bureau of Indian Affairs and take upon themselves the responsibility for programs and services provided by the federal government. "We have concluded," Nixon said in his special message on Indian affairs in 1970, "that Indians will get better programs and that public monies will be more effectively expended if the people who are most affected by these programs are responsible for operating them."

The administration urged passage of a bill that would have allowed Indian tribes, simply at their own request, to assume full control of federal Indian programs, but the law eventually passed was of a more limited nature. Indian leaders were afraid that a "takeover" bill such as Nixon advocated might be a step toward termination, and they settled instead for a system by which tribes could make contracts with federal departments for bits and pieces of educational, health care, or other programs.

The twofold policy of the government was asserted in the preamble to the law: the United States recognized its obligation to respect "the strong expression of the Indian people for self-determination by assuring maximum Indian participation in the direction of educational as well as other Federal services to Indian communities so as to render such services more responsive to the needs and desires of those communities"; and Congress declared its commitment to "the maintenance of the Federal Government's unique and continuing relationship with and responsibility to the Indian people" through a self-determination policy that would provide an orderly transition from federal domination to effective Indian participation in planning and administering programs.

The tension between the two points was not eliminated by the law, for the secretaries of the federal departments still made basic decisions about which contracts to approve. Indians charged that use of this ultimate authority negated the effects intended by Congress in the legislation. Tribal leaders spoke of massive resistance to contracting by employees of the Bureau of Indian Affairs—the "backlash of a paternalistic organization"—and insufficient technical assistance from the bureau. They objected to tying the contract process into the preexisting operation of the bureau with its line item budget, instead of allowing the tribes to shape their own programs, and to the increased burden of paper work. The law, the president of the National Tribal Chairmen's Association said, was "an extraordinary example of the institutional power and capacity of some Federal Bureaucracies to preserve and protect themselves against the will of the people they serve." Thus, representatives of the same organizations that had rejected legislation to allow tribes to assume full responsibility for programs and instead opted for a contracting scheme were now singing a different tune.

Despite the strong rhetoric of Indian leaders about the failure of the act to provide genuine self-determination, in fact a large number of contracts were concluded under its provisions. In fiscal year 1980, 370 tribes contracted for the operation of $200 million worth of programs under the Indian Self-Determination Act, and $22.3 million was paid to the tribes to cover their overhead in the contracts. By the next year 480 grants had been made to tribal governments under the act to improve their capacity to operate federal programs under contract and in general to increase their effectiveness in serving tribal members.

AMERICAN INDIAN POLICY REVIEW COMMISSION

The outbreaks of restless and frustrated Indians at the Bureau of Indian Affairs in 1972 and at Wounded Knee in early 1973 were clear evidence to many people that something needed to be done to meliorate the conditions in federal-Indian relations that had led to such violence. One proposed solution came from Senator James Abourezk of South Dakota, the leading congressional advocate of Indian rights, who urged the appointment of a congressional commission with members from both houses and from the Indian community to undertake an exhaustive review of the historical and legal elements in federal-Indian relations and to recommend legislation. What Abourezk and his supporters had in mind was a new Meriam Report that would provide a "systematic exploration of the contributing causes to the chaotic state of Indian affairs" with a "longer range objective of corrective action." The commission's report, it was hoped, would furnish a blueprint for future Indian policy.

As Abourezk's proposal became law on January 2, 1975, it established a commission of eleven members—three senators, three representatives, and five Indians (three from federally recognized tribes, one urban Indian, and one from nonrecognized groups). The commission was charged to analyze official documents to determine "the attributes of the unique relationship," review policies and practices, and collect data on Indian needs. It was directed, furthermore, to appoint investigative task forces to consider specific problems. Each task force was composed of three members, a majority of whom were to be Indians, and support staff for the task forces was authorized.

In the end there were eleven task forces, and thirty-one of the thirty-three members were Indians. They worked in the following areas: (1) trust responsibilities and federal-Indian relationship; (2) tribal government; (3) federal administration and structure of Indian affairs; (4) federal, state, and tribal jurisdiction; (5) Indian education; (6) Indian health; (7) reservation and resource development and protection; (8) urban and rural nonreservation Indians; (9) Indian law consolidation, revision, and codification; (10) terminated and nonrecognized Indians; and (11) alcohol and drug abuse. In addition, two special task force reports were prepared on Alaska Native issues and on the management of the Bureau of Indian Affairs.

The American Indian Policy Review Commission held out great promise. Indeed, an expert, historically accurate, and balanced analysis of Indian status and of the legal responsibilities of the federal government would have been of tremendous value in understanding past policies and planning future development. Unfortunately, little of this was realized, and the commission was largely a failure.

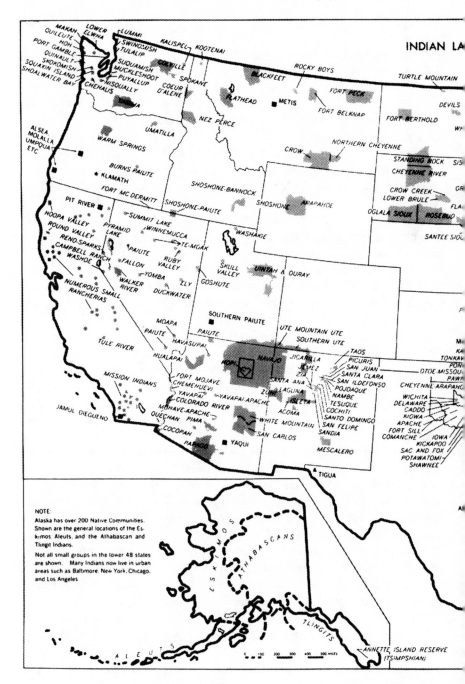

NOTE:
Alaska has over 200 Native Communities. Shown are the general locations of the Eskimos, Aleuts, and the Athabascan and Tlingit Indians.

Not all small groups in the lower 48 states are shown. Many Indians now live in urban areas such as Baltimore, New York, Chicago, and Los Angeles.

COMMUNITIES

NETT LAKE GRAND PORTAGE

LEECH LAKE
KEWEENAW BAY
RED CLIFF BAD RIVER
LAC
LAC COURTE LAC DU
OREILLES FLAMBEAU
CROIX
LAKE
SOKAOGON
MENOMINEE
HANNAHVILLE
POTAWATOMI
NER SIOUX PRAIRIE ISLAND ONEIDA
WINNEBAGO BROTHERTON
STOCKBRIDGE
MUNSEE POGAGON
POTAWATOMI

SAC AND FOX

AND FOX

WYANDOT
SHAWNEE
MIAMI
PEORIA
QUAPAW
SENECA-CAYUGA
WYANDOTTE

EE

E

OTTAWA AND CHIPPEWA
BAY MILLS

ISABELLA
POTAWATOMI

MIAMI

MOHAWK
ONEIDA
TONOWANDA ONONDAGA
TUSCARORA
CAYUGA SENECA

NIPMUC
WAMPANOAG
PEQUOT NARRAGANSET
SCATICOOK
PAUGUSETT MOHEGAN
MONTAUK
SHINNECOCK
POOSEPATUCK

MOOR
NANTICOKE
RAPPAHANOCK
UPPER MATTAPONI
MATTAPONI
PAMUNKEY
CHICKAHOMINY
AMHERST HALIWA

CUBAN
COHARIE
CHEROKEE LUMBEE
CATAWBA WACCAMAW

SUMMERVILLE

MALECITE
MICMAC
PASSAMAQUODDY

PENOBSCUT

CHOCTAW

CHOCTAW

CHOCTAW CHOCTAW CREEK
TUNICA
COUSHATTA
CHITIMACHA
HOUMA

SEMINOLE SEMINOLE
SEMINOLE
MICCOSUKEE
MICCOSUKEE

LEGEND
FEDERAL INDIAN RESERVATIONS
▲ State Indian Reservations
■ Other Indian Groups
★ Terminated (Only Klamath shown)

0   100   200   300   400   500 MILES

ALBERS EQUAL AREA PROJECTION

BUREAU OF INDIAN AFFAIRS—1971

The commission in its *Final Report*, submitted to Congress on May 17, 1977, set forth its "policy for the future" and provided 206 specific recommendations for Congress to consider, but the report and the reports of the eleven task forces on which it was based had little effect. Instead of the balanced historical and legal report called for, the commission submitted a report based on the controversial positions of inherent full political sovereignty of the tribes and broad trust responsibilities of the federal government. The vice chairman of the commission, Representative Lloyd Meeds of Washington, submitted a vigorous dissent from the commission's report on these two points, claiming that the report was "one-sided advocacy" encompassing only a tribal view of the future of American Indian law and policy.

Even without the vice chairman's dissent, however, the report of the commission could not serve as a general plan for future Indian policy. In the first place, it was caught in the theoretical dilemma that plagued the whole movement for self-determination. Although the report was premised on the concept of full political sovereignty of the tribes, most of the 206 recommendations of the commission were proposals for the federal government to appropriate funds for Indian programs or in some other way to deliver services to the "sovereign" tribes. There was, moreover, such a barrage of demands for funds or other congressional and administrative action that it was difficult to know where to begin.

In the second place, the task forces' work and their reports were by and large not of high quality. These reports in many cases were an accumulation of raw data, often not expertly gathered, and were short on convincing analysis and interpretation. They showed neither the historical nor legal understanding that the purposes of the commission demanded. Compared with the well-organized information and tightly argued conclusions provided by the technical experts who made up the Meriam survey team in the 1920s, the material published by the American Indian Policy Review Commission was unsatisfactory.

The commission and the task forces did, of course, provide some useful material, and their findings and recommendations influenced action by the executive departments and the Congress on a number of aspects of Indian policy and administration. But the *Final Report* did not furnish the blueprint for the future that had been hoped for. Piecemeal changes continued to be made, and these did move the Indian communities toward a greater degree of self-determination and protection of their rights. Unfortunately, there was no overarching plan and no solution to the inherent problems arising from the tension between self-determination of the Indian tribes and the continuing trust responsibility of the federal government.

LAND CLAIMS AND CONFLICTS

The 1970s were a decade of violent Indian protest, but they were also a period in which Indians resorted to the courts to protect their rights and to demand a righting of old wrongs. With increasing skill and considerable success, Indians and their lawyers made use of the American legal system to gain recognition of their claims and remedies for their grievances.

As Indians became more active in asserting claims, a new area of agitation opened up that soon gained the attention of the public press and the federal government. This was the claims of Indian groups in the eastern United States for land parcels that they alleged had been taken away from them illegally by eastern states. The claims were based on the Indian Trade and Intercourse Act of 1790, which in section 4 declared: "That no sale of lands made by any Indians, or any nation or tribe of Indians within the United States, shall be valid to any person or persons, or to any state, whether having the right of pre-emption to such lands or not, unless the same shall be made and duly executed at some public treaty, held under the authority of the United States."

The argument appeared first in the suits brought by the Passamaquoddy and Penobscot Indians in Maine. When the secretary of the interior, on the ground that the tribes did not fall under the government's trust responsibility, refused to undertake the Indians' suit for recovery of lands lost under agreements made after the 1790 law, the Indians sued in the federal district court in Maine. In the case of *Passamaquoddy Tribe* v. *Morton*, Judge Edward T. Gignoux held that even though the tribe had never been federally recognized, the Trade and Intercourse Act was applicable to it and that the law established a trust relationship between the United States and the tribe.

Gignoux's decision came as a bolt of lightning out of the blue, for the state's dealings with Indians outside the scope of federal Indian policy had been of long standing, without objection or interference from Washington, and it was a shock to discover the strong possibility that the agreements by which Maine (then part of Massachusetts) had cleared large areas of the land of Indian title were invalid. The decision cast a cloud over land titles in much of Maine, and the Indians, private landowners, and the state of Maine geared up for a long period of complex litigation. Such an extended court battle (during which time land titles would be in doubt) would have brought tremendous economic hardship to Maine, and it was soon evident that a negotiated settlement, with the federal government picking up the bill, was the only solution.

After long and difficult negotiations, a settlement was provided by the Maine Indian Claims Settlement Act of 1980, which ratified all transfers of land and other natural resources by the Indians and thus extinguished all their claims to the land. In return Congress established a fund of $27 million, to be held in trust by the secretary of the interior for the tribes and the income used for their benefit. Another $54.5 million created an acquisition fund from which 300,000 acres of land would be purchased for the Indians of the state. The tribes were recognized by the federal government and able to draw on the full federal services provided for Indian groups. They were, however, to be under the civil and criminal jurisdiction of the state.

Before the Maine case had reached this successful conclusion, the claims of the Narragansett Indians in Rhode Island had been settled. The tribe claimed aboriginal title to 3,200 acres of land within the town of Charlestown and asserted that the alienation of those lands between 1790 and 1880 was null and void. The lawsuits clouded the title of most of the land in the town, and after lengthy negotiations a settlement was approved by the Rhode Island Indian Claims Settlement Act of September 1978. The state transferred to a state-chartered and Indian-controlled corporation about 900 acres of state land, and Congress appropriated $3.5 million to purchase another 900 acres for the Indians. In return all tribal land claims within Rhode Island were extinguished.

A similar case was that of the Mashpee Indians, a small community on Cape Cod, who brought suit in federal court in August 1976. They asked the court to declare that they were the legal owners of much of the land in the town of Mashpee because the provisions of the 1790 law had not been followed in alienating the land. After a long trial on the question of the tribal status of the Mashpees, the jury found that although the Indians had been a federal Indian tribe in 1834 and 1842, they had ceased to be so by 1869, at which time their lands were sold to individual white purchasers, and that they were not a tribe when they brought suit in 1976. The district court approved the jury's decisions and dismissed the case in March 1978, and this action was upheld by the United States Court of Appeals, First Circuit, in February 1979. The Supreme Court declined to review the actions of the lower courts, thus ending the case unfavorably for the Indians.

A case of quite a different sort arose from a festering land dispute between the Navajos and the Hopis. The Hopis, a sedentary people relying on farming and grazing for a livelihood, had inhabited their mesa-top villages for centuries. The Navajos were later arrivals—a semi-nomadic people for whom grazing was a primary occupation—and they gradually spread from their center in northwestern New Mexico. After their return in 1868 from forced exile at the Bosque Redondo, they expanded their reservation to keep pace with increasing population and ultimately surrounded the Hopis. To meet the growing Hopi complaints about Navajo encroachment, President Chester A. Arthur on December 16, 1882, by executive order set aside a reservation of nearly 2.5 million acres for the Hopis. The Hopis actually lived in a contracted area and did not use the full 1882 reservation, although their religious traditions required the use of shrines throughout the region; and the aggressive Navajos, still growing, moved onto it with their flocks and herds. By 1960 there were perhaps eighty-five hundred Navajos occupying land within the 1882 reservation boundaries.

Attempts to settle the question about the 1882 reservation by negotiation failed, and a court settlement, which called for joint Navajo-Hopi occupancy of most of the reservation, was little more successful. The Hopis wanted a clear partition of the reservation that would affirm their rights. The Navajos wanted to stay where they were in the disputed area and to buy out the Hopi interest in those lands.

An act of December 22, 1974, provided for partition of the joint-use area. Indians who were on the wrong side of the line would be relocated, and five years were allowed to complete the relocation. As removal approached, the Navajos dug in their heels to stay, and they sought amendment or repeal of the 1974 act. Congress was sympathetic to them and, over the cries of the Hopis, provided for life estates to allow certain Navajos to stay on the land. It also authorized the acquisition of additional lands for the Navajos. This act of July 8, 1980, however, did not reverse the basic policy of partition and relocation. As a relocation commission carried out its work, the anguished cries of the Navajos continued, and the final settlement of the long and bitter conflict remained in doubt.

WATER RIGHTS AND FISHING RIGHTS

The 1970s brought a tremendous concern for the rights of Indians to water on their reservations. As population increased in the arid West, pressure on the limited water resources mounted, and the Indians were threatened by loss of water necessary for their existence. Fifty-five percent of all the Indian land and 75 percent of the Indian reservation population lay within the zone of less than twenty inches of annual rainfall (the amount generally considered necessary for successful agriculture), and as Indians sought to improve their condition through economic development, the use of water for irrigation and for other uses became of supreme importance. The activism of the Indians in the 1970s was strongly reflected in strident demands that Indian water rights be protected.

The determination of what rights the Indians had to water was a matter of judicial interpretation—which was complex and controverted. The debate revolved around three fundamental questions: what priority did Indian reservations have to the limited water resources in relation to the rights of non-Indians, what volume of water were the Indians entitled to, and to what uses of water did the Indians' rights extend? Initial formulations of answers to these questions were worked out through the decades of the twentieth century. It was agreed that Indian water rights existed independent of state water management laws, for these rights arose under federal law, and that they came into being at the date of the creation of the reservation (or in some cases from time immemorial, if the reservation was on lands owned aboriginally by the tribe). No actual diversion of water and application of it to beneficial uses was necessary to create the water rights of the Indians, nor did the principles of prior appropriation apply to their rights.

The fundamental principles rested on the case of *Winters* v. *United States*, in which the Supreme Court on January 6, 1908, established the doctrine of "reserved rights" for the Indians that were different from all other rights to water. It did not matter if non-Indians had begun to use the water first (prior appropriation) or if the Indians in fact used any of the water at all. The water necessary for the purposes for which a reservation had been created were reserved for Indian use. Later cases confirmed and extended the *Winters* decision.

Indians have seriously complained, however, that the United States government, as trustee for Indian resources, failed to fulfill its responsibility to protect their water rights. Striking cases illustrate the Indians' concern and anger on this issue. One is the diversion of waters from Pyramid Lake in Nevada, in which waters from the Truckee River that supplied the lake were diverted to the Carson River watershed as part of the Newlands Reclamation Project. The Paiute Indians, who depended upon fishing in the lake for their livelihood, found the lake practically destroyed. Another is the serious diminution of underflow and groundwater of the Santa Cruz River in southern Arizona, upon which the Papago Indian Tribe depended for irrigated agriculture. Upstream use of water by non-Indians hampered farming efforts of the Papagos. A third is the controversial Central Arizona Project, being constructed to divert waters from the Colorado River to central and southern Arizona and which seriously affects five Indian communities.

A similar issue of rights to natural resources concerned fishing and hunting off the reservations. Treaties signed with Indian tribes in the nineteenth century in some cases preserved for the Indians their traditional fishing and hunting rights in lands ceded to the federal government. For many years these clauses in the treaties were ignored or forgotten, since there was little conflict between Indians and whites over the resources. But in the mid-twentieth century, as the resources became depleted, these latent rights assumed new importance. Indian groups, in seeking to promote their economic well-being, demanded full recognition of their rights, but it was not clear what the extent of these rights was and how far the Indians were subject to state regulatory authority. Considerable litigation resulted, which by and large tended to vindicate the Indians' rights.

Much of the litigation concerned fishing rights embodied in the treaties negotiated with the tribes of the Pacific Northwest in 1854 and 1855 by Isaac I. Stevens, the governor of Washington Territory. Those treaties reserved to the Indians "the right of taking fish, at all usual and accustomed grounds and stations . . . in common with all citizens of the Territory."

A vital question was whether the Indians were entitled to a definite amount or percentage of the catch. In *United States* v. *State of Washington*, a case filed in the Federal District Court for the Western District of Washington in 1970, a group of Indian tribes sought a determination of their rights to a fair share of the catch. In 1974, after three and a half years of study, Judge George Boldt rendered his decision in an extensive opinion that thoroughly analyzed the treaties, the migratory patterns of the fish, Indian fishing patterns, and the history of state regulation. The analysis showed how Indian rights had been reduced over the years by state regulation and non-Indian encroachment, and Boldt set forth a series of principles to govern Indian fishing. He noted that the treaties reserved fishing rights for Indians that were distinct from those of other citizens, that off-reservation fishing rights extended to all places that a tribe had customarily fished, and that the state could regulate Indian fishing only to the extent needed to conserve the fish resources. The most controversial part of the decision was Boldt's determination that the right to "fish in common with the citizens of the Territory" meant not just the right of access to fishing sites but up to 50 percent of the harvestable number of fish, exclusive of catches used for subsistence or for ceremonial purposes.

Non-Indian reaction to the Boldt decision was violent, and much of the public outburst was aimed against Judge Boldt personally. Non-Indian fishermen declared that the decision constituted racial discrimination against them, and they openly violated the ruling by fishing illegally. A serious backlash against augmented Indian rights threatened to halt, if not reverse, recent Indian gains. But the Supreme Court in 1979 reviewed the Boldt decision and upheld it almost completely.

Another case involved Chippewa Indian fishing in Lake Michigan in violation of regulations promulgated by the state of Michigan. In *United States* v. *State of Michigan*, the United States District Court for the Western District of Michigan, denied the power of Michigan to regulate Indian fishing based on aboriginal use and on a treaty of 1836 that reserved "the right of hunting in the lands ceded, with the other usual privileges of occupancy, until the land is required for settlement."

INHERENT SOVEREIGNTY AND TRIBAL JURISDICTION

All elements of Indian self-determination were tied to the issue of tribal sovereignty, and the 1970s saw a culmination of the gradual reawakening of tribal identity and autonomy. The nineteenth- and early-twentieth-century attempts to divest Indians of their tribal relations and let them disappear as individual citizens into the body of the nation did not succeed. Contrary to the confident expectations of humanitarian reformers and federal officials, tribalism survived, and it became the basis for much of the legal maneuvering in the second half of the twentieth century. The tribal governments established under the Indian Reorganization Act of 1934 and other similar Indian bodies governed the reservations, and little by little federal courts recognized and protected this tribal authority. It became an accepted position that Indian tribes had retained inherent sovereignty, that they enjoyed the attributes of sovereignty that had not been taken away or given up.

The doctrine of inherent sovereign powers was accepted by the United States Supreme Court, notably in *United States* v. *Wheeler*, March 22, 1978, in which the court said:

> Before the coming of the Europeans, the tribes were self-governing sovereign political communities. . . . Like all sovereign bodies, they then had inherent power to prescribe laws for their members and to punish infractions of those laws.
>
> Indian tribes are, of course, no longer possessed of the full attributes of sovereignty. . . . Their incorporation within the territory of the United States, and their acceptance of its protection, necessarily divested them of some aspects of the sovereignty which they had previously exercised. By specific treaty provision they yielded up other sovereign powers; by statutes, in the exercise of its plenary control, Congress has removed still others.
>
> But our cases recognize that the Indian tribes have not given up their full sovereignty. . . . The sovereignty that the Indian tribes retain is of a unique and limited character. It exists only at the sufferance of Congress and is subject to complete defeasance. But until Congress acts, the tribes retain their existing sovereign powers.

In a variety of cases the courts have recognized that Indian tribes enjoy sovereign immunity from suit and are not subject to adverse possession, laches, or statutes of limitation. Tribes can exercise the right of eminent domain, tax, and create corporations. They can set up their own form of government, determine their own members, administer justice for tribal members, and regulate domestic relations and members' use of property. They can establish hunting and fishing regulations for their own members within their reservations and can zone and regulate land use. They can do a great many things that independent political entities do, insofar as federal law has not preempted their authority.

It is true, as the courts have long held, that Indian tribes are subject to the legislative power of the United States, and the courts have spoken of the plenary power of Congress over Indian affairs. The power of the United States government is not in question but rather whether Congress has in given cases exercised that power or intended to restrict tribal sovereignty. In some instances tribes are governed by general congressional legislation, in other cases not.

The question of state jurisdiction over Indian reservations has been crucial, for states have been irked by restrictions on enforcing their laws and regulations over areas within their boundaries. The courts have said that where federal law has preempted jurisdiction the states do not have authority, but the conflict between state and tribal jurisdiction is far from resolved. An especially disputed point is the extent of tribal authority over nontrust lands located within the original boundaries of the reservations.

The stickiest issue has been tribal jurisdiction over non-Indians on reservations. On March 6, 1978, the Supreme Court in the case of *Oliphant* v. *Suquamish Indian Tribe* decided against such tribal jurisdiction. Mark Oliphant, a non-Indian residing on the Port Madison Reservation in the state of Washington, had been arrested by tribal authorities and charged with assaulting a tribal officer and resisting arrest. He claimed that he was not subject to tribal authority, and the Supreme Court upheld his claim. After a consideration of historical cases involving tribal jurisdiction, the court declared: "They have little relevance to the principles which lead us to conclude that Indian tribes do not have inherent jurisdiction to try and to punish non-Indians."

Oliphant was taken by Indians as a damaging blow to their sovereign revival, a step backward in the progress made in recent years, and it emphasized the fragile nature of tribal sovereignty and the ultimate power of the federal government in determining the extent and limitations of that sovereignty. The court, in fact, on March 24, 1981, restated the *Oliphant* doctrine in *Montana* v. *United States*, which concerned the right of the Crow Indian Tribe to regulate hunting and fishing of nonmembers on fee title lands held by non-Indians within the reservation. After noting inherent tribal power over tribal domestic concerns, the court said: "But exercise of tribal power beyond what is necessary to protect tribal self-government or to control internal relations is inconsistent with the dependent status of the tribes, and so cannot survive without express congressional delegation." It repeated bluntly "the general proposition that the inherent sovereign powers of an Indian tribe do not extend to the activities of nonmembers of the tribe."

The courts were thus moving toward a clearer definition of tribal sovereignty. Retained inherent power was affirmed as it applied to tribal members; its application in given cases to nonmembers was denied. New cases will no doubt further determine tribal jurisdiction, for it remains a problem of vital importance to Indian self-determination.

CHAPTER 26

The Indians: America's Unfinished Business

The century from 1880 to 1980, which began with a strong sentiment that the Indians were the "vanishing Americans," ended with a resurgence of Indian visibility. Indian population steadily increased after 1900; the census of 1900 counted 237,196 Indians and that of 1980 counted 1,361,869. The recent census figures reflect both an increased willingness of many persons to identify themselves as Indians and natural increases. What at one time seemed an inexorable drive for complete assimilation has been slowed if not turned around, and new policies of self-determination have brought new hope to Indian communities. Indian protests and Indian legal actions have alerted the government and the general public to the continuing importance of Indians in American life.

URBAN INDIANS AND NONRECOGNIZED TRIBES

By 1980 it could no longer be said that the Indians as a whole were a reservation people. The urbanization of American Indians, which had become a major element in Indian life since World War II, did not slacken in the 1960s and 1970s. In the 1960 census, 27.9 percent of Indians enumerated lived in urban areas; in 1970 the percentage had climbed to 44.5 and in 1980 to 49. Some American cities, to which large numbers of Indians from disparate tribes migrated, became centers of Indian population that outdistanced reservations (see Table 2). Los Angeles, for example, had 48,158 Indians in 1980, and Tulsa, 38,498. Many of these urban Indians maintained tribal connections with the reservations, but second and third generations of Indians in cities often had no reservation experience at all. These city dwellers, for the most part, steadfastly maintained their identity as Indians.

TABLE 2: Urban Indians, 1970 and 1980

SMSAª	1980ᵇ	1970	SMSAª	1980ᵇ	1970
Los Angeles	48,158	24,509	Anaheim–Santa Ana–		
Tulsa	38,498	15,519	Garden Grove	12,942	3,920
Oklahoma City	24,752	13,033	Detroit	12,483	5,683
Phoenix	22,900	11,159	Dallas–Ft. Worth	11,225	6,632
Albuquerque	20,788	5,839	Sacramento	11,164	3,559
San Francisco	18,139	12,011	Chicago	10,709	8,996
San Bernardino–			Fort Smith	9,297	3,812
Riverside–Ontario	17,265	6,378	Denver–Boulder	9,117	4,348
Seattle–Everett	16,578	9,496	Anchorage	8,901	880
Minneapolis–St. Paul	15,959	9,852	Portland, Oregon	8,826	4,011
Tucson	14,927	8,837	San Jose	8,506	4,048
San Diego	14,616	5,880	Buffalo	7,113	5,775
New York	13,842	3,920	Yakima	6,656	416
			Milwaukee	6,534	4,075

SOURCE: *1980 Census of Population: Supplementary Reports, Standard Metropolitan Statistical Areas and Standard Consolidated Statistical Areas, 1980*, table 1; *1970 Census of Population*, vol. 1: *Characteristics of the Population*, part 1, section 1, table 67.
ªThese are the 25 Standard Metropolitan Statistical Areas with heaviest Indian population in 1980, with comparable 1970 figures.
ᵇIncludes Eskimo and Aleut.

Although the movement to cities was a difficult uprooting for many Indians—a break from family and reservation patterns and removal from Bureau of Indian Affairs programs—the Indians in urban areas by most indicators fared better than their reservation counterparts. Studies for the 1960s and 1970s showed higher income, improved occupational status, a considerably higher level of education, lower rates of unemployment, and superior (but still inadequate) housing compared to rural Indians.

The cultural, social, and economic changes that Indians were forced to make in the cities, nevertheless, were critical. Thrown into the white world in a more drastic way than on reservations, Indians faced conflicts between traditional behavioral patterns and urban ways. Extended families and tribal ties were diminished in the cities, and identification with one's occupation became an important element in social change. The changes—some of them in rapid and dramatic form—contributed to highly visible social pathology among urban Indians, especially alcoholism, crime, and mental illness. At the same time, the new situations stimulated a sense of social awareness and led to pan-Indian activities. In many cities "Indian centers" were established to provide social, cultural, and recreational activities for Indians residing there, to assist the Indians in developing job opportunities, and to attack the special problems (such as health and education needs) affecting urban Indians.

The Bureau of Indian Affairs, which traditionally had been the contact between the federal government and the Indians, generally was unconcerned with nonreservation Indians. Federal relations with those Indians came from other departments and agencies, in programs developed specifically to meet Indian needs and in those applicable to Indians along with other citizens. There was overlapping and competition among programs, however, and many Indians preferred to work with specially Indian-related programs. The accusation was made that urban Indians had become "victims of a Federal policy which denies services, if not thereby their very existence" to the urban Indian poor. Demands reechoed for specific programs to meet the needs of the Indians in the cities.

Comparable problems, though of considerably lesser extent, faced Indian groups that were not formally recognized by the United States government and thus were not eligible for federal protection or for many federal services. These groups petitioned for recognition, and the Bureau of Indian Affairs set up criteria and procedures.

The criteria established by regulations published on September 5, 1978, applied to groups that were "ethnically and culturally identifiable," that could establish "a substantially continuous tribal existence," and that had "functioned as autonomous entities throughout history until the present" The Bureau of Indian Affairs established a Federal Acknowledgment Branch, with a staff that included a historian, a genealogist, an anthropologist, and a sociologist, to check the evidence supplied by the petitioners and to do independent research on the status of each petitioning group. It promised to be a long process, for the branch estimated the number of nonrecognized groups as 251, living in thirty-eight states, of which 150 might submit petitions.

FEDERAL PROGRAMS FOR INDIANS

In 1980 urban Indians and reservation Indians—and in some cases Indians, too, from terminated or nonrecognized tribes—benefited from a tremendous array of federal programs. The ultimate, although sometimes unexpressed, goal of the federal spending was to assist the Indians to become self-supporting. Yet Indian communities and individual Indians continued to need outside help to bring them up to the economic and social levels of other American citizens, and the federal government assumed most of the responsibility. Programs for education, health, and social services; for construction of schools, hospitals, and roads; for irrigation systems and resources development—all were provided from federal funds. Year by year the amounts increased, as more needs were recognized and as Indian demands for goods and services became stronger and better articulated. Like other poverty-stricken groups in the nation, Indians drew upon general programs designed for all citizens, but their special relation with the United States government resulted in a continuation and proliferation of "Indian programs" that pertained to the recipients because of their special status as Indian people or Indian organizations.

The chief supplier of these programs, of course, was the Bureau of Indian Affairs in the Department of the Interior. The bureau's budget for 1980 totaled more than a billion dollars, of which education costs made up the largest share. Yet the Bureau of Indian Affairs, although still considered by the Indians and by the public as the principal federal agency concerned with Indian matters, no longer controlled even a majority of the funds appropriated by Congress for the Indians (see Table 3). The Indian Health Service, in the Department of Health and Human Services, spent more each year for health care than the Bureau of Indian Affairs spent on education; and in education, the bureau shared responsibility with the Department of Education. Because the bureau restricted its programs largely to Indians on or near reservations, to federally recognized tribes, and to trust obligations relating to land and other assets, Indians were forced to look to other agencies for social services, housing, employment assistance, and programs for economic development.

An amazing array of federal programs gave assistance to American Indians in 1980. If to those designed exclusively to benefit Indian tribes and individuals are added programs that specifically included Indians as eligible beneficiaries and those that were of special interest to Indians (without specially naming them), the total is almost overwhelming. Twelve of the executive departments had something to offer Indians: Agriculture, Commerce, Defense, Education, Energy, Health and Human Services, Housing and Urban Development, Interior, Justice, Labor, Transportation, and Treasury. In addition, eight independent agencies were concerned with Indian programs or Indian rights: Commission on Civil Rights, Environmental Protection Agency, Equal Employment Opportunity Commission, National Endowment for the Arts, National Science Foundation, Office of Personnel Management, Small Business Administration, and Smithsonian Institution.

This proliferation caused confusion and competition and considerable overlapping. It was impossible for all departments and agencies, even with

TABLE 3: Government-Wide Funding for Indian Programs, 1980
(in millions of dollars)

	Budget Authority	Actual Outlay		Budget Authority	Actual Outlay
Education	484	438	Management and		
Interior	(270)	(247)	Facilities	131	121
Education	(214)	(191)	Interior	(131)	(121)
Health Service/Nutrition	583	558	Construction	251	274
HHS	(547)	(525)	Interior	(160)	189)
USDA	(36)	(33)	HHS	(74)	(73)
Housing	867	141	Education	(17)	(12)
Interior	(19)	(17)	Other Interior Funds	153	142
HUD	(848)	(124)	Revenue Sharing	10	10
Social Services	121	106	Total Federal Funds	3,063	2,220
Interior	(87)	(78)			
HHS	(34)	(28)	Interior Trust Funds	969	794
Employment	250	237	Total	4,032	3,014
Interior	(52)	(45)			
Labor	(198)	(192)	Recapitulation		
Economic Development	88	91	Interior	1,043	972
Interior	(26)	(31)	Education	231	203
Commerce	(26)	(24)	HHS	655	626
HUD	(36)	(36)	USDA	36	33
Natural Resources	74	66	HUD	884	160
Interior	(74)	(66)	Labor	198	192
Trust Activities	51	36	Commerce	26	24
Interior	(51)	(36)	Revenue Sharing	10	10
			Total	3,063	2,220

SOURCE: "Department of the Interior and Related Agencies Appropriations for 1982," *Hearings before a Subcommittee of the Committee on Appropriations, House of Representatives, 97th Congress, 1st Session, Subcommittee on the Department of the Interior and Related Agencies* (1981), part 9, pp. 1279–80.

the establishment of special "Indian desks," to show the understanding and sympathy for Indian needs that the Bureau of Indian Affairs had developed over the decades. And there was recurring agitation for a new centralization of Indian administration at the federal level, a reversal of the sporadic but long-lived condemnation of concentrated authority in the hands of the Bureau of Indian Affairs.

Despite all the federal programs for Indians, there were still serious economic problems. Commissioner of Indian Affairs William E. Hallett described the situation candidly in 1980:

During the past decade and a half, federal monies have gone to Indian communities in unprecedented amounts. Those dollars bought better education, health care, housing, public employment and roads. In some ways, at least, they resulted in a noticeable improvement in the quality of reservation life.

What those dollars did not buy was substantive economic development. And if this trend continues, tribes may become overwhelmingly dependent upon direct and indirect government subsidies. That would be a tragedy for both the Indian people and the nation.

Without a comprehensive economic development plan as one of our foremost priorities, the goals of self-determination and self-sufficiency will eventually topple back onto the heap of good intentions.

In 1979 Forrest J. Gerard, assistant secretary of the interior for Indian affairs, described Indian activities under eleven headings: employment assistance, Indian Action Program, enterprise development, credit and financing, road maintenance, road construction, natural resources development, forestry and fire suppression, water resources, wildlife and parks, and minerals and mining. Yet his conclusion sounded like an echo from past decades. "Reservations," he noted, "lack some or all of the attributes necessary to support the economic enterprise functions. Reservations have no tax base, often are bleak and barren, remote from labor pools, raw materials, and markets; transportation and power may be minimal or non-existent." The need was clear; the programs to meet it all seemed ineffective.

One significant development was the formation in 1975 of the Council of Energy Resource Tribes (CERT), a consortium of tribes, originally twenty-two but later expanded, that had important mineral resources. Supported by government funds and with an office in Washington, D.C., CERT sought to promote the development of Indian resources on terms favorable to the tribes. It worked for the renegotiation of old leases to bring a higher return to the Indians, and its members hoped, on the model of the Organization of Petroleum Exporting Countries (OPEC), to be able to use the rich natural resources of the reservations (oil, coal, uranium) as a bargaining tool for bettering Indian conditions. But CERT was not the full answer, for it represented only the resource-rich tribes, a minority of the total number, and reduction in demand and lower prices for mineral resources dampened the original high hopes. The criticism of CERT voiced by Indians who feared that it was too closely tied to corporations and to the government also weakened its effectiveness.

TRUST RESPONSIBILITY: THE GREAT FATHER REDIVIVUS

The heavy federal support of services for Indians was justified in the minds of many Indians by a new concept in federal-Indian relations that came to the fore in the 1970s: trust responsibility. If the concept was not entirely new, it was given greatly expanded meaning. It was called "one of the most important" concepts governing relations between the United States government and the Indians and "one of the primary cornerstones of Indian law," but the precise extent of the trust responsibility was far from clear.

There was agreement that the United States government acted as trustee for Indian land and other property, both what was owned by the tribes and what belonged to individual Indians. The obligations in this regard were reasonably well defined. Much of the work of the Bureau of Indian Affairs in the twentieth century focused on trust duties—for the allotted lands held in trust under the provision of the Dawes Act, for tribal and individual funds held in the Treasury of the United States, and for other Indian properties. The Department of the Interior and the Bureau of Indian Affairs argued that their obligations, in fact, were limited to those of trustees of property and only for tribes that were federally recognized.

Indians and their advocates were dissatisfied with this restrictive legal interpretation and insisted that trust responsibility had a much wider application. The National Tribal Chairmen's Association in February 1974, for example, saw a threefold obligation of the federal government: not only the protection of tribal assets and the management of Indian funds and natural resources, but a duty to "protect . . . [the] sovereignty of Indian Tribes, so there is no further erosion of tribal sovereignty and to support tribes in their efforts to enhance tribal sovereignty" and to provide community and social services to Indian people.

Indians asserted that the federal government in fulfilling its trust responsibilities must provide Indians with education, health care, and other social services sufficient at least to bring them up to the level of the general population; that the responsibility extended to all Indians, not only to those of federally recognized tribes; and that the responsibility affected all agencies of the federal government, not only the Department of the Interior.

The diversity of interpretation of trust responsibility between the federal government and the Indians was only one cause of the murkiness that surrounded the concept, for Indian spokesmen themselves were hesitant to offer a detailed definition of trust responsibility. The American Indian Policy Review Commission, a major force in promoting the broad application of the concept, declared in 1977: "The argument against a precise definition of the trust obligations with an enumeration of specific rights and obligations is that the Federal trust responsibility is a continually evolving

concept." The commission wanted instead a general congressional statement of policy, which "would not place undue restrictions on the development of this doctrine but still would constitute an explicit recognition of
the scope of the obligation by Congress."

A fundamental problem surrounding the whole question of federal responsibilities to Indians was that of Indian self-determination versus federal paternalism. In earlier decades attempts to solve the problem of paternalism had rested on a distinction between the *person* and the *property* of
the Indians. At the time of the termination controversy in the 1950s, Felix S.
Cohen, in condemning the cry to end paternalism that was behind much of
the termination effort, fell back on the same sort of distinction. Trusteeship was a necessary means of protecting Indian property, Cohen argued,
and he distinguished it from wardship, which touched the personal action
of the Indians and which he called outmoded.

In the decade of the 1970s, Indians, by rejecting the limitation of trusteeship to property and by expanding the concept of trust responsibility to
nearly all aspects of Indian existence, reopened the Pandora's box of federal
paternalism. Even the trust responsibilities regarding land and other assets
brought a large element of paternalism. Commissioner Dillon Myer's assertion in 1953 that "you cannot have trusteeship without paternalism"
was reechoed by Interior Department officials twenty years later: "The exercise of a trust is paternalism. Indian leaders, government officials and the
general public should understand that the Indian demands that the government continue its trust responsibility for Indian assets inescapably involves paternalism. The government has to approve proposed uses or disposition of the assets under its trust responsibility. To do otherwise is to
violate the trust. If the Indians want to do otherwise—that is, have complete freedom for use of their assets—they should request legislation terminating the trust responsibility."

When the trust responsibility is extended to include health, education,
and social services to Indian people for an indefinite time, paternalism becomes almost unlimited in scope and in duration, for the federal government becomes the supplier of the Indians' essential needs. Some Indians
have noted that in the old days before the coming of the white man, the
buffalo provided all that the Indians needed: food, shelter, clothing. Then
the white man took away the buffalo and gave the Indians the government
instead—the new buffalo. The figure of the government as the "new buffalo" is to the point. But a better figure is the historical one of the Great
Father. Dependence on the federal government for schooling, health care,
legal services, technical aid in tribal government, and economic development means the Great Father redivivus in pervasive form.

UNFINISHED BUSINESS

Relations between the federal government and the American Indians have been an ever-developing continuum, but in the second half of the twentieth century changes have come at an especially rapid rate. The decade of the 1970s with its numerous laws and programs looking toward Indian self-determination (in education, religion, land and resource use, and tribal jurisdiction) was a remarkably busy time. The developments were the cumulative results of actions with roots far in the past, but they will undoubtedly be seen by later historians as a prelude to future—and perhaps radical—change in Indian-white relations.

As the nation and the Indian tribes look toward the twenty-first century, certain problems seem sure to remain prominent. First is the continuing need for sound economic development—including coal, oil, and other mineral resources as well as land—so that the Indian communities asserting self-determination can indeed reach some degree of self-sufficiency. But the search for economic progress will also heighten tensions within Indian groups between those who want to exploit the sources of wealth for the sake of economic betterment and those who insist that the environment should not be violated by strip mining or other extractive operations.

A second continuing issue of major concern is the question of inherent sovereignty of Indian tribes within their reservations and the increasing assertion of such sovereignty. How is criminal and civil jurisdiction to be divided between tribes, states, and the federal government, and especially, what jurisdiction does a tribe have over non-Indians within the reservation boundaries? Can viable and effective tribal governments be maintained to carry on the government-to-government relations with the United States that have become the announced goal of both Indian groups and the federal government? Tribal factionalism and a division between supporters of federally recognized tribal governments (many of which stem from the Indian Reorganization Act of 1934) and "traditional" Indian elders and spiritual leaders undercut effective modern government.

Government-to-government relations presume strong and well-supported tribal government structures that not only can deal with the federal government as independent political entities but can also manage and operate the programs for the Indian communities that have been the work and responsibility of the United States government. Practically, however, "government-to-government" has been understood to apply simply to Indian groups acknowledged by the Bureau of Indian Affairs as recipients of federal services provided by the bureau. In 1980 there were 278 such tribal entities, ranging from the large Navajo tribe (with a greater population than some members of the United Nations) to an array of very small bands, colonies, and communities scattered through California and Nevada, some with a population of fewer than a dozen people.

A third matter of concern is the federal government's responsibility for that half of the Indian population no longer living under tribal governments on reservations. How much responsibility does the federal government have toward urban Indians, and in what way can that responsibility be met? If the Bureau of Indian Affairs limits its concern to federally recognized tribes and emphasizes its trusteeship for land and related assets, can other agencies of the United States government adequately care for continuing needs of the numerous Indians outside the reservations?

Paternalism seems abiding (although few Indians or government officials want to admit it), but the Great Father cannot act as arbitrarily as he once did. Unilateral action of the federal government, common in the past, is difficult if not impossible in an age of increasingly sophisticated Indian initiatives. Tribal governments, with their astute lawyers and other specialists, skillfully draw upon the resources of the federal government and adapt them more and more to their own ends.

The history of government relations with the Indians over two centuries points with considerable clarity to the long-standing pressures for assimilation of the Indians into the mainstream of white American society. Only the future will show whether the heavy dependence of the Indians upon federal funds and federal management skills can be effectively lessened and whether the destiny of the Indians as prosperous groups with separate identities within a pluralistic society can be attained.

Commissioners of Indian Affairs

Commissioner	Entered Office	Commissioner	Entered Office
Thomas L. McKenney[1]	March 11, 1824	Hiram Price	May 6, 1881
Samuel S. Hamilton[1]	September 30, 1830	John D. C. Atkins	March 21, 1885
Elbert Herring	August 1831	John H. Oberly	October 10, 1888
Carey Harris	July 4, 1836	Thomas J. Morgan	June 30, 1889
T. Hartley Crawford	October 22, 1838	Daniel M. Browning	April 18, 1893
William Medill	October 28, 1845	William A. Jones	May 3, 1897
Orlando Brown	June 30, 1849	Francis E. Leupp	January 1, 1901
Luke Lea	July 1, 1850	Robert G. Valentine	June 19, 1909
George W. Manypenny	March 24, 1853	Cato Sells	June 2, 1913
James W. Denver	April 17, 1857	Charles H. Burke	May 7, 1921
Charles E. Mix	June 14, 1858	Charles J. Rhoads	April 18, 1929
James W. Denver	November 8, 1858	John Collier	April 21, 1933
Alfred B. Greenwood	May 4, 1859	William A. Brophy	March 6, 1945
William P. Dole	March 13, 1861	John R. Nichols	April 13, 1949
Dennis N. Cooley	July 10, 1865	Dillon S. Myer	May 5, 1950
Lewis V. Bogy[2]	November 1, 1866	Glenn L. Emmons	August 10, 1953
Nathaniel G. Taylor	March 29, 1867	Philleo Nash	September 26, 1961
Ely S. Parker	April 21, 1869	Robert L. Bennett	April 27, 1966
Francis A. Walker	November 21, 1871	Louis R. Bruce	August 8, 1969
Edward P. Smith	March 20, 1873	Morris Thompson	December 3, 1973
John Q. Smith	December 11, 1875	Benjamin Reifel	December 7, 1976
Ezra A. Hayt	September 20, 1877	———	———
Roland E. Trowbridge	March 15, 1880	William E. Hallett	December 14, 1979

[1]Head of Bureau of Indian Affairs

[2]Not confirmed by the Senate

Indian Population

1900 237,196	1930 343,352	1960 532,591
1910 276,927	1940 345,252	1970 792,730
1920 244,437	1950 357,499	1980 1,361,869

	1970	1980		1970	1980
Alabama	2,443	7,483	Nevada	7,933	13,201
Alaska	16,276	21,849	New Hampshire	361	1,297
Arizona	95,812	152,610	New Jersey	4,706	8,176
Arkansas	2,014	9,346	New Mexico	72,788	104,634
California	91,018	198,095	New York	28,355	38,117
Colorado	8,836	17,726	North Carolina	44,406	64,519
Connecticut	2,222	4,431	North Dakota	14,369	20,119
Delaware	656	1,309	Ohio	6,654	11,986
District of			Oklahoma	98,468	169,197
Columbia	956	996	Oregon	13,510	26,587
Florida	6,677	18,981	Pennsylvania	5,533	9,173
Georgia	2,347	7,444	Rhode Island	1,390	2,872
Hawaii	1,126	2,664	South Carolina	2,241	5,666
Idaho	6,687	10,418	South Dakota	32,365	45,081
Illinois	11,413	15,833	Tennessee	2,276	5,012
Indiana	3,887	7,681	Texas	17,957	39,374
Iowa	2,992	5,367	Utah	11,273	19,158
Kansas	8,672	15,254	Vermont	229	968
Kentucky	1,531	3,518	Virginia	4,853	9,093
Louisiana	5,294	11,950	Washington	33,386	58,159
Maine	2,195	4,057	West Virginia	751	1,555
Maryland	4,239	7,823	Wisconsin	19,924	29,318
Massachusetts	4,475	7,483	Wyoming	4,980	7,088
Michigan	16,854	39,702	Total	792,730	1,361,869
Minnesota	23,128	34,841			
Mississippi	4,113	6,131	Eskimos	28,186[1]	42,149
Missouri	5,405	12,127	Aleuts	6,352[1]	14,177
Montana	27,130	37,153	Total	827,268	1,418,195
Nebraska	6,624	9,147			

[1] Alaska only.

Suggested Readings

A bibliographical essay is given in the two-volume edition of *The Great Father*, pp. 1231–57. For more extensive lists of books and articles, see two bibliographies compiled by the author: *A Bibliographical Guide to the History of Indian-White Relations in the United States* (Chicago: University of Chicago Press, 1977), and *Indian-White Relations in the United States: A Bibliography of Works Published 1975–1980* (Lincoln: University of Nebraska Press, 1982). What is presented here is a brief list of books that can be used as supplementary reading.

Berkhofer, Robert F., Jr. *Salvation and the Savage: An Analysis of Protestant Missions and American Indian Response, 1787–1862* (Lexington: University of Kentucky Press, 1965).

Berkhofer, Robert F., Jr. *The White Man's Indian: Images of the American Indian from Columbus to the Present* (New York: Alfred A. Knopf, 1978).

Debo, Angie. *A History of the Indians of the United States* (Norman: University of Oklahoma Press, 1970).

Dippie, Brian W. *The Vanishing American: White Attitudes and U. S. Indian Policy* (Middletown, Conn.: Wesleyan University Press, 1982).

Hagan, William T. *American Indians*, rev. ed. (Chicago: University of Chicago Press, 1979).

Hagan, William T. *The Indian Rights Association: The Herbert Welsh Years, 1882–1904* (Tucson: University of Arizona Press, 1985).

Horsman, Reginald. *Expansion and American Indian Policy, 1783–1812* (East Lansing: Michigan State University Press, 1967).

Hoxie, Frederick E. *A Final Promise: The Campaign to Assimilate the Indians, 1880–1920* (Lincoln: University of Nebraska Press, 1984).

Keller, Robert H., Jr. *American Protestantism and United States Indian Policy, 1869–82* (Lincoln: University of Nebraska Press, 1983).

McLoughlin, William G. *Cherokees and Missionaries, 1789–1839* (New Haven: Yale University Press, 1984).

McNickle, D'Arcy. *Native American Tribalism: Indian Survivals and Renewals* (New York: Oxford University Press, 1973).

Mardock, Robert Winston. *The Reformers and the American Indian* (Columbia: University of Missouri Press, 1971).

Peroff, Nicholas C. *Menominee DRUMS: Tribal Termination and Restoration, 1954–1974* (Norman: University of Oklahoma Press, 1982).

Philp, Kenneth R. *John Collier's Crusade for Indian Reform, 1920–1954* (Tucson: University of Arizona Press, 1977).

Prucha, Francis Paul, ed. *Americanizing the American Indians: Writings by the "Friends of the Indian," 1880–1900* (Cambridge: Harvard University Press, 1973).

Satz, Ronald N. *American Indian Policy in the Jacksonian Era* (Lincoln: University of Nebraska Press, 1975).

Sheehan, Bernard W. *Seeds of Extinction: Jeffersonian Philanthropy and the American Indians* (Chapel Hill: University of North Carolina Press, 1973).

Spicer, Edward H. *A Short History of the Indians of the United States* (New York: Van Nostrand-Reinhold Company, 1969).

Szasz, Margaret. *Education and the American Indian: The Road to Self-Determination since 1928*, 2d ed. (Albuquerque: University of New Mexico Press, 1977).

Taylor, Graham D. *The New Deal and American Indian Tribalism: The Administration of the Indian Reorganization Act, 1934–45* (Lincoln: University of Nebraska Press, 1980).

Utley, Robert M. *Frontier Regulars: The United States Army and the Indians, 1866–1891* (New York: Macmillan Company, 1973).

Utley, Robert M. *The Indian Frontier of the American West 1846–1890* (Albuquerque: University of New Mexico Press, 1984).

Van Every, Dale. *Disinherited: The Lost Birthright of the American Indian* (New York: Morrow, 1966).

Viola, Herman J. *Thomas L. McKenney: Architect of America's Early Indian Policy* (Chicago: Swallow Press, 1974).

Washburn, Wilcomb E. *The Indian in America* (New York: Harper and Row, 1975).

White, Richard. *The Roots of Dependency: Subsistence, Environment, and Social Change among the Choctaws, Pawnees, and Navajos* (Lincoln: University of Nebraska Press, 1983).

Wilkins, Thurman. *Cherokee Tragedy: The Story of the Ridge Family and the Decimation of a People* (New York: Macmillan Company, 1970).

Consider also biographies of Indian leaders and histories of particular Indian tribes.

Index

Printed in the United States
64512LVS00007B/73